and Germany," and "The Sources of Change in Export Performance: The United States and Canada." The third essay, "The Impact of Research and Development on United States Trade," takes up the popular but rarely tested view that the United States makes its strongest showing in new, research-intensive lines of production. Also in Part II are studies on "Imitation, Innovation, and Japanese Exports," "Industrialization and Trade in Manufactures: The East Asian Experience," and "Primary Products, Preferences, and Economic Welfare: The EEC and Africa."

Part III, *International Financial Policies and the International Monetary System*, contains two essays on payments problems and three on the world's monetary system. These essays are "The Optimum Policy Mix: Convergence and Consistency," "Imports, Foreign Exchange, and Economic Development: The Greek Experience," "The Costs and Benefits of Being a Reserve-Currency Country: A Theoretical Approach Applied to the United States," "The Demand for International Reserves," and "Reserve-Asset Preferences Revisited."

Peter B. Kenen is Professor of Economics and Chairman of the Department of Economics at Columbia University. Roger Lawrence is Assistant Professor of Economics at Columbia University. The contributors to the volume are Donald B. Keesing, Helen Waehrer, Elinor B. Yudin, Merle I. Yahr, H. David Willey, J. Dirck Stryker, Terutomo Ozawa, Wontack Hong, John Patrick, Constantine Michalopoulos, John R. Karlik, and Margaret L. Greene.

One of the "Columbia Studies in Economics."

The Open Economy

ESSAYS ON INTERNATIONAL TRADE
AND FINANCE

COLUMBIA STUDIES IN ECONOMICS

1

The Open Economy

ESSAYS ON INTERNATIONAL

TRADE AND FINANCE

PETER B. KENEN

and

ROGER LAWRENCE

Editors

COLUMBIA UNIVERSITY PRESS

New York and London

1968

CONTRIBUTORS

MARGARET L. GREENE is Economist, Foreign Research Division, Federal Reserve Bank of New York.

WONTACK HONG is an Assistant Professor of Economics, University of Wisconsin-Milwaukee.

JOHN R. KARLIK is on the Professional Staff of the Hudson Institute.

DONALD B. KEESING is an Associate Professor of Economics, Stanford University.

PETER B. KENEN is a Professor of Economics, Columbia University.

ROGER LAWRENCE is an Assistant Professor of Economics, Columbia University.

CONSTANTINE MICHALOPOULOS is an Assistant Professor of Economics, Clark University.

TERUTOMO OZAWA is an Assistant Professor of Economics, Colorado State College.

JOHN PATRICK is an Instructor in Economics, Swarthmore College.

J. DIRCK STRYKER is an Assistant Professor of Economics, Yale University.

HELEN WAEHRER is an Assistant Professor of Economics, Portland State College.

H. DAVID WILLEY is Chief, Balance of Payments Division, Federal Reserve Bank of New York.

MERLE I. YAHR is an Assistant Professor of Economics, Columbia University.

ELINOR B. YUDIN is a Lecturer in Economics, New York University.

PREFACE

THE ESSAYS IN THIS BOOK summarize research sponsored by the International Economics Workshop at Columbia University. Most of them are students' work, based on dissertations or masters' essays. The Workshop itself has been supported by Columbia's School of International Affairs, with funds from Ford Foundation grants for international studies. It has been concerned with three major subjects: (1) the chief determinants of merchandise trade patterns; (2) relationships between the structure of foreign trade, economic growth, and factor movements; and (3) international financial policies and the international monetary system. The three parts of this volume deal with these themes.

The first part of the book offers five essays that examine the influence of labor skills or human capital on various aspects of the international economy—in particular on national trade patterns. The first essay, by Keesing, builds on his earlier work and shows that trade patterns can be classified according to the skill needs of each industry. Countries that export skill-intensive goods tend to import commodities that are less skill-intensive. Keesing infers that international differences in skill endowments, reflecting different rates of investment in the labor force, powerfully affect patterns of trade; nations well endowed with skills make the most of this advantage, while those short of skills arrange their foreign trade to conserve this scarce factor of production.

The essay that follows uses Keesing's inference to develop new results concerning U.S. foreign trade. Waehrer begins with Kravis' discovery that U.S. export industries pay higher wages than U.S. import-competing industries. She proceeds to verify Kravis' results using formal statistical tests, then goes on to show that much of the interindustry difference in wage levels is due to a difference in skill intensities. High skills earn high wages, and U.S. export industries are skill-intensive. In consequence, those industries pay higher wages than the less skill-intensive import competitors.

If labor skills can be viewed as embodied capital, a complement to ordinary tangible capital, the migration of skilled labor can and should be viewed as an international transfer of capital. This is the theme of Yudin's paper, which studies Americans employed overseas—their location, skills, and embodied capital. Yudin's calculations show that the rather small number of Americans abroad embody large investments and, by implication, make an important contribution to their host countries' stocks of human capital.

The fourth essay in this series deals with more recondite aspects of the problem. Yahr seeks to show that cross-country estimates of factor substitution are biased by neglect of systematic differences in labor quality, and also to demonstrate that an upgrading of a country's labor force amounts to a capital-saving shift in its production functions. In the course of her work, she furnishes new evidence that elasticities of substitution do not differ greatly from industry to industry. This finding lends great strength to the strong factor-intensity assumption, a central assumption of modern trade theory. Finally, Yahr offers a strong, direct test of Keesing's inference that skill supplies help to govern patterns of trade.

Kenen's essay tries to pull several of these thoughts together. Building on another paper, published separately, he reconstructs the two-factor, two-country, factor-endowments model by moving investment to the center of the stage. In his version of the model, capital can be invested in a country's land or labor, and must be reallocated with every change in the rates of return to land and labor. He studies the growth path of a closed economy, opens it to trade, and shows that free trade will equalize land rentals and wage rates without also equalizing national interest rates. In consequence, free trade is fully compatible with capital movements.

The second part of the book covers a wide range of issues. It opens with two essays on trade and productivity. The first, by Willey, provides a detailed comparison of productivity change in Britain and Germany. This essay shows that the interindustry pattern of economic growth has been quite similar in the two countries, so that differences in growth rates from industry to industry cannot account for Germany's spectacular performance in world markets. Willey then ascribes Germany's success—and Britain's failures—to the two countries' records in demand management. The slower growth of British productivity and exports are blamed, in part, on Britain's failure to control demand, the consequent tendencies toward labor hoarding and production for home markets, and the blunting of incentives to modernization. Stryker's study offers an ingenious comparison of productivity and export performance in the United States and neighboring Canada. He finds quite different patterns of industrial growth in the two countries and shows that the differences, industry by industry, have affected exports. In addition, he investigates economies of scale and finds weaker evidence that these, too, have influenced export sales.

The third essay in this part takes up the popular but rarely tested view that the United States makes its strongest showing in new, research-intensive lines of production. Here, Keesing correlates indices of research input with U.S. shares in world trade. He shows that the industries with large research inputs have made the best records in world trade and argues that this country does, in fact, enjoy a comparative advantage in research-laden products.

Ozawa's work on Japan involves a similar comparison. Since World War II, Japanese companies have imported new techniques under foreign license, and the Japanese government has compiled an intriguing body of statistics on the number and nature of licensing agreements. Using these statistics to measure each industry's imports of technology, Ozawa produces several strong, affirmative tests of the hypothesis that Japan's success in world markets is due largely to its imports of foreign technology.

Recent work by Hoffman, Chenery, and others discloses a remarkable regularity in patterns of industrial development. Hong's essay on Japan, Korea, and Taiwan shows that they follow the typical pattern—after due allowance for the difference in dates of industrialization. In each case industrial development led to large-scale import substitution, which spread from light consumers' goods to heavier producers' goods. Hong then shows that industrial development led to a similar sequence on the export side. As output grew and imports shrank in relation to consumption, each country's exports started to grow. Finally, Hong demonstrates that this sequence is most likely to happen in resource-poor countries; those with large endowments of arable land and large-scale exports of primary products are not likely to export manufactured products at the early stages of industrial development.

The final essay in this part deals with a different group of less-developed countries, the African affiliates of the EEC, and with a different aspect of their foreign trade. Working with techniques developed by Johnson, Lawrence has refined customs union theory to study the enlargement of an existing union or the granting of trade preferences to outsiders. He extracts a powerful, general result—that the sign of the prospective change in economic welfare depends on the relative size of the members' trading sectors. Using this theorem, Lawrence examines Common Market preferences—their impact on the European members of the EEC, on the African associates of the EEC, and on exporters of competitive products elsewhere in the world.

The third part of the book offers two essays on payments problems and three on the world's monetary system. The first essay, by Patrick, deals with a major theoretical problem. It attempts to identify sufficient conditions for the convergence of national policies toward an optimum policy mix. Patrick works with two countries, each of them armed with two policy instruments and aiming for two targets, internal balance and external balance. He shows that a proper assignment of instruments to targets usually suffices to guarantee convergence, even in the absence of formal coordination, but also proves that misassignment need not be fatal if the two countries' external targets are framed consistently.

The second essay in this part examines the balance-of-payments problems of a developing country. Michalopoulos reviews Greece's experience to ascertain whether foreign-exchange needs have constrained that country's development or whether, on the contrary, the rate of savings has been the effective constraint on Greek growth. He argues that the foreign-exchange constraint would have been effective in most postwar years had there been no U.S. aid, and that it would still be effective if earnings from shipping and tourist trade had not grown so rapidly in recent years. Michalopoulos' study sheds light on the Greek experience, but also illuminates the several limitations of simple import-constraint models.

In the next essay, Karlik examines the costs and benefits accruing to a reserve-currency country. These costs and benefits can be isolated, he argues, only by examining the growth paths a country would follow on the alternative assumptions that its currency does, or does not, have reserve-currency status. Examining the relevant arguments in the case of the United States, Karlik concludes that before 1958 this country enjoyed no net gain because of the dollar's reserve-currency role. In the period 1958–1966, however, he finds that the United States probably did benefit from the dollar's role as a reserve asset.

The essay that follows, by Kenen and Yudin, is an effort to measure the demand for international reserves. It argues that a nation's balance of payments can be treated as a simple sum of autoregressive disturbances and that the nation's demand for reserves depends on the variance of those disturbances. To test this compound hypothesis, the authors examine the payments experience of several major countries and show that changes in reserves, a measure of imbalances, can be described by a Markov process. They then use the several countries' experience through time to construct a single cross-sectional equation that explains the typical country's demand for reserve assets. They find that reserve holdings are, in fact, related to the variance of the balance of payments and, less strongly, to the duration of payments disturbances.

Knowledge of the demand for reserves is, of course, prerequisite to the proper management of the monetary system. So, too, is knowledge of the demand for particular reserve assets. This aspect of the problem is explored in the final essay. Here, Greene builds on Kenen's work, seeking to measure the central banks' demand for gold and, by implication, their demand for dollar assets. She shows that there was a sudden, marked change in central-bank behavior—a decreased demand for gold—in the early 1960s, but that one can still construct meaningful time-series regression equations for the longer period 1957–1964.

The several research projects summarized in these essays were conducted separately but, we hope, fit together and, as a group, furnish a significant addition to our knowledge of the international economy.

Two final comments are in order. By publication time our authors had scattered across the globe. Hence we undertook to correct galley and page proofs; if we have failed to spot errors or have introduced new ones, our authors must be exonerated. If, furthermore, we have come close to meeting our own deadlines, all credit is due Mrs. Sharon Thompson, who, with efficiency and good cheer, marshaled a deluge of draft chapters, deciphered a collage of corrections, and prepared the authors' index. We are very grateful.

Peter B. Kenen
Roger Lawrence

New York
April 1968

CONTENTS

Part I: Skills, Human Capital, and Patterns of Foreign Trade

Part II: Adaptation, Growth, and Trade

Part III: International Financial Policies and the International Monetary System

I

SKILLS, HUMAN CAPITAL, AND PATTERNS OF FOREIGN TRADE

DONALD B. KEESING

Labor Skills and the Structure

of Trade in Manufactures

THE HECKSCHER-OHLIN OR FACTOR THEORY attempts to explain international trade in terms of the availability of productive resources in each country. In recent years, shortcomings of this approach have been revealed which mean that the theory has to be modified drastically or be abandoned as a serious description of reality. As one authority puts it, realism demands "the consistent introduction of nontraded goods, of intermediate goods, of economies of scale, of product differentiation, of technical change as a determinant of the trade pattern, of transport costs, and of the size and nature of the home market—all of which would probably alter the model so much as to make it unrecognizable."[1]

Even regarding the link between factors and trade, the Heckscher-Ohlin theory postulates unreal causal relationships. "In the dynamic

Some of the empirical findings reported in this essay were published previously; see D.B. Keesing, "Labor Skills and Comparative Advantage," *American Economic Review, Proceedings*, LVI (May 1966), 249–58.

[1] W. M. Corden, *Recent Developments in the Theory of International Trade*, Special Papers in International Economics No. 7, International Finance Section, Princeton University, 1965, p. 31.

case, the producible factors of production, given time, adjust precisely to the pattern of final demand. It makes no sense to speak of 'original endowments' unless one is speaking of the immediate short run."[2] In other words, a series of events largely unrelated to factor availabilities could have "caused" observed patterns of location and trade, which in turn could have created factor supplies tailored to the factor requirements of the goods actually traded.

Under one causal relationship or another, a correlation between factors available in a country and the country's trade seems a reasonable anticipation. But, as Leontief first showed, aggregated capital and labor do not behave in conformity to expectations from a two-factor Heckscher-Ohlin model.[3] This richly deserved setback to a common variety of theory poses more questions: To which factors, if any, does the Heckscher-Ohlin theory apply empirically? Does the correlation between factor availability and trade extend to what Harrod calls "generic factors,"[4] or only to a multiplicity of specific factors such as particular natural resources, highly specialized skills, and specialized plant and equipment?

The influence of natural resources on trade, although strong, only partly salvages the theory. The Leontief paradox did seem to suggest "that world trading relationships depend to a greater degree on the unequal distribution of natural resources than on comparative endowments of capital and labor."[5] But the relationship with trade is clearest when natural resources are disaggregated, and at this level the factors are so specific that the theory becomes trivial. Moreover, a natural-resource theory of trade fails to account for the growing proportion of world trade consisting of complex manufactures.

Plausible partial explanations of world trade in manufactures can be found beyond the fringes of the factor theory. For example, technological innovation results in a qualitative superiority of one nation's product over the nearest substitutes. Product differentiation induces an exchange of

[2] S. Valavanis, "Leontief's Scarce Factor Paradox," *Journal of Political Economy*, LXII (December 1954), 524.

[3] W. W. Leontief, "Domestic Production and Foreign Trade: The American Capital Position Re-examined," *Proceedings of the American Philosophical Society*, XCVII (September 1953), 332–49; and "Factor Proportions and the Structure of American Trade: Further Theoretical and Empirical Analysis," *Review of Economics and Statistics*, XXXVIII (November 1956), 386–407.

[4] R. F. Harrod, "Factor-Price Relations under Free Trade," *Economic Journal*, LXVIII (June 1958).

[5] B. Swerling, "Capital Shortage and Labor Surplus in the United States," *Review of Economics and Statistics*, XXXVI (August 1954), 289.

similar products based on a variety of tastes and a taste for variety. When countries compete in the same or very similar products, the battle may be decided on the basis of economies of scale of one kind or another, affected in turn by characteristics of national markets. The fact that some products are traded internationally more than others, as well as the international location of industries, can be traced in considerable measure to transport costs. Government policies—taxes, subsidies, purchases, tariffs, exchange policies—twist the direction and composition of trade. So do private initiative and individual management talents, in ways that may not be predictable in advance.

Yet I have put forward evidence, and will add to it here, showing that differences in the skill intensity of products are reflected systematically in the pattern of trade. I infer from this evidence that difference in supplies of skills afford a factor explanation of trade and location in manufacturing industries within the framework of the Heckscher-Ohlin theory.[6] True, the theory must be modified somewhat to incorporate labor skills as key factors, and the direction of causation is not necessarily one way. Some of my own studies add to the evidence that a factor explanation does not supply the whole story.[7] Yet when occupational skills are treated as "generic" factors, the factor theory does finally show empirical results that accord with its intellectual appeal.

THE BASIC RATIONALE OF THE LABOR-SKILLS APPROACH

There is considerable logic in regarding labor skills as the underlying explanation of trade and location in manufacturing. In most industrial activities, labor is the most important factor of production, as reflected by factor-income shares. Whereas human resources are not so immutable as natural resources in terms of either international mobility or inherent transformability, in many respects the human resources of a country are subject to slower change than its man-made material resources. Financial capital and capital goods, after all, move internationally quite freely

---

[6] See D. B. Keesing, "Labor Skills and International Trade: Evaluating Many Trade Flows with a Single Measuring Device," *Review of Economics and Statistics*, XLVII (August 1965), 287–94; and "Labor Skills and Comparative Advantage," pp. 249–58.

[7] See, elsewhere in this volume, "The Impact of Research and Development on United States Trade," originally published in the *Journal of Political Economy*, LXXV (February 1966).

compared to labor; and, if a factor is freely mobile, its initial availability in one place compared to another will not influence industrial location.

If the skills of a labor force could be transformed easily and quickly while people stayed in place, such a transformation would substitute for an international movement of trained labor. Training and retraining do afford opportunities for reshaping the specific skills of a labor force in a short period of time, but only within rather narrow limits dictated by the cultural and educational background of the population involved, the availability of appropriately skilled people to supply training, and economic opportunities for learning by doing. Some occupational skills can be acquired only through a long process of professional training. The general training and experience of a population, together with its attitudes and working habits, resist rapid change. Therefore, broad classes of skills in any population can only be altered slowly. Specific skills that extend and narrow the focus of general training can, by contrast, change with such rapidity that one might expect them to exercise no deep imprint on patterns of industrial location.

Another reason for taking skills into account in trade theory is that they appear to play an important role in explaining economic growth; growth and trade are clearly intertwined. If the human-resources approach pays off heavily in studies of development, it would seem logical to incorporate skills into a modified factor theory of trade.

Altering the Heckscher-Ohlin model to incorporate skills, we can initially retain the assumptions of no transport costs, similar tastes in all countries, no economies of scale, and perfect competition in all markets. But we probably want to allow for the existence of several factors—such as natural resources, capital, skilled labor, and unskilled labor—and to assume that these factors differ in mobility. For example, natural resources are immobile, capital moves internationally at a low cost, and labor of whatever kind moves at a high cost. Economic activities can then be divided into primary activities, those that locate around the natural resources which they require as direct inputs, and secondary activities, which are free to locate away from natural resources. Since the indirect natural-resource requirements of secondary activities can be purchased in processed form, these industries will locate according to the availability of skilled and unskilled labor and capital outside the primary sector. Because movement of capital to labor is cheaper than the reverse, the chief influence on location will be the character of the labor force.

In the model I am proposing, moreover, the standard Heckscher-Ohlin framework has been modified to the extent that the international distribution of factor supplies has been allowed to vary through international factor movements, influenced by complementarities among resources. Factor supplies have become an effect as well as a cause of trade. Trade in intermediate goods has been incorporated.

The framework is open to other modifications. For example, the international distribution of factor supplies can be allowed to vary through the transformation and accumulation of factors over time, or through autonomous or induced migration. It remains to be seen, however, how effectively this or another Heckscher-Ohlin framework can be stretched to take into account new technology (including new products), technological gaps in efficiency, transport costs, economies of scale, and other influences on location and trade.[8]

The modifications just outlined could be combined with further assumptions about the character of the production function involving skilled and unskilled labor—assumptions sufficient to justify the method I use in the empirical studies reported next.

APPLYING THE LABOR-SKILLS APPROACH

To explore the role of occupational skills in international trade, I compute the skills that would have been required to produce the goods exported and imported by each of several countries, if every product in every trade flow were produced by the exact mix of occupational skills required to turn out the same value of output in the United States in a recent year. That is, I apply American skill requirements to compute the skills reflected in each trade flow.

---

[8] Possibly, new technology and new products can be handled by recognizing special activities (research and development) and factors (scientific and engineering talent) required to generate technical innovations, and by specifying a lagged process in the spread of innvoation. Gaps in efficiency can perhaps be handled, along with some kinds of technical change, in terms of contrasts in factor productivities according to the time and place. Transport costs might be introduced in a crude way by dividing secondary activities into those that are resource-oriented, footloose, and market-oriented, and by specifying a hyper-market-oriented service sector. Resource- and market-oriented activities would then move to natural resources and agglomerations of population, respectively. The skill mix of the labor force would dominate only the location of footloose secondary activities. We would then be talking about skill supplies produced by complex economic forces, including requirements in other activities.

The procedure was partly dictated by resources at hand: American skill requirements are the only detailed ones that I have found available for any country. But, under plausible assumptions, the ordering by skill intensity of the trade flows, revealed by my computations, would be nearly duplicated if the skill requirements of any of the other countries were used as a yardstick instead.

Elsewhere I have spelled out the logical requirements and limitations.[9] To summarize, only under obviously unrealistic assumptions would American requirements exactly indicate skill requirements elsewhere. Under much more relaxed assumptions, however, there would be a strong correlation between the relative skill-intensity ranking of a set of trade flows as measured by skill requirements in the United States and another country. A sufficient condition would be that the same industries are skill-intensive relative to other industries in all countries. Reversals in ordering among industries could be tolerated as long as the effects were minor compared to the international consistencies.

A parallel pattern of relative skill requirements would help to account for observed consistencies in wage rates and labor productivity in one industry compared to another as revealed by cross-national comparisons.[10] My impression, from fragments of available evidence, is that parallel skill requirements exist for professional skills, and perhaps a few others; but the parallels break down for a wide range of manual skills. European industries, such as the French, abound in specialized craftsmen. This pattern is stronger in certain of the older crafts-based industries, and is irregular.[11] The corresponding American industries use machines and semi-skilled operatives, and do not appear skill-intensive in the American data.

This point raises the uncomfortable possibility that American skill

[9] See Keesing, "Labor Skills and International Trade."

[10] See, for example, E. J. Mitchell, "An Econometric Study of Interindustrial Differences in Labor Productivity" (doctoral dissertation, University of Pennsylvania, 1966); and compare the essays of Merle I. Yahr and Helen Waehrer in this volume. Also compare B. Minhas, *An International Comparison of Factor Costs and Use* (Amsterdam: North-Holland Publishing Co., 1963); Leontief's review article of Minhas in *American Economic Review*, LIV (June 1964); and V. Fuchs, "Capital-Labor Substitution: A Note," *Review of Economics and Statistics*, XLV (November 1963). Most of their results, obtained by assuming capital to be the second factor along with labor, can be interpreted alternately in terms of skills or "human capital" as the second factor. G. D. A. MacDougall and R. M. Stern's well-known findings that the United States and the United Kingdom specialize in industries in which they have a relative advantage in labor productivity are also highly compatible with my own basic assumption of an internationally consistent ranking of industries by skill intensity.

[11] For some evidence, see D. B. Keesing, "Labor-Skills and the Factor Content of International Trade" (unpublished doctoral dissertation, Harvard University, 1961).

requirements might show American exports as skilled, and French exports as relatively unskilled; while French skill requirements would show French exports as rich in manual skill content compared to American exports. Clearly, it would be desirable to remeasure the same trade flows with several countries' occupational skill requirements as yardsticks, and to conduct detailed analyses of differences in skill requirements from one country to another. But, even if inconsistencies exist, it does not follows that American skill requirements have no wider validity and should be limited in their application to U.S. trade. U.S. technology is quite advanced, and automation of manual occupations has been pushed especially far. A trend in the same direction is appearing in many other countries. Moreover, U.S. experience suggests that the requirements for many of the newer skills associated with science and technology grow rapidly as a nation's wealth and technical know-how accumulate. Insofar as American skill requirements reflect chiefly the "new" rather than the "old" skills, the skill intensity of countries' trade flows measured with American requirements should furnish clues to the modern industrial skill component of their exports and imports, and this itself should be of interest.[12]

One problem in implementing my method is to select skill categories that are economically meaningful, in view of the capacity of human resources for being transformed by further training or job experience. In order to assume a causal connection flowing from the character of the labor force to the trade pattern, we must consider skills that cannot be acquired or changed quickly and are needed to train other new practitioners in similar skills, that is, root skills, the abundance of which sets off one labor force from another in the eyes of investors and long-range planners.

After giving some reflection to this subject, I decided to divide the labor force of each industry into eight occupational groups:

  I. Scientists and engineers.
 II. Technicians and draftsmen.
III. Other professionals.
 IV. Managers.

[12] Skill intensity could, of course, be merely a symptom of technological complexity: American industries could be skill-intensive because they change their technologies rapidly and rely on practitioners of skilled occupations to do the job. If other countries' skill requirements show parallels, the reason may be that they are struggling to master technological change in the same industries. The possibility of interpreting my skill results in terms of changing technology illustrates the difficulty of distinguishing the effects on trade or growth of human resources from those of technology.

V. Machinists, electricians, and tool- and diemakers.

VI. Other skilled manual workers.

VII. Clerical, sales, and service workers.

VIII. Semi-skilled and unskilled workers.

The first three categories involve basic professional skills. The managers category, unfortunately, must remain a catchall in the present type of analysis because any labor force needs its cadres. Their quality doubtless varies more than their numbers, reflecting the type of job—and labor force—that they are overseeing.

I selected for special treatment machinists, electricians, and tool- and diemakers because these manual skills are ubiquitously required in every manufacturing industry and, at the same time, are modern in orientation. In contrast, many of the skills grouped under "other skilled manual workers" are highly specific (foremen or repairmen of a certain type) or involve crafts that are giving way to machinery.

The seventh group comprises mainly clerical workers, typically female and low-paid but complementary to educated managers and professionals. Finally, I lump together semi-skilled and unskilled workers, all basically unskilled. By definition, a semi-skilled operative can be trained to his job in a few days, weeks, or months, given reasonable previous exposure to the kinds of experience provided by an industrial society.

I have regrouped the U.S. census data into 46 industries designed to correspond to standard international trade categories.[13] Elsewhere I have employed a separation of these industries into the first 35 that include the locationally footloose ones, and the last 11 that I consider "natural-resource-oriented," but I shall ignore this distinction in the results reported here.[14] Table 1, showing the percentage distribution of occupational

[13] This correspondence is necessarily imperfect, and so are the data. There are, for example, discrepancies between the sample census of population data, occupation by industry, on which my skill matrix is based, and data on employment collected by the census through questions to employers. There are other discrepancies between the relevant industry and trade classifications, as illustrated by a comparison between U.S. trade as reported in U.N. sources and by the U.S. Department of Commerce in *U.S. Exports and Imports as Related to Output.*

[14] My expectation, borne out in Table 3 of "Labor Skills and Comparative Advantage," and in results for the 11 industries separately, is that this influence of resource orientation on location will make skill requirements less of a determinant of patterns of long-distance trade. Of course, in this group as in the other, many of the industries are usually market-oriented, locating near the consumer; but whenever this locational influence predominates, there should be little international trade to affect my results. The findings reported below would not be very different if the natural-resource-oriented industries were excluded.

skills in each industry in the United States in 1960, gives the basic data on which my computations were based.

Tables 2 and 3 show the occupational skills, expressed as percentages of the requisite labor force, required to produce several countries' exports and imports of manufactures in 1962 with the American skill combinations shown in Table 1. The countries have been listed in an order determined by a convenient if somewhat arbitrary index. This ranking gives a negative Spearman coefficient of rank correlation of .87 between the export and import order for 13 countries. The export order for 14 countries displayed a close parallel to the per capita income of the countries in 1962, the rank correlation being .93, evidence of a powerful relationship between level of industrialization and the skill intensity of a country's exports.[15]

An interesting feature of the results was the difference between the patterns traced by the professional skills of Classes I–III, on the one hand, and the manual skills of Class V, on the other. This difference was confirmed in an examination of bilateral trade patterns among the Group of Ten countries for the year 1964. Compared with the average patterns, Canada and the Netherlands consistently exported manufactured goods abundant in professional relative to manual skills, while for Sweden the pattern was reversed. By way of illustration, Table 4 summarizes the pattern for Class I, scientists and engineers, as a percentage of the requisite labor force, and Table 5 gives the pattern for Class V.[16] Class II exhibited ordering patterns identical with those of Class I, while in Class III the

---

[15] These results are "unscientific" in that they involve only a crude index of skill intensity, weighting professional and Class V skills in a rough reflection of wage differentials. But the correlations would be much the same using any reasonable index of skill intensity. In the second comparison, per capita incomes were converted at prevailing exchange rates, based on data in United Nations, *Monthly Bulletin of Statistics* (September 1964). The puzzle, if there is any, is the direction of causation. Interestingly, the rank order for 9 countries' exports and imports remained almost unchanged compared with results previously published (Keesing, "Labor Skill and International Trade," Tables 1 and 2). The latter results were obtained using the same analytical techniques, but with trade data from 1957, a more limited group of industries, a different and cruder skill classification, U.S. skill data from the year 1950 with earlier employment weights, and a different index.

[16] Neither ordering is perfectly consistent: In Table 4, there are two "reversals" making it impossible to rank Canada, the Netherlands, West Germany, and the United Kingdom; and, in Table 5, there is one "reversal" confusing the ordering of France, Belgium, and Italy. Otherwise, if a country ranks ahead of another, its exports to the second are more intensive in the skill in question than are the exports of the lower-ranking country to the first one.

Table 1

U.S. Occupational Skill Requirements by Industry in 1960 for 46 Manufacturing Industries with Employment Weights and Trade Categories Assumed to Correspond

Industry Number	Industry	Occupational Skill Distribution (1960) (% of total labor force)								Estimated Employment per $100 Mil. Shipments (1961)	SITC Classes (Revised)
		I	II	III	IV	V	VI	VII	VIII		
1	Agricultural machinery	3.226	1.120	2.627	5.201	6.650	16.049	17.417	47.710	4,389.9	712
2	Office machinery	7.261	5.338	4.760	5.376	5.088	13.134	21.135	37.908	5,928.3	714
3	Miscellaneous machinery	4.030	2.495	2.047	5.744	16.372	13.736	14.982	40.594	7,292.6	715–719, 711 exc. 711.4
4	Electrical machinery	7.229	4.660	3.340	4.249	4.490	12.158	16.035	47.839	5,636.7	721
5	Motor vehicles	2.583	1.588	2.608	2.563	6.541	16.615	11.868	55.634	2,595.9	732
6	Aircraft and parts	12.972	4.798	4.566	2.982	8.496	17.447	17.345	31.394	5,177.5	734, 711.4
7	Shipbuilding	2.431	2.109	2.009	2.985	10.993	38.600	10.143	30.730	7,059.1	735
8	Other transport equipment	1.665	1.336	2.049	4.378	4.508	22.180	13.135	50.749	4,308.2	731, 733
9	Professional instruments	7.952	5.997	3.634	5.381	5.724	13.954	19.579	37.779	6,173.3	861.3, 861.7–861.9
10	Photographic equipment	6.642	4.469	4.091	4.606	5.925	13.556	19.643	41.068	4,259.8	861.4–861.6, 862
11	Watches and clocks	1.837	1.606	1.306	5.814	5.899	11.548	16.364	55.626	5,762.4	864
12	Fabricated structural metal products	3.073	3.284	1.437	7.517	3.325	22.933	14.125	44.306	4,926.9	691
13	Cutlery, hand tools	1.564	0.776	1.531	4.626	8.432	13.017	15.430	54.624	5,864.2	695, 696
14	Other fabricated metal products	5.286	3.124	2.925	4.974	7.060	15.288	15.961	45.382	4,736.3	692–694, 697, 698, 812
15	Synthetic fibers	4.518	4.384	2.422	1.600	2.823	19.230	7.830	57.193	3,683.3	266
16	Drugs and medicines	6.546	6.409	6.267	7.873	1.244	8.841	31.915	30.905	3,079.8	541
17	Paints and varnishes	4.652	3.989	2.042	10.452	0.834	9.225	29.344	40.462	2,784.5	533
18	Other chemicals	7.943	4.794	3.218	6.737	2.455	15.620	19.422	39.811	2,426.0	5 exc. 541, 533
19	Rubber products	2.608	1.476	1.964	4.449	2.321	11.545	14.881	60.756	4,450.6	621, 629
20	Miscellaneous wood products	0.396	0.335	0.798	6.601	1.366	14.274	9.333	66.897	7,647.8	632
21	Paper and paperboard products	1.136	0.601	2.161	5.076	2.375	13.150	16.389	59.112	4,233.0	642
22	Furniture and fixtures	0.492	0.572	0.909	5.377	1.497	22.065	19.007	58.941	6,075.9	

Code	Industry										SITC
23	Cement and concrete products	1.888	0.899	1.111	9.307	2.072	14.899	11.523	58.301	3,974.3	661
24	Structural clay products	1.431	0.678	1.101	5.144	1.556	11.098	8.963	70.029	8,373.8	662
25	Glass and glassware	1.569	1.131	2.711	3.598	3.231	12.199	11.428	64.133	5,699.3	664, 665
26	Pottery products	1.406	1.221	1.813	3.511	2.130	8.664	9.921	71.334	9,443.5	666
27	Miscellaneous nonmetallic mineral products	2.974	2.137	2.041	6.114	3.044	15.834	15.944	51.912	5,058.4	663
28	Leather	0.565	0.401	0.565	5.121	0.912	10.008	8.779	73.649	4,333.8	611
29	Leather products	0.451	0.175	0.763	6.241	1.179	6.734	11.719	72.738	8,422.5	612, 831
30	Footwear	0.116	0.071	0.478	2.718	0.883	5.409	10.706	79.619	9,656.1	851
31	Textiles	0.552	0.498	0.988	3.239	1.176	11.014	9.152	73.381	7,318.7	651–656
32	Rugs and carpets	0.878	0.591	1.626	4.845	1.391	10.505	14.002	66.162	3,716.6	657
33	Apparel, including knitting mills	0.109	0.079	0.839	3.604	0.405	5.114	9.090	80.760	8,524.9	841
34	Printing and publishing	0.144	0.193	8.819	7.454	0.345	27.801	38.799	16.445	6,190.8	892
35	Confectionery products	0.468	0.419	0.625	5.985	1.219	8.445	18.961	63.878	7,009.6	062, 073
36(NR1)	Blast furnaces and steel mills	2.275	1.238	1.498	2.287	4.421	27.206	10.683	50.392	5,017.9	671–679
37(NR2)	Nonferrous metals	3.466	1.790	2.098	4.183	5.382	18.250	13.475	51.356	3,026.8	682–687, 689
38(NR3)	Grain-mill products	1.570	1.096	1.954	10.023	1.135	15.473	18.644	50.105	1,580.5	046, 047
39(NR4)	Meat products	0.569	0.194	1.026	5.584	0.482	7.117	14.374	70.654	1,910.1	013
40(NR5)	Dairy products	0.420	1.202	0.890	8.321	0.266	8.835	18.034	62.032	2,495.0	022, 024, 029
41(NR6)	Canning and preserving	0.872	0.694	1.726	6.362	1.035	11.211	13.346	64.754	3,491.4	032, 053, 055
42(NR7)	Paper and pulp mills	1.838	2.054	2.318	3.701	2.879	16.038	11.244	59.928	3,363.7	641
43(NR8)	Sawmills and rough wood products	0.208	0.236	0.912	5.949	0.830	13.485	6.273	72.107	1,381.9	631
44(NR9)	Petroleum refining	6.063	4.625	5.272	5.868	3.028	20.310	19.951	34.883	822.2	332
45(NR10)	Beverages	0.938	0.413	1.436	8.892	1.255	12.650	19.411	55.005	8,444.5	111, 112
46(NR11)	Tobacco products	0.484	0.629	1.066	4.069	1.690	10.181	12.044	69.837	2,719.2	122

Sources: Skill composition of labor force from *U.S. Census of Population 1960, Occupation by Industry;* employment relative to value of shipments estimated from *U.S. Annual Survey of Manufacturing 1961* on the basis of a sum of available 1961 data by subindustries, except that, for industries 5, 36, and 37, shipments data were taken from U.S., Department of Commerce, *Survey of Current Business* (January 1964).

Method: Each trade flow was broken down by industries, based on U.N. trade data by SITC classes taken from *Commodity Trade Statistics.* Employment required in each industry to produce the value of goods traded was computed on the basis of estimates of employment relative to value of shipments, shown above. These labor requirements were broken down into skill classes according to the percentage distributions shown. Total labor requirements for the trade flow and their average skill composition were obtained by summing the results for the 46 industries. For a mathematical formulation, see D. B. Keesing, "Labor Skills and International Trade: Evaluating Many Trade Flows with a Single Measuring Device," *Review of Economics and Statistics,* XLVII (August 1965).

Table 2

Percentage Breakdown of Labor Requirements by Skill Class[a] to Produce 1962 Exports of 14 Countries, Using 1960 U.S. Skill Combinations, for 46 Manufacturing Industries

	I	II	III	IV	V	VI	VII	VIII	Index[b]
U.S.	5.02	2.89	2.74	4.85	8.38	14.96	15.73	45.42	.654
Sweden	3.53	2.34	2.23	4.41	8.92	18.87	13.73	45.96	.547
Germany	3.89	2.48	2.33	4.69	8.44	15.84	14.54	47.79	.541
U.K.	3.77	2.29	2.36	4.79	7.20	15.01	14.91	49.68	.484
Switzerland	3.50	2.39	2.18	5.29	7.76	12.66	15.65	50.56	.473
Canada	4.17	2.33	2.43	4.76	5.39	16.45	14.70	49.76	.467
Netherlands	3.62	2.39	2.31	4.65	5.04	15.62	14.50	51.87	.418
France	3.15	1.92	2.15	4.58	5.28	15.55	14.14	53.24	.370
Austria	2.76	1.76	1.91	4.15	5.71	15.97	12.87	54.87	.338
Belgium	2.83	1.71	1.98	3.86	4.67	17.35	12.75	54.85	.323
Italy	2.75	1.75	1.97	4.33	4.32	12.78	13.24	58.86	.293
Japan	2.48	1.66	1.78	3.96	4.56	15.15	12.04	58.38	.281
India	0.71	0.58	1.06	3.47	1.33	11.13	9.62	72.09	.084
Hong Kong	0.69	0.49	1.13	3.75	1.34	8.48	10.39	73.73	.084

[a] Skill classes are: I, scientists and engineers; II, technicians and draftsmen; III, other professionals; IV, managers; V, machinists, electricians, and tool- and diemakers; VI, other skilled manual workers; VII, clerical, sales and service workers; VIII, semi-skilled and unskilled workers.

[b] Index is computed from the following formula:

$$\text{Index} = \frac{2(\text{I} + \text{II} + \text{III}) + \text{V}}{\text{VIII}}$$

Table 3

Percentage Breakdown of Labor Requirements by Skill Class to Produce 1962 Exports of 13 Countries, Using 1960 U.S. Skill Combinations for 46 Manufacturing Industries

	I	II	III	IV	V	VI	VII	VIII	Index[a]
U.S.	2.77	1.71	2.02	4.63	3.88	13.87	13.74	57.38	.294
Germany	3.02	1.88	2.00	4.48	5.26	14.57	13.54	55.24	.345
U.K.	3.21	1.98	2.13	4.94	5.30	14.25	14.25	53.96	.370
Sweden	3.56	2.28	2.26	4.52	6.26	14.92	14.11	52.08	.431
Switzerland	3.48	2.14	2.28	4.66	6.41	15.11	14.47	51.46	.432
Austria	3.38	2.16	2.27	4.72	7.10	14.37	14.45	51.55	.441
Belgium	3.71	2.26	2.34	4.58	6.10	14.99	14.48	51.54	.441
Netherlands	3.89	2.39	2.29	4.41	6.17	14.93	13.91	52.01	.448
France	3.62	2.19	2.33	5.22	6.56	15.65	15.55	48.88	.467
Canada	4.09	2.37	2.60	4.70	7.05	14.74	15.32	49.12	.512
India	4.31	2.62	2.46	4.62	7.08	17.32	14.87	46.71	.554
Italy	4.22	2.53	2.53	4.59	7.86	16.20	14.58	47.65	.554
Japan	5.12	3.12	2.71	5.10	9.53	15.87	15.94	42.62	.737

[a] For skill classes and index, see Table 2.

1964 Bilateral Trade among the Group of Ten: Requirements of Class I, Scientists and Engineers, as Percentage of Labor Required to Produce Manufactures Traded from One Country to Another, Using 1960 U.S. Skill Combinations for 46 Industries

From	To								
	U.S.	Canada	Netherlands	Germany	U.K.	Sweden	Belgium	Italy	Japan
U.S.	—	3.9	5.0	4.7	4.4	4.8	4.1	4.5	5.3
Canada	3.7	—	5.7	6.5	2.8	5.2	4.6	5.7	4.7
Netherlands	4.5	3.8	—	5.7	3.6	3.9	3.4	4.7	9.2
Germany	3.6	3.7	3.8	—	4.2	3.7	3.8	4.1	4.6
U.K.	2.6	3.4	4.1	3.9	—	4.3	3.7	4.2	4.0
Sweden	3.4	3.7	3.1	2.8	2.6	—	3.2	3.5	5.5
France	2.5	2.0	3.6	2.7	2.7	3.24	2.9	3.5	4.2
Belgium	2.7	2.3	2.6	3.5	2.4	2.7	—	4.6	4.9
Italy	1.5	1.7	2.8	2.8	2.4	2.9	4.2	—	4.1
Japan	2.7	2.0	3.2	2.9	2.5	3.3	2.8	2.8	—

Table 5

1964 Bilateral Trade among the Group of Ten: Requirements of Class V, Machinists, Electricians, and Tool and Diemakers, as Percentage of Labor Required to Produce Manufactures Traded from One Country to Another, Using 1960 U.S. Skill Combinations for 46 Industries

From	To								
	U.S.	Germany	Sweden	U.K.	Netherlands	Canada	France	Belgium	Italy	Japan
U.S.	—	8.4	8.3	8.7	7.3	8.5	9.9	8.5	9.5	9.2
Germany	7.4	—	7.5	8.9	6.9	7.8	8.0	7.7	8.7	11.5
Sweden	7.3	6.2	—	6.8	7.8	10.7	7.9	8.5	9.0	9.0
U.K.	4.7	6.8	6.2	—	7.4	6.7	7.7	8.1	7.5	7.6
Netherlands	5.2	5.7	5.3	5.1	—	5.5	5.4	4.3	5.9	7.3
Canada	4.9	6.1	6.4	4.3	5.1	—	6.3	6.9	5.9	5.1
France	3.8	4.4	5.1	4.3	5.0	3.1	—	5.2	5.6	7.0
Belgium	4.6	4.8	5.9	4.2	3.6	4.2	5.0	—	6.6	4.9
Italy	2.6	4.1	3.2	4.6	4.0	3.4	5.7	5.2	—	8.9
Japan	3.9	4.0	3.7	5.4	5.1	3.2	5.7	4.1	4.5	—

Table 6

Net Skill Outflows Embodied in 10 Leading Industrial Countries' 1962 Trade in Manufactures, Based on 1960 U.S. Skill Requirements for 46 Industries

Net Balance in Trade (Numbers of People), by Skill Class[a]

	I	II	III	IV	V	VI	VII	VIII
U.S.	24,688	13,780	11,653	16,921	43,729	53,616	55,345	108,887
Germany	14,466	9,380	8,104	15,116	35,016	52,616	47,822	127,051
U.K.	9,398	6,257	6,236	11,324	21,706	38,165	37,689	111,320
Japan	2,191	1,709	2,302	5,890	3,916	25,167	17,450	111,247
France	2,516	1,567	2,008	3,764	3,289	16,818	12,722	66,705
Italy	-1,005	-419	257	1,418	-3,343	344	3,531	40,590
Belgium	168	79	425	813	259	10,532	3,486	28,116
Switzerland	246	415	35	973	-1,884	-1,728	2,192	2,250
Sweden	-391	-169	-254	-568	2,013	2,416	-1,811	-11,556
Netherlands	-1,357	-600	-530	-760	-3,143	-2,749	-2,644	-13,197
Total	50,900	31,999	30,246	54,891	105,326	195,197	175,782	571,483
U.S. % share	48.5	43.1	38.5	30.8	41.5	27.5	31.5	19.1

Netherlands ranked even higher, achieving what amounted to a "tie for first" with the United States.[17]

A weakness in the findings just discussed is that they apply only to the average skill intensity of a country's exports and imports of manufactures, without taking into account the absolute volume of one trade flow compared to the other. To round out the picture, it is possible to compute the net balance of requirements for each skill, that is, the skills required to produce a country's total exports of manufactures minus the skills that would be required to replace its imports of manufactures, using the same American skill coefficients. Of course, when the value of a country's exports of manufactures is greater than that of imports (or vice versa), this balance reflects a flow of goods outside the manufacturing sector, services, or credit. A more complete picture of the factor implications of trade would include natural-resource and labor requirements outside manufacturing.

Table 6 gives the net balance of each skill in the 1962 trade in manufactures of 10 leading industrial countries, again computed on the basis of U.S. skill requirements. The table reveals several interesting features. First, only 5 of the largest countries were net exporters in all the skill classes. Second, 3 countries—the United States, the Federal Republic of Germany, and the United Kingdom—supplied most of the rest of the world's net requirements for professional skills and for the manual skills of Class V. These three countries showed a combined net balance equivalent to the services of 48,552 American scientists and engineers, for example, compared to a net of 2,348 for the other seven countries, and an apparent deficit of 50,900 for the excluded countries. The last total can be regarded as the net "flow" of skill services implicit in the trade in manufactures from the industrial countries to the relatively skill-deficient, predominantly primary-producing countries not shown in the table. The total apparent net flows to these other countries showed a skill-intensive pattern well within the range measured in the first two tables.[18]

---

[17] Netherlands exports to the United States and the United Kingdom were more intensive in Class III skills than exports in the reverse direction. There were two other "reversals" in Class III, compared to the patterns for Classes I and II, involving the trade flows between France and Sweden and between Italy and France.

[18] Expressed as a percentage of total labor requirements, the apparent net flows had the following composition by skill class: Class I, 4.19; II, 2.63; III, 2.49; IV, 4.51; V, 8.66; VI, 16.05; VII, 14.46; VIII, 47.00; index .580. The results are not free of systematic bias, however, since countries other than the United States report imports c.i.f. Thus, their net balances were somewhat underestimated.

The consistency of these results emphasizes the desirability of a major effort to compare and analyze the disaggregated skill requirements of production processes in different countries. Hopefully, widening international recognition of the importance of manpower and educational planning will speed accumulation of the necessary facts.[19]

[19] Since this paper was written, a major study has appeared that adds significantly to our knowledge of labor skills in other countries. See M. A. Horowitz, M. Zymelman, and I. L. Herrnstadt, *Manpower Requirements for Planning: An International Comparison Approach* (Boston: Northeastern University, 1966). This study permits a comparison of occupational skill mixes (excluding manual workers), industry by industry, for seventeen countries. For professional, technical, and clerical skills there are such strong parallels among countries in the skill mixes of the various industries that the key assumption of this paper is thoroughly vindicated: Results very similar to those in Tables 2 and 3, above, would occur using skill matrixes from any industrial country.

HELEN WAEHRER

Wage Rates, Labor Skills, and United States Foreign Trade

IN AN INVESTIGATION OF THE RELATIONSHIP between interindustry wage differences and the commodity composition of U.S. foreign trade, Irving Kravis noted that U.S. export industries were characterized by higher labor earnings than U.S. import-competing industries.[1] This finding is not immediately reconcilable with certain implications of classical international-trade theory. The doctine of comparative advantage would lead us to believe that the wage structure will not exert a systematic influence

This essay is based on my unpublished doctoral dissertation, "Interindustry Skill Differences, Labor Earnings, and United States Foreign Trade, 1960" (Columbia University, 1966). I am indebted to Gary S. Becker for helpful suggestions and constructive criticisms of the study.

[1] Irving Kravis, "Wages and Foreign Trade," *Review of Economics and Statistics*, XXXIV (February 1956), 14–30.

on the pattern of international trade, and that the structure of trade will not diverge from the structure of comparative advantage determined by interindustry differences in productivity.[2]

To appraise this apparent inconsistency, I shall reexamine the relationship between interindustry differences in labor earnings and the structure of U.S. foreign trade. My study confirms Kravis' results, and I then test the contention that the interindustry distribution of labor skills explains why labor in export industries earns more than labor in import-competing industries.

At this juncture, it is useful to review Kravis' study of the structure of wages and foreign trade. Kravis was concerned with the interindustry pattern of U.S. hourly wage rates when industries are grouped as exporters and import competitors. He investigated three sectors—manufacturing, mining, and agriculture. The structure of U.S. exports and imports in the latter two sectors, however, is related principally to U.S. natural resources, and the structure of labor payments would not be expected to be related to trade in these commodities. In what follows, therefore, I shall be concerned solely with the manufacturing sector.

Kravis began with the 330 manufacturing industries defined in Leontief's input-output system (I-O). He classified industries as "leading" export industries if they exported $50 million or more in either 1947 or 1952, and as "leading" import-competing industries if they competed with imports amounting to $30 million or more in either year.[3] Of the 82 industries so classified, 15 were both leading export and leading import-competing industries. The computed average hourly wage rate paid by leading export industries was higher than the average hourly wage rate paid by leading import-competing industries regardless of the weighting

---

[2] The comparative cost doctrine is thoroughly described by Jacob Viner, *Studies in the Theory of International Trade* (New York: Harper & Row, 1937). Recent empirical studies testing the validity of the comparative-cost model imply that wage differencies do not greatly affect trade patterns. See G. D. A. MacDougall, "British and American Exports: A Study Suggested by the Theory of Comparative Cost, Part I," *Economic Journal*, LXI (December 1951), 679–724; and R. M. Stern, "British and American Productivity and Comparative Costs in International Trade," *Oxford Economic Papers*, XIV (October 1962), 275–96. This implication is also supported by a number of studies concerned with international comparisons of interindustry wage structures. See Karl Frocheimer, "The Role of Relative Wage Differences in International Trade," *Quarterly Journal of Economics*, LXII (November 1947), 1–30; Stanley Lebergott, "Wage Structures," *Review of Economics and Statistics*, XXIX (November 1947), 274–85; and Faith M. Williams and Edgar I. Eaton, "Payments for Labor and Foreign Trade," *American Economic Review*, XLIX (September 1959), 584–601.

[3] Kravis, "Wages and Foreign Trade," p. 15.

procedure used.[4] Kravis asserted that this pattern of wages has held for the last half-century in the United States, and offered the general conclusion that export industries tend to have higher wages than import-competing industries. The implications of this finding, however, were not explored.

The criteria and definitions Kravis adopted may be adequate for his purposes, although judgment on this score is difficult because the model underlying his investigation was not clearly specified. His definitions can be criticized, however, in that they limit the integration of his results with the comparative-cost and factor-endowments trade models, both of which assume, directly or indirectly, that the structure of international trade is determined by interindustry differences in productivity. The major deficiency is Kravis' definition of trade-oriented industries. From the standpoint of trade theory, the degree of trade involvement of an individual industry is better measured relative to that industry's own output, rather than relative to some absolute figure. In addition, his definition creates a bias against the inclusion of the small industry: An industry with annual exports or competitive imports of less than $50 million or $30 million, respectively, but with a large percentage of its own production involved in trade, was excluded from his classification.

These limitations, coupled with the problem of obtaining essential data at the level of detail used by Kravis, made it necessary to rework his empirical analysis of labor payments and trade structure. Although similar to the Kravis study, the analysis described below defines the variables and classifies the data differently.

INTERINDUSTRY DIFFERENCES IN LABOR EARNINGS AND U.S. FOREIGN TRADE, 1960

To test the Kravis relationship between wages and trade structure, I examined interindustry differences in labor earnings in U.S. manufacturing industries organized into export and import-competing groups.

[4] The difference between average hourly wage rates in export and import-competing industries was not statistically significant. In addition, 56 industries, not already classified, were treated as secondary exporters if their exports were 10 per cent or more of domestic production; the pattern of wages for this group confirmed the findings derived from the original classification.

The trade and wage data for 1960[5] were classified to correspond with the most detailed Standard Industrial Classification available for occupations by industry in the Census of Population for 1960.[6] This industry grouping will be refered to as the Census-SIC classification. It is a combination of four-digit SIC level data and more aggregative three- and two-digit data.

The Census-SIC classification comprises 59 manufacturing industries. The degree of trade involvement for each of these industries was defined as the percentage of its shipments exported or directly challenged by imports in 1960.[7] The requisite percentages were calculated by dividing the value of industry exports by the value of industry shipments and, similarly, by dividing the value of competitive imports (defined as imports of commodities produced domestically by the industry) by the value of industry shipments.[8] Average yearly earnings per employee, computed from total payroll data, were used to measure labor payments and were treated as equivalent to average wages and salaries in each industry.[9] Hereafter, they are called "yearly wages." The use of "yearly wages," rather than the average hourly wage rate, permits the inclusion of professional and technical workers as well as production workers, and allows subsequent use of the data to test the contention that differences in labor earnings are due mainly to differences in skill.

[5] 1960 was chosen because all the necessary data were available for that year.

[6] U.S., Bureau of the Census, *United States Census of Population: 1960, Subject Reports: Occupation by Industry* (Washington, D.C.: U.S. Government Printing Office, 1963).

[7] Ideally, competitive imports should be measured as a percentage of U.S. consumption or production, and exports should be measured as a percentage of world consumption or production (excluding the United States). However, lack of available data and the ordering by "net trade balance" prevented this measurement. For a detailed discussion, see Waehrer, "Interindustry Skill Differences," pp. 33–34. In addition, it would have been better to use free-trade exports and imports, but this could not be done because one cannot measure the degree of protection here and abroad.

[8] In some cases, this was not possible, and a substitute measure was used. For a complete discussion of alternative calculations and limitations involved, see Waehrer, "Interindustry Skill Differences," Technical Appendix A, pp. 184–90. The data on shipments by industry were obtained from the U.S. Bureau of the Census, *1960 Annual Survey of Manufactures, Value of Shipments of Selected Classes of Products, 1960, 1959, and 1958* (Washington, D.C.: U.S. Government Printing Office, 1962). The data for the value of exports and competitive imports were obtained from the U.S. Bureau of Labor Statistics, Division of Productivity and Technological Developments. I am grateful to Mr. J. Alterman for making available these unpublished data. The Bureau measured exports at producer value and competitive imports at U.S. port value.

[9] Average annual earnings data were obtained from the *Annual Survey of Manufactures*. Only direct labor payments were used, not wage supplements (fringe benefits). However, changes in wage supplements seem closely correlated with changes in direct wage payments.

Since many of the 59 industries had very small export and import percentages, it seemed unnecessary to include all of them in the analysis. Hence, cutoff points were selected to exclude industries that were relatively unimportant from the standpoint of international trade. I excluded those industries which, in 1960, exported or were challenged by imports amounting to a smaller percentage of their shipments than the overall average for all 59 industries. The cutoff points were 4.17 per cent for export industries and 4.90 per cent for import-competing industries. Of the 59 industries, 22 were thereby defined as export industries (because they exported at least 4.17 per cent of their shipments), and 22 as import-competing industries (because they were challenged by imports amounting to at least 4.90 per cent of their shipments). Each of these two categories contained 9 industries defined as both export and import-competing industries.[10] The double classification of these 9 industries seems to arise from aggregation: A broad range of very specific commodities, some-times at different stages of fabrication, is included within each industry. Transport costs may also be involved.

The first procedure used to study the relationship between wage differences and foreign trade involved a straightforward comparison of the unweighted means of yearly wages in the export and import-competing industries:

Industry Group	Number of Industries	Unweighted Average Yearly Wages
All industries	59	$5,027.61
All export industries	22	5,648.82
All import-competing industries	22	4,932.32

The unweighted mean yearly wage for the export group was above the mean yearly wage for all industries; the mean yearly wage for the import-competing group was below the mean for all industries. The difference between the export and import-competing mean yearly wages is statistically significant.[11]

The relationship between wages and trade would probably be more striking if industries with close links to natural resources had been excluded from the group. Two such industries illustrate this contention: In 1960, tobacco manufacturers exported 11 per cent of their shipments and paid

[10] For a list of these industries, see the Appendix.

[11] The computed value of t is 2.48; with 36 degrees of freedom, the critical value of t is 2.03 at the .05 level of significance.

the lowest wage in the export group; petroleum refiners were challenged by imports amounting to 5 per cent of their shipments and paid the highest wage in the import-competing group.

Next, a more detailed regression and correlation analysis was performed for a joint array of the "net trade balances" of the 22 export and 22 import-competing industries; that is, the percentage of shipments exported minus the percentage of shipments challenged by imports.[12] This ordering by the "net trade balances" eliminated two important deficiences of the initial procedure: its failure to take account of the dual trade orientation of many industries, and its failure to provide a continuous measure of trade involvement in a joint sample of export and import-competing industries.

The characteristics of the sample arrayed in this manner are shown in the Appendix. Although the net trade balances reduce the computed percentages of trade involvement, the positions of the industries within the array do not change substantially. The only changes occur within the 9 industries that fell into both groups. There, the shifts in position are quite noticeable.

The regression equation between the net trade balances and the values of the yearly wage is:

$$W = 5229.79 + 54.55B, \quad r = 0.43$$

where W measures the yearly wage and B measures the net trade balance. The relationship is statistically significant.[13]

This first regression equation took no account of industries that are but slightly involved in trade. A second equation was therefore derived from a trade-balance array of all 59 Census-SIC manufacturing industries, in order to determine whether the use of cutoff points had arbitrarily converted an insignificant relationship into a significant one. The equation for this array is:

$$W = 5059.72 + 59.66B, \quad r = 0.38$$

This relationship also is statistically significant.[14]

[12] The net trade balances result in a new classification of industries as net exporters or net import-competitors, but this method of classification was not used as a criterion for redefining industries significantly involved in foreign trade. It was merely superimposed on the 22 export and 22 import-competing industries obtained from the original definitions of trade involvement.

[13] The computed value of t is 2.72; with 33 degrees of freedom, the critical value of t is 2.03 at the .05 level of significance.

[14] The computed value of t is 3.13; with 55 degrees of freedom, the critical value of t is 1.65 at the .05 level of significance.

These two statistically significant relationships, together with the difference in yearly wages between the export and import-competing groups, substantiate the findings obtained by Kravis: There is a systematic relationship between interindustry wage differences and the structure of U.S. foreign trade.

THEORETICAL CONSIDERATIONS

The remainder of this essay is devoted to the formulation and testing of an additional hypothesis: Interindustry differences in skill mix account for a significant part of the tendency for labor to receive higher earnings in export industries than in import-competing industries. On this hypothesis, the wage pattern is not a determinant of the trade pattern. Rather, interindustry wage differences and the structure of U.S. foreign trade are each associated significantly with the interindustry distribution of occupational skills. This hypothesis derives from the assumption that a worker's productive skill results from his investment in himself, and that this investment earns a return embodied in the wage rate. This assumption, in turn, stems from Becker's broad definition of investment in humans as the totality of "activities which influence future real income through the imbedding of resources in people."[15]

If this argument is correct, a positive relationship should exist between interindustry differences in wages and interindustry skill-mix differences. An industry whose labor force is characterized by a relatively large proportion of highly skilled occupations should tend to pay higher wages than an industry using less skilled employees; and, on my hypothesis, export industries should be characterized by a greater skill intensity than import-competing industries. Finally, this argument offers a testable hypothesis: One would expect to observe stronger relationships between wage and skill differences and between trade and skill differences than between wage and trade differences.

The first relationship anticipated by my hypothesis, that between wages and skill, was derived from the analyses of Becker and Schultz[16] who held

[15] Gary S. Becker, "Investment in Human Capital: A Theoretical Analysis," *Journal of Political Economy*, LXX Supplement (October 1962), 9.

[16] T. W. Schultz, "Reflections on Investment in Man," *Journal of Political Economy*, LXX Supplement (October 1962), 1–8; and Gary S. Becker, *Human Capital* (New York: National Bureau of Economic Research, 1965).

that the structure of wages is primarily determined by capital investments in man: "· · · except for some pure rent (in earnings) for differences in inherited abilities, most of the differences in earnings are a consequence of differences in the amounts that have been invested in people."[17] If we assume that the capital investment in man occurred only in the form of training, and if the cost of occupational entry were a function only of the amount of training, then differences in wages paid to the various occupations would exactly reflect differences in the amounts of training required by those occupations. The concept of training used here is Becker's, and it includes formal and technical education as well as on-the-job training. For formal and technical schooling, the costs of training include the cost of tuition and, more importantly, earnings forgone while at school; some or all of these costs are usually borne by the student. In "general" as distinct from "specific" on-the-job training,[18] the employee again pays part, if not all, of the training cost by receiving a lower wage during the training period. In both cases, the individual has increased his current expense or lowered his current income in order to secure a larger lifetime earnings stream.[19]

Earnings, as defined by Becker, are net of the costs of investment and gross of the returns to investment. This definition of earnings is consistent with Marshall's long-term supply price; in the long term, the price of labor must be high enough to induce labor to provide its productive service.[20] This long-term supply price of labor must cover the worker's costs, including training costs. Assuming that workers in skilled occupations incur greater training costs than workers in relatively unskilled occupations, workers in skilled occupations should receive greater absolute earnings than those received by workers in relatively unskilled occupations.

The second relationship anticipated by my hypothesis, that between skill and the structure of trade, is derived from the contention that broad categories such as capital and labor cannot be used to predict the structure

[17] Schultz, "Reflections" p. 1.

[18] Specific on-the-job training refers to the acquisition of skills which cannot be transferred from one firm to another. Therefore, the employer will be willing to pay all the training costs. General on-the-job training can be used elsewhere. For a discussion of these differences, see Becker, *Human Capital*, pp. 11–29.

[19] *Ibid.* Chapter 2.

[20] Alfred Marshall, *Principles of Economics* (eighth ed.; New York: Macmillan Co., 1948), Book IV, Chapter 1, p. 142, and Book VI, Chapter 5, p. 577.

of trade in the Heckscher-Ohlin model.[21] Labor, for example, should be subdivided into two or more factors of production, according to degrees of skill, and, as a first approximation, international differences in relative skill supplies should help to determine which goods will be exported and imported.[22]

Using the Heckscher-Ohlin model to predict the trade structure of the United States, economists first looked to the capital/labor endowment of the United States and pointed out that the United States is relatively abundant in tangible capital—physical plant and equipment. Accordingly, they expected U.S. export industries to use larger amounts of capital per worker than its import-competing industries. Empirical tests of this prediction, however, indicated that the capital intensities of U.S. industries had no relationship to these industries' trade performance. Leontief's attempt to verify the Heckscher-Ohlin model in terms of two productive factors, capital and labor, even showed the opposite and paradoxical result that U.S. export industries are labor-intensive rather than capital-intensive.[23]

Leontief explained his paradox by suggesting that the United States is, in fact, a labor-abundant country because American labor is more efficient than foreign labor. He supported this interpretation by disaggregating labor requirement per million dollars of trade according to skill class and showing that the labor involved in export production is more highly skilled than that involved in import-competing production.[24] But Leontief did not try to forecast the trade pattern from his skill-mix data.

The next step was taken by Keesing, in his study of the skill content of international trade.[25] He sought to treat different qualities of labor as

[21] Eli Heckscher, "The Effect of Foreign Trade on the Distribution of National Income," reprinted in *Readings in the Theory of International Trade*, ed. by H. S. Ellis and L. A. Metzler for the American Economic Association (Philadelphia, Pa.: Blakiston, 1950), pp. 272–300; and Bertil Ohlin, *Interregional and International Trade* (Harvard Economic Studies, Vol. XXXIX; Cambridge, Mass.: Harvard University Press, 1933).

[22] This point was anticipated by Heckscher and Ohlin. See Heckscher, "Effect of Foreign Trade," p. 279; and Ohlin, "Interregional," p. 71.

[23] Wassily W. Leontief, "Factor Proportions and the Structure of American Trade: Further Theoretical and Empirical Analysis," *Review of Economics and Statistics*, XXXVII (November 1956), 386–407.

[24] *Ibid.*, p. 399, Table 2.

[25] Donald B. Keesing, "Labor Skills and the Factor Content of International Trade" (unpublished Ph.D. dissertation, Harvard University, 1961); "Labor Skills and International Trade: Evaluating Many Trade Flows with a Single Measuring Device," *Review of Economics and Statistics*, XLVII (August 1965), 287–97, and "Labor Skills and the Structure of Trade in Manufactures," in this book.

separate productive factors, then used the ratio of skilled to unskilled labor in a two-factor, many-country model predictive of trade structure. The skill content of exports and imports was measured for the United States, seven European countries, and Japan, using U.S. skill coefficients derived from Leontief's skill calculations. Keesing then ordered the countries by direct skill requirements in export production and, similarly, in import-competing production, and showed a symmetrical ordering of countries. Those whose exports are most skill-intensive have the least skill-intensive imports.[26] From this study, Keesing concluded that skill availability is a major factor in the determination of trade patterns.

The studies by Leontief and Keesing indicate that the United States has abundant skilled labor and tends to export goods embodying large amounts of skill while importing goods embodying large amounts of unskilled labor. I shall reproduce this finding and show that it explains the higher wages paid by export industries.

STATISTICAL CONSIDERATIONS

To test the hypothesis that interindustry differences in skill account for the wage differences observed between export and import-competing industries, one must first devise a measure of an industry's skill mix that can be applied to the industrial classification used in the empirical study of wages and trade. If the skills required by an occupation were uniquely correlated with the years of training needed to acquire those skills (formal and technical schooling, as well as on-the-job training), the years of formal education and on-the-job training displayed by the workers in each industry would provide the best measure. However, available data concerning on-the-job training are not classified according to the Standard Industrial Classification (SIC); thus, the use of this measure is precluded.[27] Instead, an "occupational index" was constructed from the Census of Population for 1960.[28] The Census of Population divides occupations

[26] Keesing, "Labor Skills and the Factor Content of Trade," pp. 81–82, Tables IV-I, II.

[27] Eckaus has calculated for 1950 the man-years of vocational training and general education required in selected industries. Unfortunately, his study came out too late to include his calculations. See Eckaus, "Economic Criteria for Education and Training", *Review of Economics and Statistics* XLVI (May 1964), 181–90.

[28] U.S. Bureau of the Census, *United States Census of Population, 1960, Index of Occupations and Industries* (Washington, D.C.: U.S. Government Printing Office, 1960).

into eleven classifications, eight of which are relevant to this study:[29]

I. Professional, technical, and kindred workers.
II. Managers, officials, proprietors, except farm.
III. Clerical and kindred workers.
IV. Sales workers.
V. Craftsmen, foremen, and kindred workers.
VI. Operatives and kindred workers.
VII. Service workers.
VIII. Laborers, except farm and mine.

Next, a definition of a skilled occupation was developed to identify the eight occupational groupings as skilled or unskilled. Three factors were used in devising this definition: the job title of each class, the detailed composition of each class, and the median years of schooling completed in each class. Using these three criteria, classes I through V and VII were defined as skilled, and classes VI and VIII were defined as unskilled.[30] The "occupational index," in turn, is defined as the percentage of employees in each industry belonging to the skilled occupational classes.[31]

EMPIRICAL RESULTS

My hypothesis suggests two testable relationships that might explain the correlation between yearly wages and the U.S. trade pattern. First, a significantly positive relationship should exist between interindustry differences in wages and interindustry differences in skill mix. Second, a statistically significant positive relationship should exist between the pattern of foreign trade and interindustry differences in skill mix. If, moreover, the observed relationship between wages and trade merely mirrors the relationships between interindustry differences in skills and wages and interindustry differences in skills and trade performance, each

[29] The other three classes (farm proprietors and farm managers, private household workers, and farm laborers and foremen) are not relevant to a study of manufacturing. The numbering of classes is my own and will be used in place of the title when referring to the classes. Service workers (VII) exclude private household workers.

[30] For a detailed discussion of this procedure, see Waehrer, "Interindustry Skill Differences," pp. 93–97.

[31] The most important limitation of this index is the amount of variation in training requirements within each of the eight general occupational classes; this variation is most conspicuous in classes III, IV, and VII.

of these relationships should be stronger than the direct association between wages and trade.

Least-squares regression and correlation analysis was used to test the first implication of my hypothesis—that a significant association exists between the level of wages and the skill content of an industry. The occupational index and the yearly wage were computed for 35 industries, classified on the Census-SIC level. (There were 22 export industries and 22 import-competing industries; but, as before, 9 of the industries were both export and import-competing.) A regression equation was fitted to the joint array of the export and import-competing industries:

$$W = 1923.44 + 67.89I, \quad r = 0.86$$

where W is average yearly wages, and I the occupational index. The relationship between annual wages and the occupational index is statistically significant,[32] and the test confirms the existence of a positive association between interindustry differences in wages and interindustry differences in skill content.

Before testing the second implication of the hypothesis, I pause to point out that the significant association between yearly wages and skill content should permit one to reproduce actual labor earnings in a particular industry by constructing an earnings figure from the wage data for each occupation and the skill-mix data for each industry. This can be attempted because wage and salary data are available on both bases. Data derived from total payroll figures have already been used as the measure of earnings in the study. Data for remuneration by occupational group were available in the *1960 Census of Population*. The former data were given by SIC, collected from an industry sample; the latter were collected by the Bureau of the Census from a 5 per cent sample of individual workers, and are given by occupational class.

Two estimates of yearly wages were computed, one from each source. The first estimate was the unweighted mean average yearly wages, already used. The second was computed from the median wage and salary figure given for each of the eight occupational classes by the *1960 Census of Population*. This median earnings figure was given separately for male and female workers in each occupational class. In each class, the female workers' earnings were lower than those of male workers.[33]

---

[32] The computed value of t is 9.39; with 33 degrees of freedom, the critical value of t is 2.03 at the .05 level of significance.

[33] See U.S., Bureau of the Census, *Occupational Characteristics*, pp. 336–55, Table XXVII.

Because of this difference, a weighted average of the two medians was computed for each occupational class to take account of interindustry differences in the sex composition of the labor force. Using the aircraft industry as an example, Table 1 shows the procedure used in constructing the yearly wage for each industry.

Constructed measures of earnings were calculated for each of the 35 export and import-competing industries classified on the Census-SIC level. These constructed measures are given in Table 2, along with the actual payroll averages (the yearly wages used elsewhere in this study). For all but 4 of the 35 industries, the yearly wage level estimated from the payroll data was higher than the yearly wage estimated from the occupational data, and these differences tend to be larger in the export sector. One possible reason for the higher payroll estimates is the differences between the methods used to collect the basic data. The occupational wage data were obtained from individual workers, and individuals tend to understate their incomes, biasing the wage estimates.

Another point may be involved (and may also account for the four cases in which the occupational yearly wage estimates were higher than the constructed payroll yearly wage estimates, and for the larger differences found in the export sector). The occupational wages are median estimates, whereas the payroll wages are mean estimates. If the distribution of earnings were symmetrical, the two would be identical. Since the earnings distribution is positively skewed, median estimates tend to be smaller than mean estimates. In addition, the less skilled an occupation, the more symmetrical is its wage distribution. This line of reasoning has been further developed by Becker.[34] His formula for earnings is:

$$Y = X + rC$$

where C measures total investment in human capital, r the average rate of return, and X measures earnings when there is no investment in human capital. He then states that:

Variations in X help explain an important difference among skill categories in the degree of skewness. The smaller the fraction of total earnings resulting from investment in human capital—the smaller rC relative to X—the more the distribution of earnings would be dominated by the distribution of X. Higher skill categories have a greater average investment in human capital and thus presumably a larger rC relative to X. The distribution of "unskilled ability," X, would, therefore, tend to dominate the distribution of earnings in relatively unskilled

[34] Becker, *Human Capital*, pp. 61–66.

Table 1

Constructed Yearly Wage, Aircraft Industry

Occupational Group (1)	National Median Wage		Number of Employees in Industry Labor Force		Sex-Weighted Median Wage (6)	Percentage of Total Employees in Industry (7)	(6) × (7)
	Male (2)	Female (3)	Male (4)	Female (5)			
I	$6,343	$3,697	134,560	6,373	$6,225.84	22.7	$1,413.27
II	6,960	3,646	18,238	977	6,791.14	3.0	203.73
III	4,761	3,014	48,370	60,372	3,791.09	17.2	652.07
IV	4,849	1,477	2,971	59	4,783.34	0.5	23.92
V	5,315	2,973	162,775	4,398	5,253.39	26.4	1,386.90
VI	4,292	2,338	148,193	27,268	3,988.33	27.7	1,104.77
VII	3,239	1,351	9,314	1,541	2,970.98	1.7	50.51
VIII	2,976	1,921	5,038	181	2,939.41	0.8	23.52
All occupations							$4,858.69

Source: U.S., Bureau of the Census, Occupational Characteristics, pp. 336–55, Table xxvii.

categories while the distribution of a product of ability and the amount invested, rC, would dominate in skilled categories. Hence, if abilities were symmetrically distributed, earnings would tend to be more symmetrically distributed among the unskilled rather than among the skilled.[35]

Assuming that differences in training and skill are attributable to differences in human capital, if the import-competing industries are less skill-intensive than the export industries, the differences between the mean and median would tend to be smaller in the former than in the latter.

Although the two earnings measures do not give identical estimates, they should be positively and significantly related if differences in occupational structure explain differences in earnings by industry. A least-squares regression equation fitted to the joint array of the 35 export and import-competing industries confirms this hypothesis:

$$W = -5426.34 + 2.49Wc, \quad r = 0.87$$

where W measures the annual wage derived from payroll data, and Wc the annual wage constructed from data on occupational earnings and the skill mix of each industry. The two estimates are positively and significantly correlated, implying that one can reproduce most of the actual structure of interindustry earnings from occupational data.

Now for the second part of my hypothesis: To compare the skill intensities of export and import-competing industries, the two groups of industries were arrayed separately, by the ratio of trade to value of shipments.

The average occupational indexes for the export and import-competing groups and for all 59 manufacturing industries are:

Industry Group	Number of Industries	Mean Occupational Index (%)
All industries	59	47.08
Export industries	35	52.84
Import-competing industries	35	42.89

The export industries, on the average, have a higher occupational index than the import-competing industries; the 9.95 percentage point difference (export average *minus* import average) is statistically significant.[36]

[35] *Ibid.*, p. 65.

[36] The computed value of t is 2.85; the critical value of t is 2.02 at the .05 level of significance.

Table 2

*Two Estimates of Yearly Wages for Census-SIC Export and
Import-Competing Industries, 1960*

Census Groups and Code Numbers		Yearly Wages Estimated from	
		Payroll Data	Occupational Earnings
Export Industries			
0713, 204	Grain mill products	$5,188	$4,487
21	Tobacco manufactures	3,871	3,612
281, 2, 284,[b] 6–9	Miscellaneous chemicals and allied products	6,189	4,667
283	Drugs and medicines	6,108	4,425
2823, 4	Synthetic fibers	5,535	4,327
295, 9	Miscellaneous petroleum and coal products	5,698	4,487
307	Miscellaneous plastic products	4,682	4,087
342	Cutlery, hand tools, and other hardware	5,275	4,179
351, 3–6, 8, 9	Miscellaneous machinery	5,943	4,723
357	Office, computing, and accounting machines	6,316	4,619
36	Electrical machinery, equipment, and supplies	5,404	4,276
372	Aircraft and parts	6,842	4,859
194,[c] 381–5	Professional equipment and supplies	5,818	4,488
Import-competing industries			
203	Canning and preserving fruits, vegetables, and seafoods	3,602	3,766
206, 9	Miscellaneous food preparations and kindred products	4,915	4,268
208	Beverage industries	5,391	4,475
225	Knitting mills	3,232	3,185
227	Floor covering, except hard surface	3,810	3,952
229	Miscellaneous textile mill products	4,314	4,018

Table 2 (continued)

Census Groups and Code Numbers		Yearly Wages Estimated from	
		Payroll Data	Occupational Earnings
242, 3	Sawmills, planing mills, and mill work	3,683	4,000
244, 9	Miscellaneous wood products	3,519	4,207
291	Petroleum refining	7,087	4,768
312, 5–7, 9	Leather products, except footwear	3,851	3,613
326	Pottery and related products	4,467	3,857
387	Watches, clocks, and clockwork-operated devices	4,959	3,837
39	Miscellaneous manufacturing industries	4,276	4,002
Export and import-competing industries			
226	Dyeing and finishing textile, except wool and knit goods	4,287	4,105
261–3, 6	Pulp, paper, and paperboard mills	5,959	4,408
311	Leather: tanned, cured, and finished	4,744	4,179
3312, 3	Blast furnaces, steelworks, and rolling and finishing mills	6,592	4,495
333–6, 3392, 9	Primary nonferrous industries	5,799	4,518
352	Farm machinery and equipment	5,451	4,625
371	Motor vehicles and motor vehicle equipment	6,486	4,521
374, 5, 9	Railroad and miscellaneous transportation equipment	5,352	4,548
386	Photographic equipment and supplies	6,735	4,488

[a] 0713 is excluded from the estimate of wages using payroll data.

[b] Except 2823 and 2824.

[c] 194 is excluded from the estimate of wages using payroll data.

In the final step in the analysis, I attempted to ascertain whether the wage-to-skill and trade-to-skill relationships are stronger than the wage-to-trade relationship established at the start of this essay. Comparing the t values of the export *less* import-competing wage and skill differences:

Sample Means	Degrees of Freedom	Computed Value of t
Assuming that standard errors of sample means are interdependent:		
Wages	36	6.00
Occupational index	44	12.61
Assuming that standard errors of sample means are independent:		
Wages	36	2.48
Occupational index	44	2.85

The skill differences between export and import-competing industries has higher statistical significance than the wage difference. The same tendency is shown by another test in which the independent association between wages and trade tends to disappear as skill intensity is introduced into the association:

	Wage Level		Total
	Above Median	Below Median	Industries
Export industries			
Above median skill	9	2	11
Below median skill	1	2	3
Total	10	4	14
Import-competing industries			
Above median skill	1	1	2
Below median skill	0	10	10
Total	1	11	12
Both export and import-competing industries			
Above median skill	5	0	5
Below median skill	2	2	4
Total	7	2	9

Yet both of these attempts to compare the wage-to-skill, trade-to-skill, and wage-to-trade associations are imperfect. A more detailed analysis is required, using the joint array of export and import-competing industries to provide a continuous ordering of industries by trade involvement according to the net trade balance. Regression and correlation analysis was performed on the relationship between the degree of trade involvement and the occupational index. I obtained the significant regression equation:

$$B = 16.25 + 0.31I, \quad r = 0.50$$

where B measures the net trade balance, and I the occupational index. The larger the percentage of workers engaged in skilled occupations, the larger is the net trade balance.

Regression analysis was also used to test the relationship between wages and foreign trade involvement for the joint array of export and import-competing industries. This provided a basis for comparing these results and those from the relationship between foreign trade and skill. The joint sample of the 35 industries was again arrayed according to the net trade balance. Then:

$$B = -18.48 + 0.003W, \quad r = 0.43$$

where B measures the net trade balance, and W the yearly wage. The relationship between B and W is positive and statistically significant.

In a comparison of these tests, the trade-to-skill ($r = 0.50$) and wage-to-skill ($r = 0.87$) relationships seem, as anticipated, stronger than the wage-to-trade relationship ($r = 0.43$). The results of this empirical investigation sustain the contention that observed differences in yearly wages between export and import-competing industries can be attributed mainly to interindustry skill differences.

APPENDIX Table 1

Trade-Involvement, Labor Payments, and Occupational Index for Census-SIC Export and Import-Competing Industries, 1960[a]

Census Groups and Code Numbers	Percentage of Trade[b]	Average Annual Labor Earnings ($)	Occupational Index (%)	Net Trade Balance[c] (%)
Export industries				
0713, 204[d] Grain mill products	+7.73	5,188	52.58	+7.15
21 Tobacco manufactures	+10.98	3,871	34.14	+10.23
281, 2, 4, 6–9[e] Miscellaneous chemicals and allied products	+6.53	6,189	63.64	+4.10
283 Drugs and medicines	+8.36	6,108	73.00	+6.69
2823, 4 Synthetic fibers	+6.26	5,535	47.39	+3.81
295, 9 Miscellaneous petroleum and coal products	+5.20	5,698	59.03	+2.84
307 Miscellaneous plastic products	+4.96	4,682	42.07	+4.33
342 Cutlery, hand tools, and other hardware	+4.61	5,275	47.85	+2.46
351, 3–6, 8, 9 Miscellaneous machinery	+12.49	5,943	61.75	+10.73
357 Office, computing, and accounting machines	+11.69	6,316	64.48	+8.51
36 Electrical machinery, equipment, and supplies	+4.32	5,404	54.59	+2.49
372 Aircraft and parts	+4.55	6,842	71.49	+3.91
194, 381–5[f] Professional equipment and supplies	+8.35	5,818	64.42	+6.43
Import-competing industries				
203 Canning and preserving fruits, vegetables, and seafoods	−5.25	3,602	38.45	−1.57
206, 9 Miscellaneous food preparations and kindred products	−9.27	4,915	48.97	−5.11
208 Beverage industries	−6.63	5,391	47.72	−6.00
225 Knitting mills	−5.11	3,232	22.82	−3.14
227 Floor covering, except hard surfaces	−10.20	3,810	36.39	−8.88
229 Miscellaneous textile mill products	−21.55	4,314	38.08	−17.39
242, 3 Sawmills, planing mills, and mill work	−8.80	3,683	29.77	−6.86
244, 9 Miscellaneous wood products	−10.20	3,519	35.00	−8.01
291 Petroleum refining	−5.08	7,087	67.80	−1.75
312, 5–7, 9 Leather products, except footwear	−8.70	3,851	28.99	−7.12
326 Pottery and related products	−21.66	4,467	30.87	−18.34
387 Watches, clocks, and clockwork-operated devices	−26.25	4,959	46.39	−25.09
39 Miscellaneous manufacturing industries	−10.20	4,276	46.35	−7.05

Export and import-competing industries[g]

Code	Industry	Percentage exports (+); percentage imports (−)[b]		Net[c]
226	Dyeing and finishing textiles, except wool and knit goods	+11.19 / −9.53	4,287	32.77	+1.65
261, 2, 3, 6	Pulp, paper, and paperboard mills	+4.94 / −16.78	5,959	43.06	−11.84
311	Leather: tanned, cured, and finished	+5.11 / −7.64	4,744	28.68	−2.53
3312, 3	Blast furnaces, steelworks, and rolling and finishing mills	+6.67 / −7.00	6,592	53.56	−0.33
333–6, 3392, 9	Primary nonferrous industries	+5.80 / −10.56	5,799	51.43	−4.76
352	Farm machinery and equipment	+13.62 / −4.92	5,451	54.96	+8.69
371	Motor vehicles and motor vehicle equipment	+10.55 / −6.39	6,486	47.34	+4.16
374, 5, 9	Railroad and miscellaneous transportation equipment	+7.71 / −4.87	5,352	52.15	+2.84
386	Photographic equipment and supplies	+10.25 / −6.19	6,735	62.08	+4.06

a Export industries are defined as those industries with at least 4.17 per cent of domestic shipments exported; import-competing industries are defined as those industries with at least 4.84 per cent of domestic shipments challenged by imports.
b Percentage exports, (+); percentage imports, (−).
c Defined as the percentage of production exported less the percentage of production challenged by imports, where (+) = net exports, (−) = net imports.
d 0713 is excluded from trade, labor payments, and index figures.
e Except 2823, 4.
f 194 is excluded from trade, labor payments, and index figures.
g Defined as industries which exported at least 4.17 per cent of their shipments and are challenged by imports amounting to at least 4.84 per cent of their shipments.

ELINOR B. YUDIN

Americans Abroad:
A Transfer of Capital

IN BACON'S SEVENTEENTH-CENTURY VISION, *The New Atlantis*,[1] the island of
Salomon's House imports knowledge and ideas, not goods, services, or
factors of production; it requires only "light" to complete its otherwise
replete natural endowment.

When the king had forbidden to all his people navigation into any part that was
not under his crown, he made nevertheless this ordinance: That every twelve
years there should be sent forth out of his kingdom two ships, appointed to several
voyages; That in either of these ships there should be a mission of three of the
Fellows or Brethren of Salomon's House; whose errand was only to give us
knowledge of the affairs and state of those countries to which they were designed,
and especially of the sciences, arts, manufactures, and inventions of all the world;
and with all to bring us books, instruments, and patterns in every kind; That the
ships, after they had landed the Brethren should stay abroad until the new
mission . . . . But thus you see we maintain a trade, not for gold, silver, or jewels;
nor for silks; nor for spices; nor any other commodity of matter; but only for
God's first creature which was *Light*; to have *light* . . . of the growth of all parts
of the world.[2]

  [1] Francis Bacon, "New Atlantis," in Hugh G. Dick (ed.), *Selected Writings* (New York:
The Modern Library, 1955).
  [2] *Ibid.*, pp. 563–64.

For Bacon, science and research, "the knowledge of Causes and secret motions of things" provide the key "to the effecting of all things possible."[3]

If the key in 1968 differs from that in 1624, the difference is not great; knowledge, enterprise, and communication remain prerequisite to growth and development. With technological advances in all forms of transportation and communication, knowledge itself is more easily transmitted today than ever before.

Modern trade analysts emphasize three vehicles for the international transmission of applied knowledge: First, trade in products places the results of one nation's innovational talents in other nations' markets, stimulating imitation and import competition where possible and necessary.[4] Second, the licensing and sale of patents provides a formal, legal vehicle for the international exchange of ideas and processes, easing their incorporation into other nations' production processes.[5] Third, and perhaps most important, the trade literature stresses the role of direct investment, which transfers production itself to foreign soil at the initiative of the parent corporation:[6]

... the multinational firm, by applying the most advanced technical and managerial skill to its operation throughout the world, facilitates the flow of technology

---

[3] *Ibid.*, p. 574.

[4] Competition is "possible" where the nation possesses or can import the factors required for domestic production. Competition, when it is possible, may be "necessary" for balance-of-payments reasons: domestic production can mitigate an adverse balance of payments or, minimally, prevent further worsening of the nation's external position. Cairncross stresses competition's role as the traditional mechanism for spreading technology, suggesting that there is a period before imitation during which every foreign innovator has monopolistic powers. The profits derived from those powers are a burden on the balance of payments of the importing country. A. K. Cairncross, "Migration of Technology," in *Factors in Economic Development* (New York: Praeger, 1962).

[5] "The major use of foreign patents and trademarks is to protect foreign sales by the U.S. parent corporation or its foreign subsidiary. But licensing . . . is becoming increasingly important as a means of profiting from these assets." J. N. Behrman, "Foreign Investment and the Transfer of Knowledge and Skills," in R. F. Mikesell (ed.), *U.S. Private and Government Investment Abroad* (Eugene, Oregon: University of Oregon Books, 1962), p. 123 and Chapter V. Hymer suggests that licensing is an alternative to direct investment as a vehicle for technological transfer, the choice between the two depending on considerations of cost and uncertainty. S. H. Hymer, *The Impact of the Multinational Firm*, (New Haven: Economic Growth Center, Yale University, May 1966 mimeo.).

[6] Hymer, *Impact*; also J. H. Dunning, *American Investment in the British Manufacturing Industry* (London: George Allen and Unwin, Ltd., 1958), p. 9; U.S., Bureau of the Budget, *The Balance of Payments Statistics of the United States: A Review and Appraisal*, E. M. Bernstein (chairman) (Washington D.C.: April 1965), Chapter 8 (cited hereafter as "Bernstein Report").

and entrepreneurial ability between countries, and helps bring about international cost equalization.[7]

Bacon's only mode of obtaining "light"—the travels of the Brethren of Salomon's House to gather knowledge and experience—has, until recently, been ignored in analyses of the flow of technology. The world, tending "to be dazzled by the apparent success of concrete and steel,"[8] has but lately become aware that

investment in capital equipment is not the single magic lever that, once provided and pulled, starts an unending cycle of growth. The machinery—political and social, as well as economic—neither tends nor reproduces itself. The pivotal force around which any modernization process must move is talented, skilled, developed man.[9]

Investment in capital equipment requires, therefore, parallel investment in the personnel who can tend and reproduce it. In this context, the knowledge, skill, and experience embodied in formally educated and trained personnel does, much as in Bacon's vision, play a major role in the international flow of technology. And the participation, direct or indirect, of these skilled persons becomes an integral part of any international capital transfer: their participation is, in effect, an international transfer of human capital.[10] Yet few analysts have explicitly considered that role.

The role of skilled persons in diffusing technology does relate, if only peripherally, to three areas of current research. And those working in these three areas have given us perspectives on that vital role, although they have not examined the link between the two forms of capital investment—tangible and human.

The first such field of inquiry deals with forces that work to counteract the international transmission of technology. It is concerned with the so-called "brain drain"—the migration of skilled personnel to the United States, and to other advanced countries, from all over the world,

---

[7] Hymer, *Impact*, p. 16.

[8] J. A. Perkins, "Foreign Aid and the Brain Drain," *Foreign Affairs*, XLIV (July 1966), 610.

[9] *Ibid.*, p. 611.

[10] G. S. Becker, *Human Capital* (New York: National Bureau of Economic Research, 1965), Chapter II. See also T. W. Schultz, "Investment in Human Capital," *American Economic Review*, LI (March 1961), 1–17; and J. Mincer, "On-the-Job Training: Costs, Returns and Some Implications," *Journal of Political Economy*, LXX Supplement (October 1962), 66.

but particularly from the less-developed nations.[11] Many fear that this "movement of high-level human resources may, to a great extent, account for the persistent and ever widening gaps between rich and poor areas."[12] The developed world may thus negate the positive effects of its own assistance programs, offering training and, later, employment to foreigners whose skills may be in great demand in their native lands. The brain drain may concentrate technology rather than diffuse it.

The first stages of research by Kindleberger and by Grubel and Scott seek mainly to determine the net balance-of-payments effects of labor migration on both the sending and the receiving countries.[13] Grubel and Scott point out the tendency for students trained in the United States to remain there for employment and the proclivity of scientists and engineers to migrate to the United States.[14] Yet the implications of the brain drain clearly extend beyond its static balance-of-payments impact. One must measure reductions in output and tax receipts and the value of the human-capital export embodied in highly skilled emigrants. The cost of this migration, in lost skill and lost growth potential, is difficult to estimate, but may be quite important. One must also estimate the benefits of this migration—the value of the migrants' remittances and any change in the sending country's per capita consumption resulting from the migrants' departure. Where, however, part of the migration is a component of foreign investment, these measures may not adequately account for the benefits obtained through migration: Migration integral to direct investment may augment the return to that investment.

The second research area—manpower planning—relates directly to the

[11] Concern with the brain drain has only begun to be apparent among American policy makers. From the American viewpoint, the estimated value of imported skill remains "of negligible importance relative to the size of the U.S. stock of human material wealth and the capacity to produce current output . . . . [Hence] we must turn to an analysis of the outflows from individual countries to find reason for the widespread concern over the 'brain drain'." H. G. Grubel and A. D. Scott, "The Immigration of Scientists and Engineers to the United States, 1949–61," *Journal of Political Economy*, LXXIV (August 1966), 371. See also Perkins, "Foreign Aid."

[12] Perkins, "Foreign Aid," p. 610.

[13] C. P. Kindleberger, "Emigration and Economic Growth," *Banca Nazionale del Lavoro: Quarterly Review*, LXXIV (September 1965), 235–54; H. G. Grubel and A. D. Scott, "The International Flow of Human Capital," *American Economic Review: Papers and Proceedings*, LVI (May 1966), 268–74.

[14] H. G. Grubel and A. D. Scott, "The Role of Foreigners in the American Economics Profession" (1966 mimeo.), and their two works cited in footnotes 11 and 13; and J. R. Gass and R. F. Lyons, "International Flow of Students," in *Policy Conference on Economic Growth and Investment in Education*, Vol. V (Paris: OECD, February 1962).

role of skilled people in the international transmission of technology, but treats them as an independent vehicle of technological advance, not as a factor complementary to capital investment. The concern of the Manpower Commission, the Development Centre, and the Mediterranean Regional Project—all of the Organization for Economic Cooperation and Development (OECD)—has directed attention to the supply of, and demand for, skilled personnel. Their studies examine current stocks of skill and estimate future skill requirements for individual countries.[15] They also analyze the role of foreign skills in economic development.[16] Maddison, Kindleberger, and Dunning all comment on the increasing frequency with which skilled personnel, professional and manual, reside abroad.[17] Professionals go abroad to teach, to consult under contract to foreign establishments, and to offer technical assistance through many agencies. Such people are directly engaged in introducing technological advances into new regions. And they constitute a separate vehicle for technological transfer, independent of trade, licensing, and direct investment.

The third research area focuses on the effects of research and development (R&D), but does relate to skilled personnel. These people remain at home, as the organizers of production, as scientists, engineers, or technicians involved in applied research and development; they contribute

[15] For the demand for and supply of skills in the OECD countries (Austria, Belgium, Canada, Denmark, France, the Federal Republic of Germany, Greece, Ireland, Italy, Netherlands, Norway, Spain, Sweden, Switzerland, Turkey, United Kingdom, United States, Yugoslavia), see *Resources of Scientific and Technical Personnel in the OECD Area* (Paris: OECD, 1965). For a more detailed breakdown of the U.S. supply, see the publications of the National Science Foundation (NSF): *Research and Development in Industry* (NSF 63-7) (Washington, D.C.: U.S. Government Printing Office, 1963); and *Scientific and Technical Personnel in Industry, 1961* (NSF 63-32) (Washington, D.C.: U.S. Government Printing Office, 1964). For a detailed occupational distribution of U.S. employment, see U.S., Department of Commerce, Bureau of the Census, "Occupation by Industry," Subject Report PC(2)-7C, in *U.S. Census of the Population, 1960* (Washington, D.C.: U.S. Government Printing Office, 1961). For less detailed breakdowns of other nations' employment, see H. Parnes, *Forecasting Educational Needs for Economic and Social Development* (Paris: OECD, Mediterranean Regional Project, 1962), Appendix C. Among other relevant OECD publications are H. Parnes, *Planning for Economic and Social Development* (Paris: OECD, Mediterranean Regional Project, 1963), and *Policy Conference on Economic Growth and Investment in Education*, Vol. I–V (Paris: OECD, 1962).

[16] A. Maddison, *Foreign Skills and Technical Assistance in Economic Development* (Paris: OECD, 1965).

[17] *Ibid.*, Chapter 2; also C. P. Kindleberger, *International Ecomonics*, 3rd ed., (Homewood, Ill.: Richard D. Irwin, Inc., 1963), Chapter 22; and Dunning, *American Investment*, Chapter 1.

indirectly to transfers of technology. Keesing has shown that R&D activities are quite intensive in professional skills.[18] Hoffmeyer notes the relative significance of R&D investment in specific industries (described as R&D-intensive) and attributes much of the U.S. comparative advantage in international trade to those very industries.[19] Lary, moreover, points to the growing role played by the same industries in many nations' foreign trade: R&D-intensive exports from the United States account for a large share of its total export flow; but, perhaps more interesting, U.S. imports of R&D-intensive products are rising at a much faster rate, implying the growth of this type of activity abroad.[20] If R&D-intensive exports give rise to foreign imitation and competition, if patents—the products of research and development—are sold or leased abroad, if the R&D results are implemented in the firms' foreign operations, the innovating personnel effectively, if indirectly, contribute to the flow of knowledge.

DIRECT INVESTMENT, MIGRATION, AND THE FLOW OF TECHNOLOGY

Information gleaned from these three research areas could, perhaps, help in analyzing interrelationships among the activities of skilled personnel, the flow of technology, and direct investment—the vehicle for technical transfer most frequently mentioned by trade theorists—but these relationships have not been treated. Several authors—Thomas, Dunning, Nurkse, and Ohlin among them[21]—do comment on a parallel

[18] D. B. Keesing, "Labor Skills and the Factor Content of International Trade" (unpublished doctoral dissertation: Harvard University, 1961); "Labor Skills and International Trade: Evaluating Many Trade Flows with a Single Measuring Device," *Review of Economics and Statistics*, XLVII (August 1965), 287–94 (cited hereafter as "Labor Skills"); and "The Impact of Research and Development on United States Trade," in this volume.

[19] E. Hoffmeyer, *Dollar Shortage and the Structure of U.S. Foreign Trade* (Amsterdam: North-Holland Publishing Co., 1958).

[20] H. Lary, *Problems of the United States as World Trader and Banker* (Princeton: Princeton University Press for the National Bureau of Economic Research, 1963); see, too, T. Ozawa, "Imitation, Innovation, and Japanese Exports," in this volume; and Behrman, "Foreign Investment."

[21] B. Thomas, *Migration and Economic Growth: A Study of Great Britain and the Atlantic Economy* (Cambridge: Cambridge University Press, 1954); Dunning, *American Investment*; R. Nurkse, "International Investment Today in the Light of Nineteenth Century Experience," *Economic Journal*, LXIV (December 1954); and B. Ohlin, *Interregional and International Trade* (Cambridge: Harvard University Press, 1933).

between direct-investment flows and the international migration of skilled people. Thus:

> The first function of United States capital is fulfilled by direct investment in manufacturing or merchandising when it carries with it improved technology, skilled personnel and fresh ideas, all elements from which even the economies of the most advanced European countries can derive higher productivity. The contribution of such investment to economic progress in Europe may be very large indeed and out of proportion to the amount of money involved in the original investment and ensuing service charges.[22]

But most references to this intriguing parallel relate to nineteenth century experience.

The scale of the simultaneous migration of labor and capital from Great Britain in the nineteenth century was extraordinary. Thomas holds that some of that migration was "an outflow . . . complementary to capital exports."[23] To support this contention, he cites U.S. Census data on the skill composition of immigrants. Technological developments occurring in the 1890's—the innovations in the electrical, chemical, and automobile industries—evoked augmented demands for professional, managerial, clerical, and skilled personnel. Census data for 1910 reveal a "marked preponderance" of British migrants embodying these specific skills.[24]

The nineteenth-century experience was unique in its scale. Yet such parallel movements of labor and capital have continued. The 1957 Census of U.S. business investments in foreign countries notes that 20,000 Americans were then employed abroad by foreign affiliates of U.S. firms and that, moreover, 13,600 of these people—about two-thirds of the group—were employed in professional and managerial positions.[25] Despite the continuation of the parallel, economists have neither explained the parallel itself nor accounted adequately for its occurrence.

Economic analysis does offer separate explanations for each of the two flows: skilled labor and capital. It treats labor's decision to migrate, permanently or temporarily, as the consequence of a comparison of

---

[22] Dunning, *American Investment*, p. 9.

[23] Thomas, *Migration*, p. 31.

[24] *Ibid.*, p. 152, Thomas also includes a table comparing the skill distributions of U.S. immigrants by selected country of origin, p. 150.

[25] U.S., Department of Commerce, Office of Business Economics, *U.S. Business Investment in Foreign Countries* (Washington, D.C.: U.S. Government Printing Office, 1960), p. 45 and Table 34, (cited hereafter as *Business Investment*).

expected real incomes, pecuniary and nonpecuniary. The decision to invest abroad similarly depends on a comparison of expected real returns. But the two-country, two-factor model of international trade holds that, where it is possible for one factor (labor, for example) to move in one direction, it will be profitable for the second factor (capital) to move in the opposite direction. Conventional trade theory precludes a parallel movement of the two factors.

How, then, can one explain reality—the continuing parallel flow of direct investment and skilled personnel? Closer study of direct investment itself may furnish clues.

Direct investment is generally considered only in its financial aspect;[26] as such, it is a capital movement and, one expects, would move in the opposite direction from labor flows. Yet, Hymer stresses that the character of direct investment is not one-sided.[27] It is, instead, multi-faceted, comprising a "*package* of management skills, technical knowledge, and capital and it should bring a triplet of benefits."[28] For Hymer, as for Behrman,[29] direct investment builds capital abroad, rather than simply effecting international capital transfers:

In most cases of direct investment the key element is the transfer of technology and entrepreneurship. Firms are very unequal in their ability to operate in industry: they vary in skill, efficiency, resources, etc., and direct investment is a way in which a firm *with some advantage* can put it to use in a foreign country.[30]

The special advantage which stimulates investment abroad is apt to be different from mere access to financial or physical capital. That advantage is more likely to arise out of the knowledge and use of new

---

[26] U.S. direct investment represents the U.S.-owned portion of foreign businesses in which U.S. residents have an "important voice in management." The Commerce Department defines the terms "resident" and "important voice in management"; see *Business Investment*, pp. 76–85. The Bernstein report evaluates the data themselves and strongly recommends another census of direct investment: "Regular reporters accounted for about 90 per cent of total direct investment at the time of the 1957 census; they may well account for a smaller proportion now, and the scattered reports that are added to regularly reported data seem unlikely to have accounted for all of the remainder." (Bernstein Report, pp. 61–68; quote from p. 67).

[27] See Hymer, *Impact*; and his "The International Operations of National Firms: A Study of Direct Investment" (unpublished doctoral dissertation: Massachusetts Institute of Technology, 1960). Subsequent references to Hymer relate to his monograph rather than the dissertation.

[28] *Ibid.*, p. 25.

[29] Behrman, "Foreign Investment," Chapters IV, V.

[30] Hymer, *Impact*, p. 15.

Table 1

Book Value of Direct Investments: All Sectors,
by Area (billions of dollars)

	1946	1950	1957	1959	1960	1962	1964	1966
All areas	7.2	11.8	25.2	29.7	31.8	37.2	44.4	54.6
Canada	2.5	3.6	8.6	10.2	11.2	12.1	13.8	16.8
Latin America	3.1	4.6	8.1	9.0	8.3	9.5	10.2	11.5
Europe	1.0	1.7	4.1	5.3	6.7	8.9	12.1	16.2
Middle East and Africa	0.2	1.0	1.8	2.0	2.1	2.5	3.0	3.7
Other	0.4	0.9	2.6	3.2	3.6	4.2	5.2	6.3

Source: U.S., Department of Commerce, Office of Business Economics, *Survey of Current Business* (Washington, D.C.: U.S. Government Printing Office), various issues.

techniques and the access to personnel who can implement those techniques. Techniques, capital, and skills—managerial and technical—migrate as a single entity, Hymer's "package." That entity is, in essence, enterprise: direct investment is the migration not of capital alone, but rather of enterprise.

When a new technique is involved, direct investment is a capital loan designed to implement that technique abroad. The loan thus consists of two complementary components: tangible capital and•human capital. The tangible-capital component, broadly defined, consists either of plant and equipment or of the financial resources necessary to purchase them abroad. The human-capital component consists of the skills that are "specific" to the migrating enterprise and not available abroad. The latter statement may require further clarification: Becker defines training as "specific" when it results in greater productivity increases for the firm providing the training than for other firms.[31] Skills produced by that training are, by extension, specific to the firm. Training, however, may be more than formal education, either in school or on-the-job; it may include the individual's accumulated experience with the particular firm, that is, his knowledge of the firm itself—its structure, its functioning, and its production techniques. Managerial and technical skills are often specific to the firm which employs them, representing qualities that are not obtainable elsewhere. The economic effectiveness of a capital transfer depends, then, on both of its components—tangible capital and human capital. A shortage of either one would reduce the expected

[31] Becker, *Human Capital*, p. 18.

return from the investment. If direct investment is the migration of enterprise, tangible-capital movements require parallel human-capital movements embodied in skills specific to the migrating enterprise. The observed parallel movements are not anomalous.

Direct investment, particularly by the United States, has risen rapidly in the postwar period. Table 1 illustrates the dramatic increase in its financial component, the conventional measure of direct investment.[32] Investment has been concentrated in the industries which, by U.S.

Table 2

Plant and Equipment Expenditures of Direct-Investment Enterprises, by Area and Sector, 1958 and 1966 (millions of dollars)

	1958	1966		1958	1966
All sectors			Petroleum		
All areas	4,097	8,768	All areas	1,854	2,558
Canada	1,311	2,366	Canada	510	611
Latin America	1,269	1,092	Latin America	577	268
Europe	976	3,293	Europe	422	778
Other	541	2,018	Other	345	901
Manufacturing			Mining		
All areas	1,180	4,626	All areas	420	807
Canada	404	1,203	Canada	170	315
Latin America	202	438	Latin America	221	229
Europe	460	2,260	Europe	—	6
Other	114	725	Other	27	257

Source: Same as for Table 1.

[32] The data presented in Table 1 measure only the U.S. capital contribution, not total capital needs. Within the context of this study, they would provide the "best" measure of the tangible capital stock if one could assume that the U.S. skill contribution depended on the U.S. capital contribution, not the total tangible capital requirements of the investment. Statements in the *Survey of Current Business* suggest the use of the net direct-investment capital outflow as an approximation to the current U.S. contribution to the tangible-capital stock. But the expansion of internal financing by these firms has roughly paralleled capital expenditure, so that the net capital outflow understates the current U.S. contribution. See U.S., Department of Commerce, Office of Business Economics, *Survey of Current Business* (September 1965), 23, and (November 1965), 15; for a discussion of current concepts of direct investment, see Kindleberger, *International Economics*, Chapter 20.

Plant and equipment expenditure, the second measure of the tangible-capital stock presented in Table 2, likewise fails to quantify total capital requirements: If these data could be summed from the start, they would provide an adequate measure. Taken year by year, however, they measure incremental capital requirements.

standards, require relatively large amounts of highly skilled manpower.[33] Table 2 offers similar indications using another measure of tangible U.S. capital abroad—the plant and equipment expenditures of the foreign affiliates of American firms.

And there has been a simultaneous migration of personnel. The number of Americans abroad has more than trebled since 1950. The data in Table 3 include military personnel; there are no analogous data surveying the civilian population alone. Yet the last decennial Census of the United States, reporting on Americans overseas, indicates that this flow, too, has grown rapidly in recent years.[34]

A proportion of that population is not only resident, but is also employed, in foreign countries. More than 138,000 Americans were employed

Table 3

American Population Resident Abroad: Selected Years

Year	Population	Year	Population
1900	91,219	1940	118,933
1910	55,608	1950	418,545
1920	117,238	1960	1,372,066
1930	89,453		

Source: E. Rubin, "A Statistical Overview of Americans Abroad," *The Annals of the American Academy of Political and Social Science*, CCCLXVIII (November 1966), Table 1, p. 2.

[33] The modifier "skill-intensive" will be used here to indicate an industry in which high-level skills—professional and technical—represent a relatively large percentage of total employment by comparison with other industries. The term compares only the relative utilization of the various skills; it implies nothing about the use of capital, liquid or tangible, or the "capital intensity" of the industry. Hence, skill-intensive industries can be identified from the occupational distribution of employment in American industries; for that distribution, see "Occupation by Industry." Keesing uses this technique ("Labor Skills"). A comparison of the industries that are skill-intensive by Keesing's standard and the industries accounting for relatively large shares of U.S. direct investment yields the conclusion in the text.

[34] This statement is based on an examination of the data in the volume which serves as the major source of statistical information on Americans privately employed abroad: U.S., Department of Commerce, Bureau of the Census, "Americans Overseas," Selected Area Report, PC(3)-1C, in *U.S. Census of the Population, 1960* (Washington, D.C.: U.S. Government Printing Office, 1964). Table 16 of that volume separates privately employed American personnel by date of arrival and suggests growth in that flow. See, too, E. Rubin, "A Statistical Overview of Americans Abroad," *The Annals of the American Academy of Political and Social Science*, CCCLXVIII (November 1966), 1–10: the whole issue of *The Annals* is devoted to an examination of various characteristics of the whole American population resident abroad.

Table 4

American Civilian Population, Resident and Employed Abroad, 1960

	Number	Per Cent	Male Number	Per Cent	Female Number	Per Cent
Total	138,174	100.0	98,967	100.0	39,207	100.0
Federal civilian employees	38,750	28.0	23,757	24.0	14,993	38.2
All private workers	96,923	70.2	74,129	74.9	22,974	58.1
Dependents of federal civilian employees	8,054		661		7,393	
Crews of merchant vessels	29,030		28,650		380	
Other citizens	59,839		44,818		15,021	
Other	2,501	1.8	1,081	1.0	1,420	3.6

Source: U.S., Department of Commerce, Bureau of the Census, "Americans Overseas," Selected Area Report, PC(3)-1C, in *U.S. Census of the Population, 1960* (Washington, D.C.: U.S. Government Printing Office, 1964), Table 3.

abroad in 1960. As shown in Table 4, almost all of them fall into two major Census categories. "Federal civilian employees," the nonmilitary employees of the U.S. Government, account for 28 per cent of the total employment of American civilians abroad; "private workers," the self-employed and the employees of private firms, account for over 70 per cent. The second category, "private workers," is made up of three subcategories: the dependents of federal civilian employees, the crews of merchant vessels, and "other citizens." The last category defined by the Census as those American civilians who are privately employed but who are neither the dependents of federal civilian employees nor serving on the crews of merchant vessels, accounts, in itself, for 43 per cent of all civilian personnel employed abroad[35].

Data surveying these "other citizens," whom I shall call "privately employed American personnel," provide the empirical basis for all subsequent statements and observations. Throughout this essay I shall assume, rather heroically, that these personnel are employed by the foreign affiliates of American firms. The available data do not identify the nationality of the respondent's employer. Yet a crude estimate of the population of privately employed American personnel abroad in 1957

[35] "Americans Overseas," Table 3; Rubin, "Statistical Overview."

does correspond roughly to the published estimates of Americans employed by foreign affiliates, given in the Commerce Department's 1957 survey of U.S. foreign investments.[36]

Ernest Rubin describes the group of Americans abroad as a "very special segment of the parent population" which is "younger, better educated, and probably more remuneratively employed than the national population."[37] Americans abroad tend to be transient; privately employed American personnel remain on foreign soil only about 2.5 years on the average, and the average for all American civilians employed abroad is even shorter.[38] Americans overseas, particularly those employed privately, are most strikingly distinguished by the distribution of skills which they embody. They comprise, by comparison with any other group, an unusually large proportion of highly skilled personnel.

In the next two tables, the distributions by skill and region of privately employed American personnel abroad are compared with those of the parent American population—a population that is generally considered to be "skill-intensive" relative to the populations of other nations.[39] Table 5A presents these data in the first of two alternative groupings (Group 1). This grouping, the more detailed of the two, attempted to distinguish the technical and managerial professions which, viewing

[36] The "crude estimates" are made using the Census tabulation of privately employed American personnel abroad by date of arrival, before 1955 or between 1955 and 1957. Of the group abroad in 1960, 25,929 had arrived before 1958, and 19,117 of these are employed in professional or managerial occupations (see "Americans Overseas," Table 16). These data describe a population larger than that estimated by the Office of Business Economics in their 1957 census of American business investments abroad—20,600 in all, of which 13,600 are professional or managerial personnel (see *Business Investments*, p. 45). There are, however, two points of interest that might be made: First, the percentage breakdown is similar for both sets of data; each is about two-thirds professional and managerial. Second, if one adopts Kenen's procedure of using only principal occupations—those most clearly related to the industrial sectors of the economy—the "crude estimates" come quite close to the published estimates. This "crude estimate" would then total 19,149 in all, 13,465 of whom are professional or managerial personnel. See P. B. Kenen and E. B. Yudin, *Skills, Human Capital and U.S. Foreign Trade: Variations on a Theme by Leontief* (New York: International Economics Workshop, Columbia University, December 1965).

[37] Rubin, "Statistical Overview," p. 9. The statement refers to the whole American population employed abroad, not only privately employed personnel, the portion of the group analyzed here. There is, however, no evidence to suggest that Rubin's statement is not applicable to that part of the group.

[38] *Ibid.*, p. 8.

[39] Keesing, "Labor Skills"; Lary, *Problems of United States*; Hoffmeyer, *Dollar Shortage*.

direct investment as the migration of enterprise, seem particularly relevant. It consists of ten skill categories:[40]

A. Scientists and engineers: chemists, engineers, and natural scientists, n.e.c.
B. Technical supporting personnel: draftsmen, surveyors, technicians.
C. Managers.
D. Managerial supporting personnel: accountants, editors and reporters, lawyers and judges, personnel and labor relations workers.
E. Other professional workers: all professional occupations not specified in A–D.
F. Clerical and kindred workers.
G. Sales workers.
H. Craftsmen and kindred workers.
J. Operatives and kindred workers: includes "occupation not reported."
K. Unskilled laborers.

Table 5A

Employment by Skill, Group 1: U.S. Males, Domestic and Foreign, Selected Areas, 1960 (percentages)

				Foreign			
Skill	Domestic	All Areas	Africa	Canada and Mexico	Other America	Asia	Europe and U.S.S.R.
A	2.70	13.90	12.30	9.59	17.65	14.02	14.14
B	1.64	3.17	2.60	1.56	4.32	2.65	2.91
C	12.75	25.14	14.14	39.63	27.94	20.69	26.50
D	1.99	4.40	2.80	2.76	5.49	5.11	4.43
E	5.93	25.37	54.75	13.91	20.50	32.31	21.83
F	8.30	4.35	1.49	1.32	3.02	4.72	5.81
G	8.18	3.13	1.31	4.42	2.30	1.78	5.83
H	23.31	10.93	5.64	8.46	12.62	11.57	6.99
J	29.20	7.49	4.21	10.64	5.12	6.25	9.60
K	5.99	2.12	0.76	7.70	1.02	0.89	1.95

Sources: Domestic data from U.S., Department of Commerce, Bureau of the Census "Occupation by Industry," Subject Report PC(2)-7C, in *U.S. Census of the Population 1960* (Washington, D.C.: U.S. Government Printing Office, 1961), Table 2; overseas data from U.S., Department of Commerce, Bureau of the Census, "Americans Overseas," Selected Area Report PC(3)-1C, in *U.S. Census of the Population, 1960* (Washington, D.C.: U.S. Government Printing Office, 1964), Table 15.

[40] The occupations specified beside each category are those occupations, defined by the Census, which make up the corresponding skill level.

Table 5B

*Employment by Skill, Group 2: U.S. Males, Domestic and
Foreign, Selected Areas, 1960 (percentages)*

Skill	Domestic	Foreign					
		All Areas	Africa	Canada and Mexico	Other America	Asia	Europe and U.S.S.R.
I	25.02	71.98	86.59	67.45	75.91	74.78	69.82
II	16.48	7.48	2.80	5.74	5.32	6.51	11.64
III	23.31	10.93	5.64	8.46	12.62	11.57	6.99
IV	29.20	7.49	4.21	10.64	5.12	6.25	9.60
V	5.99	2.12	0.76	7.70	1.02	0.89	1.95

Sources: Same as for Table 5A.

The second grouping (Group 2) summarizes the first, treating all professional and managerial personnel as one group rather than five, and combining clerical and sales personnel into one group instead of two. It consists of five skill categories:

I. Professional and managerial personnel: an aggregation of skill A through skill E above.
II. Clerical and sales personnel: an aggregation of skill F and skill G.
III. Craftsmen: identical with skill H.
IV. Operatives: identical with skill J.
V. Unskilled laborers: identical with skill K.

Table 5B presents the skill distributions of employment in this summary format.

At first glance, the comparisons appear somewhat startling. Professional skills (skill I), which account for one-quarter of total employment in the United States, account for over 70 per cent of the employment among privately employed American personnel abroad. The distributional pattern, moreover, though not identical within each region, shows little variation, regardless of the level of detail in the skill breakdown. On the more detailed level (Table 5A), however, interesting refinements emerge: At home, less than 3 per cent of the population is employed as scientists and engineers (skill A); abroad, the figure is closer to 14 per cent. At home, managerial personnel (skill C) comprise almost 13 per cent of the domestic population's employment; abroad, the percentage falls that low in just one case—Africa.

If these personnel are, in fact, employed by the foreign affiliates of American firms, the distributions of employment by skill support the contention that Americans who migrate with tangible capital provide specific managerial and technical skills. If, furthermore, direct investment is the migration not merely of tangible capital, but of enterprise—of technique, capital, and skills—the data on financial-capital transfers alone, given in Tables 1 and 2, understate the true value of direct investment. A better measure, I suggest, would include an accounting of the contribution of skilled personnel. This measure would better approximate the "investment in the international flow of technology," for the people who migrate with direct investment augment the efficiency of that investment, making it economically viable.

THE CAPITAL CONTRIBUTION OF SKILLED AMERICANS ABROAD

To estimate the contribution of Americans privately employed overseas, I adopt a procedure parallel to that Kenen used in estimating the human-capital input of U.S. export and import-competing production.[41] First,

Table 6A

Mean Wages, Based on Skill Group 2: U.S. Males, by Sector, 1959 (dollars)

Skill	Mining	Manufacturing	Public Utilities	Trade	Other
A	9,318	9,538	9,547	9,514	9,082
B	6,053	6,267	6,152	6,173	5,722
C	9,785	9,785	9,785	9,785	9,785
D	8,179	8,170	8,069	8,170	9,870
E	9,411	8,230	10,448	7,772	7,303
F	5,724	5,380	5,543	5,333	5,479
G	6,643	6,643	6,643	6,643	6,643
H	6,302	6,128	6,107	5,394	5,537
J	5,224	4,991	4,903	4,534	5,211
K	3,601[a]	4,242	4,451	3,246	3,269

Sources: Computed from stratified wage and salary data in U.S., Department of Commerce, Bureau of the Census, "Occupational Characteristics," Subject Report PC(2)-7A, in *U.S. Census of the Population, 1960* (Washington, D.C.: U.S. Government Printing Office, 1961), Table 28; weighted by distribution of occupation by industry in U.S., Department of Commerce, Bureau of the Census, "Occupation by Industry," Subject Report PC(2)-7C, in *U.S. Census of the Population, 1960* (Washington, D.C.: U.S. Government Printing Office, 1961), Table 2.

[a] Mean wage of all laborers.

[41] P. B. Kenen, "Nature, Capital and Trade," *Journal of Political Economy*, LXXIII (October 1965). For more detailed analysis of the findings, see Kenen and Yudin, *Skills, Human Capital.*

I suppose that skill differences are due wholly to differences in the quantity of capital invested in workers, and that wage differences are attributable entirely to skill differences. I then treat wage differences as the return to capital invested in a worker. Few, if any, data offer more than a bare indication of the actual earnings of privately employed American personnel in foreign countries. I have, in consequence, assumed that the opportunity cost of employment abroad is the wage that could be earned at home—I compute mean wages from data on earnings and employment in the United States, itself.

The data on U.S. mean wages which appear in the more detailed breakdown (Group 1) in Table 6A and in the summary breakdown (Group 2) in Table 6B are twice-weighted averages.[42] First, I compute a mean wage for each occupation, $\overline{W}_i$, using stratified earnings-by-occupation data as weights.[43] These mean occupational wages are then

[42] There are two exceptions to the procedure described in this paragraph; both relate to the computation of the wage of unskilled laborers—skill-level K in Group 1, skill-level V in Group 2. First, the Census does not classify any employees in mining as laborers: the mean wage reported for that sector in the text tables is the mean wage for all laborers in all sectors—$3,601. Second, the mean wage estimates for unskilled laborers in the other four sectors—manufacturing, public utilities, trade, and other—had to be calculated in three steps because data were not available in comparable detail. First, a mean wage, by sector, was computed for "laborers, n.e.c." from earnings-by-occupation data. Next, for nine specified occupations—carpenters' helpers, except logging and mining; fishermen and oystermen; garage laborers, and car washers and greasers; gardeners, except farm and groundkeepers; longshoremen and stevedores; lumbermen, raftsmen, and woodchoppers; teamsters; truck drivers' helpers; and warehousemen, n.e.c.—where the earnings and employment data were comparable, the procedure described in the text was used to obtain a mean wage estimate by sector:

	Mean Wage Estimate	
Sector	Specified Occupations	Laborers, n.e.c.
Manufacturing	$3,454	$4,310
Public utilities	4,976	4,236
Trade	3,777	3,001
Other	3,588	2,955

Finally, the two mean wage estimates for each sector were weighted by the sector's distribution of employment of unskilled laborers between the two categories to obtain the figures which appear in the text tables. The estimate for the mining sector is, again, an average, this time an employment-weighted average over the four sectors specified above.

[43] The earnings stratification is taken from U.S., Department of Commerce, Bureau of the Census, "Occupational Characteristics," Subject Report PC(2)-7A, in *U.S. Census of the Population, 1960* (Washington, D.C.: U.S. Government Printing Office, 1961), Table 28. These data are classified into eleven income groups. The midpoint of the class was used to compute mean wages in all but two instances: In the $10,000–$14,999 class, I use $12,000; in the open-ended class, I use $32,000. The procedure is analogous to that employed by Kenen and Yudin, *Skills, Human Capital.*

Table 6B

Mean Wages, Based on Skill Group 2: U.S. Males, by Sector, 1959 (dollars)

Skill	Mining	Manufacturing	Public Utilities	Trade	Other
I	9,086	8,907	9,479	9,552	8,310
II	5,819	5,897	5,630	6,302	5,550
III	6,302	6,128	6,107	5,394	5,537
IV	5,224	4,991	4,903	4,534	5,211
V	3,601[a]	4,242	4,451	3,246	3,169

Sources: Same as for Table 6A. [a] Mean wage of all laborers.

weighted again, this time by the distribution of employment within the skill group for each sector[44]—mining, manufacturing, public utilities, trade, and other—to obtain a mean wage by skill (j) and sector (k), $\overline{\overline{W}}_{jk}$. Where, for example, there are n occupations in skill group j, so that $i = 1, \ldots, n$, and N_{ik} people are employed in occupation i in the kth sector:

$$\overline{\overline{W}}_{jk} = \frac{\sum\limits_{i=1}^{n} \overline{W}_i N_{ik}}{\sum\limits_{i=1}^{n} N_{ik}}$$

To estimate the capital required to convert a man-year of crude labor to a man-year of skill, I invoke the assumption that wage differences result solely from skill differences and compute the wage differences for each sector—the excess of mean earnings of a skill group in a sector over the mean earnings of an unskilled laborer in the same sector. These wage differentials, the return to the worker's investment in human capital, are tabulated in Tables 7A and 7B.

To estimate the capital embodied in the skills earning these returns, I capitalize the value of the wage differentials at various rates of return. The rates of return used in this process—9.0 per cent, 11.0 per cent, and 12.7 per cent—are drawn from work by Mincer[45] and Becker,[46] who calculated rates of return to investment in human capital. The estimated investment in skills, the capitalized differentials, are arrayed in Tables 8A and 8B.

[44] The distribution of employment by sector is taken from "Occupation by Industry," Table 2.

[45] Mincer, "On-the-Job Training," p. 66.

[46] G. S. Becker, "Underinvestment in College Education," cited in Mincer, p. 66.

Table 7A

Wage Differentials (Excess over Laborers), Based on Skill Group 1: U.S. Males, Total[a] *and by Sector, 1959 (dollars)*

Skill	Total	Mining	Manufacturing	Public Utilities	Trade	Other
A	5,707	5,717	5,296	5,096	6,088	5,913
B	2,422	2,452	2,025	1,701	2,747	2,553
C	5,795	6,184	5,543	5,334	6,359	6,616
D	6,696	4,578	3,928	3,618	4,744	6,701
E	4,134	5,810	3,988	5,997	4,346	4,134
F	2,099	2,123	1,138	1,092	1,907	2,310
G	2,753	3,042	2,401	2,192	3,217	3,474
H	1,941	2,701	1,886	1,656	1,968	2,368
J	1,780	1,623	749	452	1,108	2,042

Sources: Wage data from Table 6A.

[a] Total differentials consist of a weighted average of the differentials for the separate sectors; the weight, in each case, is the percentage of total employment found in that sector.

I utilize these estimates of capital embodied in a worker's skill to evaluate the stock of human capital implicit in privately employed American personnel abroad. The data on Americans employed abroad appear in the volume, "Americans Overseas," part of the *Census of the U.S. Population, 1960.* Persons "employed" are those who had worked, or were temporarily absent from work, in either full-time or part-time jobs during the week immediately preceding the filing of Census form 60 PH-15 (April 1960); there is no indication of the proportion employed only part time. The data do exclude Americans temporarily abroad either on vacations or on business trips. Census data on privately employed

Table 7B

Wage Differentials (Excess over Laborers), Based on Skill Group 2: U.S. Males, Total[a] *and by Sector, 1959 (dollars)*

Skill	Total	Mining	Manufacturing	Public Utilities	Trade	Other
I	5,188	5,485	4,665	5,028	6,126	5,141
II	2,245	2,218	1,655	1,179	2,876	2,381
III	1,988	2,701	1,886	1,656	1,968	2,368
IV	2,040	1,623	749	452	1,108	2,042

Source: Wage data from Table 6B.   [a] See note a, Table 7A.

Table 8A

Capital Embodied in Skills, Based on Skill Group 1:
U.S. Males, All Sectors, 1959 (dollars per worker)[a]

Skill	Rates of Return		
	9.0%	11.0%	12.7%
A	63,407	51,878	44,934
B	26,909	22,016	19,069
C	64,386	52,679	45,628
D	74,405	60,877	52,728
E	45,938	37,586	32,555
F	23,327	19.086	16,531
G	30,588	25,026	21,676
H	21,571	17,649	15,287
J	19,781	16,184	14,018

Source: Differentials from Table 7A.
[a] For method of estimation, see the text.

American personnel, those Americans abroad in 1960 that the Census calls "other citizens," probably understate the actual population of privately employed Americans in foreign countries: filing of the form was entirely voluntary, and there is no clear standard against which to evaluate the figures.[47]

Table 8B

Capital Embodied in Skills, Based on Skill Group 2:
U.S. Males, All Sectors, 1959 (dollars per worker)[a]

Skill	Rates of Return		
	9.0%	11.0%	12.7%
I	57,649	47,167	40,854
II	24,948	20,412	17,680
III	22,084	18,069	15,650
IV	22,668	18,546	16,064

Source: Differentials from Table 7B.
[a] For method of estimation, see the text.

[47] The data on privately employed American personnel appear in "Americans Overseas," Tables 13–18. The Census offers several reasons for believing that the estimate for this particular group is low: "Some number of Americans overseas probably never learned the census was being conducted; some may have known but could not readily obtain a census form to fill; and some may have chosen not to cooperate, because the census, for them, was entirely voluntary. . . . The understatement may differ substantially from one area to another and from one type of person to another." (p. ix.)

The 59,839 people in this group are cross-classified by sex, region, and occupation. The female component, smaller than the male, numbering 15,021 as compared to 44,818 males, is concentrated in occupations removed from the industrial sectors of the economy; hence, I restrict this

Table 9A

Capital Embodied in Americans Employed Abroad, Based on Skill Group 1: U.S. Males, All Areas and by Region, 1960 (thousands of dollars)

Skill and Rate of Return	Region		
	All Areas	Europe	Canada and Mexico
At 9.0 per cent			
A	399,397.99	92,319.97	31,259.44
B	38,667.80	8,072.61	2,152.70
C	733,611.16	175,644.31	131,153.76
D	148,512.52	33,928.71	10,565.52
E	528,199.44	103,223.53	32,845.94
F	45,978.08	13,949.72	3,918.98
G	43,373.79	18,352.80	6,943.48
H	106,216.28	15,531.22	9,383.44
J	67,197.27	19,543.69	10,820.24
Total	2,111,153.28	480,566.55	239,043.49
At 11.0 per cent			
A	326,780.17	75,534.52	25,575.90
B	31,637.29	6,604.86	1,761.30
C	600,227.32	143,708.98	107,307.62
D	121,510.24	27,759.85	8,644.52
E	432,163.19	84,455.62	26,873.95
F	37,618.42	11,413.40	3,206.44
G	35,487.65	15,015.93	5,681.03
H	86,904.23	12,707.36	7,677.36
J	54,978.76	15,990.29	8,852.92
Total	1,727,307.23	393,190.81	195,581.04
At 12.7 per cent			
A	283,037.94	65,423.60	22,152.36
B	27,402.38	5,720.75	1,525.53
C	519,881.93	124,472.35	92,943.61
D	105,245.09	24,043.97	7,487.38
E	374,314.57	73,150.53	23,276.65
F	32,582.89	9,885.62	2,777.23
G	30,737.33	13,003.92	4,920.57
H	75,271.38	11,006.38	6,649.68
J	47,619.40	13,849.86	7,667.89
Total	1,496,092.88	340,558.97	169,400.90

Source: Data on capital embodied in skills, Table 8A, applied to employment data the Census, "Americans Overseas," Selected Area Report PC(3)-1C, in *U.S. Census of the*

study to males. The regional classification by the Census distributes the overseas population among six regions: Africa, America (except Canada and Mexico), Asia, Canada, and Mexico, Europe and the U.S.S.R., and other areas. The regional classification presented here is little different: The class "all areas" includes the six separate regions, but only the first five, not "other areas," are specifically reported; the region "Europe and the U.S.S.R." is treated as Europe alone, since employment of

	Region		
Other America	Asia	Africa	Skill and Rate of Return
			At 9.0 per cent
117,302.16	112,736.88	26,694.17	A
12,189.64	9,041.32	2,394.87	B
188,585.84	168,883.81	31,162.70	C
42,782.91	48,214.48	7,142.89	D
98,721.57	188,209.53	86,088.52	E
7,394.75	13,973.04	1,189.69	F
7,371.71	6,912.89	1,376.46	G
28,538.61	31,644.86	4,163.23	H
10,622.43	15,686.38	2,848.47	J
513,509.62	595,303.16	163,060.99	Total
			At 11.0 per cent
95,974.49	92,239.27	21,840.68	A
9,973.34	7,397.45	1,959.44	B
154,297.51	138,177.66	25,496.75	C
35,004.20	39,448.21	5,844.18	D
80,772.19	153,989.62	70,436.06	E
6,050.25	11,432.49	973.38	F
6,031.40	5,656.00	1,126.19	G
23,349.78	25,891.25	3,406.28	H
8,691.08	12,834.31	2,330.57	J
420,144.23	487,066.25	133,413.54	Total
			At 12.7 per cent
83,127.51	79,892.28	18,917.12	A
8,638.33	6,407.24	1,697.16	B
133,643.51	119,681.44	22,083.80	C
30,318.60	34,167.74	5,061.89	D
69,960.17	133,376.83	61,007.61	E
5,240.37	9,902.16	843.09	F
5,224.04	4,898.90	975.44	G
20,224.21	22,425.49	2,950.32	H
7,527.71	11,116.33	2,018.60	J
363,904.45	421,868.40	115,555.04	Total

on Americans privately employed abroad in U.S. Department of Commerce, Bureau of *Population, 1960* (Washington, D.C.: U.S. Government Printing Office, 1964), Table 15.

Table 9B

Capital Embodied in Americans Employed Abroad, Based on Skill Group 2:
U.S. Males, All Areas and by Region, 1960 (*thousands of dollars*)

Skill and Rate of Return	All areas	Region				
		Europe	Canada and Mexico	Other America	Asia	Africa
At 9.0 per cent						
I	1,880,739.56	414,323.05	199,868.93	458,655.10	546,627.41	170,871.51
II	84,548.86	29,887.73	9,854.47	13,921.00	20,582.12	2,395.01
III	108,744.07	15,900.84	9,606.76	29,217.79	32,397.96	4,262.31
IV	77,003.15	22,395.97	12,399.39	12,172.71	17,975.71	3,264.19
Total	2,151,035.59	482,507.58	231,729.54	513,966.59	617,583.19	180,793.01
At 11.0 per cent						
I	1,538,786.91	338,991.58	163,529.13	375,263.26	447,240.60	139,803.96
II	69,176.34	24,453.60	8,062.75	11,389.91	16,839.92	1,959.55
III	88,972.42	13,009.78	7,860.07	23,905.46	26,507.42	3,487.34
IV	63,002.58	18,323.98	10,144.95	9,959.49	14,707.40	2,670.70
Total	1,759,938.20	394,778.93	189,596.90	420,518.12	505,295.34	147,921.55
At 12.7 per cent						
I	1,332,807.56	293,614.76	141,639.40	325,031.17	387,373.75	121,090.04
II	59,916.15	21,180.28	6,983.48	9,865.27	14,585.75	1,697.25
III	77,062.73	11,268.31	6,807.94	20,705.52	22,959.18	3,020.53
IV	54,569.16	15,871.16	8,786.97	8,626.33	12,738.69	2,313.20
Total	1,524,355.94	341,934.51	164,217.79	364,228.29	437,657.38	128,121.03

Source: Data on capital embodied in skills, Table 8B, applied to employment data on Americans privately employed abroad in U.S., Department of Commerce, Bureau of the Census, "Americans Overseas," Selected Area Report PC(3)-1C, in *U.S. Census of the Population, 1960* (Washington, D.C.: U.S. Government Printing Office, 1964), Table 15.

Americans in the U.S.S.R. is minimal. The occupational classification by the Census distributed the overseas population among occupational categories essentially similar to, though slightly more aggregative than, those adopted for the domestic population. The skill-group data presented here are simple sums over the relevant occupations; the categories for the population abroad conform perfectly to those for the domestic population.

To measure the stock of human capital represented by privately employed American personnel, I assume that each individual is employed full-time overseas, providing one man-year of his particular skill at a wage at least equivalent to what he would earn at home, and that his skill, if not he himself, is in continual residence abroad. On these assumptions, if 45,000 American men were employed in foreign countries, they would represent 45,000 man-years of labor. Suppose, also, that 4,500 of these men were scientists or engineers, and that the estimated gross return to scientific and engineering skill were $50,000 per worker. Scientists and engineers abroad would then embody $275 million of human capital. The value of all human capital embodied in skilled Americans employed abroad is the sum of the contributions implicit in each skill category.

Recall, however, the composite nature of direct investment suggested in this study: direct investment is the migration of enterprise. If these privately employed American personnel are, in fact, employed by U.S. direct-investment enterprises, the skills these people provide may be deemed specific to the enterprise that hires them. As such, the skills represent "requirements" of the firm's production process which are integral to the capital transfer; the 4,5000 scientists and engineers thus comprise 10 per cent of the foreign affiliates' requirement of American skill, and the human capital embodied in those scientists and engineers represents a portion of the total capital transfer by the parent corporation.

To measure skill requirements, I assume that the privately employed American personnel do work for U.S.-affiliated firms; hence, the actual percentage distribution of employment by skill in a region (Tables 5A and 5B) reflects the production requirements of U.S. direct-investment enterprises in the same region. By applying the regional skill requirements to the various estimates of *per capita* investment in skill at home (Tables 8A and 8B), I obtain the measures of capital embodied in privately employed American personnel abroad in 1960—for all areas, together, and for five separate regions. These measures are set forth in Tables 9A and 9B.

Table 10A

*Total Capital Embodied in Americans Employed Abroad,
Based on Skill Group 1: U.S. Males, by Region, 1960
(millions of dollars)*

Area	Rate of Return		
	9.0%	11.0%	12.7%
All areas	2,111	1,727	1,496
Europe	480	393	340
Canada and Mexico	239	196	169
Other America	514	420	364
Asia	595	487	422
Africa	163	133	116

Source: Table 9A.

The total stock of capital embodied in these privately employed American personnel overseas, reproduced separately in Tables 10A and 10B, is large, ranging from a low estimate (at a 12.7 per cent return) of $1.5 billion to a high (at 9.0 per cent) of $2.2 billion.

The poor quality of the direct-investment data precludes a meaningful summation of the two capital figures—tangible capital and human capital. It might, nonetheless, be noted that these human-capital estimates go along with a book value of direct investment totaling $31.8 billion in 1960 (Table 1). And tangible-capital investments abroad, measured by the book value of direct investments or, alternatively, by

Table 10B

*Total Capital Embodied in Americans Employed Abroad,
Based on Skill Group 2: U.S. Males, by Region, 1960
(millions of dollars)*

Area	Rate of Return		
	9.0%	11.0%	12.7%
All areas	2,151	1,760	1,524
Europe	482	395	342
Canada and Mexico	232	190	164
Other America	514	420	364
Asia	617	505	438
Africa	180	148	128

Source: Table 9B.

Table 11

Human Capital per Worker, Americans Employed at Home: U.S. Males, 1959 (thousands of dollars)

	Rate of Return		
Skill Breakdown	9.0%	11.0%	12.7%
Group 1	29.81	24.39	21.12
Group 2	30.30	24.79	21.47

Sources: Tables 5A, 5B, 8A, and 8B.

accumulated plant and equipment expenditures (selected components appear in Table 2) have continued to rise from their 1960 levels. If, in fact, skilled personnel do migrate with tangible capital, the current stock of human capital abroad may be even larger than the estimates presented here.

These estimates of the stock of capital embodied in Americans privately employed in foreign countries mask the striking differences between the domestically employed population and that employed abroad. To reveal these differences, one must look next at estimates of the human capital embodied in a "typical" worker, at home and overseas. The data in Table 11 conveniently summarize this information for the domestic economy. They measure human capital per worker—capital embodied in each skill, weighted by the distribution of domestic employment in that skill.

These figures derive from data spanning the entire American economy. Variation would arise if sectors of that economy were analyzed separately, for the percentage distribution of employment by skill differs significantly among sectors. The skill distribution of all domestic employment is compared in Table 12 with the distributions Leontief used for the export and import-competing sectors.[48] It is not surprising that these divergent skill distributions yield human-capital estimates for the export and import-competing sectors that differ greatly from those for the whole economy.

The first row of Table 13 presents the results derived by applying the Leontief skill distributions for the export and import-competing sectors (Table 12) to the measures of capital embodied in skill (Table 8B); the second row reproduces Kenen's analogous results for the foreign-trade

[48] W. W. Leontief, "Factor Proportions and the Structure of American Trade," *Review of Economics and Statistics*, XXXVIII (November 1956), 399.

Table 12

*Employment by Skill, Group 2: U.S. Males,
All Sectors, 1960; Foreign-Trade Sectors,
1947 (percentages)*

Skill	All Sectors	Foreign Trade	
		Export	Import
I	25.02	13.75	12.24
II	16.48	22.07	17.00
III	23.31	15.15	11.79
IV	29.20	30.05	28.38
V	5.99	18.98	30.59

Sources: Table 5B, and W. W. Leontief, "Factor Proportions and the Structure of American Trade," *Review of Economics and Statistics*, XXXVIII (November 1956), 399.

sector of the U.S. economy. The relatively small discrepancies between the two reflect the fact that the two procedures, although similar, are not identical; the present calculation is more inclusive than Kenen's both in the detail underlying each step in the procedure and in the overall sector coverage.[49]

The discrepancies between either of these estimates and those for the whole economy are, by contrast, quite large. Their size, however, may be somewhat exaggerated. Leontief's data relate to production requirements for trade in 1947. And significant changes have occurred, both in production techniques and in the composition of trade flows. This lack of comparability precludes the possibility of more than *prima facie* inferences from the sets of estimates.

There is no need for a *caveat* with respect to the comparability of the estimates when the two sets of data being examined are those for human

[49] The mean wage estimates used here do differ from those Kenen and Yudin employed for their principal occupations; Kenen and Yudin, *Skills, Human Capital.*

Skill Level	Mean Wage Estimates	
	Principal Occupations (Kenen-Yudin)	*All Occupations* (present study)
I	$9,414	$8,789
II	5,934	5,846
III	5,982	5,587
IV	4,913	5,641
V	3,403	3,601

Table 13

Human Capital in U.S. Export Production and U.S. Import-Competing Production (thousands of dollars per man-year)

| | Rate of Return | | | | | |
| | 9.0% | | 11.0% | | 12.7% | |
Sectors	Export	Import	Export	Import	Export	Import
All sectors	23.59	20.34	19.30	16.64	16.72	14.41
Manufacturing, mining, services, agriculture	24.78	21.10	20.27	17.26	17.56	14.95

Sources: Tables 8B and 11, and P. B. Kenen and E. B. Yudin, *Skills, Human Capital and U.S. Foreign Trade: Variations on a Theme by Leontief* (New York: International Economics Workshop, Columbia University, December 1965), Table 9.

capital per worker at home and those for human capital per worker among privately employed American personnel abroad. The warnings here differ in nature. Throughout this study, I have used American wage data, assuming that the opportunity cost of employment overseas is the wage that could be earned at home. I have also assumed that each American employed abroad represents one man-year of labor in his specific skill. All Americans privately employed abroad, that is, are treated as working full time for a year, and at (minimally) an American wage.

Tables 14A and 14B speak for themselves. As one would predict from the distribution of skills (Tables 5A and 5B), the regional pattern here is

Table 14A

Human Capital per Worker, Americans Employed Abroad, Based on Skill-Group 1: U.S. Males, by Region (dollars)

| | Rate of Return | | |
Area	9.0%	11.0%	12.7%
All areas	46,078	37,700	32,654
Europe	46,049	37,676	32,633
Canada and Mexico	44,908	36,743	31,824
Other America	48,642	39,798	34,470
Asia	46,614	36,743	31,824
Africa	47,512	38,873	33,670

Sources: Tables 5A and 9A.

Table 14B

Human Capital per Worker, Americans Employed Abroad,
Based on Skill Group 2: U.S. Males, by Region (dollars)

	Rate of Return		
Area	9.0%	11.0%	12.7%
All areas	46,948	38,412	33,270
Europe	46,235	37,828	32,765
Canada and Mexico	43,534	35,618	30,851
Other America	48,685	39,833	34,501
Asia	48,358	39,566	34,270
Africa	52,679	43,101	37,331

Sources: Tables 5B and 9B.

quite uniform. As in those skill distributions, however, the pattern abroad stands in striking contrast to that for the domestic economy. It is sufficient to note that the lowest estimate in either of these two tables ($30,851 per worker, in Canada and Mexico) exceeds the highest of the domestic estimates of human capital per worker in Table 11 ($30,302 per worker). Table 15 summarizes the various estimates of human caital per worker presented here.

The uniquely skill-biased distribution of Americans privately employed abroad augments the *per capita* human-capital estimates. The capital embodied in a "typical" American overseas far exceeds that in a "typical" worker at home—in support of Rubin's contention that these people are, indeed, a special segment of the parent American population.

Table 15

Human Capital per Worker, Based on Skill Group 2:
Various Estimates (thousands of dollars)

	Rate of Return		
Estimate	9.0%	11.0%	12.7%
Domestic economy			
All sectors	30.30	24.79	21.47
Foreign-trade sectors			
Exports	23.59	19.30	16.72
Imports	20.34	16.64	14.41
Americans abroad	46.95	38.41	33.27

Sources: Tables 11, 12, and 14B.

If, however, direct investment is conceptually the multifaceted migration of knowledge, capital, and skills in a single entity—enterprise—one can say more. The flow of direct-investment funds to skill-intensive activities and the parallel flow of human capital embodied in people whose skill is predominantly professional, both technical and managerial, is not mere coincidence. Direct investment, in its nature, requires both tangible capital and the specifically skilled personnel who can tend and reproduce it. Both embody knowledge, thereby providing a major vehicle for the international transfer of technology. Capital embodied in skill represents more than a portion of an international capital transfer; it quantifies, albeit partially, the investment in the international transfer of technology. Much as in Bacon's vision, direct investment spreads "light," and the knowledge of skilled and experienced people is a major source of that illumination.

MERLE I. YAHR

Human Capital and Factor Substitution in the CES Production Function

THE FRAMEWORK

OUTLINES OF THE international pattern of factor use, of the output mix of countries, and of the forces determining these patterns have been furnished by several authors.[1] This study is a further attempt to analyze the forces determining the pattern of factor use; it concentrates on estimating the elasticity of substitution between labor and capital (σ).

The significance of this work is manifold, as the elasticity of substitution is an important parameter in numerous economic theories. The theory of income distribution, for example, becomes operational only when we

[1] See, for example, L. H. Bean, "International Industrialization and Per Capita Income," *Studies in Income and Wealth*, Vol. VIII (New York: National Bureau of Economic Research, 1946); W. G. Hoffmann, *The Growth of Industrial Economies*, (Manchester: Manchester University Press, 1958); and H. B. Chenery, "Patterns of Industrial Growth," *American Economic Review*, L (September 1960), 624–54.

know the magnitude of this parameter. Without this knowledge, one cannot assess the impact of such changes as technological progress, immigration, capital formation, or the unionization of labor on the share of income going to the various factors of production. Moreover, the factor-price equalization theorem implicitly assumes that in all industries the magnitudes of the elasticity, if constant, are equal. The validity of the assumptions made about the elasticity of substitution determines the usefulness of these theories. Empirical estimates of the elasticity of substitution thus provide a means of assessing the connection between the theories and reality.

Arrow, Chenery, Minhas, and Solow (ACMS), as well as O'Neill, have developed empirically useful methods for estimating this elasticity.[2] From their models and cross-sectional international data, I will obtain estimates of the elasticity of substitution for two- and three-digit ISIC industrial categories.

Assuming competition in both product and factor markets, ACMS have shown that, in the estimating equation:[3,4]

$$\log \frac{p_x X}{L} = a + b \log w$$

b is an estimate of the elasticity of substitution, provided product prices, p_x, are uncorrelated with wage rates, w. Here, X equals the quantity of output, and L equals the number of workers. Similarly, O'Neill has shown that, in the estimating equation:

$$\log \frac{rC}{L} = c + d \log w$$

d is an estimate of the elasticity of substitution, provided the rental price of physical capital, r, is uncorrelated with wage rates.[5] Here, C equals the quantity of the physical capital input. Furthermore, O'Neill shows

[2] K. J. Arrow, H. B. Chenery, B. S. Minhas, and R. M. Solow, "Capital-Labor Substitution and Economic Efficiency," *Review of Economics and Statistics*, XLIII (August 1961), 225–50; D. M. O'Neill, "Estimating the Elasticity of Substitution: Methodology and An Empirical Application to United States Manufacturing Industries" (unpublished doctoral dissertation, Columbia University, 1966).

[3] See Arrow, Chenery, Minhas, and Solow, "Substitution and Economic Efficiency" for the complete derivation.

[4] For simplicity, the stochastic terms of all estimating equations will be omitted throughout the exposition.

[5] See O'Neill, "Estimating Elasticity," for the complete derivation.

that when:

$$\frac{-1}{r_{rw}(S_r/S_w)} > \frac{1}{\bar{k}} - 1$$

where r_{rw} is the correlation between $\log r$ and $\log w$, $\bar{k}$ is the average cost of L over the n observations used to estimate σ, S_r is the standard deviation of $\log r$, and S_w is the standard deviation of $\log w$, then b and d will form an interval around the true value of σ. Both b and d will be on the same side of unity as σ, with b being the upper limit when $\sigma < 1$, and the lower limit when $\sigma > 1$. For this inequality to hold, r_{rw} must be less than zero; given this necessary condition, the inequality is more likely to hold, the smaller the negative correlation between r and w, the smaller the dispersion in r relative to w, and the more labor-intensive the industry. It is possible to test indirectly the assumption that this inequality exists. The results of these tests provide evidence that the interval estimates of the elasticity of substitution derived from the O'Neill model are reliable.[6] Therefore, I shall utilize O'Neill's interval method of estimation in this essay.

To estimate these two equations with international data, one must assume that there are no systematic differences between developed and underdeveloped countries. Fuchs has shown that the ACMS model yields biased results when no adjustment is made for these differences.[7] Dividing the ACMS countries into developed and underdeveloped categories, he adds a dummy variable to the ACMS equation and estimates it for their sample of countries.[8] Although ACMS obtained elasticities significantly different from unity in 14 of their 24 industries, Fuchs finds that his elasticity estimates are clustered around unity. Furthermore, his dummy variable is significantly different from zero in 17 of the 24 industries, indicating that there are systematic differences between developed and underdeveloped countries. Later, Becker suggested that the significant difference between developed and underdeveloped countries was that, in developed countries, wages are high because of investments in human capital.[9] Kenen then developed a more complete

[6] For the results of these tests, using the data described in this essay, see M. I. Yahr, "Estimating the Elasticity of Substitution from International Manufacturing Census Data" (unpublished doctoral dissertation, Columbia University, 1967).

[7] V. Fuchs, "Capital-Labor Substitution: A Note," *Review of Economics and Statistics*, XLV (November 1963), 436–38.

[8] ACMS estimated the elasticity of substitution for 24 two- and three-digit ISIC industries using data taken from the industrial censuses of 19 countries. For details, see Arrow, Chenery, Minhas, and Solow, "Substitution and Economic Efficiency," pp. 225–50.

[9] G. S. Becker, *Human Capital* (New York: National Bureau of Economic Research, 1965), p. 60.

statement of international trade theory including human capital as a factor of production in the theoretical framework. He also suggested that neglect of international differences in human capital when estimating the parameters of the production function would bias the resulting estimates of σ.[10]

Other authors have attempted to measure the human capital invested in the workers of different countries. Harbison and Meyers attempted to quantify the international differences in investments in highly skilled manpower.[11] They computed an index based on pupils currently enrolled in secondary schools and pupils currently enrolled in college-level schools expressed as a percentage of the school-age population. Values of this index, shown in Table 1, indicate that countries differ widely in their current ability to train skilled labor and, assuming that these differences existed in the past, that countries differ widely in their stocks of human capital, measured by investments in higher-level schooling.

A better proxy for the stock of human capital is a measure of the formal educational attainment of a country's population. For the few countries that took demographic censuses between 1952 and 1958, I computed the mean educational level for males aged 15 and over and produced an educational index.[12] I classified the male population aged 15 and over by the level of formal education that each age group had attained, then weighted each educational group by the fraction of the male population in that educational group. I assumed that the average educational attainment of the male population 15 and over is equal to the average educational attainment of the whole labor force, and that 15 years of age is the typical minimum age for males to enter the labor force. My index may underestimate the education of the labor forces in developed countries, for studies have shown that the labor-force participation rate of males between 15 and 19 years of age decreases with increased incomes.[13] Even so, values of my educational index shown in Table 1 indicate that the average educational level of the adult male population differs widely among countries.

[10] P. B. Kenen, "Nature, Capital, and Trade," *Journal of Political Economy*, LXXIII (October 1965), 437–60.

[11] F. Harbison and C. A. Myers, *Education, Manpower, and Economic Growth: Strategies of Human Resource Development* (New York: McGraw-Hill Book Co., 1964), pp. 31–32.

[12] For the data sources used in computing this index, see Yahr, "Estimating Elasticity."

[13] United Nations, *Demographic Aspects of Manpower: Sex and Age Patterns of Participation in Economic Activities* (1962), p. 12.

Table 1

Levels of Human Resource Development for Selected Countries,
By Harbison Index, Correa Index, and Educational Index

Country	Harbison Index	Educational Index (School Years/Worker)	Correa Index
Argentina	82.0	4.13	93.46
Australia	137.7		97.84
Brazil	20.9	2.26	68.76
Canada	101.6	7.35	92.45
Chile	51.2	4.37	69.44
Denmark	77.1		97.41
Finland	88.7		91.28
India	35.2		27.51
Japan	111.4	8.57	59.22
Korea	55.0	3.96	
Mexico	33.0	2.96	60.26
New Zealand	147.3		98.31
Norway	73.8	6.23	90.09
Pakistan		1.66	
Paraguay	22.7	3.00	78.24
Peru	30.2	3.81	
Sweden	79.2		86.97
Taiwan	53.9	3.66	
United Kingdom	121.6	9.45[a]	97.50
United States	261.3	8.47	96.23

Sources: F. Harbison and C. A. Myers, *Education, Manpower, and Economic Growth: Strategies of Human Resource Development.* (New York: McGraw-Hill Book Co., 1964), pp. 31–32; H. Correa, *The Economics of Human Resources* (Amsterdam: North-Holland Publishing Co., 1963), pp. 32–34; educational index computed from data taken from United Nations, *Demographic Yearbook, 1963.* (New York: United Nations), Table 14.

[a] Index computed from data taken from OECD, *The Residual Factor and Economic Growth* (Paris: OECD, 1964), p. 43.

To mention one more measure, Correa has developed a physiological index to measure an individual's basic capacity to perform productive tasks and has computed it for several countries.[14] He has related the actual caloric intake of the population to the caloric requirements of the population and combined his findings into an index of working capacity for each country. Values of this index shown in Table 1 indicate that nutritional levels and, therefore, capacities to do productive work, differ greatly among countries. Furthermore, Correa believes that the computed

[14] H. Correa, *The Economics of Human Resources* (Amsterdam: North-Holland Publishing Co., 1963), pp. 32–34.

values of his index underestimate the true international differences in nutritional satisfaction: In advanced countries, those sectors of the population needing more calories can obtain them, whereas, in under-developed countries, workers in occupations requiring a high caloric intake, for example, agriculture or construction, have lower-than-average wages and are less likely to obtain the additional calories they need. Even without this qualification, Correa's index indicates that there are large international differences in workers' productive capacities.

Since the various forms of human investment are additive and these indexes are positively correlated, human investments probably differ among countries more than is revealed by any single index.[15] The overall systematic differences, moreover, will seriously bias cross-sectional estimates of the elasticity of substitution derived from the ACMS and O'Neill equations, for wage rates are positively correlated with investments in human capital. Hence, it is necessary to alter the ACMS and O'Neill equations to adjust for variations in the quality of labor, Q.

The modified equations I shall employ are multiple regression equations in which the wage rate, w, and a measure of the human capital endowment of workers, Q, will be the independent variables:

$$\log \frac{p_x X}{L} = a' + b_1' \log w + b_2' \log Q$$

$$\log \frac{rC}{L} = c' + d_1' \log w + d_2' \log Q$$

In these modified equations, the elasticity estimates, b_1' and d_1', will be estimates of substitution possibilities between physical capital and labor of a given quality.[16] Substitution possibilities between workers of different qualities will not be included in these elasticity estimates. If, furthermore, the correlations between $\log p_x$ and $\log Q$, and between $\log r$ and $\log Q$, are both zero, the coefficients of $\log Q$ will yield information about the "bias" of the shift of the production function caused by a change in labor quality.[17] A negative d_2' in the O'Neill equation indicates that an increase

---

[15] For the proof of this statement, see Yahr, "Estimating Elasticity."

[16] This method of incorporating labor-quality differences into the estimating equations treats labor quality as an exogenous factor; the observed international variation in wage rates results from differences in workers' productivity, not from deliberate choices by entrepreneurs to hire skilled rather than unskilled workers. The true elasticity of substitution between physical capital and labor is assumed to be unaffected by differences in labor quality.

[17] For the proof of this statement, see Yahr, "Estimating Elasticity."

in labor quality will raise the marginal product of labor more than it raises the marginal product of capital; in Hicksian terms, this is a capital-saving shift of the production function. A positive d_2' in the O'Neill equation indicates that an increase in labor quality causes a labor-saving shift of the production function. A nonsignificant d_2' indicates that a change in labor quality causes a neutral shift of the production function (unless σ is close to zero, which outcome will bring d_2' close to zero automatically).

If, further, the partial correlation between $\log p_x$ and $\log Q$ is zero, the ACMS coefficient of $\log Q$, b_2', should always be negative (unless σ is close to zero) regardless of the type of shift of the production function caused by a change in labor quality.

THE DATA

I shall estimate these modified equations using industrial census data for 22 countries.[18] Industry estimates of σ will be obtained for 19 of the 20 two-digit ISIC industrial categories and for 37 of the 55 three-digit categories.[19] Some countries are not represented in the data for every industry, but every effort has been made to cover a large part of the manufacturing sector of each country.

Data were collected on value added, employment, and labor costs. I used value added, rather than value of shipments, as the output variable because there is no explicit allowance for raw materials inputs in the theoretical structure I am employing. Since direct estimates of payments to physical capital are not generally available, the difference between total value added and total labor cost will be used as a proxy for this variable. To measure differences in labor quality, I used the Harbison and Myers "Index of Levels of Human Resource Development" (the Harbison index). Using an index classified by country alone, rather than by country and by industry, I am implicitly assuming that differences in average labor quality are not wholly due to (or reflected in) the nations'

---

[18] For the sources and shortcomings of these data, see Yahr, "Estimating Elasticity."

[19] If σ is not the same among processes, and if there are variations among countries in an industry's product mix, the estimates of σ will be biased. At the three-digit industrial level, there is least possibility of variations in an industry's product mix; hence, I estimated σ at the three-digit level wherever possible. Additional estimates of σ at the two-digit level of industrial aggregation were used for purposes of comparison—as a check on my results.

product mixes; that there are, in fact, significant international differences in the human-capital endowments of workers employed in a particular industry. This assumption will be tested in the final section of this study.

The raw data (labor costs per worker and value added per worker) in local currency units were converted into U.S. dollars at official exchange rates or at free-market rates where multiple exchange rates prevailed. If neither an official nor a free-market rate existed, and there were multiple exchange rates, I used the rate that applied to the most general class of imports.[20] This method of conversion into dollars probably underestimates wage rates and value added in the underdeveloped countries because of the differences in price levels between developed and underdeveloped countries.[21] Since the interval-estimating procedure devised by O'Neill is an indirect means of avoiding this source of bias, O'Neill's model is especially valuable for obtaining elasticity estimates from international data.

These manufacturing census data will be used to estimate the ACMS and O'Neill models by regression techniques. My results will be analyzed in two sections. First, I shall focus on the validity of the estimating procedure. Three questions will be considered: (1) Does the model fit the data well; that is, is there, on the average, a high and significant coefficient of determination for each of the two estimating equations? (2) Do the independent variables display the expected signs, and are they significant in both equations? (3) Is the Harbison index an acceptable means of measuring differential endowments of human capital? Second, I shall focus on the economic interpretation of my regression results. Again, three questions will be considered: (1) Are my estimates of σ significantly different from unity and/or zero? (2) What can one infer from the signs and sizes of the coefficients of the labor-quality variable? (3) What can be inferred about the parameters of the CES production

[20] In principle, the failure to select "correct" exchange rates should introduce no biases into the elasticity estimates. However, since both estimating equations are modifications of the theoretically correct equations, two sources of bias are introduced via the conversion of value-added and labor costs into dollars. As both the dependent and independent variables are multiplied by the exchange rate, the elasticity estimates will be biased toward unity by an incorrect exchange rate. This error will be compounded by the omitted-variable bias of the estimating equations. The latter error depends on the magnitude of the estimated elasticity and the correlation between the wage rate and the omitted variables—the product price in the ACMS equation and the rental price of capital in the O'Neill equation.

[21] M. Gilbert, *Comparative National Products and Price Levels: A Study of Western Europe and the U.S.* (Paris: OECD, 1958).

function from these same coefficients? One additional question will be considered separately: Is there evidence of a significant dispersion in σ across industries?

The equations are estimated in two steps: The first step yields a simple regression equation with log w as the independent variable. The second step yields a multiple regression equation, with log w and log Q as independent variables.

GENERAL VALIDITY OF THE
ESTIMATING PROCEDURE

Table 2 describes the frequency distribution of the adjusted coefficients of determination, $\bar{R}^2$, at each step of the estimating procedure. A high and significant $\bar{R}^2$ indicates that much of the variability in the dependent variable has been "explained" by the independent variables. For the two-digit data (19 industries), the mean $\bar{R}^2$ for the ACMS equation is .84 at step 1 and .85 at step 2; for the O'Neill equation, it is .65 at step 1 and .69 at step 2. Table 2 shows that the mean values derived from the three-digit data do not differ greatly from the values for the two-digit data. The values of $\bar{R}^2$ at the 25th and 75th percentiles are also shown in Table 2. The small differences indicate that $\bar{R}^2$ varies little across industries. Furthermore, almost all of the $\bar{R}^2$ are statistically

Table 2

Arithmetic Means and Percentile Statistics for $\bar{R}^2$

	Step 1				Step 2			
			Top of Quartile				Top of Quartile	
	Mean	Median	First	Third	Mean	Median	First	Third
Three-Digit Industries (37)								
Equation 1	.86	.90	.83	.94	.85	.91	.84	.95
Equation 2	.61	.66	.46	.79	.62	.71	.49	.80
Two-Digit Industries (19)								
Equation 1	.84	.93	.88	.96	.85	.93	.88	.96
Equation 2	.65	.69	.59	.84	.69	.72	.64	.84

Note: Numbers in parentheses indicate the number of industries in each data set.

significant at the .05 level of significance. Taking these results together, I conclude that the model fits the data well and that the level of aggregation has little effect on the explanatory power of the model.

The first step of the estimating procedure yields simple regressions with the wage rate as the independent variable in both equations. The coefficients of the wage rate are significantly different from zero, and positive in almost all industries, implying positive elasticities of substitution (as expected). The average significance level (Student's t value) for the two-digit data is 13.92 for the ACMS equation, and 6.60 for the O'Neill equation. The average significance level is slightly lower in the multiple regression equations (step two), but remains statistically and practically significant at the .05 level of significance. At each step, however, the mean t values computed for O'Neill's equation are lower than those for the ACMS equation.[22] This is to be expected, for the mean $\bar{R}^2$ was smaller for O'Neill's equation.

TESTS OF THE HARBISON INDEX

As previously explained, I have introduced a second independent variable, an index of labor quality, into the regression equations. The difficulties involved in measuring international differences in labor quality have already been mentioned. The variable I have used (the Harbison index) is, at best, a rough approximation to a theoretically correct variable that would measure the endowment of human capital embodied in workers in each industry and country. However, it is possible to ascertain the appropriateness of the Harbison index to the requirements of the theoretical model.

The first step of my procedure was, following Fuchs, to incorporate a dummy variable into the regression equations in order to dichotomize countries into developed and underdeveloped groups. I assigned this dummy variable the value of unity for developed countries and zero for underdeveloped countries. Table 3 lists the value assigned to each country. If the regression coefficient of the dummy variable is significant,

[22] This result is probably due to the fact that $(p_x X - wL)/L$ is an indirect measure of rC/L, the cost of physical capital per worker. Random divergences from the assumptions of competition and linear homogeneity will add an unknown amount of error to this indirect measure. If, for example, there are increasing returns to scale, the value-added figure will include this return to scale, and rC/L will be overestimated by the indirect measure.

Table 3

Dummy Variable Values Assigned to 22 Countries
Used in Three-Digit Industry Regressions

Country	Dummy Value	Country	Dummy Value
Argentina	0	Israel	1
Australia	1	Japan	1
Belgium	1	Mexico	0
Brazil	0	New Zealand	1
Canada	1	Norway	1
Chile	0	Pakistan	0
Colombia	0	Peru	0
Denmark	1	South Africa	0
India	0	Sweden	1
Korea	0	Taiwan	0
United Kingdom	1	United States	1

it should correctly describe the effects on the elasticity estimates of *all* the differences between developed and underdeveloped countries. Next, I incorporated my own educational index into the equations. This index is a reasonable proxy for endowments of human capital, but is available for only a small number of countries. If a large part of the difference between developed and underdeveloped countries is attributable to differential endowments of human capital, the effect of this human-capital variable should be similar to the effect of the dummy variable. Finally, I incorporated the Harbison index into the regression equations, using the complete samples of manufacturing census data. If the Harbison index is a meaningful proxy for differential endowments of human capital, the effect of the Harbison index in the regression equations should be similar to the effect of the educational index, a better, but less readily available, measure of human capital. The statistical reliability of the results based on the Harbison index, however, will be greater than the reliability of regressions including the educational index because of the larger sample sizes.

To execute the first step of my procedure, I recomputed the ACMS and O'Neill equations with the dummy variable using the 37 three-digit industries. In most industries and both equations, the coefficient of the dummy variable was negative; the average t value of the negative coefficients was 1.50 in the ACMS equation and 1.40 in the O'Neill equation. Most of the negative coefficients were not significant at the .05 level. The reason may be that the dummy variable was highly correlated with the wage rate; the average correlation was .71. If the independent variables in a regression equation are highly correlated, that is, exhibit multicollinearity, their standard errors will be large and the net effect of each of them becomes difficult to isolate.

But the large number of negative signs of these coefficients bolsters our faith in the dummy variable, and a sign test was performed to show that this predominance of negative signs was not due to chance. On the null hypothesis that the probability of obtaining a negative or positive sign for each coefficient is .5, the binomial probabilities of observing the sample frequencies are less than .05 for both equations. I therefore reject the null hypothesis and conclude that these negative signs are not due to chance: the "true" coefficient of the dummy variable is negative.

The introduction of this dummy variable reveals meaningful differences between developed and underdeveloped countries, and shows that these differences have a systematic effect on the independent variables of the ACMS and O'Neill equations. The dummy variable, however, merely dichotomizes countries; it does not describe the differences among them. I maintain that a substantial part of the difference among these countries is the difference in endowments of human capital. Therefore, I expect that the introduction of a variable measuring these human-capital endowments will yield results similar (in terms of the signs of the coefficients) to those obtained using the dummy variable.

To test this hypothesis, I recompute each equation, using the wage rate and my educational index as independent variables. For the same group of countries, I also compute both equations with the wage rate and the Harbison index as the independent variables. I can then meaningfully compare the coefficients of these two quality indexes. Similar coefficients (in signs and significance levels) will be taken to indicate that the Harbison index is a reasonable proxy for different countries' endowments of human capital.

In 15 two-digit industries, I had more than ten observations on the three types of data—manufacturing census data, Harbison data, and educational index data—necessary to make this comparison. As in the regressions with the dummy variable, negative signs predominate for the coefficients of the labor-quality indexes. The average Student's t value of the negative regression coefficients was similar for the Harbison and education indexes. Furthermore, these indexes of labor quality had similar effects on the magnitude of the elasticity estimates. This test indicates that the Harbison index can be used as a proxy for endowments of human capital per worker. In the analysis that follows, the coefficients of the Harbison index computed from the full industrial samples will be interpreted in this way.

Consider, again, the multiple regressions computed with Harbison's index using the entire sample of industrial census data. Theoretically, the labor-quality variable could take on a positive or negative sign in the O'Neill equation. But my experiments with the dummy variable, the educational index, and the Harbison index lead one to expect that the coefficients of the Harbison index will be negative. This was true in the majority of industries, and, when I performed sign tests on these coefficients, I concluded that the frequency of negative signs was not due to chance.[23]

Although logarithmic and arithmetic forms of the labor-quality variable are theoretically possible, the partial correlations of the logarithmic form exceeded those obtained with the arithmetic form in almost all cases. Thus, I have chosen the logarithmic form as the "correct" form. But even the logarithmic form is not, on the average, statistically significant. As previously explained, this was probably due to high multicollinearity in the estimating equations: The average correlation between $\log w$ and $\log Q$ was .66 for the two-digit industries, and .69 for three-digit industries.

Summarizing the joint effect of both variables in the ACMS and O'Neill equations: The average negative partial correlation between the labor-quality index and the wage rate raises the regression coefficient of the wage rate and lowers its significance level slightly. The lower t value of the wage-rate coefficient is probably due to the high correlation between the wage rate and the labor-quality index. The wage-rate coefficient (elasticity of substitution) is positive and significant in almost all industries; the labor-quality coefficient is, on the average, negative in both equations (and with sufficient frequency to rule out pure chance occurrence), but is not usually significant. Estimates of the elasticity of substitution derived from the multiple regression equations are most likely to be correct. The coefficient of the labor-quality variable will be interpreted in human-capital terms.

[23] For 19 two-digit industries, the values of the regression coefficients for step 2 of the estimating procedure are given in the Appendix.

INTERPRETING THE RESULTS

In many empirical studies, the elasticity of substitution has been assumed to be zero (as in the fixed-input-coefficient production function) or to be unity (as in the Cobb-Douglas production function). What is the true value? I shall use two methods to answer this question: First, I will view the industry estimates of σ as sample estimates of the true σ from a population of manufacturing industries and will ask whether each is significantly different from zero and unity. Second, I will aggregate these estimates of σ into an estimate of the elasticity of substitution for the whole manufacturing sector, then ask whether this average value of σ is significantly different from both zero and unity.

I have already noted that, in both equations, the coefficients of the wage rate are significantly different from zero at the .05 level of significance. These coefficients are upper and lower bounds on the elasticity of substitution for each industry. If these industry estimates of σ are considered as samples drawn from the manufacturing sector's population, they suggest that the elasticity of substitution is significantly different from zero.

But these same regression results might be interpreted to indicate that the elasticity of substitution is not substantially different from unity. Student's t tests were used to determine whether each industry's regression estimates are significantly different from unity. In the three-digit data, 10 of 37 industries yielded a pair of coefficients that were significantly different from unity at the .05 level of significance. If the all-manu-facturing σ were unity, however, no more than 2 of 37 random drawings (industry observations) would yield coefficients significantly different from unity at the .05 level of significance. For this reason, these 10 exceptional industries indicate that the true elasticity of substitution may be different from unity. Similar results obtain in the the two-digit industries, providing additional evidence that the population σ is different from unity.

Next, I aggregated these industry elasticities into an estimate of the elasticity of substitution for the entire manufacturing sector. I computed the arithmetic mean upper bound of the three-digit elasticities and used it as the upper bound of the all-manufacturing elasticity; I computed the arithmetic mean lower bound and used it as the corresponding lower bound. For the standard error of this aggregate elasticity, I computed the square root of the sum of the component variances divided by the number of component variances.[24]

A Student's *t* test may be used to determine whether the all-manufacturing elasticity is significantly different from unity. The arithmetic mean upper bound for the 37 industries is .90 and the standard error of this mean is .02; the mean lower bound is .80 and its standard error is .03. Both boundaries are significantly different from unity at the .05 level of significance. The two-digit industries give similar results; both bounds differ significantly from unity at the .05 level of significance.[25]

Summarizing, these results clearly suggest that the elasticity of substitution between physical capital and labor of the entire manufacturing sector is not zero, and provide weaker support for the conclusion that the elasticity is smaller than unity. But, if σ differs from unity, it is by a small amount.

Stigler has suggested that substitution possibilities between physical capital and labor may be severely limited in the short run, implying production functions of the fixed coefficient type, while the long-run production function may display substantial substitution possibilities.[26] If this hypothesis is correct, one would expect international data to yield estimates of σ that differ considerably from zero, for the variability in these international data may be similar to the changes in supply conditions that would occur in one country over a long period.

The coefficients of the labor-quality index yield information about the type of shift of the production function caused by exogenous differences in labor quality (assuming that the partial correlations between r and Q, and w and Q are zero). As noted previously, these coefficients are non-significant, probably because of multicollinearity in the estimating equations. However, sign tests showed a significant number of negative signs, implying that these coefficients are not trivial; that is, the "correct" sign of this coefficient is probably negative. Fortunately, knowledge of its sign is sufficient to classify the shift of the production function caused by a change in labor quality. The negative coefficients in the O'Neill equation imply that the shifts are capital-saving; the availability of high-quality labor induces the entrepreneur to substitute labor for

[24] Using this procedure to compute the standard error, I have implicitly assumed that the component variances are independent.

[25] The mean of the upper bounds is .88 and the standard error is .03; the mean of the lower bounds is .80 and the standard error is .04.

[26] G. J. Stigler, "Production and Distribution in the Short-Run," *Journal of Political Economy*, XLVII (1939), 305–27.

physical capital, at a given set of factor prices. Furthermore, theory predicts that the labor-quality coefficient in the ACMS equation will be negative, independent of the type of shift. Thus, the large number of negative b_2' coefficients suggest that my results are meaningful.

IMPLICATIONS FOR TRADE THEORY

As usually stated, the Heckscher-Ohlin theorem impounds differences in production methods among countries and treats differential factor endowments as the most important determinants of international differences in pre-trade commodity prices.[27] Given these factor-supply differences and similar demand patterns among countries, a two-factor, two-commodity model predicts that products intensive in a country's relatively abundant factor will be relatively cheap in that country, and products intensive in a country's relatively scarce factor will be relatively expensive.[28,29] As a result, a country tends to export those products that are most intensive users of that country's abundant factor.

Neither Heckscher nor Ohlin concluded that trade would completely equalize factor prices among countries. But Samuelson has shown that free trade in commodities will result in complete factor-price equalization, both relative and absolute, among the trading countries.[30] Assumptions about the shapes of the production functions, viz., that they are linearly homogeneous and can be ranked uniquely by factor intensity (hereafter referred to as the strong factor-intensity assumption)—are strategic to Samuelson's proof. Although these assumptions have been attacked, no definitive evidence has been presented to support or refute them. Thus,

[27] See E. Heckscher, "The Effect of Foreign Trade on the Distribution of Income" (1919), reprinted in H. S. Ellis and L. A. Metzler (eds.), *Readings in the Theory of International Trade* (Philadelphia: The Blakiston Co., 1950), pp. 272–300, and B. Ohlin, *Interregional and International Trade* (Cambridge: Harvard University Press, 1933), for the original statements.

[28] Ohlin defined relative abundance in terms of the relative prices of the factors of production. This is the definition used in this study.

[29] Other assumptions are necessary to predict the pattern of foreign trade: (1) the factors of production must be homogeneous both within and among countries; (2) there must be perfect competition in all markets; (3) production functions must be homogeneous of first degree and susceptible of unique ranking by factor intensity; (4) transport costs must be zero.

[30] P. A. Samuelson, "International Factor-Price Equalization Once Again," *Economic Journal*, LIX (June 1949), 181–97.

it seems appropriate to test these assumptions with the preceding empirical results.

First, I will review the methodology and conclusions of previous empirical analyses of the strong factor-intensity assumption. Then, I will analyze the results of my own empirical tests of this proposition.

In *An International Comparison of Factor Costs and Factor Use*, B. S. Minhas presents empirical work that does not substantiate the strong factor-intensity assumption.[31] Having first estimated CES production functions, Minhas shows that empirically plausible variations in relative factor prices will induce reversals in factor intensities, that is, the relatively capital-intensive commodity will become relatively labor-intensive. These reversals are possible because his estimated elasticities of substitution are not equal. If elasticities of substitution are constant and differ from industry to industry, there will be some critical value of the factor-price ratio at which relative factor intensities will reverse.[32] Using his own

[31] B. S. Minhas, *An International Comparison of Factor Costs and Factor Use* (Amsterdam: North-Holland Publishing Co., 1963), Chapter IV.

[32] To compute this critical ratio, let

$$X = [\alpha_1 C^{-\rho} + \alpha_2 L^{-\rho}]^{-1/\rho}$$

be the generalized form of the CES production function, where $\sigma = 1/(1 + \rho)$. Taking the partial derivatives of this function with respect to L and C yields the expressions for w, the real wage rate, and r, the real rate of return to capital:

$$w = \frac{\partial X}{\partial L} = \alpha_2 \left(\frac{X}{L}\right)^{\rho+1}$$

$$r = \frac{\partial X}{\partial C} = \alpha_1 \left(\frac{X}{C}\right)^{\rho+1}$$

Therefore, the factor-price ratio, w/r, is equal to:

$$\frac{w}{r} = \left(\frac{\alpha_2}{\alpha_1}\right) \left(\frac{C}{L}\right)^{\rho+1}$$

Minhas then substitutes $x_i = (C/L)_i$ and $x_j = (C/L)_j$ in the preceding expression, obtaining:

$$x_i = \left(\frac{w}{r}\right)^{\sigma_i} \left(\frac{\alpha_1}{\alpha_2}\right)^{\sigma_i}, \quad x_j = \left(\frac{w}{r}\right)^{\sigma_j} \left(\frac{\alpha_1}{\alpha_2}\right)^{\sigma_j}$$

Taking logarithms:

$$\log x_i = \sigma_i \log \left(\frac{\alpha_1}{\alpha_2}\right) + \sigma_i \log \left(\frac{w}{r}\right), \quad \text{etc.}$$

Given α_{1i}, α_{2i}, and σ_i for two industries, these two equations can be solved simultaneously for the critical value of w/r at which the value of x_i/x_j changes from less than to more than unity, i.e., the relatively labor-intensive good became relatively capital-intensive, and vice versa.

Table 4

*Critical Values of the Factor-Price Ratio and
Corresponding Capital-Labor Ratios*

Industry	Factor-Price Ratio	Capital-Labor Ratio
Textiles–nonferrous metals	$ 1,350	$ 1,720
Dairy products–pulp and paper	2,136	4,117
Pulp and paper–basic chemicals	5,370	9,970
Dairy products–nonferrous metals	8,665	11,308
Basic chemicals–grain mill products	20,400	30,410

Source: B. S. Minhas, *An International Comparison of Factor Costs and Factor
Use* (Amsterdam: North-Holland Publishing Co., 1963), p. 38.

empirical work, Minhas identifies these critical values for five pairs of industries. His results are listed in Table 4. Minhas then points out that wage rates vary between $250 per man-year in low-income countries (Asian) and $3,600 per man-year in high-income countries (the United States and Canada). Combining these data with information on rates of return on capital, he finds that factor-price ratios can range from $1,100 to $24,000. From this evidence, Minhas concludes that the ordering of industries by relative factor intensities can change between countries.

Minhas presents another empirical test of the strong factor-intensity assumption. This assumption implies that, in any two countries, no matter how widely different their relative costs of labor and capital, the rankings of industries according to capital intensity must exactly match. To test this hypothesis, Minhas ranks 20 U.S. and Japanese industries by total capital requirements per worker. The Spearman rank correlation coefficient between the industry orderings is .328. For the same 20 industries, the Spearman correlation coefficient for the rankings by direct capital requirements is .730.[33] Minhas concludes that these rank correlations tend to invalidate the strong factor-intensity assumption.

Leontief has challenged Minhas' conclusions, questioning his empirical work.[34] He argues that Minhas' data verify rather than dispute the strong

[33] According to Walker and Lev, there is no computed table of significance for Spearman coefficients for between 8 and 25 observations. H. M. Walker and J. Lev, *Statistical Inference* (New York: Holt, Rinehart & Winston, 1953), p. 282. However, Minhas concludes that "the two orderings are so dissimilar that even the null hypothesis of zero rank correlation between them is not rejected at the .10 level of significance." (Minhas, *International Comparison*, p. 40.)

[34] W. W. Leontief, "International Factor Costs and Factor Use," *American Economic Review*, LIV (June 1964), 335–45.

factor-intensity assumption, explaining that some of Minhas' conclusions are not supported by the empirical work shown in *An International Comparison of Factor Costs and Factor Use.*

Using his own methods, Leontief estimates the parameters α_1, α_2, and σ of a CES production function:

$$X = [\alpha_1 C^{-\rho} + \alpha_2 L^{-\rho}]^{-1/\rho}$$

where $\sigma = 1/1(1 + \rho)$. He works with the 21 industries for which Minhas presented the necessary data. Using the computed parameters, he plots the 21 equations:

$$\log \left(\frac{w}{r}\right)_i = \left(\frac{\alpha_2}{\alpha_1}\right)_i + \frac{1}{\sigma_i} \log \left(\frac{C}{L}\right)_i$$

on one graph. If any two lines on this graph intersect within the empirically possible range of factor-price ratios, there is a critical factor-price ratio at which the relative factor intensities of two industries will reverse. The positions of the 21 lines on this graph are determined by their slopes, $(1/\sigma)_i$, and by $(\alpha_2/\alpha_1)_i$, their intercepts. Of the 210 theoretically possible intersection points between the 21 lines, only 17 are to be found within the empirically relevant range of factor-price ratios observed, for example, in the United States and India. Moreover, most of the 17 crossover points occur between industries whose curves are, in a practical sense, identical.

Ball has other grounds for criticizing the evidence that Minhas presents.[35] He claims that the results of Minhas' rank correlations are inconclusive, for certain of the industries included in the rankings do not satisfy the assumptions of the test. Furthermore, he shows that the test results occur only because those same industries are ranked so dissimilarly. Ball maintains that the agricultural and food-processing industries should not be included in the rankings because: (1) the categories are so broad that the output mix (share of each good) may differ between countries; (2) different natural-resource conditions affect the production processes of those industries; (3) measures of factor inputs are least reliable for those industries. His own tests show that the dissimilarity in rankings by capital intensity is reduced when the agricultural and food-processing industries are deleted.[36] Ball concludes that "to include agriculture in the rankings tests and claim that the resulting dissimilarities are caused by

[35] D. S. Ball, "Factor Intensity Reversals in International Comparison of Factor Costs and Factor Use," *Journal of Political Economy*, LXXIV (February 1966), 77–80.

[36] For the numerical values of these rank correlations, see *ibid.*, p. 78.

factor intensity reversals ignores this evidence." Furthermore, using other data that Minhas has compiled, Ball ranks a larger number of U.S. and Japanese industries. Again, he removes noncomparable and primary industries and compares the rankings of these smaller samples. These additional rank correlation tests indicate that there are meaningful similarities between the capital-intensity rankings of U.S. and Japanese industries.

Using these same criteria, Ball criticizes Minhas' demonstration of particular factor-intensity reversals (based on 5 pairs of industries). In 4 of the 5 pairs of industries Minhas examined, natural resources are a significant factor. Ball maintains that these industries should not be included in the testing procedure.

In a two-factor world, factor-intensity reversals can occur only if constant elasticities of substitution between the two factors differ among industries. O'Neill presents evidence indicating that elasticities of substitution differ significantly among industries.[37] O'Neill's elasticity estimates, however, are intervals. To obtain a point estimate, he takes the average of these interval estimates for 19 two-digit SIC industrial categories.[38] He then computes standard errors for each of these averaged elasticities. Using the two-standard-error rule, 6 of the 19 elasticities are significantly different from an all-manufacturing elasticity estimate (the expected value of the population elasticity). However, O'Neill notes that this result occurred because the standard errors of several of the elasticity estimates were quite large. Reasoning in practical terms, O'Neill concludes that there is a significant dispersion in his estimates of the elasticities of substitution.[39]

My own empirical work can also be used to determine whether elasticities of substitution between labor and physical capital differ among industries. Since these elasticity estimates are regression coefficients, I

[37] O'Neill, "Estimating Elasticity," pp. 112–13.

[38] The two-digit U.S. Standard Industrial Classification (SIC) industries are similar to the two-digit ISIC industries. See U.S., Bureau of the Budget, *Standard Industrial Classification Manual* (Washington, D.C., 1957), for a complete discussion of the component industry categories.

[39] To substantiate his "practical" conclusion, O'Neill computed estimates of the elasticity using a different set of cross-sectional data. The differences between his two sets of estimates would be large if the observed dispersion in the first set was due to sampling fluctuations. Using different sample sizes (he omits certain deviant industries on theoretical grounds), he finds that the correlation between his two sets of estimates is between .57 and .93, depending on the industries included. He concludes that the dispersion in his first set of estimates is not due to sampling variation.

Table 5

F-Ratios To Test Whether Corresponding
Regression Coefficients Are Equal

Industry Group	F-Ratio	Degrees of Freedom
Two-digit industries (19)[a]		
Upper bounds	1.14	36,261
Lower bounds	1.40	36,261
Three-digit industries (37)[b]		
Upper bounds	1.03	82,614
Lower bounds	1.48	82,614

Source: Test derived from R. J. Foote, *Analytical Tools for Studying Demand and Price Structures* (U.S.: Department of Agriculture, 1958), pp. 180–81.

[a] Critical F (40, 200) 1.69, at .01 level of significance.

[b] Critical F (75, 400) 1.47, at .01 level of significance.

can use a test specifically designed to ascertain differences among regression coefficients.[40] This test was applied separately to both bodies of data, in order to compare elasticities of substitution at comparable levels of industrial aggregation. Since each elasticity estimate is an interval, the test was performed first on each set of upper-bound estimates, and then on each set of lower-bound estimates. This is the most rigorous manner of performing the test; there will be less variability among the interval means than among the upper-bound estimates and lower-bound estimates, considered separately. I shall accept the null hypothesis that there is no difference between elasticities of substitution, if, and only if, upper-bound and lower-bound estimates each exhibit no significant variability.

Table 5 summarizes the results of this test for the two-digit and three-digit data. For both equations and both data sets, the null hypothesis is accepted at the .01 level of significance. The general conclusion that emerges from these tests is that there are no statistically significant differences among elasticities of substitution. These empirical results substantiate the strong factor-intensity assumption: Variations in relative factor prices will not induce variations in relative factor intensities.

What general conclusion can be drawn from this mélange of evidence disputing the likelihood of factor-intensity reversals? In my view, there is not sufficient empirical evidence for abandoning the strong factor-intensity assumption.

[40] The test was taken from R. J. Foote, *Analytical Tools for Studying Demand and Price Structures* (U.S., Department of Agriculture, 1958), pp. 180–1.

LABOR QUALITY AND THE PRODUCT MIX

In estimating the elasticity of substitution, I have used the same measure of skill, the Harbison index, for all industrial categories, as data limitations prevented the measurement of skill levels in each industry. Following this procedure, I have implicitly assumed that the level of skill does not vary among industries in any one country. If, however, industry skill levels vary greatly, it is possible that all the international variation in skill levels might conceivably be attributed to variations in countries' product mixes. While this view is probably too extreme, it seems likely that a country with abundant unskilled labor would tend to concentrate in industries that, on the average, do not have high skill requirements.

This view is not entirely novel: Differences in the manufacturing structure of countries at different stages of development have been delineated by several authors. From these studies, a fairly clear pattern of industrialization has emerged.[41] I shall develop one possible explanation of this pattern, emphasizing that an important constraint on development may be the skill level of a country's labor force.

Keesing has also emphasized the importance of labor skills; he has shown that there are significant differences between the skill requirements of export and import-competing industries.[42] Keesing classifies labor into eight skill categories:

    I. Scientists and engineers.
    II. Technicians and draftsmen.
    III. Other professionals.
    IV. Managers.
    V. Machinists, electricians, tool and diemakers.
    VI. Other skilled manual workers.
    VII. Clerical and sales workers.
    VIII. Unskilled and semiskilled workers.

He then assumes that countries use the same direct skill combinations used by the United States to produce a product, and demonstrates that

[41] See Bean, "International Industrialization"; Hoffmann, *Industrial Economies*, and Chenery, "Patterns," for explanations of the patterns of development.

[42] D. B. Keesing, "Labor Skills and Comparative Advantage," *American Economic Review*, LVI (May 1966), 249–58. He presents a similar thesis in "Labor Skills and International Trade: Evaluating Many Trade Flows with a Single Measuring Device," *Review of Economics and Statistics*, XLVII (August 1965), 287–94. See also "Labor Skills and the Structure of Trade in Manufactures," in this volume.

the skill requirements of export and import-competing industries differ considerably. Keesing does not present any direct evidence on the skill abundance of the countries he studies. It is possible, however, that a country's pattern of production and trade is shaped to conserve its scarce resources, such as skilled labor.

Emphasizing skills as Keesing did, I propose to show that the industries in which the underdeveloped countries specialize are those that conserve skilled labor, and that the developed countries specialize in industries requiring relatively more skilled labor.

To distinguish skill-intensive industrial categories from the less skill-intensive, I assume that industries with average wages above the mean wage rate in the manufacturing sector of the country employ large numbers of skilled workers, and that industries with average wages lower than the mean wage rate are those that employ large numbers of unskilled workers. In brief, I assume that, in any one country, the interindustry structure of wages and the interindustry differences in skill levels are positively correlated; industries characterized by a relatively large proportion of highly skilled occupations tend to pay higher wages than industries characterized by occupations requiring less skill. Waehrer provides empirical support for this assumption.[43]

Which industries pay above-average wages, and which ones pay below-average wages? To answer this question, I have computed the ratios of the industry wage rates to an unweighted mean wage rate in manufacturing, using data taken from the U.N. publication *The Growth of World Industry*.[44] These data cover 13 industrial categories which are aggregates of the two-digit ISIC categories. Next, I have asked whether the structure of wage rates is similar from country to country. To answer this question, I have computed Kendall's "coefficient of concordance" for this data matrix. The computed Kendall coefficient is .61. An F test may be used to test the significance of this coefficient; the computed value of F is 3.27 with 12,252 degrees of freedom, indicating that the coefficient is significant at the .01 level of significance. The test results

[43] Waehrer correlates an educational index and an occupational index, measures of skill, with the average yearly wages of workers in each industry. She obtains significant correlation coefficients with both indexes. See H. Waehrer, "Wage Rates, Labor Skills, and United States Foreign Trade," in this volume.

[44] United Nations Statistical Office, *The Growth of World Industry* (New York: United Nations, 1963). The definitions and possible biases of the variables taken from this publication are similar to those of the two- and three-digit industrial census data. For details, see Yahr, "Estimating Elasticity."

suggest that interindustry wage patterns are similar.[45] I have also performed sign tests on the columns (industry wage ratios) of this matrix to see which industries pay low wages, and which ones pay high wages, that is, which industries employ more skilled workers than the average of the manufacturing sector in each country. The null hypothesis for these sign tests is that, in a given industry, the probability is .5 that the ratio of the industry wage rate to the all-manufacturing wage rate is less than or greater than unity in any country. On this hypothesis, I have computed the binomial probability of observing these frequencies if the true probability was .5. At the .05 level of significance, the null hypothesis will be rejected if this binomial probability is less than .05. For all but two of the industries (30, rubber products, and 33, nonmetallic mineral products), the null hypothesis is rejected. The remaining 11 industries can be unequivocally characterized as either high-wage or low-wage industries. Categories 20–22, 23, 24, 25–26, 29, and 39 may be classified as low-wage industries; categories 27, 28, 31–32, 34, and 35–38 may be classified as high-wage industries.

I have postulated that a country varies its output mix to conserve its scarce factors of production. I also postulate that, since one scarce factor in an underdeveloped country is skilled labor, those countries will specialize in industries requiring relatively less skilled labor. The developed countries, in turn, will specialize in industries requiring relatively more skilled labor. To test this hypothesis, I have computed a matrix of ratios of value added in the ith industry to value added for the entire manufacturing sector of a particular country, using every country in the U.N. sample. If the output mix were similar from country to country, the ratios for a given industry would be identical. If, instead, the scarce resource in an underdeveloped country is skilled labor, the ratios for the low-skill industries should be negatively correlated with an index of labor quality, and the ratios for the high-skill industries should be positively correlated with an index of labor quality. Simple regressions were computed for selected groupings of the 11 industries identified as being high- or low-wage industries, using the Harbison index as a proxy for the skill level of the labor force. I aggregated similar types of production processes into one group.

[45] Other writers have also shown this to be true. See, for example: I. B. Kravis, "Wages and Foreign Trade," *Review of Economics and Statistics*, XXXVIII (February 1956), 14–30; S. Lebergott, "Wage Structures," *Review of Economics and Statistics*, XXIX (1947), 274–85.

Table 6

Regression Coefficients and Coefficients of Determination for Product-Mix Equations; Dependent Variable: Industry Value Added/Value Added of Whole Manufacturing Sector

Industry Code	Regression Coefficient (Standard Error)	Coefficient of Determination (Adjusted)
Low-skill industries		
20, 21, 22	−.12[a]	.25[a]
	(.04)	
23, 24	−.09[a]	.17[a]
	(.04)	
25, 26	+.02	.08
	(.01)	
20, 21, 22, 23, 24, 25, 26	−.20[a]	.43[a]
	(.04)	
20, 21, 22, 23, 24, 25, 26, 29	−.20[a]	.44[a]
	(.04)	
20, 21, 22, 23, 24, 25, 26, 29, 39	−.19[a]	.42[a]
	(.04)	
High-skill industries		
27, 28	+.04[a]	.16[a]
	(.02)	
35, 36, 37, 38	+.16[a]	.54[a]
	(.02)	
31, 32	−.02	.05
	(.01)	
27, 28, 31, 32, 35, 36, 37, 38	+.18[a]	.47[a]
	(.04)	
27, 28, 31, 32, 34, 35, 36, 37, 38	+.18[a]	.34[a]
	(.05)	

[a] Significant at the .05 level. All regressions are based on 26 observations, save for the last, which is based on 23.

Table 6 summarizes the results of these regressions. It shows that the coefficients of determination vary among industries and among combinations of industries, being lowest for those industries closely linked to the availability of natural resources.[46] They are also lower for more narrowly defined industrial categories than for broadly aggregated

[46] Countries might specialize in these industries if they had relatively large endowments of the specific resources related to the processes used in those industries. Keesing also argues that labor skills will not influence the trade patterns of industries to which natural resources are an important input, i.e., the availability of natural resources will obscure the role of labor skills. Keesing, "Labor Skills and International Trade," p. 288.

categories. These results seem reasonable, for the degree of specialization in specific industries must be linked to such additional factors as the availability of natural resources, markets, specific entrepreneurial skills, and social overhead capital.

The coefficients of the Harbison index are significant (with a negative sign for the low-skill industries) for all the industries except 25–26, 31–32, and 39. Two of these industries, wood products and furniture (25–26) and chemicals and chemical, petroleum, and coal products (31–32), are industries closely dependent on the availability of natural resources. The regression coefficient of miscellaneous manufacturing (39) is nonsignificant, and it does not have the expected negative sign. Since the components of this industry often vary among countries, it may not be correct to classify this category as a low-(or high-)wage industry; the correct procedure may be to omit this category from the analysis. For this reason, Table 6 shows the aggregate unskilled industry group with and without category 39. (As that category contains only 2.06 per cent of the value added of the manufacturing sector, omitting it makes little difference for the size or sign of the coefficient of the aggregate regression equation.)

The regression results in Table 6 provide consistent support for the supposition that a country varies its manufacturing output mix to conserve its scarce factor. The underdeveloped countries specialize in industries requiring relatively more unskilled labor; the developed countries specialize in industries requiring relatively more skilled labor.

If labor intensities—workers per unit of output—are similar among industries, the same relationships should hold when the dependent variable is the ratio of the number of workers employed in an industry to the number of workers employed in the entire manufacturing sector. I computed simple regressions between these employment ratios and the Harbison index for the 11 high-wage and low-wage groupings and, using the same aggregated categories as before, for several combinations of these groups.

Table 7 summarizes the results of these regressions. They are similar to those obtained with value-added ratios as the dependent variables. The coefficients of determination vary among industries, and are higher when the dependent variable is an aggregate of the low-skill (or high-skill) industries. The regression coefficients are significant, with the correct signs, for all industries except 25–26, 31–32, and 39. Again, these regression results indicate that a country chooses its manufacturing output mix to conform to the skill mix of its population. The underdeveloped

Table 7

*Regression Coefficients and Coefficients of Determination for Product-Mix
Equations; Dependent Variable—Industry Employees/Employees
of Whole Manufacturing Sector*

Industry Code	Regression Coefficient (Standard Error)	Coefficient of Determination (Adjusted)
Low-skill industries		
20, 21, 22	−.09[a]	.16[a]
	(.04)	
23, 24	−.10[a]	.21[a]
	(.04)	
25, 26	−.02	.05
	(.01)	
20, 21, 22, 23, 24, 25, 26	−.18[a]	.43[a]
	(.04)	
20, 21, 22, 23, 24, 25, 26, 29	−.18[a]	.43[a]
20, 21, 22, 23, 24, 25, 26, 29, 39	−.17[a]	.41[a]
	(.04)	
High-skill industries		
27, 28	+.03[a]	.19[a]
	(.01)	
35, 36, 37, 38	+.16[a]	.53[a]
	(.03)	
31, 32	−.02	.02
	(.02)	
27, 28, 31, 32, 35, 36, 37, 38	+.17[a]	.44[a]
	(.04)	
27, 28, 31, 32, 34, 35, 36, 37, 38	+.18[a]	.42[a]
	(.04)	

[a] Significant at the .05 level. All regressions are based on 27 observations, save for the last, which is based on 23.

countries specialize in relatively low-skill industries; the developed countries specialize in relatively high-skill industries.

In this final section, I showed that underdeveloped countries conserve skilled labor by varying the output mix in manufacturing. However, specialization in relatively unskilled industries may not be extensive enough to rectify completely shortages of skilled labor. If unskilled labor is not easily substituted for skilled labor and specialization by industry is incomplete in the underdeveloped countries, the wage paid to a skilled worker in these countries will be relatively high, compared to what it is in the developed countries; that is, underdeveloped countries will pay higher premiums for skills. This hypothesis can be tested.

Table 8

Summary Statistics for Coefficient of Variation Regressions:
Two- and Three-digit Data Sets

Data Set (Number of Observations)	Regression Coefficient (Standard Error)	$\bar{R}^2$
Three-digit data (21)	−.0006 (.0005)	.07
Two-digit data (17)	−.0007 (.0005)	.06

Assume, as before, that wage rates are highly correlated with skill levels. If there are residual skill shortages in the underdeveloped countries, the average level of wages in the skill-intensive industries will be higher, compared to the national average, than in the developed countries. Furthermore, a country endowed with relatively few skilled workers will have a greater interindustry wage variability than a country endowed with relatively more skilled workers.

To test this hypothesis, I computed separately for each country the coefficients of variation of wage rates among industries for the two- and three-digit data sets. These coefficients measure wage-rate variability relative to the country's mean wage rate. The hypothesis above proposes that wage-rate variability will be higher in the underdeveloped countries, which are conserving skilled labor incompletely. Next, I computed simple regressions between these coefficients of variation and the Harbison index. The results of these regressions are summarized in Table 8. The regression coefficients are negative, indicating that wage variability is relatively high in the underdeveloped countries, and that specialization by product mix is probably incomplete. However, these coefficients are not significant at the .05 level.

CONCLUSION

It was the intention of this study to enlarge our knowledge of the elasticity of substitution between labor and capital by estimating the ACMS and O'Neill models from international data and allowing the labor input to be heterogeneous in quality. The principal conclusion that emerges from this work is that differences in the quality of the labor input affect the elasticity of substitution. Furthermore, it was suggested that, in a two-factor model, labor quality, viewed as an exogenous factor to the entrepreneur, raises the marginal product of labor more than it raises the marginal product of capital, causing substitutions of labor for capital. Finally, it was shown that the level of skill of the labor force may be an important constraint on development. This work suggests that the neglect of differences in labor quality has probably led to biases in previous estimates of σ.

My work also indicates that the elasticity of substitution for all manufacturing industries is slightly less than unity, but, for many individual industries, σ is not significantly different from unity. The all-manufacturing σ is significantly different from zero, as are the elasticities for separate industries. Finally, I have argued that there are no significant differences among the industry elasticities.

APPENDIX

Regression Coefficients for Step 2 of the Estimating Procedure for 19 Two-Digit ISIC Industries

Industry	b_1'	b_2'	$\bar{R}^2$	d_1'	d_2'	$\bar{R}^2$
20. Food manufacturing industries, except beverages	.85 (.10)	−.22 (.14)	.92	.76 (.16)	−.34 (.23)	.72
21. Beverage industries	.81 (.18)	(.01) (.23)	.68	.77 (.23)	−.01 (.29)	.54
22. Tobacco manufactures	.53 (.35)	−.16 (.33)	.08	.44 (.44)	−.24 (.42)	−.06
23. Manufacture of textiles	.87 (.06)	−.14 (.07)	.96	.76 (.10)	−.26 (.12)	.82
24. Manufacture of footwear, other wearing apparel, textile goods	.81 (.06)	−.09 (.06)	.95	.63 (.12)	−.20 (.13)	.69
25. Manufacture of wood and cork except furniture	.86 (.07)	−.05 (.09)	.96	.71 (.13)	−.08 (.17)	.81
26. Manufacture of furniture and fixtures	.88 (.06)	−.01 (.08)	.96	.75 (.11)	−.03 (.15)	.84
27. Manufacture of paper and paper products	.99 (.08)	−.16 (.09)	.95	.97 (.12)	−.25 (.15)	.86
28. Printing, publishing, and allied industries	.83 (.06)	.09 (.07)	.96	.68 (.12)	.17 (.14)	.82
29. Manufacture of leather and leather products except footwear and wearing apparel	.94 (.08)	−.27 (.10)	.92	.86 (.16)	−.50 (.19)	.65
30. Manufacture of rubber products	.87 (.08)	−.18 (.11)	.89	.75 (.14)	−.30 (.19)	.63
31. Manufacture of chemicals and chemical products	1.01 (.08)	−.17 (.11)	.93	.99 (.13)	−.23 (.16)	.84
32. Manufacture of products of petroleum and coal	.95 (.21)	−.45 (.23)	.55	.93 (.28)	−.61 (.31)	.38
33. Nonmetallic mineral products, except products of petroleum and coal	.89 (.05)	−.07 (.08)	.97	.81 (.09)	−.12 (.13)	.88
34. Basic metal industries	1.04 (.21)	−.47 (.24)	.72	1.05 (.28)	−.71 (.32)	.72
35. Manufacture of metal products, except machinery, transport equipment	.95 (.04)	−.16 (.06)	.98	.89 (.08)	−.28 (.11)	.91
36. Manufacture of machinery, except electrical	.98 (.05)	−.09 (.08)	.96	.96 (.10)	−.15 (.19)	.84
37. Manufacture of electrical machinery, appliances, and supplies	.86 (.08)	−.09 (.11)	.90	.73 (.15)	−.15 (.19)	.64
38. Manufacture of transport equipment	.89 (.11)	−.11 (.15)	.88	.75 (.20)	−.15 (.27)	.57

Note: Numbers in parentheses are standard errors of regression coefficients.

99

PETER B. KENEN

Toward a More General Theory
of Capital and Trade

MOST THEORIES OF PRODUCTION, GROWTH, AND TRADE treat capital as
though it were an ordinary input. The stock of capital appears directly
in the production function, just like land or labor, and has a separate
marginal product. Processes are classified by capital intensity, and
countries are classified by capital scarcity.[1] Elsewhere, I have offered a

[1] For examples in growth theory, see R. M. Solow, "A Contribution to the Theory of
Economic Growth," *Quarterly Journal of Economics*, LXX (1956), J. E. Meade, *A Neo-
Classical Theory of Economic Growth* (London: George Allen & Unwin, 1961); and H.
Uzawa, "On a Two-Sector Model of Economic Growth," *Review of Economic Studies*, XXIX
(1961–62), and XXX (1963). For examples in trade theory, see E. Heckscher, "The
Effects of Foreign Trade on the Distribution of Income," in *Readings in the Theory of
International Trade*, H. E. Ellis and L. A. Metzler (eds.) (Philadelphia: Blakiston, 1949);
B. Ohlin, *Interregional and International Trade* (Cambridge: Harvard University Press,
1933); J. E. Meade, *Trade and Welfare* (London: Oxford University Press, 1955); and W.
P. Travis, *The Theory of Trade and Protection* (Cambridge: Harvard University Press, 1964).
For important empirical applications, see K. J. Arrow, H. B. Chenery, B. S. Minhas, and
R. M. Solow, "Capital-Labor Substitution and Economic Efficiency," *Review of Economics
and Statistics*, XLIII (1961); W. W. Leontief "Factor Proportions and the Structure of
American Trade: Further Theoretical and Empirical Analysis," *Review of Economics and
Statistics*, XXXVIII (1956); and B. S. Minhas, *An International Comparison of Factor Costs
and Factor Use* (Amsterdam: North-Holland Publishing Co., 1963).

different approach.[2] Capital can be regarded as the progenitor of other inputs, having an indirect marginal product. Combined with land and labor, the "natural endowment," it furnishes the service flows used in production. This essay will illustrate the merits of my new approach. It will reexamine several propositions in the pure theory of foreign trade, reworking the familiar Heckscher-Ohlin model in order to secure more plausible results than trade and growth theories have been able to supply using the conventional concept of capital.

The theory of capital developed here has several antecedents. Its fundamental supposition, that capital and nature are complementary, is basic to the Austrian theory of capital and has sometimes crept into writings on foreign trade.[3] My own views, however, derive from the more recent works of Vanek,[4] Schultz,[5] and Becker.[6] Vanek postulates a complementarity between capital and land, then argues that U.S. trade may conserve scarce land rather than scarce capital, answering Leontief's celebrated paradox.[7] Schultz and Becker postulate a complementarity between capital and labor. They suggest that outlays on schooling and training are forms of investment, and that the capital invested in man contributes importantly to total output. Combining these suggestions in a formal model, I shall treat each input stream, the service flows from land and labor, as though they were produced by acts of investment, assigning a pervasive role to capital formation.

THE ALLOCATION OF INVESTMENT

Let each country have a fixed stock of labor, N_1 men, and a fixed stock of land, N_2 acres. Suppose, however, that these stocks must be improved before they can contribute to current production. More formally, let

[2] P. B. Kenen, "Nature, Capital and Trade," *Journal of Political Economy*, LXXIII (1965).

[3] See C. Iverson, *International Capital Movements* (London: Oxford University Press, 1935); and R. Nurkse, "Causes and Effects of Capital Movements," in *Equilibrium and Growth in the World Economy: Economic Essays by Ragnar Nurkse*, G. Haberler and R. M. Stern (eds.) (Cambridge: Harvard University Press, 1961).

[4] J. Vanek, *The Natural Resource Content of United States Foreign Trade* (Cambridge: MIT Press, 1963).

[5] T. W. Schultz, "Reflections on Investment in Man," *Journal of Political Economy*, LXX Supplement (1956).

[6] G. S. Becker, "Investment in Human Capital: A Theoretical Analysis," *Journal of Political Economy*, LXX Supplement (1956).

[7] Leontief, "Factor Proportions."

there be a single, malleable capital good that can be used with equal ease to make all improvements in the "natural endowment," and let it be combined with that endowment to generate a single, undifferentiated service flow from labor and a second flow from land. Further:

1. Let all markets be purely competitive, all inputs be fully employed, and all decision units have perfect foresight.
2. Let all accounts be kept in real terms, with the price of the capital good as *numeraire*.
3. Let all investments have the same lifespan (v years), and let them depreciate by sudden death.
4. Let all production functions be homogeneous of first degree in the factor services, be twice differentiable with diminishing marginal products, and have an invariant ranking by factor intensity.
5. Let demand conditions be independent of the income distribution, with unitary income elasticities of demand for all final products.

The first of these assumptions is common to most models built at a comparable level of abstraction. The second gives a simple way to value all assets and incomes. The third permits us to avoid several intractable problems in capital theory, pertaining to the heterogeneity of capital goods and their varied ages.[8] The fourth and fifth assumptions allow us to ignore the influence of scale on both sides of the market; they are especially helpful in tracing the growth path of a closed economy and in the study of foreign trade.

Now let each investment in the "natural endowment" be financed by a loan from a central fund (whose total claims will measure the capital stock); let each worker and landlord borrow from that fund in order to improve himself or his holdings, then earn income by selling the factor-service flows that come from the improvement. Furthermore, let each investor maximize the present value of his income stream (let there be no preference for present over future earnings). Under these additional assumptions, a loan from the central fund will be repaid in equal annual instalments spanning the v-year life of the factor-service flow produced by the investment for which the loan was made.[9] A worker will borrow in order to train himself and will have repaid his debt when he leaves the

---

[8] See J. Robinson, "Accumulation and the Production Function," *Economic Journal*, LXIX (1959); and P. A. Samuelson, "Parable and Realism in Capital Theory: The Surrogate Production Function," *Review of Economic Studies*, XXIX (1962).

[9] Meade, *Neo-Classical Theory*, pp. 134–44.

labor force; a landlord will borrow in order to improve his land and will have repaid his debt when his land reverts to its natural state.

To study the behavior of a single investor, define:

z_i The annual supply of the ith factor service (input) flowing from a unit of the ith natural factor ($i = 1$ for labor, $i = 2$ for land).

k_i The number of units of the homogeneous capital good needed to evoke the flow z_i.

w_i The real annual wage earned by a unit of the ith factor service (its money wage divided by the price of the capital good).

y_i The real annual income earned by the owner of a unit of the ith natural factor (his money wage divided by the price of the capital good).

r The interest rate.

g The gross amortization rate linking the yearly debt-service payment (interest and principal) to the face value of the corresponding loan.

Now relate k_i, an act of investment, to z_i, the steady v-year service flow to which it gives rise. Write:

$$z_i = f_i(k_i), \quad i = 1, 2 \tag{1}$$

such that $f_i(0) = 0$, $f_i' = \eta_i(z_i/k_i) > 0$, and $f_i'' = (\eta_i - 1)(f_i'/k_i) < 0$, where the η_i are constant (and, by implication, fall between zero and unity). The first of these restrictions on the factor-service supply functions asserts that the "natural endowment" is wholly inert until it is improved by an act of investment; it does not furnish services useful in production. The second and third restrictions convey another important assumption— that investment in the "natural endowment" is subject to diminishing factor-service returns.

As all investments are financed by loans from the central fund, k_i represents the real value of the debt incurred by an investor, while gk_i represents his annual debt-service payment. In consequence, his income is:

$$y_i = w_i z_i - gk_i, \quad i = 1, 2 \tag{2}$$

Furthermore, the present value of the stream gk_i must equal k_i, so that:

$$k_i = gk_i \sum_{t=1}^{v} (1 + r)^{-t} = gk_i \frac{(1 + r)^v - 1}{r(1 + r)^v} \tag{3}$$

As z_i is a steady flow lasting v years, a worker or landlord will maximize the present value of his income stream by maximizing y_i. To reproduce his behavior, differentiate (2) with respect to k_i and set the derivative equal to zero:[10]

$$w_i f_i' = g, \quad i = 1, 2 \tag{4}$$

A worker or landlord will borrow and invest up to the point at which the marginal revenue from factor-service sales equals the marginal debt-service cost of investing in himself or his holdings.[11]

Now let us pretend that optimal (income-maximizing) quantities of capital have been invested in each of the nation's N_1 workers and each of its N_2 acres, and that past investments have been spaced out evenly. On these suppositions, N_i/v of "old" investments will die off each year, and:

$$\left. \begin{aligned} Z_i &= N_i z_i \\ K_i &= \frac{N_i}{v} k_i \\ Y_i &= N_i y_i = w_i Z_i - v g K_i \\ K &= \sum_i K_i \end{aligned} \right\} \quad i = 1, 2 \tag{5}$$

Here, Z_i is the aggregate annual supply of the ith factor service; K_i is the aggregate annual investment required to sustain Z_i; Y_i is the real annual income earned by all the owners of the ith natural factor; and K is the aggregate annual investment required to sustain the two factor-service flows (and measures the annual output of the capital good).[12]

The level of investment, K, also represents the real value of new lending in this stationary state, while gK represents the aggregate annual

---

[10] The sufficient second-order condition for maximum y_i is $w_i f_i'' < 0$, and is satisfied by the third restriction imposed on (1).

[11] Note, further, that (3) and (4) give:

$$y_i = w_i z_i (1 - \eta_i)$$

The income derived from factor-service sales is a steady, v-year stream of positive quasi-rents, bearing a close resemblance to land rent in the Ricardian model. Its sign derives from the assumption of diminishing factor-service returns to investment in the "natural endowment." The analogy is completed below, when it is shown that net capital formation reduces the interest rate and raises y_i, just as population growth reduces the real wage and raises land rent in the Ricardian model.

[12] Note the vital difference between z_i and Z_i. The former is a v-year flow; the latter is perpetual. Similarly, k_i is a single act of investment, while K_i is the annual flow needed to perpetuate a stationary state.

debt-service payment required to amortize a single year's lending. The balance outstanding on all past loans measures the capital stock, and is given by:[13]

$$C = \frac{K}{r}\,(vg - 1) \tag{6}$$

Interest income is defined in relation to this stock:

$$rC = K(vg - 1) \tag{6a}$$

Hence, one can go on to measure national income:

$$Y = Y_1 + Y_2 + rC = w_1 Z_1 + w_2 Z_2 - K = w_2 Z_1 (w + R) - K \tag{7}$$

where $w = w_1/w_2$, henceforth described as the wage-rate ratio, and $R = Z_2/Z_1$, henceforth described as the gross factor ratio. This equation measures national income as gross national product at factor cost *less* depreciation, K, on the stock of capital (including both human and tangible capital). Alternatively, write:

$$Z_i = Z_{ik} + Z_{in}, \quad i = 1, 2 \tag{8}$$

where Z_{ik} is the amount of the ith factor service required to produce the capital good, while Z_{in} is the amount left for the production of final output. Furthermore, write:

$$K = \beta_k(R_k, 1) Z_{1k} \tag{9}$$

where $R_k = Z_{2k}/Z_{1k}$. As w_i is the real wage rate of the ith factor service in the capital-goods industry:

$$w_1 = \beta_k(R_k, 1) - \beta_k{}' \cdot R_k$$

$$w_2 = \beta_k{}' \tag{10}$$

[13] If all debt-service payments are made at the start of the year, the unpaid balance on a loan t years after issue is defined by:

$$C_t = K(1 + r)^t - gK[(1 + r)^{t-1} + \cdots + (1 + r) + 1]$$
$$= K(g/r)[1 - (1 + r)^{t-v}], \quad t < v$$

In effect, each amortization payment earns interest from the time it is made through the start of year t. The balance outstanding on all past loans is then defined by:

$$C = \sum_{t=0}^{v} C_t = K(g/r) \sum_{t=0}^{v} [1 - (1 + r)^{t-v}]$$

so that:

$$K = w_1 Z_{1k} + w_2 Z_{2k} \tag{8a}$$

Therefore:

$$Y = w_1 Z_{1n} + w_2 Z_{2n} = w_2 Z_{1n}(w + R_n) \tag{7a}$$

where $R_n = Z_{2n}/Z_{1n}$, henceforth described as the net factor ratio.[14]

In order to complete the two-factor model, let there be two final products, X_1 and X_2, with $R_1 < R_2$ at all w. Here, of course, $R_1 = Z_{21}/Z_{11}$ and $R_2 = Z_{22}/Z_{12}$, where Z_{ij} is the input of the ith factor service to the jth final product. For full employment, let:[15]

$$Z_{in} = \sum_j Z_{ij}, \quad i = 1, 2; \; j = 1, 2 \tag{11}$$

and write:

$$\left. \begin{aligned} X_j &= \beta_j(R_j, 1) Z_{1j} \\ \frac{w_1}{p_j} &= \beta_j(R_j, 1) - \beta_j' \cdot R_j \\ \frac{w_2}{p_j} &= \beta_j' \end{aligned} \right\} j = 1, 2 \tag{12}$$

where p_j is the price of the jth final product expressed in units of the capital good.

Finally, write:

$$Q = \frac{X_2}{X_1} \tag{13}$$

and:

$$Q^c = \theta(p) \tag{14}$$

where $p = p_1/p_2$, the product-price ratio, and Q^c is the ratio in which X_1 and X_2 are consumed at each and every level of national income.

[14] One more variant will be used below. Write:

$$K = w_2 Z_{1k}(w + R_k)$$

and:

$$Y = w_2[Z_1(w + R) - Z_{1k}(w + R_k)] = w_2 Z_{1n}(w + R_n)$$

so that:

$$(R - R_n) = (R_k - R)(Z_{1k}/Z_{1n})$$

One can always rank the three factor ratios by ranking any pair. When $R_k > R$, then $R > R_n$; when $R_k = R$, then $R = R_n$; and when $R_k < R$, then $R < R_n$.

[15] In consequence:

$$(R_2 - R_n) = (R_2 - R_1)(Z_{11}/Z_{1n})$$

We have, in all, 38 equations in 42 unknowns.[16] But in a closed economy:

$$Q = Q^c \tag{15}$$

If, then, N_1, N_2, and K are given, we can solve for all the other terms in the system.

Yet one can write a simpler version of the system, to solve for g, r, p, w, Q^c, Q, k_1, k_2, R, R_n, R_k, R_1, and R_2, given N_1, N_2, and K:

$$g - \frac{r(1+r)^v}{(1+r)^v - 1} = 0 \tag{16}$$

$$g - \frac{w \cdot \beta_k' \cdot \eta_1 \cdot f_1(k_1)}{k_1} = 0 \tag{17}$$

$$p - \frac{\beta_2'}{\beta_1'} = 0 \tag{18}$$

$$Q^c - Q = 0 \tag{19}$$

$$Q^c - \theta(p) = 0 \tag{20}$$

$$\frac{w \cdot \eta_1 \cdot f_1(k_1)}{k_1} - \frac{\eta_2 \cdot f_2(k_2)}{k_2} = 0 \tag{21}$$

$$R \cdot N_1 f_1(k_1) - N_2 f_2(k_2) = 0 \tag{22}$$

$$N_1 k_1 + N_2 k_2 - vK = 0 \tag{23}$$

$$\beta_2(R_2, 1)(R_n - R_1) - Q \cdot \beta_1(R_1, 1)(R_2 - R_n) = 0 \tag{24}$$

$$(R - R_n)N_1 f_1(k_1) - \frac{(R_k - R_n)K}{\beta_k(R_k, 1)} = 0 \tag{25}$$

$$\beta_k'(R_k + w) - \beta_k(R_k, 1) = 0 \tag{26}$$

$$\beta_1'(R_1 + w) - \beta_1(R_1, 1) = 0 \tag{27}$$

$$\beta_2'(R_2 + w) - \beta_2(R_2, 1) = 0 \tag{28}$$

This simpler system and variants on it will serve as the basis for subsequent analysis.

[16] These 38 equations are the two equations (1), the two equations (2), equation (3), the two equations (4), the seven equations (5), equations (6) and (7), the two equations (8), equation (9), the two equations (10), the two equations (11), the six equations (12), equation (13), equation (14), and the definitions of R, R_n, R_1, R_2, R_k, w, and p. The 42 unknowns are N_1, N_2, z_1, z_2, k_1, k_2, w_1, w_2, y_1, y_2, r, g, Z_1, Z_2, K_1, K_2, K, Y_1, Y_2, Y, C, Z_{1n}, Z_{2n}, Z_{1k}, Z_{2k}, Z_{11}, Z_{12}, Z_{21}, Z_{22}, X_1, X_2, p_1, p_2, R, R_n, R_1, R_2, R_k, Q, Q^c, w, and p.

DISPLACEMENT AND ADJUSTMENT
IN A CLOSED ECONOMY

Once the stock of capital is optimally allocated, satisfying these equations, changes in N_1, N_2, and K will cause systematic changes in the economy.[17] To study displacement and adjustment in this system, write out the total derivatives of equations (16) through (28):

$$g^* - \left[1 - \frac{vr}{(1+r)[(1+r)^v - 1]}\right]r^* = 0 \qquad (29)$$

$$g^* - \left[w^* + \frac{\beta_k''}{\beta_k'}R_k \cdot R_k^* - (1 - \eta_1)k_1^*\right] = 0 \qquad (30)$$

$$p^* - \left[\frac{\beta_2''}{\beta_2'}R_2 \cdot R_2^* - \frac{\beta_1''}{\beta_1'}R_1 \cdot R_1^*\right] = 0 \qquad (31)$$

$$Q^{c*} - Q^* = 0 \qquad (32)$$

$$Q^{c*} - \left(\frac{dQ^c}{dp}\right)\left(\frac{p}{Q^c}\right) \cdot \left(\frac{dp}{dw}\right)\left(\frac{w}{p}\right)w^* = 0 \qquad (33)$$

$$(1 - \eta_1)k_1^* - (1 - \eta_2)k_2^* - w^* = 0 \qquad (34)$$

$$\eta_1 k_1^* - \eta_2 k_2^* + R^* - (N_2^* - N_1^*) = 0 \qquad (35)$$

$$\left(\frac{K_1}{K}\right)k_1^* + \left(\frac{K_2}{K}\right)k_2^* - \left[K^* - \left(\frac{K_1}{K}\right)N_1^* - \left(\frac{K_2}{K}\right)N_2^*\right] = 0 \qquad (36)$$

$$\frac{R_n(R_2 - R_1)R_n^*}{(R_2 - R_n)(R_n - R_1)} - \left[\frac{R_2(R_n + w)R_2^*}{(R_2 + w)(R_2 - R_n)} + \frac{R_1(R_n + w)R_1^*}{(R_1 + w)(R_n - R_1)}\right]$$
$$- Q^* = 0 \qquad (37)$$

$$\left(\frac{R - R_n}{R}\right)\eta_1 k_1^* - \left(\frac{Z_{2n}}{Z_2}\right)R_n^* - \left(\frac{Z_{2k}}{Z_2}\right)\left(\frac{R_n + w}{R_k + w}\right)R_k^* + R^*$$
$$- \left(\frac{R - R_n}{R}\right)(K^* - N_1^*) = 0 \qquad (38)$$

[17] An increase in N_1 represents an increase in the nation's labor force. An increase in N_2 can, perhaps, be viewed as an increase in its stock of land or, more plausibly, as a proxy for "disembodied" technological progress affecting that stock's quality (its susceptibility to improvement by investment). An increase in K represents net saving; it measures the increase in stationary-state replacement investment corresponding to a permanent change in the stock of capital (the total claims of the central loan fund).

$$\left(\frac{\beta_k''}{\beta_k'}\right)R_k \cdot R_k^* + \left[\frac{w}{(R_k + w)}\right]w^* = 0 \tag{39}$$

$$\left(\frac{\beta_1''}{\beta_1'}\right)R_1 \cdot R_1^* + \left[\frac{w}{(R_1 + w)}\right]w^* = 0 \tag{40}$$

$$\left(\frac{\beta_2''}{\beta_2'}\right)R_2 \cdot R_2^* + \left[\frac{w}{(R_2 + w)}\right]w^* = 0 \tag{41}$$

where asterisks denote relative rates of change ($g^* = dg/g$, $w^* = dw/w$, and so on).

To make this system more compact, use (39) through (41) to replace R_k^*, R_1^*, and R_2^* wherever they appear, then use (29) through (38) to solve for r^*, g^*, p^*, w^*, Q^*, k_1^*, k_2^*, R^*, and R_n^*. From (29), obtain:

$$r^* = e_{rg} \cdot g^*, \quad e_{rg} = \left[1 - \frac{vr}{(1+r)[(1+r)^v - 1]}\right]^{-1} > 0 \tag{29a}$$

because $vr < [(1+r)^v - 1]$. Rewrite (30), as:

$$g^* = \left(\frac{R_k}{R_k + w}\right)w^* - (1 - \eta_1)k_1^* \tag{30a}$$

Then rewrite (31), as:

$$p^* = e_{pw} \cdot w^*, \quad e_{pw} = \frac{w(R_2 - R_1)}{(R_1 + w)(R_2 + w)} > 0 \tag{31a}$$

because $R_1 < R_2$ at all factor prices.[18] From (32) and (33), obtain:

$$Q^* = e_{cp} \cdot e_{pw} \cdot w^*, \quad e_{cp} = \left(\frac{dQ^c}{dp}\right) \cdot \left(\frac{p}{Q^c}\right) > 0 \tag{33a}$$

[18] Note, in passing, that (18) and (31a) can be invoked to reaffirm factor-price equalization in a two-country, two-product model. As β_1' and β_2', the arguments of (18), are functions of w, one can write (18) in the general form:

$$p = h(w), \quad w = h^{-1}(p)$$

As (31a) asserts that the first of these functions is single-valued and monotonic, the second is likewise single-valued and monotonic. If, then, two countries have identical production functions for X_1 and X_2, if trade between them fosters an equality in product prices, and if neither country is completely specialized in X_1, or X_2 (so that β_1' and β_2' exist in both countries), the two countries will display the same wage-rate ratios, w, and the same factor-service prices, w_1 and w_2.

with well-behaved demand functions. From (34) and (36), derive:

$$k_1^* = \frac{[R(\eta_2/\eta_1) + w][K^* - (K_1/K)N_1^* - (K_2/K)N_2^*] + [R\phi/(1-\eta_1)]w^*}{w + R\phi} \quad (34a)$$

$$k_2^* = \frac{\phi[R + w(\eta_1/\eta_2)][K^* - (K_1/K)N_1^* - (K_2/K)N_2^*] - [w/(1-\eta_2)]w^*}{w + R\phi} \quad (36a)$$

where $\phi = (1 - \eta_1)\eta_2/(1 - \eta_2)\eta_1$.[19] From (35), obtain:

$$R^* = \eta_2 k_2^* - \eta_1 k_1^* + (N_2^* - N_1^*) \quad (35a)$$

Rewrite (37), as:

$$Q^* = e_{QR_n} \cdot R_n^* - e_{Qw} \cdot w^*, \quad e_{QR_n} = \frac{R_n(R_2 - R_1)}{(R_2 - R_n)(R_n - R_1)} > 0,$$

and

$$e_{Qw} = -\frac{w(R_n + w)}{(R_2 - R_n)(R_n - R_1)}\left[\frac{\beta_2'(R_n - R_1)}{\beta_2''(R_2 + w)^2} + \frac{\beta_1'(R_2 - R_n)}{\beta_1''(R_1 + w)^2}\right] > 0 \quad (37a)$$

because $R_1 < R_2$ at all w,[20] while $\beta_1'' < 0$ and $\beta_2'' < 0$ when all production functions display diminishing marginal products. Finally, from (38), write:

$$R_n^* = \left(\frac{Z_2}{Z_{2n}}\right)\left[R^* + \left(\frac{R - R_n}{R}\right)(\eta_1 k_1^* - K^* + N_1^*)\right] + \left(\frac{Z_{1k}}{Z_{2n}}\right)\left(\frac{R_n + w}{R_k + w}\right)\left(\frac{w}{R_k + w}\right)\left(\frac{\beta_k'}{\beta_k''}\right)w^* \quad (38a)$$

Now use (34a), (35a), (36a), and (38a) to write out the changes in k_1, k_2, R, and R_n that could happen with a constant wage-rate ratio (those that would come about in consequence of N_1^*, N_2^*, and K^*, were $w^* = 0$):

$$k_1^{**} \equiv \frac{R(\eta_2/\eta_1) + w}{w + R\phi}\left[K^* - \left(\frac{K_1}{K}\right)N_1^* - \left(\frac{K_2}{K}\right)N_2^*\right]$$

$$= \left[\frac{R(\eta_2/\eta_1) + w}{w + R\phi}\right]\left[K^* - \frac{w \cdot N_1^* + R(\eta_2/\eta_1) \cdot N_2^*}{w + R(\eta_2/\eta_1)}\right] \quad (42)$$

[19] These formulations derive from (21) and (23), which yield:
$$(K_1/K) = 1 - (K_2/K) = w/[w + R(\eta_2/\eta_1)]$$

[20] When $R_1 < R_2$ and neither X_i is zero, $R_1 < R_n < R_2$ (see note 15).

$$k_2^{**} \equiv \phi\left(\frac{\eta_1}{\eta_2}\right)k_1^{**} \tag{43}$$

$$R^{**} \equiv (\phi - 1)\eta_1 k_1^{**} + (N_2^* - N_1^*) \tag{44}$$

$$R_n^{**} \equiv \left(\frac{Z_2}{Z_{2n}}\right)\left\{(N_2^* - N_1^*) - \left(\frac{R - R_n}{R}\right)(K^* - N_1^*)\right.$$

$$\left. + \left[(\phi - 1) + \left(\frac{R - R_n}{R}\right)\right]\eta_1 k_1^{**}\right\} \tag{45}$$

Reinserting these new terms into the equations that were used to define them:

$$k_1^* = k_1^{**} + \frac{R\phi \cdot w^*}{(w + R\phi)(1 - \eta_1)} \tag{46}$$

$$k_2^* = \phi\left(\frac{\eta_1}{\eta_2}\right)k_1^{**} - \frac{w \cdot w^*}{(w + R\phi)(1 - \eta_2)} \tag{47}$$

$$R^* = R^{**} - e_{Rw} \cdot w^*, \quad e_{Rw} = \left(\frac{\eta_2}{1 - \eta_2}\right)\left(\frac{w + R}{w + R\phi}\right) > 0 \tag{48}$$

$$R_n^* = R_n^{**} - e_{R_nw} \cdot w^*, \quad e_{R_nw} = \left(\frac{w + R_n}{R_n}\right)\left(\frac{Z_1}{Z_{1n}}\right)$$

$$\times \left[\left(\frac{\eta_2}{1 - \eta_2}\right)\left(\frac{R}{w + R\phi}\right) - \left(\frac{Z_{1k}}{Z_1}\right)\left(\frac{\beta_k'}{\beta_k''}\right)\frac{w}{(w + R_k)^2}\right] > 0 \tag{49}$$

The sign of e_{R_nw} derives from the fact that $\beta_k'' < 0$.

To complete this version of the basic model, use (33a), (37a), and (49) to write:

$$w^* = \frac{e_{QR_n} \cdot R_n^{**}}{e_{cp} \cdot e_{pw} + e_{QR_n} \cdot e_{R_nw} + e_{Qw}} \tag{50}$$

so that the change in w depends on the change in the net factor ratio induced by K^*, N_1^*, and N_2^*. Then use (29a), (30a), and (46) to write:

$$r^* = e_{rg}\left[\frac{w(R_k - R\phi)w^*}{(R_k + w)(R\phi + w)} - (1 - \eta_1)k_1^{**}\right] \tag{51}$$

so that the change in r depends on the signs of $(R_k - R\phi)$, w^*, and k_1^{**}.

When w^* is zero, we shall speak of product-market balanced growth.

When r^* is zero, we shall speak of capital-market balanced growth. And, when $w^* = r^* = 0$, we shall speak of full-scale balanced growth.

How can the last result occur? Clearly, it requires that R_n^{**} be zero. But it also requires that k_1^{**} be zero. Otherwise, r^* would not vanish when w^* had vanished. When k_1^{**} is zero, however, equation (42) becomes:

$$K^* - N_1^* = \frac{R(\eta_2/\eta_1)}{w + R(\eta_2/\eta_1)} (N_2^* - N_1^*) \tag{52}$$

And (45) becomes:

$$R_n^{**} = \left(\frac{Z_2}{Z_{2n}}\right)\left[\frac{w + R_n(\eta_2/\eta_1)}{w + R(\eta_2/\eta_1)}\right](N_2^* - N_1^*) \tag{53}$$

Hence R_n^{**} is not zero when k_1^{**} is zero unless $N_1^* = N_2^*$ and, from (52), $K^* = N_1^* = N_2^*$. This is the only instance of full-scale balanced growth. All other sets of changes in the "natural endowment" and capital stock will alter the wage-rate ratio, the interest rate, or both.

One could, of course, devise a series of cases in which r^* would vanish, and another set of cases in which w^* would vanish. Furthermore, wage-rate change will affect R_n^{**} and can force the economy toward product-market balanced growth. But this result is far from certain; changes in K, N_1, and N_2 may, instead, induce continuous changes in w and r.

To study such a case of continuous change, set $\eta_1 = \eta_2 = \eta$, so that:[21]

$$k_1^{**} = (K^* - N_1^*) - \left(\frac{R}{R + w}\right)(N_2^* - N_1^*) \tag{54}$$

$$R_n^{**} = \left(\frac{Z_2}{Z_{2n}}\right)\left(\frac{Z_{1k}}{Z_{1n}}\right)\left[\left(\frac{Y}{K}\right)\left(\frac{w + R_k}{w + R}\right)(N_2^* - N_1^*)\right.$$
$$\left. + \left(\frac{R - R_k}{R}\right)(1 - \eta)k_1^{**}\right] \tag{55}$$

$$r^* = -e_{rg}\left[\frac{w(R - R_k)w^*}{(w + R_k)(w + R)} + (1 - \eta)k_1^{**}\right] \tag{56}$$

When, then, $k_1^{**} > 0$, the signs of the changes in w and r come to depend on $(N_2^* - N_1^*)$ and on $(R - R_k)$. When, for instance, $N_2^* \geqslant N_1^*$ and $R > R_k$, the net factor ratio will rise, raising the wage-rate ratio, and the increase in the latter will depress the interest rate. When, instead,

---

[21] This is the "linear version" of the general model (so named because the gross factor ratio is not affected by capital formation); it is the one that was used in my earlier paper, cited in note 2.

Table 1

Changes in the Rate of Interest (with $\eta_1 = \eta_2 = \eta$ and $k_1^{**} > 0$)

Rankings	R_n^{**} and w^*	Wage-Induced r^*	Total r^*
With $N_2^* > N_1^*$, and			
$R > R_k$	+	−	−
$R = R_k$	+	0	−
$R < R_k$	?	?	?
With $N_2^* = N_1^*$, and			
$R > R_k$	+	−	−
$R = R_k$	0	0	−
$R < R_k$	−	−	−
With $N_2^* < N_1^*$, and			
$R > R_k$	?	?	?
$R = R_k$	−	0	−
$R < R_k$	−	−	−

$N_2^* < N_1^*$ and $R < R_k$, the net factor ratio will decline, reducing the wage-rate ratio, but, as before, the interest rate will fall. In each instance, moreover, two forces are at work on the rate of interest; k_1^{**} induces a "primary" change, and w^* induces a "secondary" change. The full range of results (for $k_1^{**} > 0$) is set out in Table 1. Notice that r^* is always negative, save when $N_2^* > N_1^*$ while $R < R_k$, and when $N_2^* < N_1^*$ while $R > R_k$.

Now let $K^* = N_1^*$ and let $N_2^* = 0$, so that:

$$R_n^{**} = \left(\frac{Z_2}{Z_{2n}}\right)\left(\frac{Z_{1k}}{Z_{1n}}\right)\left(\frac{w + R_k}{w + R}\right) T \cdot K^* \tag{57}$$

where:

$$T = \left(\frac{R - R_k}{R_k + w}\right)(1 - \eta) - \left(\frac{Y}{K}\right) \tag{58}$$

and where:

$$dT = -(1 - \eta)\left(\frac{R}{R + w}\right)\left[\frac{R - R_k}{R_k + w} - \frac{Y}{K}\right]K^* - \frac{w^*}{R_k + w}\left\{\eta R_k\left(\frac{R + w}{R_k + w}\right)\right.$$
$$\left. - \left(\frac{w}{R_k + w}\right)\left(\frac{R + w}{R_k + w}\right)\left(\frac{\beta_k'}{\beta_k''}\right)(1 - \eta) + w\left(\frac{R - R_k}{R + w}\right)\left[\frac{R - R_k}{R_k + w} - \frac{Y}{K}\right]\right\} \tag{59}$$

Here, we must compare $[(R - R_k)/(R_k + w)]$, $[(R - R_k)/(R_k + w)]$ $(1 - \eta)$, and (Y/K), and this is done in Table 2. When, for instance,

$$[(R - R_k)/(R_k + w)](1 - \eta) > (Y/K),$$

Table 2

Changes in R_n^{**} (with $\eta_1 = \eta_2 = \eta$, $K^* = N_1^*$, and $N_2^* = 0$)

Ranking	T, R_n^{**}, and w^*	Change in R_n^{**}		
		K effect	w effect	Total
$\dfrac{R - R_k}{R_k + w}(1 - \eta) > \dfrac{Y}{K}$	$+$	$-$	$-$	$-$
$\dfrac{R - R_k}{R_k + w}(1 - \eta) = \dfrac{Y}{K}$	0	$-$	0	$-$
$\dfrac{R - R_k}{R_k + w} > \dfrac{Y}{K} > \dfrac{R - R_k}{R_k + w}(1 - \eta)$	$-$	$-$	$+$	?
$\dfrac{R - R_k}{R_k + w} = \dfrac{Y}{K}$	$-$	0	$+$	$+$
$\dfrac{Y}{K} > \dfrac{R - R_k}{w + R_k} > 0$	$-$	$+$	?	?
$\dfrac{R - R_k}{R_k + w} < 0$	$-$	$+$	$+$	$+$

R_n^{**} and w^* are positive, as is $[(R - R_k)/(R_k + w)] = (Y/K)$. In consequence, all arguments of (59) are unambiguously negative, and R_n^{**} declines. But, when R_n^{**} and w^* have fallen to zero, the first argument of (59) is still negative, so that R_n^{**} has also to turn negative. Product-market balanced growth is not a stable state.

To end this exploration of the closed economy, consider one more simple case in which R_n^{**} will always go to zero. Let $K^* > N_1^* = N_2^*$ (which includes the simpler case of capital formation without any change in the "natural endowment"). In this instance:

$$R_n^{**} = \left(\frac{Z_2}{Z_{2n}}\right)\left(\frac{Z_{1k}}{Z_{1n}}\right)\left(\frac{R - R_k}{R}\right)(1 - \eta)(K^* - N_1^*) \qquad (60)$$

This case is covered by the middle section of Table 1; for all orderings of R and R_k, the interest rate declines. In this case, moreover, R_n^{**} will go to zero from any starting point, for $(\partial R/\partial w)(w/R) < 0$ [see equation (48)] and $(\partial R_k/\partial w)(w/R_k) > 0$ [see equation (39)]. Factor-market balanced growth will occur eventually and, once it is attained, will be self-perpetuating. When it has been reached, however, r^* will take the sign of $(K^* - N_1^*)$, declining with an increase in capital per worker.

TRADE AND INVESTMENT IN A TWO-COUNTRY MODEL

To study foreign trade and foreign investment, let there be two countries, I and II, and adopt five more assumptions:

1. That both final products, X_1 and X_2, are traded without transport cost, but there is no trade in the capital good.
2. That both countries have identical production functions, and each country produces both final products.
3. That demand conditions are the same in both countries (with unitary income elasticities).
4. That all factor-service supply functions have the same elasticities $(_I\eta_i = {}_{II}\eta_i = \eta)$ and all investments have the same factor-service lives $(_Iv = {}_{II}v = v)$.
5. That the two countries' natural endowments yield a strict ordering of gross factor ratios: $_IR < {}_{II}R$ whenever $_Iw = {}_{II}w$ and $_Ir = {}_{II}r$.[22]

Under the first of these assumptions, free trade will equalize the two countries' product prices. Under the second, equation (18), linking p and w, exists and is the same in the two countries. Hence, free trade will equalize the two countries' factor prices.[23]

But, with factor-price equalization and identical demand conditions, the two-country model can be set out with common p and w, with common R_k, R_1, R_2, and Q^c (all of which depend on p or w), and in terms of $_Ig$, $_{II}g$, $_Ir$, $_{II}r$, $_IQ$, $_{II}Q$, $_Ik$, $_{II}k$, $_Ik_2$, $_{II}k_2$, $_IR$, $_{II}R$, $_IR_n$, and $_{II}R_n$, given $_IK$ and $_{II}K$, $_IN$ and $_{II}N_1$, and $_IN_2$ and $_{II}N_2$. To solve this whole system, we need twenty equations: the (common) equations (18), (20), (26), (27), and (28); the two sets of equations (16), (17), (21), (32), (24), and (25); and one new equation linking the common Q^c with global production:

$$Q^c = \left(\frac{_IX_2 + {}_{II}X_2}{_IX_1 + {}_{II}X_1}\right) = \frac{\beta_2(R_2, 1)}{\beta_1(R_1, 1)}\left[\frac{(_IR_n - R_1) + (_{II}R_n - R_1)U}{(R_2 - {}_IR_n) + (R_2 - {}_{II}R_n)U}\right] \quad (61)$$

where

$$U = \left(\frac{w + {}_IR_n}{w + {}_{II}R_n}\right)\left(\frac{_{II}Y}{_IY}\right) = \left(\frac{w + {}_IR_n}{w + {}_{II}R_n}\right)\left(\frac{v \cdot {}_{II}g - \eta}{v \cdot {}_Ig - \eta}\right)\left(\frac{_{II}K}{_IK}\right)$$

[22] The role of this iso-interest restriction is clarified in note 25.

[23] See note 18; see also P. A. Samuelson, "The Prices of Factors and Goods in General Equilibrium," *Review of Economic Studies*, XXI (1953–54).

With identical demand conditions, moreover, the output ratios $_IQ$ and $_{II}Q$ determine the pattern of trade. If $_{II}Q > _IQ$ at the common product prices fixed by free trade, country I will export X_1 and country II will export X_2. It is, in fact, sufficient to know the net factor ratios if one wants to forecast the structure of trade. When prices are equal in the two countries:

$$_{II}Q - _IQ = \frac{\beta_2(R_2, 1)}{\beta_1(R_1, 1)} \left[\frac{(R_2 - R_1)(_{II}R_n - _IR_n)}{(R_2 - _{II}R_n)(R_2 - _IR_n)} \right] \tag{62}$$

so that $_{II}Q > _IQ$ whenever $_{II}R_n > _IR_n$.

Thus far, then, this model gives familiar results. It generates equality in factor-service prices whenever the conventional assumptions are fulfilled, and, with the conventional restrictions on final demand, it generates a pattern of merchandise trade reflecting the physical factor endowments (net factor ratios) of the trading countries. But the model also offers several new results concerning international trade and investment.[24]

The net factor ratios $_IR_n$ and $_{II}R_n$ are not directly descriptive of capital supplies; they are not the same as the capital-to-labor ratios featured in conventional two-country models. Nor are the factor ratios R_1 and R_2 directly descriptive of capital requirements; they cannot be used to order the production functions according to capital intensity. Hence, statements about the capital intensities of export and import-competing production have no true counterparts in the model studied here. Yet, one can still measure capital scarcity by comparing interest rates. Furthermore, a difference in national interest rates will affect the ordering of net factor ratios, thereby affecting the pattern of trade. On the fourth assumption introduced above, one can rank the two countries' net factor ratios when those two countries face the same prices:

$$_{II}R_n - _IR_n = _{II}\left(\frac{Y+K}{Y}\right)\left(\frac{w + _{II}R_n}{w + _{II}R}\right)\left[(_{II}R - _IR)\left(\frac{w + _IR_n}{w + _IR}\right)\right.$$
$$\left. - (_IR_n - _IR)\left(\frac{_{II}g - _Ig}{_{II}g}\right)\left(\frac{w + _{II}R}{w + _IR}\right)\right] \tag{63}$$

When interest rates are equal in the two countries, the gross amortization rates will be equal too, and the second argument of (63) will vanish

---

[24] Some of these results, concerning the effects of changes in demand on international movements of capital and the similar effects of import tariffs, were set out in my earlier paper (cited in note 2) and will not be repeated here.

completely. The ordering of net factor ratios will depend on the ordering of gross factor ratios, and the latter will reflect an underlying difference in "natural endowments."[25] When interest rates are different in the two countries, reflecting a difference in capital scarcity, the second argument of (63) will come into play. If, for instance, $_{II}r > {}_{I}r$ (so that $_{II}g > {}_{I}g$), while $R_k > {}_{I}R$ (so that $_{I}R_n < {}_{I}R$), the difference in interest rates will augment the iso-interest difference in net factor ratios, making for more trade. If, instead, $R_k > {}_{I}R$, the same difference in interest rates will narrow the difference in net factor ratios, making for less trade (and may even overturn the iso-interest difference, reversing the pattern of merchandise trade).[26]

A difference in capital scarcity will also cause a difference in net factor incomes. Free trade will align the factor-service prices, w_i, but will not always equalize the net factor incomes, y_i. These incomes will differ

[25] The constant-elasticity factor-service supply function can be written in the form:

$$Z_i = N_i(\gamma_i \cdot k_i^{\eta_i})$$

where γ_i is a constant reflecting factor quality. But (4) can be written as:

$$g = w_i \cdot \eta_i \cdot \gamma_i \cdot k_i^{\eta_i - 1}$$

so that:

$$\log Z_i = \log N_i + \frac{1}{1 - \eta_i} \log \gamma_i + \frac{\eta_i}{1 - \eta_i} [\log w_i + \log \eta_i - \log g]$$

And:

$$\log R = \log \left(\frac{N_2}{N_1}\right) + \frac{1}{1 - \eta_2} \log \left(\frac{\gamma_2}{\gamma_1}\right) - \frac{\eta_2}{1 - \eta_2} \log \left(\frac{w\eta_1}{\eta_2}\right)$$
$$+ \frac{\eta_2 - \eta_1}{(1 - \eta_1)(1 - \eta_2)} [\log (w_1\eta_1) + \log \gamma_1 - \log g]$$

With $_{I}w = {}_{II}w$ and $_{I}\eta_i = {}_{II}\eta_i = \eta_i$, then:

$$\log \left(\frac{{}_{II}R}{{}_{I}R}\right) = \left[\log {}_{II}\left(\frac{N_2}{N_1}\right) - \log {}_{I}\left(\frac{N_2}{N_1}\right)\right]$$
$$+ \frac{1}{1 - \eta_2} \left[\log {}_{II}\left(\frac{\gamma_2}{\gamma_1}\right) - \log {}_{I}\left(\frac{\gamma_2}{\gamma_1}\right)\right]$$
$$+ \frac{\eta_2 - \eta_1}{(1 - \eta_1)(1 - \eta_2)} \left[\log \left(\frac{{}_{I}g}{{}_{II}g}\right) + \log \left(\frac{{}_{II}\gamma_1}{{}_{I}\gamma_1}\right)\right]$$

The first argument of this equation measures the difference in relative quantities (in acres per worker). The second measures the difference in relative quantity. The third combines two terms relating to absolute quality and to relative capital scarcity, but this term vanishes when, as in the text, $\eta_2 = \eta_1$.

[26] This inference assumes that $_{II}R > {}_{I}R$. When $\eta_I \neq \eta_2$, however, the ordering of gross factor ratios can itself be altered by a difference in interest rates (see note 25).

between countries if those countries' "natural endowments" differ in quality or if they embody different investments.[27] In consequence, the model set forth here furnishes a comprehensive explanation of international differences in real incomes. These may be ascribed to national differences in supplies of tangible capital and labor-force participation (the elements that enter conventional models), but can also be ascribed to national differences in stocks of "human capital" and in the quality of "natural endowments."[28]

I come now to the most important new proposition furnished by this model of capital formation. In the conventional Heckscher-Ohlin construct, free trade will equalize national interest rates, and capital movements are wholly redundant.[29] An act of net saving in country I, for example, will not cause it to invest in country II, for interest rates will be aligned by changes in the terms of trade resulting from country I's domestic investment. In the model studied here, free trade will not equalize two countries' interest rates; it is not a substitute for capital

---

[27] By way of proof, use the arguments of notes 11 and 25 to write:

$$\log \left(_{\mathrm{II}} y_i / _{\mathrm{I}} y_i \right) = \log \left[\left(_{\mathrm{II}} g / _{\mathrm{I}} g \right) \left(_{\mathrm{II}} k_i / _{\mathrm{I}} k_i \right) \right]$$

$$= \frac{\log \left(_{\mathrm{II}} \gamma_i / _{\mathrm{I}} \gamma_i \right) - \eta_i \log \left(_{\mathrm{II}} g / _{\mathrm{I}} g \right)}{1 - \eta_i}$$

Differences in factor incomes can then be attributed to differences in quality $\left(_{\mathrm{II}} \gamma_i / _{\mathrm{I}} \gamma_i \right)$ and, inversely, to differences in capital scarcity $\left(_{\mathrm{II}} g / _{\mathrm{I}} g \right)$.

[28] Denoting the (conventional) supplies of labor and capital by L' and K', the corresponding real wages by w_1' and w_2', and the total population by N, gross national product per capita can be written in the form:

$$G/N = (L'/N)[w_1' + w_2'(K'/L')]$$

Because free trade will equalize the w_i' between countries, differences in national outputs per capita must be due to differences in tangible capital per worker (K'/L') and in labor-force participation (L'/N). In the model studied here:

$$G/N = (N_1/N) z_1 (w_1 + w_2 \cdot R)$$

Once again, free trade will equalize the w_i between countries, but differences in national outputs per capita can now be due to differences in (N_1/N), labor-force participation, in z_1, the labor-service flow from a single worker, and in R, land-service flow per unit of labor-service flow. Differences in z_1 and R, moreover, can reflect differences in capital scarcity and in the quality of "natural endowments."

[29] See P. A. Samuelson, "Equalization by Trade of the Interest Rate along with the Real Wage," in Trade, Growth and the Balance of Payments R. E. Caves, H. G. Johnson and P. B. Kenen (eds.) (Chicago: Rand-McNally, 1965).

movements serving to optimize world production.[30]   I shall prove this proposition by a simple illustration that does not require any new formulae, and will then examine it somewhat more thoroughly.

Suppose that $_{\mathrm{I}}r = {}_{\mathrm{II}}r$ initially, and that $_{\mathrm{I}}R = {}_{\mathrm{II}}R = R_k$ at a common set of prices in the two countries.   Under these conditions, $_{\mathrm{I}}R_n = {}_{\mathrm{II}}R_n$, and there will be no trade.   Now, disturb this situation by an act of net saving in country I, and let that saving be invested inside country I itself.   There will be no change in $_{\mathrm{I}}R_n$, for $_{\mathrm{I}}R_n^{**} = 0$ when $_{\mathrm{I}}R = R_k$ [see equation (55)].   Hence capital formation will not cause a change in prices and will not bring on trade.   Yet $_{\mathrm{I}}r$ will decline with this capital formation, falling by $e_{r_g}(1 - \eta)_{\mathrm{I}}K^*$ [see equation (56)], and some of country I's net saving must be moved to country II in order to restore interest-rate equality.   Notice, moreover, that this transfer of capital will not lead to trade, for $_{\mathrm{II}}R_n^{**} = 0$ when, as here, $_{\mathrm{II}}R = R_k$.   In brief, free trade cannot substitute for capital movements, and movements of capital need not bring on trade.[31]

This proof was contrived to forestall foreign trade, but similar results obtain when the two countries are trading initially.   To study such a case,

[30] This result, it should be stressed, does not depend on my assumption that there is no trade in the capital good or, more generally, on my combination of two traded products with three factors of production, Z_1, Z_2, and K. Capital is not a factor of production in the ordinary sense. Hence, the addition of one more commodity (or trade in the capital good) would not serve to equalize national interest rates. My results, below, should be compared with Samuelson's ("Equalization by Trade"). He shows that a model with one primary factor (labor) and reproducible capital goods that enter directly into production will, in fact, equalize national interest rates and take on Ricardian properties. When free trade has equalized the two countries' interest rates, their production functions can be regarded as "the simple linear ones of the Ricardian labor-theory-of-value, constant-cost case." My model, by contrast, posits two primary factors, land and labor, and assumes that the reproducible capital good is not used directly in production. In consequence, interest rates must be equalized by international lending (by transfers between the two countries' loan funds). Once they have been equalized (and if there are no differences in factor quality), my model becomes a straightforward Heckscher-Ohlin construct, not a Ricardian construct, with trade based on differences in land and labor endowments.

[31] The last statement is not quite accurate. A capital movement always requires an offsetting flow of goods; so does the interest payment to which it gives rise. When country I lends to country II, the latter will use the loan proceeds to buy some of every final product in country I, releasing its own factor services to produce additional capital goods and expand its output. With no saving in country II, even at the higher level of net geographic product, that country will not repay its debts. Instead, country I will obtain a perpetual interest-income stream from country II and will use that income stream to buy some of country II's final output. But neither of these trade flows is based on the principle of comparative advantage; each one involves a one-way flow of both final products.

define:

$$s \equiv \frac{{}_{II}r'}{{}_{I}r'} \tag{64}$$

and let $s = 1$ to start. Then use (54) and (56) to write:

$$\left. \begin{aligned}
s^* &= ({}_{II}r^* - {}_{I}r^*) \equiv s_w{}^* + s^{**} \\
s_w{}^* &\equiv -e_{rg}\left[\frac{w({}_{II}R - {}_{I}R)}{({}_{I}R + w)({}_{II}R + w)}\right]w^* \\
s^{**} &\equiv -e_{rg}(1 - \eta)({}_{II}k_1^{**} - {}_{I}k^{**})
\end{aligned} \right\} \tag{65}$$

Since $s_w{}^* \neq 0$ when ${}_{I}R \neq {}_{II}R$ and $w^* \neq 0$, any change in factor-service prices can create a difference in national interest rates. Hence, factor-price equality (${}_{I}w = {}_{II}w$ and ${}_{I}w^* = {}_{II}w^*$) does not guarantee interest-rate equality.

But what happens to w^* when the k_1^{**} are different from zero; what are the effects of capital formation and changes in the nations' "natural endowments"? To answer this question, one must differentiate equation (61) and solve it for w^*. First, write:

$$
\begin{aligned}
e_{cp} \cdot e_{pw} \cdot w^* = &(R_2 - R_1)(1 + U)V[{}_{I}R_n \cdot {}_{I}R_n{}^* + {}_{II}R_n \cdot U \cdot {}_{II}R_n{}^*] \\
&+ \left\{\frac{w}{(w + R_1)^2}\left(\frac{\beta_1{}'}{\beta_1{}''}\right)\left[\frac{(w + {}_{I}R_n) + (w + {}_{II}R_n)U}{({}_{I}R_n - R_1) + ({}_{II}R_n - R_1)U}\right]\right. \\
&\left. \times \frac{w}{(w + R_2)^2}\left(\frac{\beta_2{}'}{\beta_2{}''}\right)\left[\frac{(w + {}_{I}R_n) + (w + {}_{II}R_n)U}{(R_2 - {}_{I}R_n) + (R_2 - {}_{II}R_n)U}\right]\right\}w^* \\
&+ UV(R_2 - R_1)({}_{II}R_n - {}_{I}R_n)U^* \tag{66}
\end{aligned}
$$

where

$$V \equiv \frac{1}{[({}_{I}R_n - R_1) + ({}_{II}R_n - R_1)U][(R_2 - {}_{I}R_n) + (R_2 - {}_{II}R_n)U]} > 0$$

and where:

$$
\begin{aligned}
U^* = &\left(\frac{{}_{I}R_n \cdot {}_{I}R_n{}^*}{w + {}_{I}R_n} - \frac{{}_{II}R_n \cdot {}_{II}R_n{}^*}{w + {}_{II}R_n}\right) + \frac{w({}_{II}R_n - {}_{I}R_n)w^*}{(w + {}_{I}R_n)(w + {}_{II}R_n)} \\
&+ \left(\frac{vg}{vg - \eta}\right)\left(\frac{s^{**} + s_w{}^*}{e_{rg}}\right) + ({}_{II}K^* - {}_{I}K^*) \tag{67}
\end{aligned}
$$

When $s = 1$, however, equation (63) gives:

$$\frac{w(_{II}R_n - {}_IR_n)w^*}{(w + {}_IR_n)(w + {}_{II}R_n)} = \left(\frac{Y + K}{Y}\right)\frac{w(_IR - {}_{II}R)w^*}{(w + {}_IR)(w + {}_{II}R)}$$

$$= -\left(\frac{vg}{vg - \eta}\right)\left(\frac{s_w{}^*}{e_{rg}}\right) \quad (68)$$

so that:

$$U^* = \left(\frac{_IR_n \cdot {}_IR_n{}^*}{w + {}_IR_n} - \frac{_{II}R_n \cdot {}_{II}R_n{}^*}{w + {}_{II}R_n}\right) - \left(\frac{vg}{vg - \eta}\right)$$

$$\times (1 - \eta)(_{II}k_1^{**} - {}_Ik_1^{**}) + (_{II}K^* - {}_IK^*) \quad (67a)$$

Returning, now, to (66), use (67a) and (49) to replace U^*, $_IR_n{}^*$, and $_{II}R_n{}^*$, then solve for w^*:

$$w^* = \frac{V(R_2 - R_1)}{e_{cp} \cdot e_{pw} + e_{v_1w} + e_{v_2w}}\left\{W\left[\frac{_IR_n \cdot {}_IR_n^{**}}{w + {}_IR_n} + \frac{_{II}R_n \cdot U \cdot {}_{II}R_n^{**}}{w + {}_{II}R_n}\right]\right.$$

$$+ U(_{II}R_n - {}_IR_n)\left[(_{II}K^* - {}_IK^*)\right.$$

$$\left.\left. - \left(\frac{vg}{vg - \eta}\right)(1 - \eta)(_{II}k_1^{**} - {}_Ik_1^{**})\right]\right\} \quad (69)$$

where:

$$W \equiv (w + {}_IR_n) + (w + {}_{II}R_n)U > 0$$

$$e_{v_1w} \equiv VW(R_2 - R_1)\left[\frac{_IR_n}{w + {}_IR_n}(_Ie_{R_nw}) + \frac{_{II}R_n \cdot U}{w + {}_{II}R_n}(_{II}e_{R_nw})\right] > 0$$

$$e_{v_2w} \equiv -VW\left\{\frac{w}{(w + R_1)^2}\left(\frac{\beta_1'}{\beta_1''}\right)[(R_2 - {}_IR_n) + (R_2 - {}_{II}R_n)U]\right.$$

$$\left. + \frac{w}{(w + R_2)^2}\left(\frac{\beta_2'}{\beta_2''}\right)[(_IR_n - R_1) + (_{II}R_n - R_1)U]\right\} > 0$$

$$(70)$$

Consider, now, the leading cases. First, let $_IK^* = {}_IN_1{}^* = {}_IN_2{}^*$, and $_{II}K^* = {}_{II}N_1{}^* = {}_{II}N_2{}^*$, giving full-scale balanced growth in each country. Here, of course, $_Ik_1^{**} = {}_{II}k_1^{**} = 0$, and, in consequence, $_IR_n^{**} = {}_{II}R_n^{**} = 0$, so that s^{**} vanishes completely. Furthermore, (69) gives:

$$w^* = \frac{V(R_2 - R_1)U(_{II}R_n - {}_IR_n)(_{II}K^* - {}_IK^*)}{e_{cp} \cdot e_{pw} + e_{v_1w} + e_{v_2w}} \quad (71)$$

If, then, $_{II}K^* > {}_IK^*$ while $_{II}R > {}_IR$, w will rise, and (65) tells us that $_{II}r$ will fall relative to $_Ir$. Capital must flow to country I, the slower-growing country, in order to equalize the two countries' interest rates.[32] Put differently, full-scale balanced growth does not preclude capital movements unless it proceeds at the very same rate in the two countries.

Next, let $_IK^* > {}_IN_1^*$, let $_{II}K^* > {}_{II}N_1^*$, and let $_IN_1^* = {}_IN_2^* = {}_{II}N_1^* = {}_{II}N_2^*$ (an instance of net capital formation per worker but uniform growth in "natural endowments"). Here, $_Ik_1^{**} > 0$, $_{II}k_1^{**} > 0$, and $_{II}k_1^{**} - {}_Ik_1^{**} = {}_{II}K^* - {}_IK^*$ [see equation (54)], while $_IR_n^{**}$ takes its sign from $_IR - R_k$ and $_{II}R_n^{**}$ takes its sign from $_{II}R - R_k$ [see equation (60)]. Here, too:

$$w^* = \frac{V(R_2 - R_1)}{e_{cp} \cdot e_{pw} + e_{v_1 w} + e_{v_2 w}} \left\{ W \left[\frac{{}_IR_n \cdot {}_IR_n^{**}}{w + {}_IR_n} + \frac{{}_{II}R_n \cdot U \cdot {}_{II}R_n^{**}}{w + {}_{II}R_n} \right] \right.$$
$$\left. + U({}_{II}R_n - {}_IR_n) \left[\frac{\eta(vg - 1)}{vg - \eta} \right]({}_{II}K^* - {}_IK^*) \right\} \quad (72)$$

When, then, $_{II}K^* \gg {}_IK^*$ (so that $s^{**} < 0$), while $_{II}R > {}_IR \gg R_k$, w will rise, s_w^* will be negative, and capital must flow from country II to country I. Conversely, when $_{II}K^* \ll {}_IK^*$, while $R_k \gg {}_{II}R > {}_IR$, w will fall, s_w^* will be positive, and capital must flow from country I to country II. Notice, however, that, when $_{II}K^* > {}_IK^*$ while $R_1 \gg {}_{II}R$, or when $_{II}K^* < {}_IK^*$ while $_IR \gg R_k$, the sign of the capital flow is thoroughly ambiguous. In the first of these two cases, s^{**} is negative; there will be a "primary" growth-induced flow from country II to country I. In the same case, however, $_IR_n^{**} < 0$ and $_{II}R_n^{**} < 0$, so that the signs of w^* and s_w^* are uncertain. In the second of these cases, s^{**} is positive; there will be a "primary" growth-induced flow from country I to country II. But $_IR_n^{**} \gg 0$ and $_{II}R_n^* > 0$, so that the signs of w^* and s_w^* are again uncertain.

Consider, now, the simplest case, one in which $_IK^* = {}_{II}K^*$ and there is no change in "natural endowments." Here, s^{**} is zero, as with full-scale balanced growth; there is no "primary" capital flow. When $_{II}R > {}_IR \gg R_k$, however, $_IR_n^{**} \gg 0$ and $_{II}R_n^{**} > 0$, so that w will rise, s_w^* will be negative, and capital must flow from country II to country I. When, instead, $R_k \gg {}_{II}R > {}_IR$, w will fall, s_w^* will be positive, and capital

[32] If, of course, $_IR > {}_{II}R$, w will fall, but s_w^* will still be negative and capital will still flow to the slower-growing country. If, finally, $_IR = {}_{II}R$, there will be no capital transfer despite the difference in growth rates.

must flow from country I to country II. When, finally $_{II}R > R_k > {}_IR$, the signs of w^* and s_w^* are uncertain; capital can flow in either direction, or may not flow at all.

This final case deserves a bit more attention, for one can show that wage-rate change must lead the system to this zone, and that, eventually, capital will cease to move. When $_IK^* = {}_{II}K^* = K^*$ and there is no change in "natural endowments," the sign of the change in the wage-rate ratio is given by:

$$\frac{_IR_n \cdot {}_IR_n^{**}}{w + {}_IR_n} + \frac{_{II}R_n \cdot U \cdot {}_{II}R_n^{**}}{w + {}_{II}R_n}$$

$$= U(1 - \eta)\left(\frac{w + {}_{II}R_n}{w + R_k}\right)\left(\frac{K}{Y}\right)\frac{Y + K}{Y} M \cdot K^* \quad (73)$$

where:

$$M = \left(\frac{_IR - R_k}{w + {}_IR}\right)\left(\frac{_IK}{{}_{II}K}\right) + \left(\frac{_{II}R - R_k}{w + {}_{II}R}\right) \quad (74)$$

But $_IR$ and $_{II}R$ decline when w^* is positive [see equation (48)], while R_k rises in the same circumstance [see equation (39)]. When, then, M is positive and w rises, M itself must fall; when M is negative and w falls, M itself must rise. With capital formation proceeding at the same rates in the two countries, the system will converge on product-market balanced growth and, once there, will stay there.

II

ADAPTATION, GROWTH,

AND TRADE

H. DAVID WILLEY

Growth Patterns and Export Performance: Britain and Germany

THE POST-WORLD WAR II CONCERN with economic growth as an objective of national economic policy has given rise to considerable discussion of the relation between economic growth and exports. Although most writers agree that a nation's exports must increase if economic growth is not to be impeded by balance-of-payments deficits, there has been much controversy over the functional relation between exports and the growth process. Nurkse has stressed a rivalry between exports and economic growth, arguing that exports draw away resources needed for domestic investment.[1] Others have emphasized the role of exports as a spur to economic growth. Kindleberger has noted the stimulus of exports to innovation and technical progress.[2] Beckerman has seen rising exports as

---

[1] R. Nurkse, "The Relation between Home Investment and External Imbalance in the Light of British Experience, 1954–1955," *The Review of Economics and Statistics,* XXXVIII (May 1956), 121–54.

[2] C. P. Kindleberger, *Foreign Trade and the National Economy* (New Haven and London: Yale University Press, 1962), p. 194.

strengthening the confidence of entrepreneurs about the future growth of demand for their products.[3]

These discussions have often touched upon the contrasting economic performance of Britain (i.e., the United Kingdom) and Germany (i.e., the Federal Republic)—two industrial countries with widely divergent growth rates for both income and exports during the 1950s. The average annual growth rates of Britain's real national product and of the volume of her goods and service exports were 2.5 per cent and 2.8 per cent, respectively, from 1951 to 1962. Comparable German rates were 6.8 per cent and 12.1 per cent. Manufactures are critical to this comparison, because in both countries they account for about half the exports of goods and services, four-fifths the exports of goods, and between one-third and one-half of the gross domestic product.

This study examines the relation between exports and economic growth through a comparison of British and German manufacturing performance. To make this comparison, a number of growth rates have been calculated for a twelve-sector breakdown of manufacturing industry in each country. These rates include each sector's exports, output, labor and capital inputs, and a measure of total productivity—the "residual." The German growth rates for these variables grew markedly faster than the British in all sectors. Despite this fundamental difference, there were two striking similarities. First, the "residual" accounted for approximately the same proportion of output growth in both countries. This does not indicate that productivity growth in Britain was truly satisfactory, for a country with almost no growth in labor input must depend more on productivity progress to assure an adequate advance in output. Second, the ranking by sector of changes in output and productivity corresponded closely in both countries. This similarity may have been an important reason for the inconclusive statistical results obtained from an attempt to explain relative export performance by relative changes in productivity and labor cost. Nevertheless, there is some evidence that in the early years of the 1951–1962 period, when German price competitiveness and Germany's share of world manufacturing exports rose strongly, the ranking by sector of British and German export change was inversely related.

The British-German comparison suggests the importance of increases in labor and capital inputs as an explanation of relative growth in both the output and export of manufactures. The remainder of this essay

---

[3] W. Beckerman, "The Determinants of Economic Growth," in P. D. Henderson (ed.), *Economic Growth in Britain* (London: Weidenfeld and Nicolson, 1966), pp. 55–83.

reviews and interprets the evidence for this conclusion: the next section discusses relative export performance and competitiveness, and the succeeding two sections examine some of the reasons for change in each country's international competitive position and growth.[4]

BRITISH AND GERMAN
INTERNATIONAL COMPETITIVENESS

Superior German export performance is *prima facie* evidence that German exports were more competitive, and the following analysis indicates that German export competitiveness improved with respect to that of Britain in both price and nonprice aspects during the 1951–1962 period.

German exports of manufactures rose more than four times as fast as British manufactured exports over the period, although the German advantage had diminished to something like twice the British rate by the end of the period. (These rates and a number of other indications of international competitiveness are shown in Table 1.) As a result of faster German export growth, the German share in total world exports of manufactures rose from 10 per cent in 1951 to 20 per cent in 1962, while the British share declined from 22 per cent to 15 per cent in the same period. Germany recaptured roughly the same share of world manufactured exports that it held before World War II (by all of Germany, including the East); British performance marked a continuation of the long-term decline in the British share noted by Tyszynski, and attributed by him to Britain's competitive shortcomings in markets for iron and steel and engineering products.[5]

With respect to the post-World War II decline in the British share, Wells concluded that Germany almost always gained where Britain lost.[6] But data developed for this study suggest that German gains at the expense of Britain were concentrated early in the 1951–1962 period. The correlation between export growth rates for the two countries, using a twelve-part cross section of manufactured exports, reveals a negative

[4] For a more detailed treatment of the subject, see H. D. Willey, "Growth of British and German Manufacturing, 1951–62" (unpublished doctoral dissertation, Columbia University, 1966).

[5] H. Tyszynski, "World Trade in Manufactured Commodities, 1899–1950," *Manchester School*, XIX (September 1951), 272–304.

[6] S. J. Wells, *British Export Performance. A Comparative Study* (Cambridge: Cambridge University Press, 1964), p. 14.

Table 1

Evidence of International Competitiveness
(average annual growth rates in per cent)

	1951–1954	1954–1959	1959–1962	1951–1962
Manufacturing exports (value)				
German[a]	16.1	13.1	9.4	12.9
British	1.2	4.9	3.7	3.6
Manufacturing prices				
German export[a]		0.7	2.0	
German producer[a]	−1.6	1.2	3.0	0.9
British wholesale	0.3	2.2	1.9	1.6
Labor productivity in manufacturing				
German	4.4	5.6	5.4	5.2
British	2.0	2.5	3.4	2.6
Hourly labor payments in manufacturing				
German[a]	4.8	8.0	13.0	8.5
British	6.8	6.2	7.2	6.6

Source: See Appendix.

[a] Adjusted for 1961 revaluation of the Deutsche mark.

relation for the 1951–1954 period ($\tau = -.30$), a very small positive relation for 1954–1959 ($\tau = .09$), and a stronger positive relation for 1959–1962 ($\tau = .45$).[7] German gains were, in fact, highest in the early years of the 1951–1962 period. British losses were more persistent, the largest occurring in 1960. Some of the British losses in later years may have been to Japan and Italy, which raised their shares by 2 per cent each during the period. German gains were also at the expense of the United States, whose share of manufactured exports fell from 27 per cent to 20 per cent.

Evidence concerning the relative price *levels* of British and German manufactures is scanty and inconclusive. Gilbert's study of relative purchasing power for 1950 reveals that one dollar would have purchased more clothing, household goods, transport equipment, and producers' durables in Britain than in Germany.[8] By 1955, however, the British

[7] Using the rank correlation coefficient, τ. M. G. Kendall, *Rank Correlation Methods* (New York: Hafner Publishing Co., 1955). With a double-tail test and 12 observations, a τ of .36 or more is significant at the .10 level.

[8] M. Gilbert and associates, *Comparative National Products and Price Levels. A Study of Western Europe and the United States* (Paris: OECD, 1958), pp. 31, 56, 79.

advantage in producers' durables had narrowed to $.09 from the $.14 margin recorded for 1950; 1955 data for other manufacturing categories are not available. Gilbert's data for general purchasing power show a $.07 British advantage in 1950 and an $.08 German advantage in 1955. These figures show nothing, however, about the price of goods actually exported or about actual export prices, which may have differed considerably from comparable internal prices. Thus, the level of German export prices could have been less than the level of British export prices during the early 1950s, even though the Gilbert figures suggest the reverse.

By 1959, however, British prices were probably higher than German prices, since wholesale prices of manufactures had risen much more rapidly in Britain than in Germany. The 5 per cent German revaluation of 1961 was an important factor accounting for the more rapid rise in German prices from 1959 to 1962. For the whole period, nonetheless, German prices rose at a slower pace than British prices.

The advance of labor costs per unit of output was also slower in Germany than in Britain. Although labor costs represent approximately a third of the value of output, changes in labor costs also influence the price of materials and fuel, and are thus a very important influence on prices.[9] German labor productivity (output per man-hour) and hourly labor payments each increased more rapidly than those of Britain. However, the rise in hourly labor payments was more in line with the pace of labor productivity, so that labor costs rose more slowly in Germany than in Britain.

Statistical assessment of the relationship between prices or labor costs and export performance has been complicated by the inadequacy of the data. In a recent study, Junz and Rhomberg, using rather poor price data, found that "while there is a clear association between movements in relative prices and export performance, it is apparent that nonprice factors play an important role in the determination of a country's exports."[10]

Junz and Rhomberg found that the geographic structure of exports was one nonprice factor of considerable assistance to German sales abroad. German exports are heavily concentrated in the rapidly growing European Economic Community. German exports to this area ranged

[9] E. Nevin, "The Cost Structure of British Manufacturing, 1948–61," *Economic Journal*, LXXIII (December 1963), 642–64. Similar relations are probably true of German manufacturing as well.

[10] H. B. Junz and R. R. Rhomberg, "Prices and Export Performance of Industrial Countries, 1953–63," *International Monetary Fund Staff Papers*, XII (July 1965), 224–71.

from 25 per cent of total German foreign sales in 1954 to 31 per cent in 1962, while the comparable figures for Britain are 11 per cent and 18 per cent.[11] British exports, on the other hand, were directed strongly to slower-growing sterling area countries; almost half of all British exports went to this area in 1954 (though the proportion had dropped to 34 per cent by 1962). About 8 per cent of German exports went to sterling area countries during this period.

The commodity structure of exports apparently gave little advantage to either country. Both Junz and Rhomberg and the British National Institute of Economic and Social Research (NIESR) came to this conclusion, the latter from a study based on a forty-commodity breakdown of the machinery, transport equipment, and chemicals sectors.[12] The NIESR found that the British share of fast-growing commodity exports in these groups was not significantly lower than the share of slow-growing exports. The German commodity pattern, however, appeared to be biased somewhat toward the faster-growing commodities.

These studies contradict the conclusion reached by Barna, from a study of net exports (i.e., exports less imports) of manufactures, that poor British performance in relation to Germany could be explained by the British shortfall in fast-growing machinery and chemicals products.[13] Barna's use of net exports makes performance more dependent on domestic demand and supply conditions than would have been the case had he used exports alone. An important reason for superior German performance may have been that German manufacturing industry was better able to supply both foreign and domestic demand than was British industry. Barna apparently did not believe this to be a dominant reason, for he attributed the British shortfall to "backwardness."

More direct evidence concerning the possible "technical backwardness" of British production is mixed. On the one hand, a number of "unsuccessful" British exporters replying to an NIESR survey in October 1960 cited the superior quality of foreign competitors' products as a reason for their own lack of success.[14] On the other hand, British expenditures for research and development in manufacturing are relatively

[11] "Trends of United Kingdom and World Exports of Manufactures in 1964," *Board of Trade Journal*, CLXXXIX (December 3, 1965), viii, ix.

[12] "Fast and Slow-Growing Products in World Trade," *National Institute Economic Review*, No. 25 (August 1963), 22–39.

[13] T. Barna, "Export Growth Retarded by Technical Backwardness; Britain Compared with U.S. and Germany," The *Times* (London), April 3, 1963, p. 19.

[14] *National Institute Economic Review*, No. 13 (January 1961), 32–33.

large, and, as noted below, are positively related to the growth of British manufacturing output and productivity.

In one important facet of exporting, that of marketing, the British have clearly fallen short of the Germans. Granick was impressed by the "extraordinarily export-minded" German executives who placed a premium on marketing, while Barna has scored the backwardness of senior British managers and their lack of interest in sales promotion.[15]

Another nonprice factor, the availability of easy export credit, has sometimes been cited as a reason for German export success. Wells has concluded, however, that this factor does not explain a substantial part of German export performance.[16]

In summary, Germany had the advantage in both price and nonprice aspects of competitiveness. Until late in the period, Germany's prices and labor costs were rising at a much less rapid rate than Britain's, and Germany had the advantage in geographic structure of exports and in marketing. The much faster rise of German manufacturing output presumably also tended to make the elasticity of export supply greater there. The next sections examine the growth of each country's manufacturing output and its relation to international competitiveness.

BRITISH MANUFACTURING GROWTH AND INTERNATIONAL COMPETITIVENESS

To facilitate the analysis of British manufacturing and to permit ready comparison with changes in German manufacturing, a simple model has been used. This model apportions the growth of net output among labor input, weighted by the share of labor in net output (α), capital input, weighted by the share of capital ($1 - \alpha$, or β), and a "residual".[17] The model assumes that labor is paid its marginal product and posits a unitary elasticity of substitution between capital and labor and neutral

---

[15] D. Granick, *The European Executive* (Garden City, New York: Doubleday and Co., Inc., 1962), pp. 158–60; T. Barna, *Investment and Growth Policies in British Industrial Firms*; National Institute of Economic and Social Research, Occasional Papers No. XX (Cambridge: Cambridge University Press, 1962), especially pp. 54–62.

[16] Wells, *British Export*, pp. 78–81.

[17] This model was used by R. Solow in "Technical Change and the Aggregate Production Function," *Review of Economics and Statistics*, XXXIX (August 1957), 312–20. The "residual" was so named by E. Domar, in "On the Measurement of Technological Change," *Economic Journal*, LXXI (December 1961), 709–29.

Table 2

Growth rates in British Manufacturing Output, Inputs, and
Productivity

	Output	α × Labor	β × Capital	"Residual"
1951–1954				
Rates	2.9	= 0.64 × 0.9 +	0.36 × 4.0 +	0.9
(Apportionment)	(100)	(18)	(50)	(32)
1954–1959				
Rates	2.6	= 0.64 × 0.1 +	0.36 × 4.4 +	1.0
(Apportionment)	(100)	(3)	(60)	(37)
1959–1962				
Rates	2.7	= 0.64 × −0.7 +	0.36 × 4.4 +	1.6
(Apportionment)	(100)	(−16)	(58)	(58)
1951–1962				
Rates	2.7	= 0.64 × 0.1 +	0.36 × 4.3 +	1.1
(Apportionment)	(100)	(3)	(56)	(41)

Source: See Appendix.

Note: Output, inputs, and productivity are expressed as annual average rates of change in per cent; α is labor's share in the value of net output, and β is 1 − α, or capital's share; apportionment of output change is in per cent.

productivity shifts in a Cobb-Douglas production function. Output changes have been measured by the industrial production index, labor input changes by man-hours worked, and capital-input changes by the stock of capital in a base period plus (or minus) gross fixed-capital formation in constant base-period prices. The labor weight, α, is calculated as the ratio of wages and salaries paid (adjusted for working proprietors' and employers' contributions to social insurance) divided by the value of net output at factor cost. The assumptions underlying the model probably depart somewhat from reality, and the data used in the model are imperfect, but the picture presented seems to be a fairly good representation of British developments during this period. The results derived from this model are shown in Table 2.

Despite temporary rises and falls during the period from 1951 to 1962, manufacturing production rose at a fairly constant rate during those years. The faster-growing sectors were refining and chemicals, and vehicles and aircraft; the textile industry, for which output actually declined, was at the low end of the scale. (See Table 4.)

Labor input increased very slowly during the period. A 0.8 per cent rate of increase in employment—reflecting mainly a low (0.3 per cent) average annual increase in the working-age population—was nearly offset by a decline in average hours worked. Most of the decline in average hours was concentrated in the 1959–1962 subperiod, and led to an actual decline in total hours worked between those years. Labor input thus accounted for only a small part of the increase in output over the entire period.

The labor force, furthermore, was fully employed throughout the period, the highest rate of unemployment reaching only 2.2 per cent in 1959, and in many years unfilled vacancies exceeded unemployment by a considerable margin. Dicks-Mireaux found excess demand for labor (vacancies less unemployment) to be a statistically significant explanatory variable for wage and price changes,[18] and the tight labor situation was probably an important reason for the often-criticized practice of labor hoarding. Labor's position also may have strengthened those elements in trade unions that have been attacked for being stagnant and conservative. It thus seems probable that the tight labor market permitted a higher rate of wage and price increase and slowed the rate of productivity advance.

The capital measure is subject to considerable uncertainty, but approximates the more sophisticated calculations made by Dean.[19] The higher growth rate of the capital stock in the latter two subperiods reflects the investment booms of 1955–1957 and 1959–1961, and is one indication that recurrent demand restrictions have not appreciably inhibited capital investment. Investment was sufficiently high, in fact, for Nurkse to view investment and exports as rival claimants to the output of capital-goods industries, and Harrod doubted that a further substantial increase in investment "in the next dozen years could be put to good use."[20] Firms reporting to NIESR surveys believed that more spare capacity existed in late 1962 than at any time since the end of World War II.[21] Statements about spare capacity, however, do not take explicit account of how modern existing capacity was, and how much scope existed for substituting new machinery for labor or for modernizing plant and equipment. British

[18] L. A. Dicks-Mireaux, "The Interrelationship between Cost and Price Changes, 1946–1950. A Study of Inflation in Post-War Britain," *Oxford Economic Papers*, XIII N.S. (October 1961), 267–92.

[19] G. Dean, "The Stock of Fixed Capital in the United Kingdom in 1961," *Journal of the Royal Statistical Society*, Series A, CXXVII (1964), 327–51. Dean's figures give a growth rate of 4.2 per cent per year for the manufacturing capital stock (excluding textiles and including construction) between 1951 and 1962.

[20] Nurkse, "Relation between Home Investment and External Imbalance"; R. Harrod, *The British Economy* (New York: McGraw-Hill Book Co., Inc., 1963), p. 199.

[21] *National Institute Economic Review*, No. 19 (February 1963), 22.

managers have often been criticized for failing to recognize the need for modernization. Nevertheless, manufacturing investment on a much greater scale would almost certainly have been impossible for the British economy without some reduction in the share of national income going into other uses. And increases in the capital stock did account for more than half the output gain in manufacturing registered for 1951–1962.[22]

Productivity gains accounted for somewhat less than half the rise in output. Productivity changes, as measured by the "residual," reflect not only true technological changes but also changes in utilization, economies of scale, organizational progress, and input quality. It will also reflect any change in specification errors (in the applicability of the basic model). The increase in the "residual" from subperiod to subperiod reflects in large part a decline in average hours worked, which was offset by more efficient utilization of labor. The "residual" may also reflect progress stemming from research and development efforts by the government and by private industry. The statistically significant rank correlation between this expenditure, sector by sector, and the "residual" for each sector, is consistent with such an interpretation.[23] The "residual" also bears a statistically significant relation to total output change by manufacturing sector ($\tau = .47$, for 1951–1962 rankings). This could reflect the presence of economies of scale, or perhaps, as suggested by Lamfalussy, better management when demand is expanding rapidly.[24]

---

[22] To the extent that technical progress is embodied in renewal of the capital stock, the increase in capital stock also accounted for productivity change. The embodiment thesis has been forwarded by E. S. Phelps, "The New View of Investment: a Neoclassical Analysis," *Quarterly Journal of Economics*, LXXVI (November 1962), 548–67, and taken up by R. Solow, "Investment and Technical Progress," in K. J. Arrow, Samuel Karlin, and Patrick Suppes (eds.), *Mathematical Methods in the Social Sciences, 1959* (Stanford: Stanford University Press, 1960), pp. 89–104, as well as in "Technical Progress, Capital Formation, and Economic Growth," *American Economic Review: Papers and Proceedings*, LII (May 1962), 76–86. In the model of the present study, technical progress embodied in the changing age structure of the capital stock would appear imperfectly in the "residual."

[23] The correlation of sector rankings by "residual" for 1951–1962 with sector rankings by total 1961–1962 expenditure on research and development resulted in a τ of .64. This was significant at the .10 level (double-tail test). Expenditure data came from United Kingdom, *Annual Report of the Advisory Council on Scientific Policy, 1961–2* (London: HMSO, Cmnd. 1920), pp. 36–37. This survey, for firms with 100 or more employees, provided data for an eight-sector division of manufacturing industry. To make the sectors used in the present study comparable, the appropriate sector "residual" rates were combined using net output weights.

[24] A. Lamfalussy, *Investment and Growth in Mature Economies. The Case of Belgium* (London: Macmillan & Co., Ltd., 1961).

The relation, however, might be a statistical fluke resulting from the fact that output change itself is an important element in the "residual."

A limitation on "residual" advance, probably important, has been the often criticized "backward" attitudes of labor and management. If British managers lack initiative to attain efficiency in operations and marketing at home, one would expect them to be relatively unresponsive to the requirements of foreign sales, which sometimes entail the establishment of extensive selling organizations, the adaptation of existing products, etc. The rapid rise in prices at home made it easier to pass on cost increases and to sell there rather than abroad.

In a country like Britain, where the size of labor and capital increases has been limited by circumstances, the rate of increase in productivity has been of special importance. Owing to the rapid increase in wages, a more rapid rise in productivity during this period would have been essential for maintaining British international price competitiveness. And, to the extent that productivity changes represent technical and organizational progress, they influence the nonprice factors affecting international competitiveness. For these reasons, raising the rate of productivity advance has been of special concern to official policy makers and to academic economists. Productivity teams have publicized shortcomings in British performance, and a number of economists have proposed that Britain steadily increase domestic demand at a higher rate in an effort to improve productivity growth.[25]

My analysis leads to the conclusion that the latter course would probably raise wages faster than productivity. And, even if Britain could pursue this course by international borrowing or by a change in the sterling parity, the further deterioration in international competitiveness would probably eventually force a policy reversal. Operation of the economy so that the labor market was not so close to its capacity limitation might give much better results. Some increase in unemployment would give managers the opportunity to utilize labor more efficiently, might reduce the pace of wage increases, and might make labor more receptive to plant improvements. If the demand limitations necessary to bring about this change affected consumption primarily, resources could be

---

[25] This general point of view has been expressed by a number of writers including Beckerman, "Projecting Europe's Growth," *Economic Journal*, LXXII (December 1962). 912–25; Harrod, *British Economy*, pp. 20–22, A. Maddison, *Economic Growth in the West: Comparative Experience in Europe and North America* (New York: The Twentieth Century Fund, 1964), pp. 18–21; and Wells, *British Export*, p. xii.

gradually shifted toward investment and exports. A less inflationary home market might encourage producers to take a greater interest in foreign markets. More competitive attitudes might also be fostered by Britain's joining the European Economic Community or even by unilateral reduction of British tariff barriers.

GERMAN MANUFACTURING GROWTH AND INTERNATIONAL COMPETITIVENESS

A model of German manufacturing growth analogous to that for Britain in the preceding section is set forth in Table 3. The measures for the different variables and parameters are the same as for Britain with the exception of capital input, which uses the perpetual inventory data developed by Krengel of the Berlin Deutsches Institut für Wirtschaftsforschung.

German manufacturing output grew at nearly three times the British rate between 1951 and 1962, but tended to decelerate through the period. The vehicles and aircraft sector recorded the fastest rate of growth, and

Table 3

Growth rates in German Manufacturing Output, Inputs, and Productivity

	Output	$\alpha \times$ Labor	$\beta \times$ Capital	"Residual"
1951–1954				
Rates	9.2	$= .65 \times 4.9 +$	$.35 \times 6.7 +$	3.7
(Apportionment)	(100)	(34)	(26)	(40)
1954–1959				
Rates	7.9	$= .65 \times 2.3 +$	$.35 \times 8.2 +$	3.6
(Apportionment)	(100)	(19)	(36)	(45)
1959–1962				
Rates	7.0	$= .65 \times 1.6 +$	$.35 \times 7.7 +$	3.4
(Apportionment)	(100)	(15)	(38)	(47)
1951–1962				
Rates	8.0	$= .65 \times 2.8 +$	$.35 \times 7.6 +$	3.6
(Apportionment)	(100)	(23)	(33)	(44)

Source: See Appendix.

Note: Output, inputs, and productivity are expressed as average annual rates of change in per cent; α is labor's share in the value of net output, and β is $1 - \alpha$, or capital's share; apportionment of output change is in per cent.

Table 4

Selected Growth Rates by Manufacturing Sector, Britain and Germany,
1951–1962 (per cent per annum)

Sector	Britain			Germany		
	Exports Value	Output Volume	"Residual"	Exports[a] Value	Output Volume	"Residual"
Food, drink, and tobacco	3.0	2.5	0.2	13.2	7.3	3.9
Refining and chemicals	6.9	5.5	1.7	12.6	10.8	4.8
Iron and steel	6.8	1.4	−0.7	8.8	5.7	2.3
Nonferrous metals	7.6	1.7	−0.4	10.6	6.6	1.8
Engineering	5.9	3.0	1.0	13.6	8.4	2.5
Vehicles and aircraft	3.9	4.6	2.5	20.4	14.2	6.5
Textiles	−5.7	−0.8	0.8	5.8	4.0	2.6
Leather, fur, and clothing	−1.1	1.4	2.0	16.2	7.0	3.8
Bricks, pottery, and glass	0.3	2.5	0.9	8.0	6.9	2.7
Timber and furniture	10.1	1.0	1.1	10.9	5.2	4.1
Paper, printing, and publishing	4.1	3.4	1.2	6.0	7.2	2.6
Other	0.9	3.4	1.4	16.3	12.5	3.5
Manufacturing industry	3.6	2.7	1.1	12.9	8.0	3.6

Source: See Appendix.
[a] Adjusted for 1961 revaluation of the Deutsche mark.

textiles the lowest. (See Table 4.) This suggests a structural parallel with British output, and, in fact, the rank correlation of sectors' output growth between the two countries was statistically significant ($\tau = .78$, for 1951–1962 rankings). Furthermore, the measure of labor's share in the value of net output was almost the same in both countries. The difference between the two countries was thus largely one of scale. German output simply grew faster across the board.

Labor input in Germany rose at a substantially higher rate than in Britain and accounted for considerably more of the change in output. Employment rose between 1951 and 1962 at an average annual rate of 4.0 per cent, but average hours worked declined at a rate of 1.2 per cent. Man-hour input rose faster during the early years when large-scale unemployment—resulting mainly from the huge influx of refugees—was being wiped out, and when the tendency for average hours to decline had not become marked. Unemployment dropped from 10.2 per cent of the labor force in 1951 to 0.4 per cent in 1962, and by the late 1950's the labor market had become very tight. The tightness occurred despite increasing use of foreign workers, who accounted for 4.4 per cent of manufacturing employees by September 1963.[26] As in Britain, the pace of wage increases accelerated with the drop in enemployment and the increase in unfilled vacancies.[27] In contrast to British unions, however, German labor unions were noted for their lack of aggressiveness in raising wages and for their acceptance of new working methods, etc.[28] Certainly, the pace of German wage increases was more in line with the rise of productivity than was the case in Britain.

Capital input grew almost twice as fast in Germany as in Britain, although it directly accounted for less of the change in output. Much of this increase, especially in the earlier years, was needed to provide plant and equipment for new employees, but the emphasis gradually turned toward rationalization (i.e., equipment to reduce the need for new employees and to incorporate technical improvements).[29] The rapid increase in German capital was facilitated by the destruction during World War II and the dismantling thereafter. Krengel points out that this loss prematurely retired much plant and equipment,[30] thus permitting use of a higher percentage of gross investment for net new, as opposed to replacement, investment; it was an important factor in speeding the modernization of German capital stock. The capital increase was also facilitated by the lesser proportion of national income accounted for by consumption. Gilbert has calculated German consumption with U.S. quantity weights as 66 per cent of gross national product in 1950 and

[26] "Die Beschäftigung ausländischer Arbeitskräfte in Deutschland 1882 bis 1963," *Wirtschaft und Statistik* (February 1963), 93–95.

[27] See H. Scherf, "Zur Frage der Beziehungen zwischen Löhnen und Preisen in der Bundesrepublik Deutschland 1951 bis 1961," *Weltwirtschaftliches Archiv*, Vol. 93 (1964), 44–78. Scherf, in a time-series study, related wage rates to the cost of living, the percentage of unemployment, and a "political" factor (zero up to 1953, one thereafter); he also related wage drift to average hours worked and labor productivity, and related the cost of living to earnings rates and import prices.

[28] United Nations, Economic Commission for Europe, *Some Factors in Economic Growth in Europe during the 1950's*; Part 2 of the *Economic Survey of Europe in 1961* (Geneva: United Nations, 1964), pp. VI-2 and VI-3.

[29] Yearly surveys conducted by the Munich I.F.O.-Institut für Wirtschaftsforschung from 1955 to 1958 revealed that German firms placed increasing emphasis on rationalization and less on capacity expansion as time progressed. See B. R. Williams, *International Report on Factors in Investment Behavior* (Paris: OECD, 1962), pp. VII.5 and VII.9.

[30] R. Krengel, "Some Reasons for the Rapid Economic Growth of the German Federal Republic," *Banca Nazionale del Lavoro*, *Quarterly Review*, LXIV (March 1963), 121–44.

63 per cent in 1955. Comparable British rates were 73 per cent and 68 per cent.[31] In contrast to Britain, Germany could thus both invest and export.

The total German fixed investment in manufacturing over the period was nonetheless not strikingly larger than Britain's. The German total in 1955 prices was $27–28 billion, depending on whether the conversion rate used dates from before or after the 1961 revaluation; British investment in 1955 prices totaled between $24 billion and $25 billion, depending on whether the conversion rate is in terms of current dollars or the OEEC index of purchasing power.[32] About 80 per cent of German fixed investment went into plant and machinery and about 20 per cent into buildings. (The dividing line between plant and buildings is, of course, somewhat arbitrary.) These proportions are closely comparable to those for Britain, where approximately 75 per cent of fixed investment was for plant and machinery and 25 per cent for buildings. In both countries, the increase in the capital stock was generally in sectors with the more rapid increases in output and exports. These relations were statistically stronger in the German case, but too much should not be made of this comparison because of the statistical weakness of capital measures.

According to Krengel's data, German capital utilization in manufacturing reached a peak in 1955 and remained, with some variation, quite high thereafter.[33] The restoration of plant and equipment that had been impaired by World War II and its aftermath brought rapid gains in output with relatively small investment, and aided in reducing the pool of unemployed labor.

Manufacturing productivity, as measured by the "residual," grew in Germany at somewhat more than three times the rate in Britain during the period, although there was a tendency for the German rate to decelerate as the period progressed. The "residual" accounted for approximately the same proportion of output growth as in Britain, and the rank correlation of British and German manufacturing sectors by size of

[31] Gilbert, *Comparative National Products*, pp. 86–87.

[32] The German total is not changed by use of the OEEC purchasing-power index for conversion. The source of this OEEC index is: Gilbert, *Comparative National Products*, p. 56. Data for German investment in Deutsche marks came from data prepared by Krengel and published in the *Vierteljahrshefte zur Wirtschaftsforschung* (first issue 1961, and fourth issue 1963). Data for British investment, in pounds, came from United Kingdom, Central Statistical Office, *National Income and Expenditure*.

[33] R. Krengel, "Produktionsvolumen und Produktions Faktoren der Industrie im Gebiet der Bundesrepublik Deutschland," *Vierteljahrshefte zur Wirtschaftsforschung* (fourth issue, 1964), 367.

"residual" was statistically significant ($\tau = .61$, for 1951–1962). This is additional evidence that manufacturing growth in Germany was structurally similar to that in Britain. This similarity may have been an important reason for the statistical insignificance of cross-sectional regressions relating relative export performance in 1951–62 to relative changes in productivity for the same period. Nevertheless, as discussed above, the generally faster growth of German productivity probably was a significant factor underlying superior German export performance.

There are three major identifiable reasons why German productivity grew at a much faster rate than British productivity: the German increase in utilized capacity, the faster German modernization of capital stock, and German labor and management attitudes favorable to economic growth.

The advance to fuller capacity operation between 1951 and 1954 added almost a full percentage point to the average annual growth rate of the "residual" for this subperiod, and "residual" progress was highest in the sectors with the largest increases in capacity utilization ($\tau = .79$, for 1951–1954). Change in utilization also appears to account for the statistically significant relation between sector rankings by output change and by the size of the "residual." If the "residual" is calculated with utilized capital rather than total capital, the rank correlation between output and the "residual," although still positive, is reduced to statistical insignificance.[34] The relation between output and productivity may have been further complicated by economies of scale. The ranking of sectors by "residual" calculated with utilized capital was significantly related to sector rankings by a crude measure of economies of scale, the growth rate of output per firm ($\tau = .64$, for 1951–1954).

Although the benefits from the increase in capacity utilization were primarily limited to the early years of the 1951–1962 period, rapid modernization probably played a continuing role. The faster modernization of German capital stock was the result of both higher gross investment and the use of a larger proportion of this gross investment for net new investment. Data are inadequate to make a detailed statistical analysis of the rate of modernization and its contribution to productivity, but some idea can be gained by a comparison of Dean's and Krengel's

---

[34] Correlation between rankings by output and the "residual" calculated with total capital resulted in a τ of .65 for 1951–1954, and a τ of .52 for 1954–1959. Ranking by the "residual" calculated with utilized capital reduced τ to .30 and .15 for the respective subperiods.

estimates of the age of the manufacturing capital stock in Britain and Germany, respectively.[35] At the beginning of 1957, 55 per cent of the capital stock in the German consumer-goods sectors and 61 per cent in the investment-goods sectors was of post-World War II vintage. By as late as the end of 1961, the British capital stock was not yet this modern. At that time, 50 per cent of the capital stock in the British consumer-goods sectors and 46 per cent in the investment-goods sectors were of post-World War II vintage.

A third major German advantage was the favorable attitude of labor and management. Wallich has described Germany as "production oriented," and Mendershausen noted German trust in the social order.[36] Attitudes in Germany may have stemmed from a simple desire to rebuild an economy broken by war. They may have been reinforced, however, by bitter memories of the inflation that followed World War I[37] and by relatively high unemployment before the late 1950's.

Faster German output growth in conjunction with increasing international competitiveness was thus principally the result of circumstances: those stemming from World War II and its aftermath, such as capital loss, the low capacity utilization of capital, and the influx of refugees. Other factors, such as acceptance of a relatively low percentage of national income devoted to consumption and attitudes favorable to growth and export sales, were presumably also influenced by the War's aftermath. Although this view of German performance makes official policy measures a secondary explanation, economic policy played an important, although perhaps not completely conscious, role.

Monetary policy was the primary policy tool. The German money supply rose at a rapid and steady annual rate of about 14 per cent during the period.[38] This expansion allowed the domestic economy to advance

[35] G. Dean, "Stock of Fixed Capital," and R. Krengel, *Anlagevermögen, Produktion und Beschäftigung der Industrie im Gebiet der Bundesrepublik von 1924 bis 1956*: Deutsches Institut für Wirtschaftsforschung, Sonderheft, New Series No. 42 (Berlin: Duncker & Humblot, 1958), pp. 52–53.

[36] H. C. Wallich, *Mainsprings of the German Revival* (New Haven: Yale University Press, 1962), p. 31; Mendershausen, *Two Postwar Recoveries of the German Economy* (Amsterdam: North-Holland Publishing Co., 1966), p. 60.

[37] On this point, see J. W. Angell, *The Recovery of Germany* (New Haven: Yale University Press, 1929); and Mendershausen, *Two Postwar Recoveries*.

[38] The money supply is defined as note and coin circulation excluding credit institutions' cash holdings, plus deposits (sight, time, and saving) of other German financial institutions. The series was constructed so as to avoid distortion from inclusion of the Saar. Deutsche Bundesbank, *Monthly Report*, XVII (February 1965), 34.

at a rapid pace. Two facts about the monetary expansion are especially noteworthy. The first is that the 1948 currency reform severely reduced the stock of money. As a result, income velocity at the beginning was quite high. By 1962, expansion of the money supply brought income velocity to about the same level as in Britain, where velocity had been rising.[39] The second is that the steady growth of the money supply occurred despite recurrent periods of tight monetary policy.

Maddison has noted the quick German enforcement of monetary restraint when inflation loomed,[40] and monetary discipline was one of the fundamental principles of the current official political philosophy, *soziale Marktwirtschaft*.[41] Indeed, the avowed principal aim of German monetary authorities was price stability.[42] Monetary policy apparently had an important effect on the German economy, for the yearly percentage range around the average rate of national product growth was wider in Germany than in Britain, where "stop-go" policies have come under heavy criticism. German restrictions had the salutary effect of aiding its international competitiveness by inhibiting the rise in prices and assuring that there was generally sufficient available capacity to meet both home and export demands. Even so, high domestic demand in boom years apparently had an adverse effect on export performance.[43]

The almost complete reliance on monetary measures for anticyclical policy attracted funds from abroad which, when added to the domestic money supply, reduced the effectiveness of monetary restrictions; this dilemma led to revaluation in 1961. A better balance between fiscal and monetary policy might have reduced Germany's balance-of-payments surpluses and might have been even more effective in restraining inflation.

---

[39] Calculated as the ratio of gross national product in current market prices to the money supply. The British money supply was defined as average estimated circulation of notes and coin with the public plus gross deposit liabilities of London clearing banks, Scottish banks, and Northern Ireland banks. United Kingdom Central Statistical Office, *Annual Abstract of Statistics*, 1964, Tables 345–48, and 1962, Tables 330, 331, and 336. For Irish bank deposit liabilities, United Kingdom, Committee on the Working of the Monetary System, *Principal Memoranda of Evidence*, Vol. 2 (London: HMSO, 1960), Statistical Appendix, Table 4.

[40] Maddison, *Economic Growth*, p. 138.

[41] P. Boarman, *Germany's Economic Dilemma* (New Haven and London: Yale University Press, 1964), p. 22.

[42] J. Hein, "The Mainsprings of German Monetary Policy," *Economia Internazionale*, XVII (May 1964), 317–24.

[43] This is the conclusion of the Sachverständigenrat zur Begutachtung der gesamtwirtschaftlichen Entwicklung. See its *Jahresgutachten 1964–65, Stabiles Geld-stetiges Wachstum* (Stuttgart and Mainz: W. Kohlhammer GmbH, 1965), p. 6.

British experience, at least, seems to have shown that fiscal restriction is often more effective than monetary policy in restraining domestic demand.[44]

Fiscal measures in Germany probably did exert an important influence in favor of economic growth. On the expenditure side, fiscal policy included investment in bottleneck industries (aided by Marshall Plan funds) and in social overhead projects. The latter type of investment was especially necessary because of wartime destruction and the large influx of unemployed refugees. On the revenue side, tax concessions for investment were an important source of investment funds in manufacturing.[45] There is, however, some controversy concerning the consciousness of German fiscal actions relating to economic growth. Reuss alleges that these policies were deliberately aimed at economic growth, but Senf, examining the revenue side, denies any conscious policy to this end.[46]

Another aspect of German economic policy, the encouragement of economic competition, has been credited by Sohmen, Boarman, Hennessy, and others with being a major factor underlying German economic performance.[47] "Freedom in the realm of goods" was, along with monetary discipline, one of the principal elements of the social market philosophy, but it is difficult to judge the extent to which market conditions were freer in Germany than in other countries, and the degree to which such

[44] P. B. Kenen, in *British Monetary Policy and the Balance of Payments 1951–57* (Cambridge, Massachusetts: Harvard University Press, 1960), p. 247, concluded that the orthodox "credit squeeze" may accomplish little, because investment demand may prove extremely inelastic and credit rationing may not cause spending to decline. The Radcliffe Committee suggested that one reason why monetary policy was not so effective was that monetary changes did not always substantially affect long-term interest rates; United Kingdom, Committee on the Working of the Monetary System, *Report* (London: HMSO, 1959), p. 178. Dow argued that direct controls, such as those over hire-purchase and capital issues, are the more effective forms of financial restriction [J. C. R. Dow, *The Management of the British Economy 1945–60* (Cambridge: Cambridge University Press, 1964), p. 329].

[45] K. Haüser, "West Germany," in a Conference Report of the National Bureau of Economic Research and the Brookings Institution, *Foreign Tax Policies and Economic Growth* (New York: National Bureau of Economic Research, 1966), p. 117; and K. W. Roskamp, *Capital Formation in West Germany* (Detroit: Wayne State University Press, 1965), p. 162.

[46] R. G. Reuss, *Fiscal Policy for Growth without Inflation. The German Experiment* (Baltimore: The Johns Hopkins Press, 1963), p. 2; P. Senf, Discussion of Haüser's "West Germany," pp. 160–62.

[47] E. Sohmen, "Competition and Growth: The Lesson of West Germany," *American Economic Review*, XLIX (December 1959), 986–1003; Boarman, *Germany's Economic Dilemma*; and J. Hennessy, "The German Miracle," in *Economic "Miracles"* (London: The Institute of Economic Affairs; Andre Deutsch Ltd., 1964), pp. 1–73.

conditions might have favored German economic growth. Wallich has cited the inclination of German managers to form cartels rather than to compete aggressively in the home market,[48] and the many other reasons advanced above for faster German growth appear sufficient to account for at least most of the more successful German economic performance.

CONCLUSION

Given the circumstances in the United Kingdom during this period, it is highly improbable that British producers could have increased their production at anything like the German rate. Labor was scarce, and vacancies outstripped unemployment; the relatively high proportion of national product devoted to consumption, as well as the need to export, limited the amount of national product that could be allocated to enlarging and modernizing industrial capacity; and "backward" attitudes of labor and management further limited productivity advances. Owing to these limitations, overexpansion of demand during periods of "go" led to rapid wage and import increases. Productivity was raised as industrial capacity came closer to its potential maximum, but there is doubt that the gain was more than temporary. The ensuing relatively rapid rise in British prices and a lack of export aggressiveness were important factors which inhibited the growth of British exports, and they helped bring about an important decline in the British share of world exports of manufactures.

In contrast with the United Kingdom, Germany had a number of enormous advantages. The huge influx of population immediately after World War II—including many workers with valuable skills—and the additional flows before construction of the Berlin Wall provided a great source of new employees. The existence of this labor force also permitted a rapid industrial expansion without an inordinate rise in wages or prices, and provided new demand for industrial output. Industrial growth was also aided by the much larger proportion of German national product that could be devoted to investment. Primarily because consumption was a smaller proportion of national product and defense expenditures did not swell the government's share, Germany could both export and invest. Owing to wartime destruction and post-World War II dismantling, more investment was devoted to new expansion, and

[48] Wallich, *Mainsprings*, pp. 213–16, 336.

manufacturing capacity was much more rapidly modernized. German price competitiveness and export aggressiveness brought fast export gains and an enlarged German share in world exports of manufactures. Largely because of this export growth, the expansion of demand could proceed without a balance-of-payments constraint.

It seems clear that the more successful German performance was in significant part the result of "special" factors. This view is reinforced by the narrowing German advantage as the German labor market and industrial capacity became tight. Nevertheless, at least one general policy conclusion emerges from the British-German comparison. Economic authorities should attempt to keep domestic demand from approaching the capacity limitations of the domestic economy. These limits and the extent to which they can be approached without adverse consequences may vary from country to country. But the risk of deteriorating international competitiveness is great enough to outweigh the seemingly temporary benefits to output and productivity which come from overly rapid advances in domestic activity. Economic growth and export performance can, and must, advance together.

APPENDIX

TABLE 1: EVIDENCE OF INTERNATIONAL COMPETITIVENESS

a. *Manufacturing exports.* German data are for the export sales of larger industrial firms. They were adjusted in 1959 by the ratio of *beteiligten* gross turnover to *hauptbeteiligten*, owing to a change in the published data. The series was linked in 1960, figures prior to that time being published without the Saar and figures subsequent to that time being published with the Saar. Data are from the *Statistisches Jahrbuch*. British data have been assembled from figures published in the *Accounts Relating to Trade and Navigation of the United Kingdom*, Table II. They include food, drink, and tobacco manufactures.

b. *Manufacturing prices.* German export prices were calculated by combining indices of export price change for individual groups of manufactures by net output weights for 1954. German producer prices based on 1950 were linked in 1959 to 1958-based prices. The indices for sectors were combined with 1954 net output weights. Data are from the *Statistisches Jahrbuch*. British wholesale prices are from the *Board of Trade Journal* and the *Annual Abstract of Statistics*.

c. *Labor productivity in manufacturing* is the change in the ratio of manufacturing output to hours worked.

German output is the index of net industrial production. The individual series for this index were shifted from their original 1950 base to a 1954 base and aggregated with net output weights for 1954. Hours worked is the product of employment and average hours worked. Employment indices were constructed from industrial data for larger firms (10 or more employers). For 1962, the number of employees in the Saar was subtracted from the total for Germany including the Saar. Average hours worked were computed by dividing the number of hours actually worked by the the average number of workers—both series for the larger industrial firms. For 1951, the number of workers for larger industrial firms was not published. It was therefore necessary to estimate the number of workers by taking the proportion of workers to total employees as determined in the 1951 census. For 1962, both the hours worked and the average number of workers included the Saar. Data are from the *Statistisches Jahrbuch*.

British output is from the industrial production index. Where necessary, series have been linked and sectors combined with 1954 net output weights. Data are from the *Annual Abstract of Statistics*. Employment was based on the 1948 Standard Industrial Classification for the years 1951, 1954, and 1959. The 1962 figures, based on the 1958 SIC, were linked with the 1948 series in 1959. Employment figures are midyear national insurance accounts from which the yearly average of unemployed persons has been deducted. The average of April and October figures for average hours worked per operative, adjusted for the general change in paid holidays between 1951 and 1954, form the basis for the average hours worked. Data for employment net hours are from the *Ministry of Labour Gazette*. Holiday data are from the Ministry of Labour and National Service, *Time Rates of Wages and Hours of Labour*.

d. Manufacturing hourly labor payments. The German series was calculated from the ratio of total wages and salaries to total hours worked. The source of both figures is industrial data from the *Statistisches Jahrbuch*. The British series is the change in the ratio of total wages and salary payments to hours worked. The hours worked are described above. Total wages and salaries are from *National Income and Expenditure*.

TABLES 2 AND 3: MANUFACTURING OUTPUT, INPUTS, AND PRODUCTIVITY

a. Output was calculated as described above.

b. α is the ratio of wages and salaries paid to net output in 1954. The value of wages and salaries for Germany was estimated by multiplying total employment (including handicraft workers) by average labor payments per employee and by a factor representing employer social security contributions. Total employment was given by the 1954 census for industrial firms, but it was necessary to estimate handicraft employment for 1954 on the basis of the 1950 and 1956 censuses of the handicraft sector. Average labor payments per employee were computed by summing wages and salaries actually paid in 1954 and by dividing this figure by the number of employees, both series for larger industrial firms. The adjustment factor for employer social security contributions was based on data for the entire economy, not only the manufacturing sector. Net output was calculated by adjusting the national income account figure for manufacturing to approximate factor cost. The value of wages and salaries for Britain was determined by figuring the average labor payment and multiplying this payment by the number of employees, including self-employed. These series for 1954 were from the Board of Trade, *Report on the Census of Production for 1958*, Part 133, Table 3 (London: HMSO, 1962), pp. 33–47. This product was then further adjusted for employers' contributions to wages and salaries for all manufacturing industry based on the *National Income and Expenditure* accounts, as was the value of net output.

c. *Labor* is the man-hours series described for Table 1.

d. β is $1 - \alpha$.

e. *Capital* is an estimate of the change in real gross fixed capital. For Germany, the estimates are calculated from figures prepared by R. Krengel and published periodically in the *Vierteljahrshefte zur Wirtschaftsforschung*. The Krengel series without the Saar were linked to the series with the Saar in 1960. For Britain, the estimate is calculated by combining estimates made by T. Barna for the capital stock in buildings and plant in mid-1955 with national income estimates of gross fixed-capital formation in buildings and plant for previous and subsequent years. The Barna data are described in his article, "The Replacement Cost of Fixed Assets in British Manufacturing Industry in 1955," *Journal of the Royal Statistical Society*, Series A, CXX, Part I (1957), 1–47. The estimates of capital formation were taken from *National Income and Expenditure*, and were deflated to constant prices by implicit indexes, one for plant and machinery and another for buildings and works.

f. The "*residual*" was calculated for both countries as the difference between the rate of growth of output and the weighted sum of the rates of growth of labor and capital inputs.

TABLE 4: SELECTED GROWTH RATES BY MANUFACTURING SECTOR

These rates were derived as explained for Table 1 (exports and output) and Tables 2 and 3 (the "residual").

J. DIRCK STRYKER

The Sources of Change in
Export Performance:
The United States and Canada

THE RELATIONSHIP OF LABOR PRODUCTIVITY, wages, and unit costs to the structure of United States and United Kingdom exports has been investigated by MacDougall,[1] Stern,[2] and Balassa.[3] This study extends this type of analysis to include the role of capital inputs as well as that of labor inputs. In addition, the importance of differences in technology, economies or diseconomies of scale, and relative factor prices is investigated.

The assistance of the members of the Statistics Division, U.S. Internal Revenue Service, who provided some of the data used in this study is gratefully acknowledged.

[1] G. D. A. MacDougall, "British and American Exports: A Study Suggested by the Theory of Comparative Cost, Part I," *Economic Journal*, LXI (December 1951), 697–724; "British and American Exports: A Study Suggested by the Theory of Comparative Costs, Part II," *Economic Journal*, LXII (September 1952), 487–521.

[2] Robert Stern, "British and American Productivity and Comparative Costs in International Trade," *Oxford Economic Papers*, XIV (October 1962), 275–96.

[3] Bela Balassa, "An Empirical Demonstration of Classical Comparative Cost Theory," *Review of Economics and Statistics*, XLV (August 1963), 231–38.

Furthermore, this study is concerned primarily with changes in the productivity, factor-price, and export variables over time, whereas previous work has used data for a series of single years. The time period covered here is 1949–1962; the countries considered are the United States and Canada.

The first part develops a two-country, partial-equilibrium model which explores some of the factors underlying international price competition and sets forth the hypotheses to be tested later. The second part discusses the statistical tests employed and mentions some of the principal problems involved in their use. Next, the empirical results are discussed. Finally, a Statistical Appendix provides information concerning the sources of data and a series of tables which underlie the text.

THE THEORETICAL MODEL

Consider two countries, the United States and Canada, which sell to each other and to an outside world at a common set of international prices. Suppose that the demand and supply curves of the outside world are perfectly elastic. Each country is assumed to produce a variety of products, some quantity of each product being produced in each country. The production functions are assumed to be of the form:

$$O = AL^\alpha K^\beta + R \qquad (1)$$

where O is the quantity of output produced; L is labor input; K is capital input; R is raw material input; A is a proportionality parameter; α and β are the elasticity coefficients of value added ($V = O - R$) with respect to labor and capital, respectively.[4]

Initially, it is assumed that the manufacturing production function is subject to constant returns (i.e., $\beta = 1 - \alpha$). Labor and capital are each assumed to be homogeneous, with capital earning rental payments similar to the wages of labor. Raw materials are obtained from outside the manufacturing sector and are assumed, initially, to be supplied solely by domestic sources. It is supposed that the production of raw materials is subject to decreasing returns.

Perfect competition is assumed to prevail in all markets, and all firms are assumed to be in long-run equilibrium, so that a single set of factor prices faces each industry within a given country. But there are barriers

[4] V is used here and throughout to represent real value added.

to factor mobility between countries, and there are differences in factor prices between countries.[5]

We may imagine that each industry's supply curve consists of two parts. The average cost of manufactured value added is constant, and thus equal to the marginal cost of value added. Thus, if the cost to the industry of its raw materials inputs were constant, the supply curve of the industry

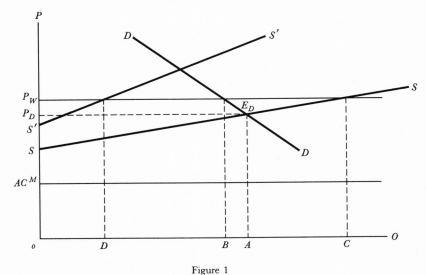

Figure 1

would be perfectly elastic.[6] But it is assumed that the production of raw materials is subject to increasing cost. Hence the average cost of final output from the manufacturing industry will rise as output expands. With perfect competition in the product market, product price will be an increasing function of output; the supply curve will be upward sloping to the right.[7]

Figure 1 illustrates the case of an individual industry before and after the opening of trade. P_W is the world price at which the product can be

[5] Factor-price equalization will not occur through trade, since the assumptions necessary for this condition are not fulfilled. For example, the parameters of the production functions are assumed to differ between countries.

[6] This also assumes that there are no nonpecuniary economies or diseconomies of scale which are external to the firm but internal to the industry.

[7] It is assumed here that the raw materials for each industry are partly or wholly specific to the industry, so that an expansion of final output results in a substantially increased demand for the raw materials used in that industry. Furthermore, the type of production function assumed does not allow the substitution of capital or labor for raw materials in the production process.

exported or imported, assuming, initially, zero transportation costs. Average cost in the manufacturing sector, excluding raw material costs, is given by AC^M. The supply curve of the industry, SS, is the vertical sum of this cost and raw material costs for each quantity of output produced. The domestic demand curve is represented by DD.

Before the opening of trade, the economy produces and consumes at E_D. The domestic price P_D is less than P_W, so that, with the opening of trade, the country is able to export this product. Total production will be oC, with oB being consumed at home and BC exported.

Supply curve $S'S'$ indicates the case of a product which is imported after the opening of trade. The quantity oD is produced and consumed at home, while DB is imported for domestic consumption. Note that one cannot infer whether the product is being imported or exported merely by examining the post-trade price. It is only from pre-trade prices that the pattern of trade can be predicted.

The usual practice at this juncture is to relax the assumption of zero transportation costs.[8] Let us assume that the world price is the price prevailing abroad. The domestic demand curve for the good produced overseas will then be shifted downward, and the supply curve facing the foreign market will be shifted upward, by the amount of the transportation cost. The results are depicted in Figure 2. If the industry supply curve at home is SS, then exports will be GE instead of BC. If the supply curve is $S'S'$, imports will be HF, not DB.

If these two supply curves are the industry supply curves for our two countries, the United States and Canada, and if we assume that domestic demand conditions are the same in the two countries (represented by a single demand curve in the diagram), a knowledge of post-trade domestic prices allows us to predict which country is exporting and which is importing the product. But notice that we cannot predict the quantity of goods traded. Consider a product which both countries export to the outside world. In Figure 3, the supply curve S_{US} is below the curve S_{Ca} for the same quantities of product. With identical demand conditions in the two countries, the exports of the United States, AC, exceed the exports of Canada, AB.[9]

[8] Jagdish Bhagwati, "The Pure Theory of International Trade: A Survey," reprinted in *Surveys of Economic Theory, Vol. II: Growth and Development* (New York: St. Martin's Press, 1965), p. 164.

[9] This conclusion does not depend in any way on the particular assumptions made to explain why the supply curves are upward-sloping. It depends only on the assumptions that they are of this general shape, that world demand is infinitely elastic, and that transportation costs are the same for both countries.

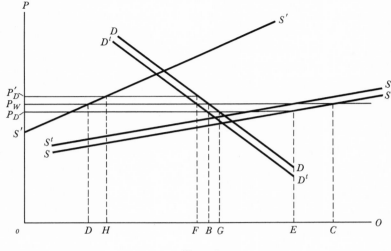

Figure 2

But because we have assumed constant returns to scale in the manufacturing sector, we should be able to predict, albeit roughly, relative
export quantities by examining the differences in average costs at this
stage of the production process. As an extreme case, assume that the
supply functions for raw materials are precisely the same in the two
countries. If domestic demand conditions are also the same, it can be

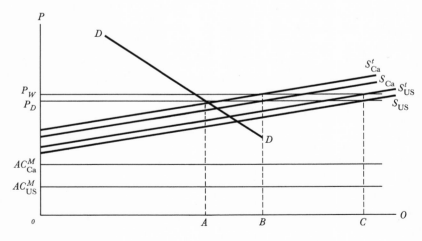

Figure 3

seen from Figure 3 that the difference in export quantities depends only on the difference in average costs in manufacturing.

It is not even necessary to assume identical supply functions for raw materials, but only to relax the previous assumption of international immobility of these materials so as to permit trade in raw materials and intermediate products. If both countries have access to material inputs at the same set of international prices, the relative prices of final products will be determined solely by relative costs in the manufacturing sectors. The assumption that each country pays the same prices for raw materials is not very realistic, however, if transportation costs are large relative to the value of the materials. A country with abundant supplies of raw materials may have a strong comparative advantage in the production of goods that are intensive in the use of these inputs.[10] For this reason, and for others elaborated later, the relationship between exports and manufacturing costs will be formulated not in terms of levels, but in terms of relative rates of change over time.

Allowance for trade in raw materials and intermediate products causes the quantity of exports of each country to be indeterminate, since the supply curve of each final product is now perfectly elastic. One way of avoiding this problem is to assume that there is a difference between the post-trade domestic price and the foreign price of each good. This price differential is assumed to persist because at least some producers require a positive monetary incentive to overcome the risks and additional costs involved in marketing their products abroad.[11] Furthermore, it is assumed that producers vary in their willingness to take risks and in their knowledge of overseas markets. The supply of exports of a particular product is thus some positive function of the ratio of the foreign to the domestic price of the product. For a given country, this relationship may be written in the following way:

$$\frac{dX/dt}{X} = E \cdot \frac{[d(P_W/P_D)]/dt}{P_W/P_D} = E\left[\frac{dP_W/dt}{P_W} - \frac{dP_D/dt}{P_D}\right] \qquad (2)$$

where E is the supply elasticity of exports with respect to this price ratio and is assumed to be a constant and equal for both countries. The difference in the relative growth rates of exports between the two countries

[10] This is a very important consideration in the case of Canada, for which the proportion of raw materials and semifinished products in total exports is quite large.

[11] Charles P. Kindleberger, *Foreign Trade and the National Economy* (New Haven: Yale University Press, 1962), pp. 15–20.

is, then, a function of the difference between the relative rates of change of domestic prices:

$$\left(\frac{dX/dt}{X}\right)_{US} - \left(\frac{dX/dt}{X}\right)_{Ca} = E\left[\left(\frac{dP_D/dt}{P_D}\right)_{Ca} - \left(\frac{dP_D/dt}{P_D}\right)_{US}\right] \tag{3}$$

If the ratio of the average manufacturing cost to the average cost of material inputs is roughly the same in the two countries and the final product price is equal to the sum of these two components of total cost, this relationship can be approximated by the following equation:

$$\left(\frac{dX/dt}{X}\right)_{US} - \left(\frac{dX/dt}{X}\right)_{Ca} = E\left[\left(\frac{dAC^M/dt + dAC^R/dt}{P_D}\right)_{Ca}\right.$$

$$\left. - \left(\frac{dAC^M/dt + dAC^R/dt}{P_D}\right)_{US}\right] = E\left(\frac{AC^M}{P_D}\right)\left[\left(\frac{dAC^M/dt}{AC^M}\right)_{Ca} - \left(\frac{dAC^M/dt}{AC^M}\right)_{US}\right]$$

$$+ E\left(\frac{AC^R}{P_D}\right)\left[\left(\frac{dAC^R/dt}{AC^R}\right)_{Ca} - \left(\frac{dAC^R/dt}{AC^R}\right)_{US}\right] \tag{4}$$

where AC^R is the average cost of material inputs. If the relative rates of change of these input costs are equal, the last term of equation (4) drops out.

Consider, now, the production of a single product in a single country. Focusing our attention on the manufacturing component of average cost, we may write this as $AC^M = [wL + rK]/V \cdot (V/O)$, where w is the wage of labor, and r is the rental return to capital. We can then multiply and divide through by $L^\alpha K^{(1-\alpha)}$ to obtain:

$$AC^M = \frac{L^\alpha K^{(1-\alpha)}}{V} \cdot \frac{wL + rK}{L^\alpha K^{(1-\alpha)}} \cdot \frac{V}{O} \tag{5}$$

From equation (1) and our assumption of constant returns, the first term of this expression is equal to $1/A$. Furthermore, we may assume that differences in A indicate differences in technology, or in the effective use of technology, which are factor-neutral in the Hicksian sense.[12] The

---

[12] Hicksian neutrality means that differences in technology do not affect the ratio of the marginal products of capital and labor. Since α and $(1 - \alpha)$ are parameters of the production function which do not change with neutral differences in technology, an increase of technology which, for example, doubles the marginal products of capital and labor will also double the average products of capital and labor $[\alpha = (\partial V/\partial L) \cdot (L/V)$, $(1 - \alpha) = (\partial V/\partial K) \cdot (K/V)$, where both α and $(1 - \alpha)$ are held constant]. This, in turn, can be treated as a twofold increase in A.

second term in (5) is the total labor and capital cost of manufacturing divided by a geometrically weighted average of inputs. The final term is simply the ratio of value added to total output, reflecting the fact that average cost in the manufacturing sector refers to total output, not merely to that part of total output which is generated at this stage.

With some additional algebraic manipulation, we can show that:

$$\frac{wL + rK}{L^{\alpha}K^{(1-\alpha)}} = r \cdot \left(\frac{K}{L}\right)^{\alpha}\left(\frac{wL}{rK} + 1\right) \tag{6}$$

With perfect competition in the factor markets, the long-run equilibrium production technique chosen by the firm will equate the ratio of marginal products to the ratio of factor prices. Therefore, the ratio of the coefficients α and $(1 - \alpha)$ will equal the ratio of total wage payments to total rental payments:

$$\frac{\alpha}{1 - \alpha} = \frac{\partial V/\partial L}{\partial V/\partial K} \cdot \frac{L/V}{K/V} = \frac{w \cdot L}{r \cdot K} \tag{7}$$

Furthermore:

$$\frac{K}{L} = \frac{w}{r} \cdot \frac{(1 - \alpha)}{\alpha} \tag{8}$$

Substituting (7) and (8) into (6):

$$\frac{wL + rK}{L^{\alpha}K^{(1-\alpha)}} = r\left(\frac{w}{r} \cdot \frac{(1 - \alpha)}{\alpha}\right)^{\alpha}\left(\frac{\alpha}{1 - \alpha} + 1\right) \tag{9}$$

Additional algebra yields the following:

$$\frac{wL + rK}{L^{\alpha}K^{(1-\alpha)}} = r \cdot \left(\frac{w}{r}\right)^{\alpha}\left(\frac{1}{\alpha^{\alpha} \cdot (1 - \alpha)^{(1-\alpha)}}\right) \tag{10}$$

Substituting equation (10) into equation (5), we obtain:

$$AC^{M} = \frac{L^{\alpha}K^{(1-\alpha)}}{V} \cdot r \cdot \left(\frac{w}{r}\right)^{\alpha} \cdot \left(\frac{1}{\alpha^{\alpha} \cdot (1 - \alpha)^{(1-\alpha)}}\right) \cdot \frac{V}{O} \tag{11}$$

The second term, r, of this expression gives us the effect of the general level of factor prices on average costs in manufacturing. The third term shows the influence of the factor-price ratio. It should be noted that the latter effect depends not only on the factor price ratio itself but also on the relative size of the coefficients α and $(1 - \alpha)$.[13] The expression $r(w/r)^{\alpha}$

[13] This is true despite the fact that, with the Cobb-Douglas type of production function, we are implicitly assuming an elasticity of substitution equal to unity.

is entirely symmetrical:

$$r\left(\frac{w}{r}\right)^{\alpha} = r^{(1-\alpha)} \cdot w^{(\alpha-1)+1} = w\left(\frac{r}{w}\right)^{(1-\alpha)}$$

The fourth term of the expression depends solely on the relative values of the elasticity coefficients. It indicates that, the greater the imbalance in the size of the coefficients, the greater will be the output produced, all other things being equal.

At this point, the assumption of constant returns in the manufacturing sector can be relaxed to allow for economies or diseconomies of scale. These scale effects are industry-wide and may consist, wholly or in part, of economies or diseconomies which are external to the firm but internal to the industry. If all scale effects are external to the firm, our other assumptions continue to hold without difficulty. But if some economies or diseconomies are internal to the firm, some theoretical questions arise. If the firms in certain industries experience increasing returns, is the assumption of perfect competition at all reasonable? If decreasing returns are experienced, why should any firm produce above minimum average cost, since other firms can enter the industry and produce at lower cost? Should a firm producing in the area of decreasing returns to scale equate its price to average cost instead of marginal cost?[14]

Although there is no easy theoretical way to escape these difficulties, it should be noted that the assumption of perfect competition in the product market, which generates these problems, is not necessary to the analysis. We can, instead, imagine that certain imperfections exist to determine the size of firms and that monopoly or oligopoly elements prevail in certain industries. To use the framework set out here, it is necessary only to assume that all firms engage in average-cost pricing, an assumption which may not depart too drastically from reality.[15] We continue to suppose, however, that perfect competition prevails in

[14] It is necessary to consider the case of firms experiencing decreasing returns, despite its theoretical improbability, because the empirical estimates of α and β, used later, indicate that this condition exists in certain industries. Furthermore, the manner in which these estimates are used assumes that expansion in these industries takes place in the firms experiencing decreasing returns and not through the entry of new firms. However, the estimates are subject to a number of statistical limitations to be discussed later.

[15] See Richard B. Heflebower, "Full Costs, Cost Changes, and Prices," in A Conference of the Universities-National Bureau Committee for Economic Research, *Business Concentration and Price Policy* (Princeton: Princeton University Press, 1955), pp. 361–92, for a discussion of "full-cost" pricing, especially the section dealing with pricing practices in oligopoly industries.

international markets, so that the firms of each country face a single world price.

The existence of scale effects in manufacturing causes the product supply curve to be either more or less steeply sloped. But it does not fundamentally change the analysis. Equation (5) may now be written:

$$ AC^M = \frac{L^\alpha K^\beta}{V} \cdot \frac{L^{\alpha/(\alpha+\beta)} K^{\beta/(\alpha+\beta)}}{L^\alpha K^\beta} \cdot \frac{wL + rK}{L^{\alpha/(\alpha+\beta)} K^{\beta/(\alpha+\beta)}} \cdot \frac{V}{O} \tag{12} $$

Again, the first term is equal to $1/A$. The second term, however, shows the effects of scale. If $(\alpha + \beta)$ is greater than unity, then the scale effects are positive and $L^{\alpha/(\alpha+\beta)} K^{\beta/(\alpha+\beta)}/L^\alpha K^\beta$ is less than one. If $(\alpha + \beta)$ is less than unity, this term is greater than one. If $(\alpha + \beta)$ is equal to unity, we have the constant-returns case described above with $L^{\alpha/(\alpha+\beta)} K^{\beta/(\alpha+\beta)}/L^\alpha K^\beta = 1$. The third term of equation (12) is similar to the second term of equation (5), except that each coefficient is divided by $(\alpha + \beta)$ to adjust the sum to unity. If constant returns were assumed, of course, this term would be identical with the second term in equation (5). In both cases, the term is equal to total costs in manufacturing divided by a geometrically weighted average of the inputs.

The equation comparable to equation (11) and derived in a similar fashion is the following:

$$ AC^M = \frac{L^\alpha K^\beta}{V} \cdot \frac{L^{\alpha/(\alpha+\beta)} K^{\beta/(\alpha+\beta)}}{L^\alpha K^\beta} \cdot r \cdot \left(\frac{w}{r}\right)^{\alpha/(\alpha+\beta)} \cdot \left(\frac{\alpha + \beta}{\alpha^{\alpha/(\alpha+\beta)} \cdot \beta^{\beta/(\alpha+\beta)}}\right) \cdot \frac{V}{O} \tag{13} $$

It can easily be seen that this equation reduces to equation (11) if $\alpha + \beta = 1$.

The ratio of average manufacturing cost for Canada to average manufacturing cost for the United States can now be equated to the product of the corresponding ratios for each term of equation (13). Taking the logarithms of each side of this equation, we have:

$$
\begin{aligned}
\log AC^M_{Ca} - \log AC^M_{US} = &\ [\log A_{US} - \log A_{Ca}] \\
&+ \left[\log \left((L^\alpha K^\beta)^{(\alpha+\beta-1)/(\alpha+\beta)}\right)_{US} - \log \left((L^\alpha K^\beta)^{(\alpha+\beta-1)/(\alpha+\beta)}\right)_{Ca}\right] \\
&+ [\log r_{Ca} - \log r_{US}] + \left[\log \left(\left(\frac{w}{r}\right)^{\alpha/(\alpha+\beta)}\right)_{Ca} - \log \left(\left(\frac{w}{r}\right)^{\alpha/(\alpha+\beta)}\right)_{US}\right] \\
&+ \left[\log \left(\frac{\alpha + \beta}{\alpha^{\alpha/(\alpha+\beta)} \cdot \beta^{\beta/(\alpha+\beta)}}\right)_{Ca} - \log \left(\frac{\alpha + \beta}{\alpha^{\alpha/(\alpha+\beta)} \cdot \beta^{\beta/(\alpha+\beta)}}\right)_{US}\right] \\
&+ \left[\log \left(\frac{V}{O}\right)_{Ca} - \log \left(\frac{V}{O}\right)_{US}\right]
\end{aligned}
\tag{14}
$$

As stated earlier, we are primarily interested in the changes in these variables over time. And, if we want to consider the effects of technological change, we must permit the parameter A to vary. Let us then assume that the effect of technological change is such as to cause this parameter to increase exponentially with respect to time; write the parameter as $A_o e^{\lambda T}$, where T is time.[16] We can now differentiate equation (14) with respect to time to obtain:

$$
\left(\frac{\dot{AC}^M}{AC^M}\right)_{Ca} - \left(\frac{\dot{AC}^M}{AC^M}\right)_{US} = [\lambda_{US} - \lambda_{Ca}]
$$

$$
+ \left[\left(\frac{\alpha + \beta - 1}{\alpha + \beta}\left(\alpha\frac{\dot{L}}{L} + \beta\frac{\dot{K}}{K}\right)\right)_{US} - \left(\frac{\alpha + \beta - 1}{\alpha + \beta}\left(\alpha\frac{\dot{L}}{L} + \beta\frac{\dot{K}}{K}\right)\right)_{Ca}\right]
$$

$$
+ \left[\left(\frac{\dot{r}}{r}\right)_{Ca} - \left(\frac{\dot{r}}{r}\right)_{US}\right] + \left[\left(\frac{\alpha}{\alpha + \beta}\frac{(\dot{w/r})}{w/r}\right)_{Ca} - \left(\frac{\alpha}{\alpha + \beta}\frac{(\dot{w/r})}{w/r}\right)_{US}\right]
$$

$$
+ \left[\left(\frac{\dot{V/O}}{V/O}\right)_{Ca} - \left(\frac{\dot{V/O}}{V/O}\right)_{US}\right] \tag{15}
$$

The dots above certain variables indicate first derivatives with respect to time.

The next section will combine equations (4) and (15) to test the hypothesis that differences in the relative rates of change of exports between the United States and Canada, $(\dot{X}/X)_{US} - (\dot{X}/X)_{Ca}$, are related to the various terms on the right-hand side of equation (15).

THE STATISTICAL TESTS

The first step in the empirical procedure was to obtain estimates of each of the terms on the right-hand side of equation (15) for 24 industries in both the United States and Canada. These variables were then related to each industry's rate of export change in a cross-sectional analysis.

If it is assumed that the relative rates of change of the material inputs costs are the same for both the United States and Canada, and that the supply elasticity of exports and the ratio of average manufacturing cost to the price of the final product are the same in all industries, then

[16] This implies that technological change is of the disembodied variety.

equation (4) may be written to explain interindustry differences in relative rates of export growth. For the ith industry:

$$\left[\left(\frac{\dot{X}}{X}\right)_{US} - \left(\frac{\dot{X}}{X}\right)_{Ca}\right]_i = b\left[\left(\frac{\dot{AC^M}}{AC^M}\right)_{Ca} - \left(\frac{\dot{AC^M}}{AC^M}\right)_{US}\right]_i \tag{16}$$

The terms on the right-hand side of equation (15) can then be substituted for $(\dot{AC^M}/AC^M)_{Ca} - (\dot{AC}_M/AC_M)_{US}$, and a least-squares regression analysis can be performed across industries.

The validity of these assumptions is essentially an empirical question. For example, while it would appear that Canadian industries are able to purchase many raw materials at lower costs than industries in the United States, it is not nearly so certain that this cost advantage has increased over time. If the proportionate change in the cost of transporting these materials is approximately equal to the change in the cost of producing the materials, the rates of change of the total cost of the materials to industries in each of the countries should be nearly equal.

There are several other advantages in expressing the variables in terms of relative rates of change. First, tariffs will affect the exports of two countries differently at any moment in time, but changes in relative cost advantages will not be affected as long as the tariff rates are not changed during the period considered. Second, changes in external demand do not affect the analysis of changes in exports, because this demand is reflected in a change of international prices, which affects all countries equally.[17] Third, the estimation of the terms on the right-hand side of equation (15) requires the use of data on the quantities of output produced and the quantities of capital inputs used by the two countries. Since each of the industries included in this study produces a number of different products and uses many types of capital equipment, it is necessary to use deflated value figures for these variables. Although there are price indexes which permit us to adjust for changes in prices over time, there are no data permitting price comparisons to be made between the United States and Canada for any single year.

To estimate the terms on the right-hand side of equation (15), two sets of estimates of the coefficients α and β were used.[18] One set consists of the

[17] This assumes that changes in P_w are not so great as to cause a product which was previously exported to be imported. This possibility will be discussed at greater length later.

[18] Initial attempts to estimate α, β, and λ directly, using time-series regressions, were unsuccessful. This appeared to be due partly to a relatively high degree of multicollinearity between the time and capital variables and partly to errors in the data.

estimates obtained by Hildebrand and Liu from least-squares regression of value added on labor and capital across states, using data from the *U.S. Census of Manufactures, 1958.*[19] All variables were divided by the number of establishments in each state in order to adjust each variable to the size of the "representative" establishment. To use this set of estimates, we must assume that the coefficients for the United States also apply to Canada. In general, the sums of α and β do not equal unity. The other set of estimates was obtained by assuming that constant returns prevailed in each industry and that the share of labor in total value added is a measure of the coefficient α. The capital coefficient is then assumed to equal $(1 - \alpha)$. Though this set of estimates does require the assumption of constant returns, it does not require that the coefficients be the same for both countries. Table A in the Statistical Appendix lists both sets of coefficients by industry. It shows that the two sets vary considerably for some industries. Footnotes to the table, describing some of the difficulties connected with each set of estimates, help to explain why these differences exist.

Under the assumptions required for the use of our first set of coefficients, we can substitute equation (15) into equation (16) and rearrange terms to obtain:

$$\left[\left(\frac{\dot{X}}{X}\right)_{\text{US}} - \left(\frac{\dot{X}}{X}\right)_{\text{Ca}}\right]_i = b[\dot{r}_{\text{Ca}} - \dot{r}_{\text{US}}] + b[\lambda_{\text{US}} - \lambda_{\text{Ca}}]_i$$
$$+ b\left[\frac{\alpha + \beta - 1}{\alpha + \beta}\left(\left(\alpha\frac{\dot{L}}{L} + \beta\frac{\dot{K}}{K}\right)_{\text{US}} - \left(\alpha\frac{\dot{L}}{L} + \beta\frac{\dot{K}}{K}\right)_{\text{Ca}}\right)\right]$$
$$+ b\left[\frac{\alpha}{\alpha + \beta}\left(\left(\frac{\dot{w/r}}{w/r}\right)_{\text{Ca}} - \left(\frac{\dot{w/r}}{w/r}\right)_{\text{US}}\right)\right]_i$$
$$+ b\left[\left(\frac{\dot{V/O}}{V/O}\right)_{\text{Ca}} - \left(\frac{\dot{V/O}}{V/O}\right)_{\text{US}}\right]_i \qquad (17)$$

All terms of this equation can vary from industry to industry, except the first term, which will be the same for all industries under our assumption

[19] George H. Hildebrand and Ta-Chung Liu, *Manufacturing Production Functions in the United States, 1957* (Ithaca: The New York State School of Industrial and Labor Relations, 1965). Production functions were estimated by Hildebrand and Liu for only 17 major industries. Where industries used in this study are defined more narrowly, it is assumed that the coefficients of these narrower industries are the same as those of the larger industry groups to which these industries belong.

that the same factor prices face all industries within each country. This term accounts not only for different general price-level changes in the United States and Canada, but also for any changes in the exchange rate. In the cross-sectional regressions, this term was not estimated; it forms part of the intercept coefficient. Similarly, the difference between the relative rates of change of the factor-price ratios of the two countries is assumed to be invariant between industries and to form part of the regression coefficient applied to $\alpha/(\alpha + \beta)$.[20]

The parameter λ was estimated from time-series data for each industry and each country for the period 1949–1962. The regression equation used to obtain this estimate is:

$$\log V - \alpha \log L - \beta \log K = \log A_o + \lambda T \tag{18}$$

The estimates of the variables value added, labor, and capital are also discussed in the Appendix. Value added is in constant dollars. Labor input is in man-hours of production and nonproduction workers. The capital variable was estimated as the deflated book value of the gross capital stock.[21]

The industries used in this study do not, in fact, account for all the manufacturing processes that go into each final product. In addition to raw materials, labor, and capital, the inputs of each industry include intermediate manufactured products. In addition, the outputs of many of the industries undergo further processing before they are consumed at home or exported. Only if we had information about the determinants of cost at each such prior or subsequent stage of production could we use V/O to measure the relative importance of manufacturing costs in the industry considered. Since we do not have this information, it is assumed that any changes that took place in V/O were the same for both countries, and the final term of equation (17) will no longer be considered.

To use the second set of α and β estimates, we must assume that constant returns prevail so that the elasticity coefficients may be represented by the share of each input in value added. Doing so, we obtain another industry

[20] Relative rates of change of factor-price ratios were estimated directly only to check the statistical results obtained.

[21] Ideally, a measure of the flow of capital services should be used as the capital-input variable to this production function, but data on stocks are the only ones available. On the advisability of using a gross measure of the capital stock instead of a value which is net of depreciation, see Edward F. Denison, *The Sources of Economic Growth in the United States* (New York: Committee for Economic Development, 1962), p. 98.

equation in the same manner that we obtained equation (17):

$$\left[\left(\frac{\dot{X}}{X}\right)_{\text{US}} - \left(\frac{\dot{X}}{X}\right)_{\text{Ca}}\right]_i = b\left[\left(\frac{\dot{r}}{r}\right)_{\text{Ca}} - \left(\frac{\dot{r}}{r}\right)_{\text{US}}\right] + b[\lambda_{\text{US}} - \lambda_{\text{Ca}}]_i$$

$$+ b\left[\left(\alpha\,\frac{\dot{w/r}}{w/r}\right)_{\text{Ca}} - \left(\alpha\,\frac{\dot{w/r}}{w/r}\right)_{\text{US}}\right]_i \quad (19)$$

The last term may be divided into two parts:[22]

$$b\left[\left(\alpha\,\frac{\dot{w/r}}{w/r}\right)_{\text{Ca}} - \left(\alpha\,\frac{\dot{w/r}}{w/r}\right)_{\text{US}}\right]_i = b\left[\left(\frac{\dot{w/r}}{w/r}\right)_{\text{US}}(\alpha_{\text{Ca}} - \alpha_{\text{US}})\right]_i$$

$$+ b\left[\alpha_{\text{Ca}}\left(\left(\frac{\dot{w/r}}{w/r}\right)_{\text{Ca}} - \left(\frac{\dot{w/r}}{w/r}\right)_{\text{US}}\right)\right]_i \quad (20)$$

The first term of this expression is the effect on exports of an international difference in the share of labor in value added, given the rate of change of the U.S. factor-price ratio. The second term is the effect of an international difference in the rates of change of the factor-price ratios, given the share of labor in Canadian value added. In the estimating equation, $(\dot{w/r}/w/r)_{\text{US}}$ and $(\dot{w/r}/w/r)_{\text{Ca}} - (\dot{w/r}/w/r)_{\text{US}}$, which are assumed to be the same for all industries, form part of the cross-sectional regressive coefficients, and only α_{Ca} and $(\alpha_{\text{Ca}} - \alpha_{\text{US}})$ are used as variables. The only other differences between equations (17) and (19) are that no scale term is included in (19) and that the values of λ used in (19) were estimated from equation (18) using factor shares as the estimates of the coefficients α and β.

In each cross-sectional regression equation shown below, three dependent variables are used. The first is the difference between the relative rates of change of exports to third markets (all countries other than the United States and Canada). This is the variable to which our theoretical model conforms if we assume that both countries are exporting each

[22] In logarithmic form:

$$\alpha_{\text{Ca}}\log\left(\frac{w}{r}\right)_{\text{Ca}} - \alpha_{\text{US}}\log\left(\frac{w}{r}\right)_{\text{US}} = \alpha_{\text{Ca}}\log\left[\left(\frac{w}{r}\right)_{\text{US}}\cdot\frac{(w/r)_{\text{Ca}}}{(w/r)_{\text{US}}}\right] - \alpha_{\text{US}}\log\left(\frac{w}{r}\right)_{\text{US}}$$

$$= \log\left(\frac{w}{r}\right)_{\text{US}}(\alpha_{\text{Ca}} - \alpha_{\text{US}}) + \alpha_{\text{Ca}}\left[\log\left(\frac{w}{r}\right)_{\text{Ca}} - \log\left(\frac{w}{r}\right)_{\text{US}}\right]$$

Taking the derivatives with respect to time of this equation, we have equation (20).

product. Since each country exports *and* imports products within most industry classes, the second dependent variable used is the difference between the relative rates of growth of reciprocal exports. This variable gives us a convenient way to examine the effects of average cost changes on both exports and imports, since exports from the United States to Canada are the same as imports of Canada from the United States, and conversely. But limitations on the growth of demand in the two countries prevent this from being an adequate test of the basic hypothesis; supply conditions, by themselves, cannot possibly determine the growth rates of bilateral trade. Perhaps the best results might be expected from the third dependent variable, the difference between the relative rates of growth of total exports, since the exports of each country may go to any foreign market.

Rates of export growth were determined from linear regressions of the value of exports on time, using annual export data for the years 1951–1964.[23] No attempt was made to deflate the value of exports, since the difference between the relative rates of change of the value of exports is equal to the difference between the relative rates of change of export quantities if, as here, we assume that export prices are the same for both countries.[24] The values of the dependent and independent variables for each industry are given in Tables A and B of the Appendix.

Before examining the empirical results, a few of the more important problems involved in this procedure should be mentioned.[25] It has already been noted that the production function used here is one which assumes that the elasticity of substitution between the inputs, capital and

---

[23] Adequate export data are not available for years before 1951.

[24] If values of exports are substituted for export quantities, we have:

$$\frac{[d(p \cdot X_{US})/dt]}{p \cdot X_{US}} - \frac{[d(p \cdot X_{Ca})/dt]}{p \cdot X_{Ca}} = \frac{[p \cdot (dX_{US}/dt)] + [X_{US} \cdot (dp/dt)]}{p \cdot X_{US}}$$

$$- \frac{[p \cdot (dX_{Ca}/dt)] + [X_{Ca} \cdot (dp/dt)]}{p \cdot X_{Ca}}$$

$$= \left(\frac{dX_{US}/dt}{X_{US}} + \frac{dp/dt}{p}\right) - \left(\frac{dX_{Ca}/dt}{X_{Ca}} + \frac{dp/dt}{p}\right)$$

$$= \left(\frac{\dot{X}}{X}\right)_{US} - \left(\frac{\dot{X}}{X}\right)_{Ca}$$

[25] For a more thorough discussion of these and other problems related to this empirical procedure, see J. D. Stryker, "United States and Canadian Manufacturing Production and Exports" (unpublished doctoral dissertation, Columbia University, 1967).

labor, is equal to unity. Another type of production function developed
by Arrow, Chenery, Minhas, and Solow assumes a constant elasticity of
substitution which is not restricted to unity.[26] One has then to ask whether
our estimates of λ are biased by the particular type of production function
specified. One can only say that, at present, the evidence for the CES
production function is mixed.[27] Furthermore, Nelson has indicated that,
within a wide range of elasticities, the conclusions drawn from the use of
the CES function differ little from those drawn from the use of the simpler
function employed here.[28]

Another difficulty is that each industry considered produces a large
number of different products, rather than the single homogeneous good
assumed in our model. There are also aggregation problems related to
the use of a single production function to describe an industry made up
of many firms.[29] Even if aggregate production functions could be
satisfactorily estimated, the heterogeneity of industry output carries with
it a number of implications for appraisals of changes in trade patterns.
Our hypothesis has assumed that each product is exported by each
country. In reality, of course, many of the products produced by each
industry will be imported rather than exported. Furthermore, the export
changes actually measured will consist of changes in the quantity of
existing exports and in the kinds of products exported. But we must
pretend that changes in the level of average manufacturing costs result in
changes in the total exports of all of an industry's products equal to the
change one would expect in exports of a single homogeneous product.
Another implication of product heterogeneity is that product differentiation, as well as price, may be important in competition.[30]

Of the statistical problems discussed in the Statistical Appendix, two
are noteworthy. One relates to the fact that value-added and labor data
are collected on an establishment basis, whereas capital-stock data are

[26] Kenneth J. Arrow, H. Chenery, B. Minhas, and R. Solow, "Capital-Labor Substitution and Economic Efficiency," *Review of Economics and Statistics*, XLIII (August 1962),
225–50.

[27] See, for instance, C. E. Ferguson, "Cross-Section Production Functions and the
Elasticity of Substitution in American Manufacturing Industry," *Review of Economics and
Statistics*, XLV (August 1963), 305–13.

[28] Richard R. Nelson, "Aggregate Production Functions and Medium-Range Growth
Projections," *American Economic Review*, LIV (September 1964), 577.

[29] A. A. Walters, "Production Functions and Cost Functions: an Econometric Survey,"
Econometrica, XXXI (January–April 1963), 1–66.

[30] This would result in a downward-sloping demand curve facing each industry in each
country.

collected from firms, and the two are not always classified into the same industry. The other difficulty is that the price-index series used to deflate value added is quite inadequate.

EMPIRICAL RESULTS

Before examining the findings when both capital and labor are included in the analysis, it is useful to consider the relationship between export growth and the growth of labor productivity (value added divided by labor input).[31] The following table gives the regression results obtained from a cross-sectional analysis of 24 industries, using the equation:

$$\left[\left(\frac{\dot{X}}{X}\right)_{\text{US}} - \left(\frac{\dot{X}}{X}\right)_{\text{Ca}}\right]_i = a + b\left[\left(\frac{\dot{V/L}}{V/L}\right)_{\text{US}} - \left(\frac{\dot{V/L}}{V/L}\right)_{\text{Ca}}\right]_i \qquad (21)$$

Dependent Variable	a	b	$\bar{R}^2$
Third-market exports	−.0219	+1.9750* (.8712)	.1528*
Reciprocal exports	−.0186	+1.7150* (.8231)	.1277*
Total exports	−.0235	+1.9265* (.7280)	.2074*

Note: $\bar{R}^2$ is the coefficient of determination adjusted for the number of degrees of freedom. Standard errors of the b coefficients are found in parentheses below the value of the coefficients. Coefficients which are statistically significant at the .05 level are marked with an asterisk. A one-tailed Student's t test was used to test the significance of the regression coefficients. (These notes also apply to the regression results listed later in the text.)

In each case, the b coefficients and the coefficients of determination are significantly different from zero at the .05 level of significance, though the $\bar{R}^2$'s are not very high.

Given this evidence concerning the importance of labor productivity, we can ask if the changes in labor productivity which took place were offset by increases in the amount of capital employed in production or were primarily due to technological innovation. Using the first set of estimates

---

[31] The empirical work of MacDougall, Stern, and Balassa was primarily concerned with the relationship between exports and labor productivity.

of α and β taken from Hildebrand and Liu, we estimated the equation:

$$\left[\left(\frac{\dot{X}}{X}\right)_{\text{US}} - \left(\frac{\dot{X}}{X}\right)_{\text{Ca}}\right]_i = a + b_1[\lambda_{\text{US}} - \lambda_{\text{Ca}}]_i + b_2 \cdot \frac{\alpha + \beta - 1}{\alpha + \beta}$$

$$\times \left[\left(\alpha\frac{\dot{L}}{L} \times \beta\frac{\dot{K}}{K}\right)_{\text{US}} - \left(\alpha\frac{\dot{L}}{L} + \beta\frac{\dot{K}}{K}\right)_{\text{Ca}}\right]_i + b_3 \cdot \left(\frac{\alpha}{\alpha + \beta}\right)_i$$

Dependent Variable	a	b_1	b_2	b_3	$\bar{R}^2$
Third-market exports	+.1878	+1.7352* (.7841)	+17.6330* (9.5535)	−.3129* (.1035)	.3634*
Reciprocal exports	+.1168	+1.6821* (.8174)	+.7104 (.9960)	−.2089* (.1078)	.2091
Total exports	+.1422	+1.7192* (.6779)	+12.6475 (8.2594)	−.2506* (.0894)	.3624*

Here we see that, in the case of exports to third markets, all the coefficients are significant (though the standard error of b_2 is quite high and the coefficient is just barely significant). In the other cases, b_2 is not significant, although it is always positive; the evidence for the influence of scale effects on the growth of exports is rather weak. This may be due to the difficulties involved in the estimation of the elasticity coefficients mentioned above.

The coefficient of $\alpha/(\alpha + \beta)$ is always negative, suggesting [from equation (17)] that the ratio of wages to rentals rose at a faster rate in the United States than in Canada. To see if this was actually so, data were collected on average hourly earnings in manufacturing, interest rates on high-quality corporate bonds, and price indexes of producers' durables and construction for the years 1949 and 1962. The factor-price ratio was then computed for each year.[32] The results indicate that there was an increase of about 3 per cent in the ratio of wage rates to rental rates on capital from 1949 to 1962 in the United States; there was no change in this ratio for the same period in Canada. Thus, there is some evidence supporting the validity of the coefficient b_3, though the evidence is not very strong. It should be noted, however, that the calculation of factor-price ratios may be subject to a considerable degree of error.

Using the second set of estimates of α and $(1 - \alpha)$ obtained from the relative shares of labor and capital, regression analyses were performed on

[32] In computing the factor-price ratio, the implicit rental on capital was calculated from the present value of future returns to capital (assumed equal to the cost of the existing stock), the rate of interest, and the average length of service life of capital.

the following equation:

$$\left[\left(\frac{\dot{X}}{X}\right)_{\text{US}} - \left(\frac{\dot{X}}{X}\right)_{\text{Ca}}\right]_i = a + b_1[\lambda_{\text{US}} - \lambda_{\text{Ca}}]_i + b_2[\alpha_{\text{Ca}} - \alpha_{\text{US}}]_i + [b_3\alpha_{\text{Ca}}]_i$$

The coefficients of this equation were all insignificant, with the exception of b_1, which was always significantly different from zero. Since the standard errors of b_2 and b_3 were very large, these variables were dropped from the equation to yield the following results:

Dependent Variable	a	b_1	$\bar{R}^2$
Third-market exports	−.0335	+1.6601* (.9541)	.0814
Reciprocal exports	−.0337	+1.9928* (.8467)	.1653*
Total exports	−.0361	+1.7569* (.7954)	.1448*

The poor results obtained for the variables $(\alpha_{\text{Ca}} - \alpha_{\text{US}})$ and α_{Ca} may be due to problems involved in estimating α and $(1 - \alpha)$ by the factor-shares method. At the same time, they may simply reflect relatively small changes in the factor-price ratio. The latter interpretation would be consistent with our empirical evidence on changes in relative factor prices. Again, however, this evidence may be of limited value.

It does seem clear, at least, that the relationship between changes in exports and changes in labor productivity has not been offset by changes in the capital stock. In every case but one, the difference in relative rates of growth of exports was significantly related to the term $(\lambda_{\text{US}} - \lambda_{\text{Ca}})$. This may be seen even more clearly by relating the difference in the relative growth rates of labor productivity directly to the difference in the relative growth rates of both capital and labor productivity. For this purpose, the second two independent variables of equation (17) are added together, since increases in labor productivity may result from both technological change and from increasing returns to scale. Correlating these variables for both sets of α and β, we have, for the Hildebrand and Liu estimates:

$$\left[\left(\frac{\dot{V/L}}{V/L}\right)_{\text{US}} - \left(\frac{\dot{V/L}}{V/L}\right)_{\text{Ca}}\right]_i = -.0041 + .8835*\left[(\lambda_{\text{US}} - \lambda_{\text{Ca}})\right]$$
$$(.1134)$$
$$+ \frac{\alpha + \beta - 1}{\alpha + \beta}\left\{\left(\alpha\frac{\dot{L}}{L} + \beta\frac{\dot{K}}{K}\right)_{\text{US}} - \left(\alpha\frac{\dot{L}}{L} + \beta\frac{\dot{K}}{K}\right)_{\text{Ca}}\right\}\right]_i \qquad \bar{R}^2 = .7219*$$

and for the factor-shares estimates:

$$\left[\left(\frac{\dot{V/L}}{V/L}\right)_{US} - \left(\frac{\dot{V/L}}{V/L}\right)_{Ca}\right]_i = -.0047 + .7135^*(\lambda_{US} - \lambda_{Ca})_i \quad \bar{R}^2 = .4359^*$$
$$(.1648)$$

In both cases, we see that the correlations are fairly high.

In summary, it can be said that the evidence is fairly strong that, for these two countries, the growth of exports over time has been related to the differing rates of technological progress taking place within manufacturing industries. There is also some indication that scale effects have had an influence on export growth, but the evidence here is very weak. Finally, there is at least the possibility that a faster growth rate of wages relative to capital costs in the United States than in Canada may have contributed to a decline in the international competitiveness of the products of the more labor-intensive U.S. industries.

CONCLUSIONS

The empirical evidence presented above supports the hypothesis that changes in the structure of U.S. and Canadian exports were related to relative changes in average manufacturing costs during the period examined. Furthermore, these comparative-cost changes appear to have been due to changes in the productivity of both capital and labor and to changes in the ratio of factor prices.

Previous attempts to study the empirical relationship between comparative costs and exports have assumed that these costs may be adequately represented by labor productivity. Although for some purposes this variable may be a useful proxy for total factor productivity, it tells us little of the underlying causes of differences in productivity. In this study, a particular type of production function has been specified, and productivity changes have been examined in terms of the parameters of the function. In particular, an attempt has been made to attribute these changes to technological progress, represented by time, and to the effects of changes in the scale of production.

The United States and Canada are two countries that differ considerably in size, giving scope for differential scale effects which might be quite large. Because of their geographical proximity and extensive economic interrelations, however, there is some reason to expect that the technology used in both countries might be approximately the same. Yet, a glance at the last three columns of Table B in the Appendix shows that the effect of different rates of technological change on comparative costs has been much more important than the effects of scale changes. This is also supported by the stronger correlations of differential export growth rates with the time-trend variable than with the scale variable. This result may be due to statistical problems in the estimation of the elasticity coefficients or to the fact that these coefficients are estimates for the United States and may not be applicable to the Canadian industries. But there is some presumption, at least, that technological change has taken place at different rates in the two countries, and that this has been a relatively more important influence on the structure of trade.

The results also suggest that wages have risen relative to rentals at a faster rate in the United States than in Canada, and that this has tended to reduce the competitiveness of labor-intensive industries in the United States. One cannot say whether this difference in factor-price changes was due to different growth rates of factor supplies, to changes in the structure of demand, or to non-neutral technological change. Nevertheless, the effect on the structure of trade is evident.

Finally, it should be noted that this study has been able to explain little more than one-third of the variation in export growth-rate differentials. Whether this is due to the statistical problems mentioned here or to other factors which influence trade patterns is a matter for future research.

STATISTICAL APPENDIX

The industry classification system used in this study is based on the U.S. Standard Industrial Classification, the Canadian Standard Industrial Classification, and the Standard International Trade Classification. Each of these classifications was adjusted to obtain a single classification which is comparable for data on value added, labor, capital, and exports. Adjustments were also made for various revisions in the classification systems made during the period of time considered. The major problem remaining after the adjustments is that value added and labor data are reported by establishment, whereas capital data are reported by firm. In some cases, where large firms own plants in several industries, part of the value of the capital stock reported for a particular industry exists in establishments classified in another industry. Certain industries for which this discrepancy is very large were excluded from the analysis.[33]

[33] These industries were: petroleum and coal products, paints and varnishes, other leather products, and confectionery. Tobacco products and printing and publishing were excluded because estimates of α and β were not obtained for these industries by Hildebrand and Liu. The dairy-products industry was excluded because data are inadequate for the first part of the period. All other manufacturing industries have been included in the analysis.

Table A

Industry, Estimates of α and β from Hildebrand and Liu, and Estimates of α for the United States and Canada Derived from the Share of Labor in Value Added

No. and Industry	Hildebrand and Liu[a]		Share of Labor[b]	
	α	β	U.S.	Canada
1. Meat products	.536	.618	.570	.526
2. Canned and preserved fish, fruits, and vegetables	.536	.618	.382	.428
3. Grain mill and bakery products	.536	.618	.464	.506
4. Alcoholic beverages	.536	.618	.327	.213
5. Miscellaneous foods	.536	.618	.322	.303
6. Rubber products	.716	.358	.521	.415
7. Boots and shoes	.824	.118	.635	.647
8. Textiles	.841	.027	.605	.597
9. Apparel	.501	.289	.604	.616
10. Lumber and wood products	.443	.462	.585	.542
11. Furniture	.730	.110	.565	.630
12. Paper products	.669	.345	.469	.426
13. Agricultural machinery	.763	.269	.535	.769
14. Nonferrous metals and fabricated metal products	.708	.290	.541	.452
15. Primary iron and steel	.764	.303	.484	.462
16. Machinery, machine tools, and electrical appliances	.763	.269	.549	.403
17. Other electrical machinery and equipment	.584	.337	.545	.555
18. Motor vehicles	.887	.252	.447	.557
19. Miscellaneous transportation equipment	.887	.252	.516	.728
20. Nonmetallic mineral products	.669	.337	.470	.435
21. Drugs	.801	.209	.260	.275
22. Soaps and toilet preparations	.801	.209	.234	.251
23. Other chemical products	.801	.209	.350	.403
24. Miscellaneous products	.666	.362	.554	.534

[a] The estimates of α and β listed here were obtained using simple, least-squares regression analyses across states. Hence, they are subject to a number of biases, summarized elsewhere by Nerlove and by Walters. See Marc Nerlove, *Estimation and Identification of Cobb-Douglas Production Functions* (Chicago: Rand McNally and Company, 1965), pp. 18–29, and A. A. Walters, "Production Functions and Cost Functions: An Econometric Survey," *Econometrica*, XXXI (January–April 1963), pp. 1–66.

[b] Factor shares were computed for each industry in a year in which the industry was at or near full capacity, usually either 1955 or 1956. There are several problems connected with the use of relative factor shares as estimates of α and (1 − α). If constant returns do not actually exist, the labor coefficient will be biased downward under increasing returns, and upward under decreasing returns. Furthermore, if gross value added should be adjusted for depreciation before taking factor shares, the labor coefficient will be biased in the downward direction when this adjustment is not made. Finally, the incidence of corporate income tax might be such that the tax is either shifted forward onto the consumer or backward onto labor, resulting in biased coefficients when we assume that the tax is paid out of the return to capital.

Table B

Differences between Relative Rates of Change of Exports and Associated Production Variables[a,b]

Ind. No.	$\Delta\left(\dfrac{\dot{X}}{X}\right)^3$	$\Delta\left(\dfrac{\dot{X}}{X}\right)^R$	$\Delta\left(\dfrac{\dot{X}}{X}\right)^T$	$\Delta\lambda^{HL}$	$\dfrac{\alpha+\beta-1}{\alpha+\beta}\Delta\left(\alpha\dfrac{\dot{L}}{L}+\beta\dfrac{\dot{K}}{K}\right)$	$\Delta\lambda^{FS}$
1	.0816	.1321	.1191	.0215	−.00219	.0201
2	.0170	.0453	.0376	.0193	.00044	.0197
3	.1084	.1363	.1096	.0001	−.00019	−.0013
4	.0467	−.1044	−.0687	−.0269	−.00217	−.0218
5	−.0786	.0139	−.0379	.0196	−.00495	.0240
6	.0714	.0664	.0551	.0124	.00033	.0196
7	−.1204	−.1063	−.1105	−.0073	.00004	−.0068
8	−.1113	.0480	−.0572	.0018	.00058	.0047
9	−.1560	−.0236	−.0942	−.0070	−.00200	−.0089
10	.0507	.0496	.0434	.0255	.00311	.0270
11	−.1455	−.0606	−.1192	−.0082	.00114	−.0131
12	.0304	.0594	.0629	.0019	.00015	.0016
13	.1001	.0066	.0124	.0583	−.00017	.0458
14	.0043	.0232	.0156	.0081	.00000	.0145
15	−.1164	−.1137	−.1022	−.0130	−.00197	−.0046
16	−.0658	−.1039	−.0668	−.0056	.00022	−.0072
17	.0104	−.0809	−.0326	.0051	−.00067	.0083
18	−.0350	−.0755	.0152	.0388	−.00154	.0343
19	.0269	−.1444	−.0210	−.0118	.00210	−.0161
20	.0411	−.0305	−.0130	−.0060	−.00010	−.0034
21	−.0482	.0073	−.0401	.0088	−.00002	.0384
22	−.1254	−.0511	−.1022	.0014	−.00011	.0065
23	.0359	.0424	.0590	.0194	−.00016	.0238
24	−.1365	−.1120	−.1494	.0095	−.00027	.0114

[a] See the text and body of Appendix for a discussion of sources.

[b] The superscripts 3, R, and T indicate that these export variables refer to third-market exports, reciprocal exports, and total exports, respectively. The superscripts HL and FS refer to estimates of λ assuming α and β to equal the Hildebrand and Liu estimates and the factor-shares estimates, respectively. Each variable is the value for the United States minus the value for Canada.

Data on value added and labor were taken from censuses and surveys of manufactures for the United States and Canada.[34] Value-added figures were deflated by available price indexes, in most cases the wholesale price indexes for each industry. The unavailability of value-added indexes for this purpose presents certain difficulties. In particular, during the Korean War period, the rapid rise

[34] U.S. Bureau of the Census, *Annual Survey of Manufacturers* and *Census of Manufacturers*, (Washington, D.C.: Government Printing Office, various years); Canada, Dominion Bureau of Statistics, *General Review of the Manufacturing Industries of Canada*, (Ottawa: various years).

in the price of raw materials tends to give the price indexes for some industries an upward bias. In the worst cases, value-added data for the years before 1954 were not used. Instead, indexes of industrial production for these industries were linked to the deflated value-added series for the later years. Although this helped to correct the worst cases, it must be realized that the deflated value-added series suffer in quality because of the lack of appropriate price indexes.

Labor data are in man-hours per year and cover all employees. Man-hours for U.S. production workers were taken directly from the data source. Man-hours for Canadian production workers were computed by multiplying the number of such workers by the average number of hours worked per year, assuming a 50-week work year. Nonproduction man-hours were computed by assuming that each of these employees worked 40 hours per week, 50 weeks per year. These figures should be reasonably comparable for the United States and Canada.

Book values of fixed, reproducible capital assets for each industry were taken from tax-return sources for the two countries.[35] These values were then converted to constant (1949) prices using the following deflator:

$$D = \frac{BV_{t-1} + I_t - W_t}{K_{t-1}^* + I_t^* - W_t^*}$$

where D is the value of the deflator used, BV_{t-1} is book value at the end of year $t-1$, I_t is the value of investment in year t in current prices, W_t is the value of write-offs in year t in current prices, K_{t-1}^* is the value of the capital stock at the end of year $t-1$ in constant prices, I_t^* is the value of investment in year t in constant prices, and W_t^* is the value of write-offs in the year t in constant prices.[36] The choice of these particular input variables was determined by the variables used by Hildebrand and Liu to obtain their estimates of the elasticity coefficients, α and β. Thus, no effort was made to include other capital variables such as inventories, intangibles, or land.

Data on exports were obtained from United Nations, *Commodity Trade Statistics*. All exports are valued in U.S. dollars.

[35] U.S., Internal Revenue Service, *Statistics of Income* (Washington, D.C.: Government Printing Office, various years); Canada, Department of National Revenue, *Taxation Statistics* (Ottawa: various years).

[36] For a discussion of the estimates used for each of these variables, see Stryker, "United States and Canadian Manufacturing."

DONALD B. KEESING

The Impact of Research and
Development on United States Trade

A NUMBER OF PEOPLE HAVE ARGUED that what gives the United States
its ability to compete in world markets despite its high wages is its ability
to supply a steady flow of new products.[1] New products can be attributed
partly to research and development. This article tests the hypothesis that

Reprinted from the *Journal of Political Economy* (Vol. 75, No. 1, pp. 38–48) by permission
of the University of Chicago Press. Copyright 1967. I owe a special debt to my chief
research assistants, Earl L. McFarland and Elinor B. Yudin, for their valuable ideas and
hard work. I also thank Peter B. Kenen, Harry G. Johnson, Raymond Vernon, Charles
P. Kindleberger, and Irving B. Kravis for constructive criticisms and encouragement.

[1] For the background of this idea, see J. H. Williams, "The Theory of International
Trade Reconsidered," *Economic Journal* (June 1929), and his later writings; T. Balogh,
The Dollar Crisis: Cause and Cure (Oxford: Blackwell, 1949); I. B. Kravis, " 'Availability'
and Other Influences on the Commodity Composition of Trade," *Journal of Political
Economy* (April 1956); D. MacDougall, *The World Dollar Problem* (London: Macmillan
and Co., Ltd., 1957); E. Hoffmeyer, *Dollar Shortage* (Amsterdam: North-Holland
Publishing Co., 1958); J. Drèze, "Quelques réflections sereines sur l'adaptation de
l'industrie belge au Marché Commun, *Comptes Rendus des Travaux de la Société Royale
d'Economie Politique de Belgique* (December 1960); S. B. Linder, *An Essay on Trade and
Transformation* (Uppsala: Almqvist and Wiksells, 1961); M. V. Posner, "International
Trade and Technical Change," *Oxford Economic Papers* (October 1961); R. Vernon,
"Solutions: Trade Policy," in S. E. Harris (ed.), *The Dollar in Crisis* (New York: Har-
court, Brace & World, 1961); C. P. Kindleberger, *Foreign Trade and the National Economy*
(New Haven: Yale University Press, 1962), and *International Economics* (Homewood, Ill.:
Irwin, 1963); H. B. Lary, *Problems of the United States as World Trader and Banker* (New
York: National Bureau of Economic Research, 1963); S. Hirsch, "The United States
Electronics Industry in International Trade," *National Institute Economic Review* (November
1965); G. C. Hufbauer, *Synthetic Materials and the Theory of International Trade* (London:
Gerald Duckworth & Co., 1966); and R. Vernon, "International Investment and Inter-
national Trade in the Product Cycle," *Quarterly Journal of Economics* (May 1966).

R&D activity is associated with American competitive ability in manufacturing industries, and also tests this hypothesis against other hypotheses
advanced to explain American trade patterns.

One would expect, at most, an imperfect correlation between American
competitive ability and R&D activity in each industry. Exports of new
products consisting of military and space equipment are not freely
permitted. Probably not all R&D affect exports in the industry that
performs the R&D; some affect other industries. The link between
R&D activity and new products is far from routine, and other countries
engage in R&D in competition with the United States.[2]

In addition, the available indicators of R&D and U.S. competitive
ability are far from perfect. U.S. competitive ability is measured throughout this study by 1962 U.S. exports in each industry as a percentage of the
total 1962 exports of the leading industrial countries known as the Group
of Ten (the United States, United Kingdom, Federal Republic of Germany, France, Italy, Belgium, Netherlands, Sweden, Canada, and
Japan).[3] Indicators of R&D in each industry are taken from data
published by the National Science Foundation.[4] In every case, the
information is limited to R&D performed by industrial companies,
either for themselves or under contract.[5] Data on R&D expenditure

[2] Further research is certainly needed on the relationships prevailing in other countries,
especially since a correlation between U.S. R&D patterns and trade performance would
not itself establish an American superiority in R&D sufficient to overcome the competitive
handicap of high wages. A superficial examination of R&D data for other countries
(the United Kingdom, Canada, Japan, and Sweden) leads me to believe that the same
industries attract the most R&D elsewhere as in the United States, so that the United
States does compete successfully in exports based on R&D.

[3] Though this is the only indicator of U.S. trade performance that is reported here,
others have also been tested—for example, U.S. exports minus imports divided by
manufacturers' shipments, and U.S. exports divided by imports. They give essentially
the same results, but the correlations are weaker. None of these measures is ideal. The
measure used has the peculiarity that the United States cannot export to itself but others
can; thus it is a mixed measure reflecting U.S. resistance to imports as well as successful
exports. In some respects an ideal measure, as H. G. Johnson has suggested to me, would
be shares of world consumption.

[4] The data come from surveys of companies undertaken for NSF by the Bureau of the
Census. Research and development are defined to include "basic and applied research
in the sciences and engineering and design and development of products and processes."
The definition excludes "quality control, routine products testing, market research, sales
promotion, sales service, research in the social sciences or psychology, or other non-
technological activities or technical services." See National Science Foundation, *Research
and Development in Industry 1960*, NSF 63-7 (Washington, D.C., 1963), p. 109.

[5] In 1960 three-fourths of U.S. R&D by value was performed by industrial firms. The
remaining one-fourth was done by government laboratories, universities, and other non-
profit organizations. NSF, *Research and Development*, p. ix.

by industry are seriously flawed because R&D is classified according to the main industry of the company performing the task, though firms that perform R&D characteristically spread their efforts over many product fields.[6] Information on applied R&D expenditure by product field is available only for a rather unsatisfactory set of product fields.[7] The best of the available indicators of R&D activity is perhaps the scientists and engineers in R&D as a percentage of the labor force of each industry, classified according to the industry of the establishment in which people work.

THE ASSOCIATION BETWEEN R&D AND COMPETITIVE TRADE PERFORMANCE

For eighteen industries, Table 1 compares scientists and engineers in R&D, as a percentage of the industry's total employment in January 1961, with 1962 U.S. exports as a percentage of Group of Ten exports.[8] The correlation is much too high to be attributed to chance. The linear correlation is .88, and the Spearman coefficient of rank correlation is .94.[9]

This finding is confirmed, though the correlations are not always so high in tests using other indicators of R&D. For example, for 22 product fields, taking as a measure of R&D the funds spend on applied R&D in each product field as a percentage of value added by the corresponding industry in 1960, the linear correlation with my measure of trade performance is .66; the Spearman rank correlation is .78.[10]

[6] In several industries, less than half the R&D relates to the corresponding product field, and conversely, in some product fields less than half the R&D is performed by the corresponding industry. NSF, *Research and Development*, Tables A-18 and A-19.

[7] Fields in which little R&D are performed are virtually unrepresented. See Appendix Table 2.

[8] While this choice of years implies a one- to two-year lag between R&D and their effect on trade, the correlations are not sensitive to the years chosen: the structure of R&D expenditure by industry and the pattern of American competitive export performance have been quite stable in recent years.

[9] A linear correlation above .59 would be statistically significant at the .01 level. Spearman coefficients of rank correlation are reported in the text throughout because this measure is so familiar, but inferences from small numbers of observations have been checked with the Kendall coefficient. In this instance, the Kendall coefficient is .80 where anything above .45 would be statistically significant at the .01 level.

[10] The data are presented in Appendix Table 2. In this case, unlike others reported, the linear correlation is significantly improved (to .78) by use of logarithms. On grounds that exports of new products were scarcely permitted, a number of product fields were excluded from the comparisons, as Appendix Table 2 shows.

Table 1

Competitive U.S. Trade Performance in Comparison with Research and Development, for 18 Industries

Industry	U.S. Exports as % of Group of Ten Exports, 1962	Scientists and Engineers Engaged in R&D as % of Employment, January 1961
Aircraft	59.52	7.71
Office machinery	35.00	5.09
Drugs	33.09	6.10
Other machinery	32.27	1.39
Instruments	27.98	4.58
Chemicals, except drugs	27.32	3.63
Electrical equipment	26.75	4.40
Rubber	23.30	0.95
Motor vehicles	22.62	1.14
Petroleum refining	20.59	2.02
Fabricated metal products	19.62	0.51
Nonferrous metals	18.06	0.69
Paper and allied products	15.79	0.47
Stone, clay, glass products	15.22	0.60
Other transport equipment	13.71	0.46
Lumber and wood products	11.68	0.03
Textile mill products	10.92	0.29
Primary ferrous metals	9.14	0.43

Sources: U.S. exports as % of Group of Ten exports computed from United Nations *Commodity Trade Statistics 1962*; scientists and engineers engaged in R&D as percentage of employment computed from data in National Science Foundation, *Scientific and Technical Personnel in Industry*, NSF 63-32 (Washington, D.C., 1963). Underlying NSF data and standard international trade classifications assumed to correspond to each industry are shown in Appendix Table 1.

From data on R&D expenditure by industry, it is possible to gain some insight into the separate impact on trade of federally financed and company-financed R&D.[11] As Table 2 shows, apparently the two types of R&D have a cumulative effect. One might expect company R&D to exert a greater impact on trade, dollar for dollar, than federal R&D, but there is only inconclusive evidence that it does.[12]

[11] The shortcomings of the industry classification of R&D expenditure, discussed previously, reduce the value of this test.

[12] Information on this point was sought by means of a least-squares regression, $T = \alpha + \beta_1 C + \beta_2 F + \epsilon$, where T represents U.S. exports as a percentage of Group of Ten exports, C is company-funded R&D, and F is federally funded R&D, in the forms shown in Table 2. The correlation of .33 between the two types of R&D is not significant at the .05 level so that this regression does not involve multicollinearity. However, the difference between the resulting estimates of β_1 and β_2 (2.79 as compared with 1.73, with α equal to 13.79) is not nearly significant, and the adjusted R^2 is not improved by separating C and F, compared to lumping all R&D together.

Table 2

Federal and Company Funds Spent for the Performance of Research and Development in Comparison with Trade Performance, for 16 Industries

Industry	U.S. Share of Group of Ten Exports, 1962	Company R&D as Percentage of Sales, 1960	Federal R&D as Percentage of Sales, 1960	Total R&D as Percentage of Sales, 1960
Aircraft	59.52	2.6	19.9	22.5
Scientific and mechanical measuring equipment	36.52	4.1	7.7	11.8
Drugs	33.09	4.7	0.1	4.8
Machinery	32.50	2.7	1.6	4.3
Chemicals, except drugs	27.32	3.4	0.7	4.1
Electrical equipment	26.75	3.7	7.2	10.9
Rubber products	23.30	1.4	0.7	2.1
Motor vehicles and other transport equipment	22.62	2.4	0.7	3.1
Other instruments	21.62	4.4	2.1	6.5
Petroleum refining	20.59	1.0	0.1	1.1
Fabricated metal products	19.62	1.0	0.5	1.5
Nonferrous metals	18.06	0.9	0.2	1.1
Paper and allied products	15.79	0.7	0.0	0.7
Lumber, wood products, furniture	12.26	0.5	0.1	0.6
Textiles and apparel	10.26	0.4	0.2	0.6
Primary ferrous products	9.14	0.6	0.0	0.6
Rank correlation with first column		.84	.73	.92
Linear correlation with first column		.59	.84	.90

Sources: First column, see Table 1. Next three columns, National Science Foundation, Research and Development in Industry 1960, NSF 63-7 (Washington, 1963), Tables A-20 and A-22. Federal R&D funds were computed from and assumed to represent the difference between company and total funds. Chemicals were adjusted for the exclusion of drugs. Drugs were adjusted, based on raw values, to eliminate a discrepancy in the original tables.

Departing from the method used up to now, one can also illustrate the basic relationship if one is willing to regard as a technical requirement the proportion of scientists and engineers in each industry who are engaged in R&D. On this basis, scientists and engineers engaged in R&D represented 2.87 per cent of the labor force "required" to produce U.S. manufactured exports, but just 1.21 per cent of the labor force that would have been "required" to replace manufactured imports in 1961.[13]

ARE OTHER CAUSAL RELATIONSHIPS INVOLVED?

In these tests, a correlation between R&D and competitive ability has been confirmed, but, as in any statistical association, conflicting causal interpretations could be advanced. The association might be partly incidental to cross-relationships of R&D with other variables associated with successful export performance. Some plausible relationships resist quantification. For example, R&D probably appeal to, and can best be afforded by, companies that enjoy wide profit margins and large accumulated funds, for whatever reason.[14] Thus, there may be a "feedback loop" of causality running from trade success to performance of R&D.

Here I will test the relative explanatory power and cross-relationship with R&D of four proposed explanations of U.S. competitive trade performance—capital requirements, natural-resource requirements, labor-skill requirements, and economies of scale.

The United States appears to enjoy a relatively plentiful supply of "capital," whichever way that ambiguous concept is understood. This abundance of capital is not reflected, however, by American exports of capital-intensive products.[15] This Leontief paradox continues to hold for manufacturing industries today. The point can be shown with the

[13] For the underlying data and method, see footnote and data in Appendix Table 1.

[14] Cross-relations might exist with monopoly power, enterprising management, or any number of other intangibles. It is also worth noting that past successes in performing R&D may be reflected better by the present level of a company's R&D out of its own and government funds than by its spending when its successes were germinated!

[15] See, especially, W. W. Leontief, "Factor Proportions and the Structure of American Trade," *Review of Economics and Statistics* (November 1956). There, capital-intensity was judged by ratios of the value of man-made "physical" capital requirements to output. Even the inclusion of an allowance for "human capital" barely evens the balance between the capital-intensity of American exports and competitive imports. See P. B. Kenen, "Nature, Capital, and Trade," *Journal of Political Economy* (October, 1965).

Table 3

Hickman's U.S. Capital-Output Ratios in Comparison with Trade Performance and Research and Development, for 10 Industries

Industry	U.S. Exports as Percentage of Group of Ten Exports, 1962	Net Capital-Output Ratio, 1960	Scientists and Engineers in R&D as Percentage of Employment, January, 1961
Nonautomotive transport equipment	39.1	.44	5.36
Machinery	32.5	.40	2.83
Chemicals	28.0	.84	4.00
Rubber	23.3	.60	0.95
Motor vehicles	22.6	.56	1.14
Petroleum and coal products	20.6	2.43	ˋ2.02
Stone, clay, glass	15.2	.85	0.60
Paper	13.1	.96	0.47
Primary metals	11.3	1.46	0.50
Textiles	10.9	.88	0.29

Sources: U.S. share of Group of Ten exports computed from U.N. *Commodity Trade Statistics 1962;* net capital-output ratios from Hickman, *Investment Demand and U.S. Economic Growth* (Washington, D.C.: Brookings, 1965), Tables 12 and 13; scientists and engineers in R&D as a percentage of employment computed from National Science Foundation, *Scientific and Technical Personnel in Industry 1961,* as in Table 1.

help of recent estimates of "long-term net capital output ratios" for 1960, made by Bert G. Hickman.[16]

Table 3 relates his estimates of capital requirements in ten manufacturing industries to 1962 U.S. exports as a percentage of Group of Ten exports, and to scientists and engineers in R&D as a percentage of employment in January 1961.[17] These ten industries exhibit a strong negative correlation between capital requirements and trade performance.[18] This evidence merely scratches a little more of the surface of this interesting subject, but it suggests that an inverse association between

[16] B. G. Hickman, *Investment Demand and U.S. Economic Growth* (Washington, D.C.: The Brookings Institution, 1965), p. 76 and *passim.* The ratios represent estimates of desired or equilibrium capital requirements derived from the regression of net investment (investment minus depreciation) on current and lagged output, time, and lagged capital stock between 1949 and 1960.

[17] The ten industries are drawn from thirteen in the original; but "other durables" (0.42), "food and beverages" (0.45), and "other nondurables" (0.24) are hard to relate to trade categories. Their inclusion would undoubtedly weaken but not reverse the relationships discussed next.

[18] There are Spearman rank correlations of −.78 between an industry's capital requirements and its competitive trade performance, and of −.58 between Hickman's capital-output ratios and scientists and engineers in R&D as a percentage of employment. These

capital requirements and R&D in manufacturing industries probably contributes to the Leontief paradox. In any event, since there is no reason for assuming *low* capital requirements to be a chief reason for locating an industry in the United States, this evidence makes it safe to dismiss the relationship of R&D with physical capital requirements as a cause of my previous results.

The geographical availability of natural resources clearly exerts a powerful influence on American trade patterns in certain industries.[19] In natural-resource-oriented industries, the United States may lack competitive ability because of its resource limitations, whereas the low level of R&D in the industry might merely reflect the fact that R&D cannot overcome the problem. However, if one drops from the original comparison petroleum refining, primary ferrous metals, nonferrous metals, paper, and lumber and wood products,[20] for the remainder of the industries shown in Table 1 the linear correlation is still .85 and the rank correlation .95. Thus, the basic association cannot be attributed to the effects of natural-resource shortages.

My own previous studies have demonstrated that U.S. exports of manufacturers are considerably more skill-intensive than U.S. imports would be if produced under American conditions.[21] U.S. competitive ability in industries characterized by intensive R&D may relate to the skill intensity of other aspects of the same industries.[22]

Table 4 shows certain key features of the occupational skill pattern in the eighteen industries previously encountered in Table 1, along with an indicator of economies of scale to be discussed. Near the bottom, the table gives the linear correlation between the data in each column and the

---

people, however, show a .93 rank correlation with trade performance. To use a different measure of U.S. trade performance, in the five industries having the highest capital output ratios, but not in the others, the United States is a net importer.

[19] See especially J. Vanek, *The Natural Resource Content of United States Foreign Trade, 1870–1955* (Cambridge: M.I.T. Press, 1963).

[20] In the other industries, I assume that raw materials are more universally available or more easily transported, so that sources of supply have a lesser impact on location.

[21] D. B. Keesing, "Labor Skills and International Trade: Evaluating Many Trade Flows with a Single Measuring Device," *Review of Economics and Statistics* (August 1665); "Labor Skills and Comparative Advantage," *American Economic Review, Proceedings* (May 1966); and "Labor Skills and the Structure of Trade in Manufactures," in this book.

[22] Conversely, however, as Richard R. Nelson has pointed out to me, nonroutine tasks required in the production of new products may be an important explanation of the presence of a highly skilled labor force in one industry compared to another. I was led to the present study partly by the strength of patterns of requirements for scientists and engineers in my previous studies; the role of new products may help to explain my skill results.

Table 4

Selected Skill Categories as a Percentage of Employment, 1960, and Value Added per Establishment, 1958, for 18 Industries

Industry	Scientists and Engineers		Other Professions	Skilled Manual Workers	Semiskilled and Unskilled	Value Added per Establishment ($ thous.)
	In R&D	Outside R&D				
Aircraft	8.20	4.77	9.36	25.94	28.04	4,413.0
Office machinery	4.62	2.64	10.10	18.22	34.92	2,806.4
Drugs	2.45	4.10	12.68	10.09	26.47	1,542.3
Other machinery	1.27	2.68	4.47	29.42	38.32	386.9
Instruments	4.00	4.17	8.93	19.47	36.72	824.2
Chemicals, except drugs	2.83	4.57	7.74	17.57	36.89	1,022.8
Electrical equipment	3.88	3.35	8.00	16.65	44.56	1,284.9
Rubber products	1.16	1.39	3.23	14.24	56.38	734.4
Motor vehicles	0.89	1.69	4.20	23.16	51.74	2,957.1
Petroleum refining	1.51	4.55	9.90	23.34	31.73	4,751.1
Fabricated metal products	0.92	3.41	5.29	23.26	42.62	380.2
Nonferrous metals	0.65	2.82	3.89	23.63	47.64	839.1
Paper and allied	0.35	1.14	3.57	17.22	55.61	1,082.7
Stone, clay, and glass products	0.58	1.35	3.02	15.91	57.72	367.7
Other transport equipment	0.49	1.75	3.93	43.74	32.51	584.0
Lumber and wood products	0.03	0.17	1.07	12.57	72.13	84.0
Textile mill products	0.22	0.31	1.37	12.03	70.58	633.0
Primary ferrous metals	0.39	1.88	2.74	31.63	46.60	3,192.4
Linear correlation with U.S. exports as percentage of Group of Ten exports, 1962	.91	.67	.69	-.02	-.63	.44
Linear correlation with first column		.66	.71	-.04	-.59	.44

Sources: Data relating to scientists and engineers computed from U.S. Census Population 1960, Occupation by Industry; percentage of scientists and engineers in R&D based of NSF data shown in Appendix Table 1. The table omits managers and clerical and sales workers. Value added per establishment computed from U.S., Census of Manufactures 1958.

industry's competitive ability, and also the correlation of each other column (with the first one representing scientists and engineers in R&D). Scientists and engineers engaged in R&D "explain" American competitive trade performance considerably better than any other skill group, though there are some systematic associations between R&D and general skill requirements.[23]

Even stronger evidence can be obtained from multiple regressions in which 1962 U.S. exports as a percentage of Group of Ten exports are "explained" by scientists and engineers engaged in R&D, in conjunction with other scientists and engineers, other professionals, unskilled plus semiskilled labor, and value added per establishment, or any combination of the above. The partial correlation coefficient for scientists and engineers in R&D always turns out to be statistically significant at the .01 level, but, with this variable included, the partial coefficient for the other skill groups (or for value added per establishment) is never significant at the .05 level.[24]

It seems fair to conclude that, while a cross-relationship with skill requirements may strengthen the observed correlations, R&D possess a distinct and especially potent effect in shaping American competitive trade performance.

One would expect the United States, as the largest national market, to enjoy a competitive advantage in industries featuring especially strong economies from large-scale production. Unfortunately, little quantitative knowledge is available regarding many relevant dimensions of economies of scale, and no really good indicator is available. One measurable dimension, however, is the size of an average plant in each industry. The average value added per establishment in 1958 was, accordingly, included as the final column in Table 4.[25]

The results were very similar to those for skill requirements. It would

[23] Using the method of regarding scientists and engineers in an industry as a technical requirement, out of 2,495 scientists and engineers "required" to produce an average billion dollars of manufactured exports in 1961, 1,174 (47.1 per cent) were engaged in R&D, whereas of 1,401 "required" to replace an average billion dollars of manufactured imports, only 521 (37.2 per cent) were engaged in R&D. Still another test, not independent of those already reported, is worth mention—NSF has estimated the percentage of Scientists and Engineers in each industry engaged in R&D (see Appendix Table 1, column 2). These percentages themselves show a .74 correlation and a .73 Spearman rank correlation with my indicator of American competitive ability.

[24] The adjusted R^2 in every case falls from above .8 when scientists and engineers in R&D are included in the regression, to .4 or less when they are taken out.

[25] Such an averaging procedure has inherent problems; the average size of establishments may fall short of the optimum in an inconsistent way from one industry to another, while averaging may conceal divergent patterns of sub-industries, and divergences in the

appear that value added per establishment does not closely rival R&D as an explanation of American competitive ability, but there is nonetheless a positive association between R&D and economies of scale. Interestingly, the linear correlation between value added per establishment and U.S. competitive ability rises to .76 when five natural-resource-oriented industries are excluded.[26] At least one industry that weakens the correlation, the machinery industry, may owe its competitive ability to economies of scale despite the small average size of an establishment.

The cross-relationship is not surprising in that there are indivisibilities in development and marketing costs for new products. R&D are more attractive, other things being equal, when there are prospects for large-scale production. American firms probably owe part of their success in industries marked by economies of scale to attractive technical possibilities for R&D in the same industries.[27] One would hardly analyze the results of recent competition among American and European producers in such industries as aircraft, computers, and automobiles without reference to both economies of scale and American abilities in R&D.

CONCLUSION

There is a powerful correlation between the intensity of R&D activity in American industries and their export performance. The association is probably heightened by a tendency for industries that conduct intensive R&D activity to exhibit at the same time economies of scale and high requirements for skills in production. Capital requirements, however, are inversely associated with R&D.

R&D "explain" competitive trade success in manufacturing industries much better than any other variable tested. This finding is consistent with a view that the world economic role of the United States involves the systematic export of new products.

---

steepness with which costs decline as a function of plant size. Other dimensions of economies of scale are neglected—though on the whole, the industries characterized by this calculation as having large plants are also marked by concentration into large firms. Cf. U.S., Bureau of the Census, *Concentration Ratios in Manufacturing Industry 1958*, Report Prepared for the Subcommittee on the Judiciary, U.S. Senate (Washington, D.C., 1962).

[26] As previously, the excluded industries were petroleum refining, primary ferrous metals, nonferrous metals, paper, and lumber and wood products. For the remaining industries, the linear correlation between R&D and value added per establishment is .68.

[27] An ingenious empirical literature explores these connections. See, for example, F. M. Scherer, "Firm Size, Market Structure, Opportunity, and the Output of Patented Inventions," *American Economic Review* (December 1965); E. O. Mansfield, "Size of Firm, Market Structure and Innovation," *Journal of Political Economy* (December 1963); and Scherer's bibliography.

APPENDIX

Appendix

National Science Foundation Data and Trade Classification

Industry	NSF Estimates for Jan. 1961 of		Commodity Trade Categories Assumed To Correspond (SITC, Revised)
	Scientists and Engineers as Percentage of Employment	Percentage of Scientists and Engineers Engaged in R&D	
Aircraft	12.2	63.2	734, 711.4
Office machinery	8.0	63.6	714
Drugs	16.3	37.4	541
Other machinery	4.3	32.2	71 exc. 714, 711.4
Instruments	8.3	55.2	861, 862, 864
Chemicals, except drugs	9.5	30.2	266, 5 exc. 541
Electrical equipment	8.2	53.7	72
Rubber products	2.1	45.4	62
Motor vehicles	3.3	34.5	732
Petroleum refining	8.1	24.9	332
Fabricated metal products	2.4	21.2	69, 812
Nonferrous metals	3.7	18.7	68 exc. 681, 688
Paper and allied products	2.0	23.6	64
Stone, clay, and glass products	2.0	30.0	66 exc. 667
Other transport equipment	2.1	21.7	731, 733, 735
Lumber and wood products	0.5	16.3	234, 631, 632
Textile mill products	0.7	41.9	65
Primary ferrous metals	2.5	17.2	67

Sources: First two columns: National Science Foundation, *Scientific and Technical Personnel in Industry 1961*, NSF 63-32 (Washington, 1963), Tables A-3, A-7, A-9; fourth and fifth columns (except items marked with a superscript in fifth column), *Annual Survey of Manufacturers 1961*; sixth computed from fourth and fifth; seventh computed from second and sixth; exports and imports based on U.S., Department of Commerce, *U.S. Commodity Imports and Exports as Related to Output, 1961 and 1960*, Table 1-C.

Table 1

Underlying Table 1 and Certain Subsequent Computations

Employment, 1961	Sales, 1961 ($ bils)	Employment per $1 Bil. Sales, 1961	Scientists, Engineers in R&D per $1 Bil. Sales, 1961	Exports, 1961 ($ mils)	Imports, 1961 ($ mils)
694,970	13.42	51,786	4245	1174.1	149.8
139,663	2.36	59,180	2733	323.9	95.6
102,051	3.31	30,831	755	272.1	44.1
1,234,806	32.08	38,491	490	3097.7	347.3
342,642	6.20	55,265	2483	461.2	179.3
612,606	26.57	23,056	652	1810.9	380.3
1,364,450	24.00[a]	56,852	2207	1148.0	366.3
372,983	6.00[a]	62,164	720	158.1	117.1
604,328	23.28[a]	25,959	231	1129.6	367.4
128,859	15.67	8,223	124	439.0	671.2
1,050,517	20.16[a]	52,109	478	500.3	156.6
313,983	9.72[a]	32,303	209	421.5	824.1
573,246	13.56[a]	42,275	148	453.2	1054.5
569.924	9.12[a]	62,492	362	205.3	220.4
206,658	3.56	58,050	282	199.2	55.8
553,306	7.87	70,306	23	182.9	526.8
871,453	14.64[a]	59,525	133	319.5	593.9
791,363	15.00[a]	52,758	206	471.0	444.3

Note: Computation in text on scientists and engineers "required" to produce U.S. exports and replace U.S. imports in 1961 was obtained by multiplying estimates in seventh column by corresponding exports and imports, columns 8 and 9.

[a] Based on data from *Survey of Current Business,* monthly averages shown on p. S-5.

Appendix Table 2

Research and Development by Product Field versus Competititive Trade Performance

Product Field	R&D, 1960 ($ mil.)	R&D as Percentage of 1960 Value Added in Industry	SITC Categories Assumed To Correspond	U.S. Exports as Percentage of Group of Ten Exports, 1962
Aircraft	1,132	17.21	734, 711.4	59.52
Farm machinery	75	7.97	712	40.95
Scientific and mechanical measuring instruments	153	8.41	861.3, 861.8, 861.9	36.52
Office machinery	314	24.25	714	35.00
Metalworking machinery	53	1.97	715	34.94
Other chemicals	202	4.89	5 not elsewhere classified	34.53
Drugs	175	7.43	541	33.09
Engines and turbines	93	9.30	711, exc. 711.4	30.78
Plastics and synthetics	324	14.36	231.2, 266, 581	30.68
Construction and other machinery	208	2.46	717, 718, 719	29.57
Other electrical equipment, except communication	133	3.31	725, 726, 729, exc. 729.3	29.37

Agricultural chemicals	39	7.38	561, 599.2	25.68
Industrial chemicals	215	4.23	512, 513, 514, 521, 531	23.92
Rubber products	56	1.48	62	23.30
Motor vehicles	533	5.27	732	22.62
Other instruments	68	3.40	Other 861, 862, 864	21.62
Electrical distributing and industrial equipment	146	4.39	722, 723	21.29
Fabricated metal products	153	1.48	69, 812	19.62
Nonferrous metals	51	1.39	68 exc. 681, 688	18.06
Stone, clay, and glass products	53	0.83	66 exc. 667	15.22
Other transport equipment	29	1.68	731, 733, 735	13.70
Primary ferrous metals	70	0.72	67	9.14

Sources: R&D by product field, 1960, from National Science Foundation, Research and Development in Industry 1960, NSF 63-7, Table A-18; 1960 value added taken from Dept. of Commerce, Annual Survey of Manufactures 1961; export data from United Nations, Commodity Trade Statistics 1962.

Note: The following product fields were excluded from the computations: atomic energy devices ($556 mil. of R&D in 1960), communications equipment and electronic components ($2,152 mil.), guided missiles ($2,223 mil.), and ordnance ($90 mil.) on grounds that R&D spending was primarily on military systems in most of which trade was forbidden; food and kindred products ($96 mil.) and petroleum refining and extraction ($137 mil.), because of difficulties in aligning trade categories; and "other, not elsewhere classified" ($622 mil., much of it military) partly for the same reason.

TERUTOMO OZAWA

Imitation, Innovation, and Japanese Exports

TECHNOLOGY-CENTERED
INTERNATIONAL TRANSACTIONS

SINCE THE END OF WORLD WAR II, the world economy has undergone a widespread transformation in industrial structure and has taken steps to liberalize trade and capital movements. Manufacturing and marketing have been increasingly integrated among the industrialized countries; hence, as economies have grown in material wealth, the external effects on production and consumption have become more pervasive. Behind these developments lie the rapid progress of industrial and managerial technology and the ever-widening horizon of the entrepreneur. The economic universe has grown technology-conscious and international in outlook.

This essay is based on my "Imitation, Innovation, and Trade: A Study of Foreign Licensing Operations in Japan" (unpublished doctoral dissertation, Columbia University, 1966). I am grateful to Donald B. Keesing for his valuable comments.

The evolutionary character of the national economy was stressed by Joseph Schumpeter. The economic system is, in his words, "incessantly being revolutionized *from within* by new enterprise, i.e., by the intrusion of new commodities or new methods of production or new commercial opportunities into the industrial structure as it exists at any moment." [1] This same view applies to the international economic system. With the decrease of barriers to trade and investment, firms in different countries are exposed to new competition and to opportunities in world markets. The only successful survivors are those who can innovate or adapt to a changing environment.

In today's highly competitive markets, national and international, research and development activity is requisite to the survival of individual firms. And, from investment in research and development, new technologies are consciously generated. The United States, moreover, plays a strategic role in this process. Raymond Vernon argues as follows: (1) U.S. firms have a comparative advantage in exporting new labor-saving products ahead of other countries because "the United States market consists of consumers with an average income which is higher than that in any other national market," and "is characterized by high unit labor costs and relatively unrationed capital compared with practically all other markets." (2) As the new products become standardized in specifications and production methods, with the major "bugs" eliminated, firms in other countries are motivated to follow the United States, thereby replacing U.S. exports and even exporting to the U.S. market at a later stage in the "product cycle." [2]

But firms in other industrialized countries may, by their own research or by imitation, emulate U.S. leaders at the early stages of the "product cycle," thereby accelerating the standardization of new products. During this foreshortened process, adaptive innovations are likely to be generated to adjust U.S.-oriented products or production methods to new manufacturing and marketing environments. The product-cycle leader may also accelerate the "product cycle" by direct investment or licensing in order to maximize income. Through direct investment, the leaders can retain monopolistic control over price and output, and can then resort to market segmentation through which each layer of buyers, different in

[1] J. A. Schumpeter, *Capitalism, Socialism and Democracy* (New York: Harper & Row, 1950), p. 31.

[2] Raymond Vernon, "International Investment and International Trade in the Product Cycle," *Quarterly Journal of Economics*, LXXX (May 1966), 192.

income levels, may be tapped by a gradual reduction of price. This strategy enables the leaders to capture Marshallian consumer's surplus and to maximize total profits. Furthermore, licensing may be used to establish cooperation between leaders and potentially successful followers, particularly when the exportation of new products encounters import restrictions.

The advanced firms' desire to achieve and retain monopolistic power has been identified by Stephen Hymer as a powerful influence on the international flow of direct-investment capital.[3] The promptness with which firms resort to overseas operations, including licensing, will vary with the rate of technological progress within the firm (i.e., rate of obsolescence of existing technology produced by research and development) and with the intensity of technological competition among firms (i.e., how fast other firms, at home and abroad, will assimilate or create similar technology). Firms have four basic ways of operating overseas: (1) by licensing technology to an existing foreign firm; (2) by trading technology for an equity interest in an existing foreign firm; (3) by forming a new company in partnership with a foreign firm (a joint venture); or (4) by establishing a plant (or plants) in a foreign country (a subsidiary or a branch plant). A combination of these options is possible and is often employed: in particular, options (2), (3), and (4), which are varying forms of direct investment, can be combined with licensing. In other words, licensing can be either competitive with or complementary to direct investment. But nonexclusive licensing arrangements by themselves create the least conflict with local interests, whereas wholly foreign-owned operations create the most conflict.[4]

Thus, the combined findings of Vernon and Hymer are: Research-oriented exports from high-labor-cost countries (which are normally high-income countries) tend to be "ephemeral" in their life expectancy. The reason is that firms in other countries may soon produce similar products, by their own research or by imitation, and will follow the leaders. Moreover, exports that embody monopolistic advantages (such

[3] Stephen H. Hymer, "The International Operations of National Firms. A Study of Direct Foreign Investment" (unpublished doctoral dissertation, Massachusetts Institute of Technology, June 1960).

[4] It should be mentioned, however, that wholly foreign-owned operations are perhaps free from internal managerial conflict since all decision-making power resides in the advanced firms. Licensing arrangements and joint ventures, on the other hand, may be plagued by internal conflicts because managerial authority on price and output decisions may be more diffused.

as patents) are often confronted with import restrictions, which stimulate the development of substitutes in foreign markets. In order to prolong their technological advantages, advanced firms in high-labor-cost countries may therefore engage in licensing operations, attempt to forestall foreign imitation by operating directly overseas, or cooperate with foreign firms in joint ventures, capitalizing on lower production costs overseas. Hence, research-oriented exports from high-labor-cost countries such as the United States are predestined to destroy themselves by their very success and, eventually, to metamorphose from "merchandise trade" transactions into "invisible trade" transactions.

This essay is an empirical study of the relationships between technological leaders and a major "follower," with particular attention to the latter's export performance. The study selects Japan as the "follower" because it has been most active and successful in technological assimilation and in the export of manufactures during the postwar period. I will explore two hypotheses: first, that the acquisition of advanced foreign technology through licensing made a fundamental contribution to the postwar growth of Japanese exports of manufactures; second, that the unprecedented prevalence of joint ventures in postwar Japan was a reflection of advanced foreign firms' desire to maintain direct control of their technological advantage in the Japanese market.

JAPANESE EXPORT PERFORMANCE AND THE ACQUISITION OF FOREIGN TECHNOLOGY

Various studies have examined the phenomenal growth of Japan's exports during the postwar period. For example, Junz and Rhomberg's study, reproduced in Table 1, indicates that Japan had the highest export expansion of the 11 countries studied during the period 1953–1955 to 1956–1959, and the second highest during the period 1956–1959 to 1960–1963.[5] Moreover, the portion of the increase in Japanese exports left to be explained by "residual factors" (i.e., changes in relative prices and nonprice factors) was the highest among the 11 countries for both

[5] Helen B. Junz and Rudolf R. Rhomberg, "Prices and Export Performance of Industrial Countries, 1953–63," *International Monetary Fund Staff Papers*, XII (July 1965), 85–99.

Table 1

Effect of Geographic and Commodity Composition on the Growth of Exports to Industrial Markets, 1953–1955 to 1956–1959 and 1956–1959 to 1960–1963[a]

Country	Actual Change in Value of Exports of Manufactures, % (1)	Change Explained by	
		Growth of Markets and Shifts in Commodity Composition of Demand, % (2)	Other Factors (Residual), %: Col. 1 — Col. 2 (3)
1953–1955 to 1956–1959			
Austria	+57.4	+57.2	+0.2
Belgium	+41.6	+49.2	−7.6
Canada	+20.3	+49.3	−29.0
France	+52.4	+52.9	−0.5
West Germany	+76.6	+52.4	+24.2
Italy	+93.6	+58.9	+34.7
Japan	+142.1	+47.1	+95.0
Netherlands	+51.6	+57.0	−5.4
Sweden	+62.0	+57.0	+5.0
United Kingdom	+44.9	+57.8	−12.9
United States	+40.8	+48.3	−7.5
1956–1959 to 1960–1963			
Austria	+53.2	+81.8	−28.6
Belgium	+51.5	+61.2	−9.7
Canada	+13.1	+37.8	−24.7
France	+96.4	+71.7	+24.7
West Germany	+69.5	+68.1	+1.4
Italy	+129.8	+69.9	+59.9
Japan	+94.2	+32.5	+61.7
Netherlands	+72.7	+72.7	—
Sweden	+72.0	+72.3	−0.3
United Kingdom	+37.1	+56.4	−19.3
United States	+32.6	+36.7	−4.1

Source: Helen B. Junz and Rudolf R. Rhomberg, "Prices and Export Performance of Industrial Countries, 1953–63," *IMF Staff Papers* (July 1965), 228.

[a] Changes in the total value of exports of each country to the other 10 countries and Switzerland are compared with changes computed on three alternative assumptions: first, that countries maintained their market shares of the previous period in the industrial market as a whole, i.e., in the combined market of the other 10 countries and Switzerland; second, that they maintained their market shares in the market of each of the industrial countries; and third, that they maintained their market shares in each of three commodity groups in each of the industrial countries. The three commodity groups are SITC 5 (chemicals), 7 (machinery and transport equipment), and 6 plus 8 (basic manufactures and miscellaneous manufactured products) of the revised United Nations Code.

periods, accounting for approximately 65 per cent of the total change during each period.[6]

Lacking data on nonprice factors, Junz and Rhomberg analyzed the residual cell only in terms of changes in prices. Their result showed rather poor correlations between percentage changes in market shares and percentage changes in relative prices. They consequently concluded that "The degree to which changes in the price indices used in the study fall short of 'explaining' the observed variation in relative export performance is an indication both of imperfections in these indices and of the influence of nonprice factors." [7] In the case of Japan, the coefficients of determination are zero. Considering the magnitude of the "residual factors" in Japan's export growth, the "indication both of imperfections in these indices and of the influence of nonprice factors" would seem to be of real importance, and the influence of nonprice factors may well be the more important.

This possibility is strongly suggested by the extremely high productivity growth in Japanese manufacturing relative to that of other countries. Drawing on Bela Balassa's study, we can detect a close rank correlation between changes in productivity and in export shares.[8] Table 2 indicates this correlation. Note that Japan showed the highest growth in both variables during the period 1953–1961. Productivity growth influences costs and prices, but it also works through improvements in the quality and variety of output. Increases in productivity often stem from improvements in the quality of the goods used as inputs and from the development of new capacity in highly productive branches of industry. Hence, a substantial rise in productivity, such as took place within a short space of time in Japan, was no doubt accompanied by changes in quality and variety, as well as in price. In this connection, A. Maizels' observation is relevant: "It is now generally accepted that the quality of Japanese goods exported since the early 1950's has been well up to "western" standards, though this was not the case before the war . . . . Moreover,

[6] P. R. Narvekar, in an earlier study, found that about 70 per cent of Japan's export growth from 1953 to 1957 was due to "increased competitiveness," a term that corresponds to Junz and Rhomberg's "price and other factors." See P. R. Narvekar, "The Role of Competitiveness in Japan's Export Performance, 1954–58," *International Monetary Fund Staff Papers*, VIII (November 1960), 85–100.

[7] Junz and Rhomberg, "Prices and Export Performance," p. 258.

[8] Bela Balassa, "Recent Developments in the Competitiveness of American Industry and Prospects for the Future," in U.S. Congress, Joint Economic Committee, *Factors Affecting the United States Balance of Payments*, 87th Congress, 2nd Session (Washington, D.C.: U.S. Government Printing Office, 1962).

Table 2

Changes in Output per Man-Hour in Manufacturing Industry and Changes in Export Shares of Manufactures of Seven Industrial Countries, 1953–1961

Country	(1) Output per Man-Hour in Manufacturing, 1961 (1953 = 100)	Rank	(2) Export Shares in Manufacturing (%) 1953	1961	Percentage Change	Rank
Japan	197	1	4.3	8.1	+88	1
Italy	167	2	3.9	6.7	+72	2
France	165	3	10.9	11.2	+3	4
West Germany	152	4	16.0	24.1	+51	3
Belgium	143	5	7.8	6.9	−11	5
United States	124	6	31.4	24.4	−22	6
United Kingdom	122	7	25.7	18.6	−28	7

Source: (1) and (2) from Tables 3 and 7, respectively, in Bela Balassa, "Recent Developments in the Competitiveness of American Industry and Prospects for the Future," in U.S. Congress, Joint Economic Committee, *Factors Affecting the United States Balance of Payments*, 87th Congress, 2nd Session, 1962, pp. 36 and 40. Export shares were calculated by dividing the export value of the manufactures of a given country by the total export value of the manufactures of all seven countries.

Note: Spearman's coefficient of rank correlation is .96. Countries whose productivity rose by more than about 50 per cent appear to have gained in export shares over the period under review. The only country upsetting an otherwise perfect relationship is France. She had high growth in productivity, but this rise in the efficiency of domestic production was not reflected in her export performance.

the range of products in which Japan offers serious competition in world markets has widened appreciably." [9]

How did Japan succeed in bringing the quality and variety of her exports "well up to 'western' standards" since the early 1950s? To be sure, the Japanese made innovations of their own, but the main effort to raise industrial technology was concentrated on the adaptation of advanced western technologies. Hence, the answer to my question may perhaps be found in the trend of Japanese imports of technology through licensing, and in the nature of imported technologies. These are shown in Tables 3 and 4, respectively.

[9] A. Maizels, *Industrial Growth and World Trade* (London: Cambridge University Press, 1963), p. 202.

Table 3

Number of Foreign Licenses Acquired by Selected Japanese Industries, 1950–1962

Industry	1950	1951	1952	1953	1954	1955	1956	1957	1958	1959	1960	1961	1962	Total	Percentage
A. Electrical machinery	5	11	24	43	22	17	20	29	26	39	99	59	82	476	23.7
1. Power-generating equipment		2	2	2	4	1	5	1	1	3	7	8	2	38	
2. Wire and Cable	2	3	6		1	1	1		7	4	2	1		28	
3. Communication equipment	2	3	12	36	16	7	6	26	13	10	60	25	50	266	
4. Other electrical	1	3	4	5	2	8	8	2	5	22	30	25	30	144	
B. Transport equipment	9	6	8	6	7	8	12	2	6	6	17	24	17	120	6.0
C. Nonelectrical machinery	3	33	38	19	14	16	20	25	23	31	71	101	94	494	24.7
1. Power-generating equipment	3	9	12	4		2	4	3		2	3	5	3	52	
2. Metal working machinery				3	1	2		2	2	2	4	5	3	24	
3. Textile machinery	2	2	1	1		2	1			2	2	2	4	23	
4. Other nonelectrical	4	22	25	11	13	10	15	16	19	26	61	89	84	395	
D. Metals	1	9	16	8	4	7	18	11	12	25	19	27	22	179	9.0
E. Chemicals	8	23	16	14	22	17	46	30	11	33	77	59	83	439	21.9
1. Synthetic fibers		1	1		5		6	2		3	2		14	34	
2. Pharmaceuticals	3	11	4	10	6	4	5	2	2	6	14	10	7	90	
3. Organic and inorganic	4	11	7	2	8	9	33	18	7	21	51	40	54	265	
4. Other chemicals	1		4	2	3	4	2	2	2	3	10	9	8	47	
F. Textiles		4	5	7	8	1	12	7	3	7	8	23	3	88	4.5
G. Petroleum refining	1	1	14			3	5	2	5	4	7	5	5	51	2.5
H. Rubber and leather		6	3		2	1	5	7	2	3	8	8	2	52	2.6
I. Construction		1	2			1	2	3		1		1	1	16	0.8
J. Stone, clay, and glass	1	2	2	4	3		2			3		7	12	42	2.1
K. Paper and pulp		4	2	2		1	2	1	1		7	7	6	25	1.3
L. Utility supply	1	1								1	1			3	0.2
M. Entertainment	1										1			2	0.1
N. Printing			1			1	1	1	1				1	5	0.3
O. Food processing											4			6	0.3
Total	27	101	133	103	82	72	144	118	90	153	327	320	328	1,998	100.0

Source: Japanese Science and Technology Agency, *Kagaku Gijitsu Hakusho* (Survey Report on Science and Technology), 1964.

Note: The numbers represent a complete enumeration of class A licensing agreements validated and registered under the Foreign Investment Law. These agreements have an effective life of more than one year; payments of royalties are to be made in foreign currency. There is another category, class B licensing agreements, including agreements calling for royalty payments in yen or with an effective life of less than one year. Class B agreements normally cover such incidental arrangements as invitations of foreign engineers or acquisitions of drawings. No detailed studies on class B agreements have been made by government agencies, but, since class A agreements are about 10 times as large as class B agreements, measured by total royalty payments over 1950–1963, the former are far more important than the latter. We can probably assume that class A agreements reflect the major trend in technological assimilation through most of the period under study. Until the Japanese government substantially eased its restrictions on licensing in 1959, class A agreements usually covered major transfers of know-how. After the relaxation of controls, agreements relating to trademarks seem to have increased, but, since we are concerned mainly with the 1950s, this recent tendency is not likely to affect our basic supposition or greatly to distort the analysis.

Table 4

Number of New Products, New Processes, and Improved Products Attributable to Foreign Licenses, 1950–1960

Industry	Number of New Products	Number of Improved Products	Number of Improved Processes	Number of Other Kinds of Improvement[a]	Total
Electrical machinery	154 (50.8%)	62 (20.5%)	52 (17.2%)	35 (11.5%)	303 (100.0%)
Nonelectrical machinery	142 (40.7%)	79 (22.6%)	55 (15.8%)	73 (20.9%)	349 (100.0%)
Chemicals	114 (30.7%)	39 (10.5%)	136 (36.7%)	82 (22.1%)	371 (100.0%)
Transport equipment	46 (45.1%)	16 (15.7%)	18 (17.7%)	22 (21.5%)	102 (100.0%)
Base metals	35 (30.1%)	9 (7.7%)	46 (39.6%)	26 (22.4%)	116 (100.0%)
Textiles	14 (24.1%)	15 (25.9%)	19 (32.8%)	10 (17.2%)	58 (100.0%)
Other industries	45 (25.1%)	22 (12.3%)	60 (33.5%)	52 (29.0%)	179 (100.0%)
Total	550 (37.2%)	242 (16.3%)	386 (26.1%)	300 (20.3%)	1,478 (100.0%)

Source: Japan, Ministry of International Trade and Industry, Gaikoku Gijitsu Dohnyu no Genjoh to Mondaiten (Current Situation and Problems of Foreign Technology Absorption), 1962.

Note: The total number of foreign technologies acquired (i.e., 1,478) does not match the total number of licenses shown in Table 3 because the former came from a sample. The sample covered 77 per cent of the total population of license-acquiring companies. The breakdown given in the table provides some evidence of the effects of foreign licenses on the quality and variety of Japanese products, but great value should not be attached to the classification itself, because the line of demarcation is necessarily arbitrary. Moreover, one licensing agreement often embraces more than one technology.

a Includes improvements in facilities, installation, control system, etc.

The Japanese readily acknowledge the contribution of imported technology to the improvement of their output:

> ... it cannot be denied that, as the outcome of the technology acquired from overseas, there has been notable achievement in many fields of industry in connection with modernization of equipment, improvement of quality of equipment, improvement of the quality of products, development of new products, and reduction of costs. Access to advanced technology has had no small effect upon the postwar change of Japan's industrial structure, and has been the key factor in bringing about the so-called technological transformation.[10]

It is thus undeniable that Japanese productive capacity was greatly enlarged by technological borrowing, and one may put forth a formal hypothesis: The fundamental impulse to Japanese export expansion after World War II came from advanced foreign technologies acquired through licensing.[11]

Let us examine this hypothesis by performing a cross-sectional rank correlation between the size of technological borrowing (i.e., the number of licenses acquired by an industry divided by that industry's total value added to eliminate mere size effects) and the increase in the industry's export volume. Table 5 presents the basic data for this correlation: the Spearman coefficient of rank correlation is .47. If we confine our analysis to six major industries (i.e., electrical machinery, nonelectrical machinery, chemicals, primary metals, transport equipment, and textiles), the coefficient is .94. These industries were the largest users of foreign licenses (accounting for approximately 90 per cent of the total number of licenses acquired in the 1950s), and were also the largest exporters (responsible for about 65 per cent of the total value of exported manufactures in 1961).

A time-series regression analysis relating foreign licenses to export shares in each of these six industries also reveals a substantial correlation. In accordance with our assumption that foreign licenses introduce improvements in the quality and variety of Japanese products, changes in the export shares are used as the dependent variable (Y), and the number of foreign licenses as the independent variable (X). In this

---

[10] *The Oriental Economist* (February 1959), 70.

[11] Licensing is the only form of technological diffusion considered in this study, although it is but one of several methods for the transmission of technology. A comprehensive study would also examine flows of technical literature, the extent of education abroad, and employment of foreign technicians, imports of capital goods, and direct investment. This study deals with direct investment, but only in its relationship with licensing operations.

Table 5

Relation between Foreign Licenses and Export Growth

Industry	Foreign Licenses Acquired,[a] 1950–1960	(A) Rank among 9 Industries	(B) Rank among 6 Major Industries	Index of Export Volume in 1961 (1953 = 100)	(C) Rank among 9 Industries	(D) Rank among 6 Major Industries
Electrical machinery	.744	1	1	2,140	1	1
Nonelectrical machinery	.664	2	2	590	4	2
Chemicals	.557	3	3	477	5	3
Rubber and leather	.416	4	—	996	3	—
Transport equipment	.178	5	4	447	6	4
Metals	.165	6	5	298	8	6
Textiles	.123	7	6	312	7	5
Clay, stone, and glass	.101	8	—	210	9	—
Paper and pulp	.080	9	—	1,248	2	—

Sources: Number of foreign licenses from Table 3: Value added from Office of the Prime Minister, Japanese Government, *Japan Statistical Yearbook*; index of export volume from Bela Balassa, "Recent Developments in the Competitiveness of American Industry and Prospects for the Future," in U.S. Congress, Joint Economic Committee, *Factors Affecting the United States Balance of Payments*, 87th Congress, 2nd Session, 1962, Table 10, p. 45, except metals, rubber and leather, clay, stone, and glass, and paper and pulp. The indices for these items were computed from the United Nations, Statistical Office, *Commodity Trade Statistics*: Original SITC was employed; metals = 67 and 68 (worked metal products excluded); rubber and leather = 61 and 62; clay, stone, and glass = 66; paper and pulp = 25 and 64.

[a] The ratios of the number of foreign licenses to value added (1960).

regression analysis, three different methods are employed. In the first, Japan's export share in a given year is assumed to be related to the total number of foreign licenses acquired over the preceding three years; in the second, over the preceding four years; and in the third, over the preceding five years. These groupings embody the hypothesis that the effect of foreign technology on competitiveness weakens after a lapse of time. The three sets of relationships can be summarized mathematically as follows:

$$Y_t = a + b \sum_{i=t-1}^{t-k} x \qquad (k = 3, 4, \text{ and } 5)$$

where Y is an export share in a given year, x is the number of foreign licenses acquired in a given year, and t is the point in time (a given year). The results of these regressions are summarized in Table 6.

Although there is evidence of autocorrelation in some of the regression residuals, casting doubt on the validity of the corresponding equations, the results of the statistical analysis offer considerable support for the basic hypothesis connecting export competitiveness and licensing, especially for industries that absorbed large numbers of foreign licenses over the whole period. The nonelectrical machinery and chemical industries, for example, show high association without evidence of autocorrelation, whereas the textile industry shows a relatively small correlation.

Although the statistical methods are crude, all our findings indicate that Japan's export competitiveness *is* related to her acquisition of foreign technology. This, of course, is not decisive proof of causation; the connection between Japan's acquisition of licenses and her export performance may not be a one-way relationship. Thus, electrical machinery, nonelectrical machinery, chemicals, and transport equipment are the items for which postwar world demand grew rapidly,[12] and this expansion of demand might have caused the increase of Japanese exports. Japan's export expansion, in turn, could have stimulated an interest in advanced technologies available overseas. But one thing seems true in any case: Technological borrowing, whether autonomous or induced by expanding demand, did *in the end* contribute to the development of new productive capacity in sectors which experienced an increase in world demand. This process, moreover, involved a high rate of capital formation and, as a consequence, a rapid rate of economic growth in Japan. How the acquisition of foreign technology fostered Japan's capacity building through high investment is well described in the following observation made by the Japanese Government in 1962:

Generally speaking, equipment investments in connection with technological innovation have been increasingly poured in during the past ten years . . . . There are various factors which have caused an increase in equipment investments recently. Although it is natural that competition is intense under a free enterprise system, efforts toward bringing up the level of technology to that of advanced countries is one factor which has created competition in the induction of foreign technology, which, in turn, has resulted in excessive investment competition. Also, by expanding their production capacity, the various enterprises are engaging in a

---

[12] See A. Maizels, "Fast and Slow-growing Products in World Trade," *National Institute Economic Review* (London), No. 25 (August 1963), 22–35.

Table 6

*Regression of Changes in Market Share (Percentage) on
the Number of Foreign Licenses Acquired*

$$\left(Y_t = a + b \sum_{i=t-1}^{t-k} x_i \right)$$

Industry	a	b	Coefficient of Determination, R^2	Standard Error of Estimate, $S_{yx}(\%)$
$k = 3\ (1953–1963)$				
Electrical machinery	.459	.047	.54[a,b]	2.88
Nonelectrical machinery	1.767	.004	.34	.52
Chemicals	2.160	.013	.93[b]	.21
Base metals	3.063	.089	.54[b]	1.53
Transport equipment	4.361	.042	.10[a]	1.79
Textiles	15.567	.233	.27	3.35
$k = 4\ (1954–1963)$				
Electrical machinery	.312	.041	.50[a,c]	2.96
Nonelectrical machinery	1.506	.005	.67[b]	.32
Chemicals	2.049	.012	.93[b]	.21
Base metals	2.897	.075	.59[a,b]	1.45
Transport equipment	4.102	.046	.12[a]	1.76
Textiles	17.687	.132	.24	2.01
$k = 5\ (1955–1963)$				
Electrical machinery	.768	.035	.48[a,c]	2.83
Nonelectrical machinery	1.467	.005	.59[c]	.38
Chemicals	2.710	.006	.27	.20
Base metals	2.929	.065	.51[c]	1.71
Transport equipment	4.458	.039	.13	1.32
Textiles	18.926	.085	.17	1.59

Sources: The market shares for 1953–1960 are from Bela Balassa, "Recent Developments in the Competitiveness of American Industry and Prospects for the Future," in U.S. Congress, Joint Economic Committee, *Factors Affecting the United States Balance of Payments,* 87th Congress, 2nd Session, 1962. The market shares for 1962 and 1963 are derived from the same primary sources, i.e., Organization for Economic Cooperation and Development, *Foreign Trade Statistics,* and United Nations, *Commodity Trade Statistics.* The shares were calculated by dividing the value of Japanese exports by the total of the seven countries' exports. The seven countries are the United States, Belgium-Luxembourg, France, West Germany, Italy, the United Kingdom, and Japan.

[a] Residuals significantly autocorrelated at the .01 level.

[b] Statistically significant at the .01 level.

[c] Statistically significant at the .05 level.

fierce competition to secure as large a share of the market as possible without considering their margin of profit . . . investments for investment goods industries had increased greatly and as a result, the demand and supply balance of related industries had tended to become tight, which, in turn, resulted in more investments. This is the so-called effect of "investments, creating more investments." [13]

The word "induction" in this quotation refers to the government-controlled acquisition of foreign licenses under the Foreign Investment Law enacted in 1950.[14] William W. Lockwood made a similar observation connecting economic growth, rising productivity, and technologies imported by Japan:

Hailed sometimes as a "miracle," there is nothing mysterious about Japan's high-pitched growth. The factors immediately at work are well known . . . . The principal gain . . . has come from a sustained rise in the productivity of labor . . . . *A key impulse to this productivity gain has come from the great wave of technical borrowing from abroad since the occupation.* The isolation and destruction of the war had caused Japan to lag well behind the West in the industrial arts. As soon as possible her businessmen and public agencies moved energetically to repair the gap, importing the latest technologies over a wide front to rebuild their industrial plant.[15]

All this suggests that the high rate of capital formation provided the link between Japan's acquisitions of foreign technology and her export performance, and that Japanese export expansion was concomitant to the development of new productive capacity under the main stimulus of technological borrowing.[16]

[13] Japan, Economic Planning Agency, *Economic Survey of Japan* (1961–62), 27.

[14] The purpose of the Foreign Investment Law was to guarantee to foreign nationals the remittance of their royalties, dividends, and interest arising from licensing operations and investment in Japan over a specified period. The Foreign Investment Commission Law established the Foreign Investment Commission to act as an administrative organ for validating (1) the conclusion of licensing agreements between a foreign licenser and a Japanese licensee, and (2) the acquisition of the stocks and the debentures of a Japanese concern by a foreign investor. Thus, the acquisition of both foreign technology and capital was controlled under the Foreign Investment Law, since both involved an outflow of foreign exchange in the form of royalty and interest payments.

[15] William W. Lockwood, "Political Economy," in Harbert Passin (ed.), *The United States and Japan* (Englewood, N.J.: Prentice-Hall, Inc., 1966), p. 103. Emphasis added.

[16] Another important link between the imported technologies and export performance was R&D activities in Japan. Undoubtedly, the imported technologies stimulated Japanese research activities because of the necessity of adapting foreign technologies to Japanese production and marketing requirements. These increased efforts in R&D have, in turn, raised Japan's capacity to absorb advanced technologies from abroad and have led to the development of indigenous technologies. *The Economist* (London) cites an example: "They built the best foreign machinery under license and quickly applied the most advanced techniques. With strong Government support—the Ship Research Institute is part of the Ministry of Transport—Japanese shipbuilders have since improved

TECHNOLOGICAL TRANSFER AND
FOREIGN BUSINESS OPERATIONS
IN JAPAN

When the pros and cons of licensing are discussed, the "nurturing of future competition" is always listed as one possible disadvantage to the licenser. Licensing operations involve a substantial risk of fostering future competition. Consequently, some firms make it a policy never to license. One American company explains that "It has no intention of teaching a licensee what the licensee needs to become a well-equipped competitor in a few years." [17] These policies have sometimes slowed Japanese progress. Around 1956, for example, the Japanese machine tool industry, which had acquired a relatively small number of foreign licenses, was thought to be backward compared with related industries that had acquired relatively large numbers of licenses. Swiss and West German manufacturers of high-grade precision tools were reluctant to provide the necessary technology to Japan, because they thought it would become a competitor.[18] By and large, however, the Japanese were successful in finding suppliers of technology or in obtaining technologies from western manufacturers who were previously unwilling to supply them. What factors, then, induced western manufacturers to impart technology to the Japanese even at the risk of fostering future competition?

One obvious factor is the income that western companies could obtain by licensing patents and accumulated know-how that were doomed to early obsolescence in this fast-moving world of science and technology. In fact, some companies cite this reason explicitly, and have received enormous amounts in royalties.[19] The National Industrial Conference Board's study cites an aircraft company's executive as stating that "his

---

on many of the designs they previously built under license and now offer the rest of the world the highly effective result of their own original research." ["Reconsider Japan," *The Economist* (November 28, 1964), 1013.] A study of Japanese research and development, both adaptive and creative, is presented in Ozawa, "Imitation, Innovation, and Trade."

[17] Quoted in "Liking for Licensing," *Chemical Week* (May 30, 1964), 55.

[18] See *The Oriental Economist* (February 1957), 74.

[19] "For several of the U.S. companies interviewed, royalty income from Japan already exceeds $1 million a year." See James C. Abegglen, "Changing Japan: Its Challenge to U.S. Industry," *The McKinsey Quarterly* (fall 1964), 5.

company feels relatively secure in releasing current know-how to licensees, because of his company's greatly superior research facilities, and the rapid rate of technological change and new product development in the industry." [20] Thus, the foreigner's willingness to supply technology appears to be related to the rate of technological progress within his industry, as well as within his company. Interestingly enough, the National Industrial Conference Board advises that "if the company's assets as a licenser are small and its susceptibility to competitive damage great, it should probably refrain from licensing altogether." [21] But what happens if other companies in the same industry are making technological progress? Even if one company jealously guards its industrial arts, its competitive advantage in foreign markets may not be undisturbed. Other companies are likely to supply similar or sometimes superior technology. Inter-company competition, then, is an additional force inducing technological leaders to supply their knowledge to foreign competitors.

A similar inducement is generated by intercountry competition. This is well reflected in a report of a British business group that visited Japan:

It is only during the past three or four years, during which over 1,000 more technical agreements have been arranged, that *British manufacturers have appreciated the wisdom of selling "know-how" to Japan (in the knowledge that if they do not, others are willing to)* and the number of Anglo-Japanese technical agreements have risen to around 150 and there are many others known to be in the pipe line.[22]

A similar story is likely to be told by businessmen in other countries.

The nationalities of foreign licensers are shown in Table 7. The Japanese were heavily dependent on the United States, which accounted for 62 per cent of total licenses acquired, but other major western countries increased their supply of licenses in the late 1950s.[23] Thus, the United States was the leader in introducing advanced technologies into Japan, and in making other western countries appreciate "the wisdom of selling 'know-how' to Japan."

[20] National Industrial Conference Board, *Foreign Licensing Agreements*, Studies in Business Policy, No. 91, p. 66.

[21] *Ibid.*, p. 66.

[22] Emphasis added. The group visited the Far East under the auspices of the London and Birmingham Chambers of Commerce in 1965. Part of their report is quoted by Richard Bullard, in "There's Business Waiting To Be Won in the Far East," *Commerce*, Journal of the London Chamber of Commerce (May 1965), 14.

[23] Since American companies often establish trading companies in other countries, such as Switzerland, Panama, and Liechtenstein, for the purpose of manipulating taxes on royalties, the percentage for the United States shown in the table is probably understated.

Table 7

Nationality of Foreign Licensers in Japan and Number of Licenses, 1950–1962

Country	1950	1951	1952	1953	1954	1955	1956	1957	1958	1959	1960	1961	1962	Total	%
1. United States	21	74	88	72	58	44	85	61	63	92	200	187	202	1,247	62.4
2. Switzerland	3	16	8	11	6	2	6	10	8	9	18	22	25	148	7.3
3. West Germany			12	6	5	9	11	7	6	16	45	40	46	203	10.1
4. France		2	5	4	1	4	6	4	1	7	5	10	8	57	2.8
5. United Kingdom		1	3	3	1	3	11	3	2	7	10	16	12	72	3.6
6. Italy			1	1	8		10	3	1	1	8	1	5	39	1.6
7. Canada			8	4	1	2	3	2	2	2	2	7	2	35	1.8
8. Holland			1			1	2	18		9	7	7	13	38	2.9
9. Sweden		6	5		1	1	1	2	2	3	8	8	6	43	2.2
10. Panama		2	1	1		4	4	2	1	1	7	8	3	34	1.7
11. Denmark	1			1					2	2		2		8	0.4
12. Norway							1	3		1	1	3		9	0.5
13. Venezuela								3			5	5		15	0.8
14. Austria						1	2				2			5	0.3
15. Liechtenstein						1	1		1	1	3	1		8	0.4
16. Australia							1			1	2			4	0.2
17. French Morocco					1									1	0.05
18. Belgium										1	2	2	3	8	0.4
19. Other											2	1	3	6	0.3
20. Total	27	101	133	103	82	72	144	118	90	153	327	320	328	1,998	100.0

Source: Japan, Science and Technology Agency, Kagaku Gijitsu Hakusho (Report on Science and Technology), 1964, pp. 232–33.

Why, one may ask, was the United States so willing to provide technology for Japan, ahead of, for example, Western European countries? Interfirm competition was probably important, but other forces were at work. Albert O. Hirschman has pointed out that, in contrast to the industrial countries of Europe, particularly England and Germany, which "viewed with concern and alarm the building of foreign industries," the United States has been less concerned about transmitting her technology and helping other countries to industrialize.[24] According to Hirschman, U.S. exports are, on the whole, geared to high and expanding levels of income and the United States is less dependent on foreign sources of supply that might be cut off by industrialization abroad. In addition, the licensing of Japanese firms, aggressive imitators, served as a means of extracting maximum profits from the followers.

It is interesting to note that the U.S. and Japanese industries most actively involved in licensing are those in which both countries' research and development efforts are significant. This relationship is depicted in Table 8. The ordering of industries in terms of research and development expenditure is quite similar in the two countries. However, approximately one-third of Japan's research and development outlay was used for adapting imported technology.[25]

But one may still ask why U.S. firms resorted to licensing rather than direct investment. First, there were restrictions on foreign direct investment in Japan. But, more importantly, U.S. firms were not interested in establishing Japanese affiliates in the early 1950s, for the Japanese market was small, and "most technical agreements were the result of Japanese initiative."[26] Royalties were generally high, at 9 to 10 per cent of sales, and contract periods were normally as long as 15 years.[27] Hence, the Japanese market for technology was highly competitive and especially

[24] Albert O. Hirschman, "Effects of Industrialization on the Markets of Industrial Countries," in Hoselitz (ed.), *The Progress of Underdeveloped Areas* (Chicago: University of Chicago Press, 1952).

[25] The proportion of Japanese research and development outlays used for adapting foreign technologies is estimated from a study made by the Japanese Ministry of International Trade and Industry in November, 1962; 1,937 companies were selected for the survey. All the companies with capital assets worth more than 100 million yen were included. The remainder of the sample comprised half of the total number of Japanese companies with assets of 50–100 million yen. The number of companies that responded to the survey was 1,039. Thus, the rate of response was about 54 per cent. The technologies covered in the survey were those developed during the period January 1957–November 1962. See Ozawa, "Imitation, Innovation, and Trade," Chapter VI.

[26] Abegglen, "Changing Japan," p. 5.

[27] *Ibid.*, p. 5.

Table 8

Research and Development Expenditures as Percentage of Net Sales in the United States, and American Licenses Supplied to Japan

Industry	(A) U.S. R&D Expenditures as Percentage of Net Sales, 1960–1961 Average	Rank	(B) Japanese R&D Expenditures as Percentage of Net Sales, 1960–1961 Average	Rank	(C) American Licenses Supplied to Japan,[a] 1950–1960	Rank
Electrical machinery	10.6	1	1.9	1	0.382	2
Chemicals	4.6	2	1.1	2	0.284	3
Nonelectric machinery	4.5	3	0.9	5	0.251	4
Transport equipment	3.0[b]	4	1.1[c]	3	0.131[c]	6
Rubber and leather	2.1[d]	5	1.0	4	0.168	5
Stone, clay, and glass	1.8	6	0.7	6	0.053	9
Petroleum refining	1.1	7	0.3	11	0.637	1
Metal products	1.1	8	0.7	7	0.022	11
Primary metals	0.8	9	0.5	9	0.059	8
Paper and pulp	0.7	10	0.4	10	0.052	10
Textiles	0.6	11	0.6	8	0.085	7

Sources: (A) from National Science Foundation, *Research and Development in Industry, 1961*, 1964; (B) from Japanese Science and Technology Agency, *Kagaku Gijitsu Yoran* (Science and Technology Summary), 1965; (C) from Japanese Ministry of International Trade and Industry, *Gaikoku Gijitsu Dohnyu no Genjoh to Mondaiten* (Current Situation and Problems of Foreign Technology Absorption), 1962. The total number of American licenses supplied to Japan over 1950–1960 was 904. The distribution shown in the table is based on a sample of 714.

Note: Spearman's coefficient is .86 between (A) and (B), .69 between (A) and (C), and .36 between (B) and (C). (A) and (B) include both public and private funds.

[a] Number of American licenses divided by the value added (1960) of each Japanese industry to eliminate the size effect of the industry.

[b] Aircraft is excluded.   [c] Aircraft is included.   [d] Leather products are excluded.

conductive to licensing arrangements, rather than to direct investment. Stephen Hymer's work is relevant here. He maintains that, as long as the market is highly competitive (i.e., as long as there are many potential buyers of technology), licensing operations are more desirable than direct investment, because the market system allows the seller of technology to appropriate the full return to his monopolistic advantage. When, by contrast, there is an imperfection in the foreign market (i.e., when there are only a few firms), cooperation through licensing becomes difficult, and entrepreneurial coordination supersedes market coordination.[28]

With the subsequent growth of the Japanese economy and the increasing availability of technology in Japan and abroad, the bargaining balance shifted from western licensers to Japanese licensees. Royalties dropped to a range of 3 to 5 per cent, and normal contract periods to 5 years.[29] As early licensing agreements neared expiration, then, many foreign licensers were threatened with a loss of royalty income and confronted with "serious problems for their future efforts to capitalize on Japan's profit opportunities."[30] As a solution, foreign licensers, particularly big American companies, began to combine their supply of technology with direct investment in order to retain a foothold in Japanese markets. With this turn of events, conflict arose between the foreign possessors of technological advantages and the Japanese government, stemming from the latter's controls on direct foreign investment.[31] While officially espousing an "open economy," the government had restricted large equity holdings by foreign nationals. In 1964, the American Chamber of Commerce in Japan openly protested the government's attitude, declaring that "screening delays are getting longer and qualifications rules are becoming more stringent."[32]

The establishment of joint ventures emerged as the means of accommodating conflicting interests, and was often connected with continued licensing. Table 9 shows the parallel movement between the foreign licenses acquired by Japanese firms and the dollar value of joint-venture shares acquired by foreigners. With the relaxation of controls on capital transactions and licensing operations in Japan after 1959, the dollar value of joint-venture shares rose rapidly, together with the number of foreign licenses. Unfortunately, I was unable to obtain data indicating how many of these foreign licenses were actually combined with joint ventures.

[28] Hymer, "International Operations," p. 51.

[29] Abegglen, "Changing Japan," p. 5.

[30] *Ibid.*, p. 5.

[31] Japan is not the only country that resists American direct investment yet wants to have American technology. France provides another example: ". . . the dilemma is best seen in France. The French can block any investment that they feel they don't need, but they don't want to run the risk of falling behind in technology. Thus, the French government acquiesced in General Electric's acquisition of Machines Bull, the computer maker, recognizing France's inability to go it alone in this field." See "Why Europe Wants More U.S. Investment," *Business Week* (November 27, 1965), 74–76.

[32] The New York *Times* (October 25, 1964), 1.

Table 9

The Number of Foreign Licenses Supplied and the Dollar Value
of Joint-Venture Shares Acquired by Foreign Companies

Year	Number of Foreign Licenses	Value of Joint-Venture Shares Acquired by Foreign Companies (in $ thous.)
1950	27	2,572
1951	101	11,646
1952	133	7,166
1953	103	2,687
1954	82	2,467
1955	72	2,309
1956	144	5,360
1957	118	7,282
1958	90	3,698
1959	153	14,561
1960	327	31,593
1961	320	40,170
1962	328	22,618
1963	565	42,656

Source: "Foreign Capital Induction," *The Oriental Economist* (September 1964), 604. Compiled from Foreign Investment Council's data.

But there is evidence that this combination does exist. In 1963, the Japanese Ministry of International Trade and Industry conducted a survey on joint ventures. As of March 31, 1963, there were 111 joint ventures in Japan, of which 104 were covered by the survey. Thus, the information obtained and summarized in Table 10 represents about 94 per cent of the total. It is noteworthy that the foreign partners contributed technology as an asset, while Japanese partners did not, and in so doing the foreigners received royalties in addition to dividends. A tax benefit was obtained from this arrangement, because in Japan royalties are deductible from taxable income and are payable whether or not profits are earned, whereas dividends are paid only when profits are made.

Table 11 shows the distribution of joint ventures among Japanese industries, by foreign equity interest, and by the partners' nationalities. Foreign ownership was generally less than half of total equity, owing largely to the government's standard policy of limiting foreign capital to 50 per cent or less of equity. To be sure, foreign manufacturers themselves sometimes preferred joint ventures to whole ownership. First, they did not need to risk much of their capital, because substantial funds were advanced

Table 10

Asset Contribution of Joint-Venture Partners in Japan at Establishment (millions of yen)

Industry	Japanese Yen		Foreign Currencies		Facilities		Technical Knowledge		Others		Total	
	Japanese	Foreign	Japanese	Foreign	Japanese	Foreign	Japanese	Foreign	Japanese	Foreign	Japanese	Foreign
Electrical machinery	1,621	13	0	355	228	14	0	909	118	0	1,967	1,291
Nonelectrical machinery	1,269	147	0	660	120	0	0	193	0	0	1,389	1,000
Chemicals	11,420	2,340	0	2,160	2,600	0	0	7,061	0	976	14,020	12,537
Metals	508	5	0	233	1,024	0	0	532	76	0	1,608	770
Textiles	424	40	0	109	1	83	0	0	0	65	425	297
Other manufacturing	301	94	0	72	0	0	0	0	0	0	301	166

Source: Japan, Ministry of International Trade and Industry, *Wagakuni no Gobengaisha no Jittai* (Joint Ventures in Japan), 1964.

Table 11

Distribution of Joint Ventures as of March 31, 1963

Industry	By Percentage of Foreign Capital					By Partner Country				
	Total	Under 29%	30-49%	50%	Over 51%	U.S.	Switzerland	West Germany	U.K.	Others
Electrical machinery	10	0	10	0	0	9	0	0	0	1
Nonelectrical machinery	33	4	15	10	4	27	0	2	0	1
Chemicals	37	5	15	15	2	26	5	1	2	3
Metals	6	0	5	0	1	1	1	1	3	3
Textiles	5	0	3	1	1	3	0	1	1	0
Other manufacturing	5	1	2	2	0	4	0	0	0	1
Manufacturing industry	96	10	50	28	8	70	6	5	6	9
Other industries	8	2	3	2	1	4	1	1	1	1
Total	104	12	53	30	9	74	7	6	7	10

Source: Same as for Table 10.

by the Japanese partners. Second, the Japanese provided various local facilities for production, an arrangement reflected in the asset contributions shown in Table 10. But the fundamental reason for the growth of joint ventures was the Japanese government's regulation of wholly foreign-owned operations. Joint ventures have thus served as a compromise designed to minimize the conflict between foreign possessors of advanced technology and local Japanese interests.

WONTACK HONG

Industrialization and Trade

in Manufactures:

The East Asian Experience

A CONSIDERABLE BODY OF LITERATURE attests to the fact that economic development is accompanied by regularities in the changing composition of manufactured output and of manufactured imports.[1] Past studies, however, have generally analyzed separately the patterns of change in the composition of manufactured output and of manufactured imports. In

[1] W. G. Hoffman, *The Growth of Industrial Economies* (Manchester: Manchester University Press, 1958); A. Maizels, *Industrial Growth and World Trade* (London: Cambridge University Press, 1963); Colin Clark, *The Conditions of Economic Progress* (London: Macmillan and Co., Ltd., 1957); H. B. Chenery, "Patterns of Industrial Growth," *American Economic Review*, L (September 1960), 624–53; R. E. Baldwin, "The Commodity Composition of Trade: Selected Industrial Countries, 1900–54," *Review of Economics and Statistics*, XL, Part 2, Supplement (February 1958), 50–71; H. Tyszynski, "World Trade and Manufactured Commodities, 1899–1950," *Manchester School of Economic and Social Studies*, XIX (September 1951), 272–304; A. K. Cairncross, "World Trade in Manufactures since 1900," *Economia Internazionale*, VIII (November 1955), 715–41; Ingvar Svennilson, *Growth and Stagnation in the European Economy* (Geneva: United Nations, 1954); A. O. Hirschman, *National Power and the Structure of Foreign Trade* (University of California Press, 1945); and F. Hilgerdt, *Industrialization and Foreign Trade* (Geneva: League of Nations, 1945).

this study, I hope to add to our knowledge of these changing patterns by attempting to relate them explicitly. Furthermore, other studies have failed to uncover a well-established pattern of change in manufactured exports during the process of development. One of my purposes is to search for such a pattern in the experience of certain East Asian countries.

The Heckscher-Ohlin theorem states that, under certain assumptions, the factor endowment of a country compared to that of the rest of the world determines the country's trade pattern. A dynamic version of this theory states that, with systematic changes in a country's factor supplies relative to those of the rest of the world, the trade pattern changes systematically. If, in addition, we allow for systematic changes in demand, we may be able to obtain a theoretical explanation for changes in the composition of output and trade as a country undergoes economic development. In developing countries, the level of skill, the size of markets, the available capital supply, and organizational ability limit the industrial processes that can be undertaken. The demand for manufactured products cannot be wholly satisfied by domestic production. With systematic changes in demand patterns and productive capacity, then, the composition of manufactured output and imports will change systematically.

Moreover, industrialization changes productive capacity, the range of potential exports, and the actual export pattern. If there is a uniform pattern of change in absolute factor supplies and productive capacity, and if the factor endowment of the rest of the world remains more nearly constant, developing countries with similar resource endowments will tend to display similar export patterns as industrialization proceeds. But international demand conditions and the factor endowments of the rest of the world differ for each developing country, according to the time at which that country undergoes industrialization; countries which are passing through the early phase of industrialization now are apt to display a pattern of change in exports different from that of countries which passed through this stage in 1900.[2]

In the experience of most developed countries, economic development

---

[2] A similar set of arguments applies to imports. For imports, however, more emphasis might be given to changing tastes and technological progress. It is also argued that the absolute amount of imports is likely to depend on the size of the country. "Small countries are likely to be more dependent on imports than large ones, both because their range of natural resources available for industrial development is likely to be more restricted, and because they may have too small a home market for the efficient operation of optimum sized plants. In general, it seems that the import-content is inversely associated with population size in countries in a similar stage of economic development." A. Maizels, *Industrial Growth*, p. 13.

brings a relatively rapid rise in the demand for capital goods, chemicals, and durable consumer goods, and a relatively slow expansion in the demand for food, beverages, tobacco, textiles, and clothing.[3] Many empirical studies also show that an increase in per capita income is accompanied by a rise in the share of manufactured output in total national output, and that there exist significantly different growth patterns for the various branches of industry. Hoffman's study of developed countries has led him to conclude that industrialization has been characterized by a steady increase in the share of capital-goods industries in total manufactured output. A more detailed cross-country regression study has been made by Chenery.[4] The existence of uniform growth patterns is confirmed by high correlation coefficients for almost all industries.[5] According to Chenery, moreover, a fairly typical pattern of change in imports of manufactured products also exists, although the effects of a country's size are more pronounced than in the case of production. Maizels' later results, based on time-series analysis, differ from Chenery's in some respects, especially concerning the sign of the regression coefficient for textiles, but they also "support the view that economic growth is associated with a drastic shift in the pattern of imports (as well as of demand and output)." [6]

Less work has been done on the export pattern. Maizels is content to assert that, as a country's per capita manufactured output increases, its exports are increasingly dominated by manufactured products.[7]

THE STANDARD OF COMPARISON
AND COMPARABLE PERIODS

My analysis of changes in manufactured output and trade patterns deals with Korea, Taiwan, and Japan; the Korean analysis covers the period 1911–1965; Taiwan, 1902–1965; and Japan, 1881–1965. I shall compare the changing patterns in each country with one another and with the "typical" patterns of change suggested by Chenery and Maizels, to

[3] Maizels, *Industrial Growth*, p. 42.

[4] Hoffman, *Growth of Industrial Economies*, pp. 2–38; Chenery, *Patterns*, pp. 624–53.

[5] Chenery calculated "growth elasticities" and "size elasticities" from a linear logarithmic regression equation in which the per capita value added (or import value) of each manufactured product depends on per capita income and population.

[6] Maizels, *Industrial Growth*, p. 182.

[7] *Ibid.*, pp. 60–63.

Table 1

Estimates of Per Capita National Product, and Gross and Net Value (Value Added) of Manufactured and Agricultural Products: Korea, Taiwan, and Japan (1951 dollar prices)

Annual Average	Per Capita Net Value of Manufactured Product (A)	Per Capita Net Value of Agricultural Product (B)	(A)/(B)	Per Capita National Product
Korea				
1911–1915	1.1	23.4	.05	39.1
1916–1920	1.9	25.4	.07	42.5
1921–1925	2.9	29.2	.10	50.8
1926–1930	4.5	36.8	.12	66.0
1931–1935	6.4	41.7	.15	79.0
1936–1940	11.9	43.1	.28	91.4
1951–1955[a]	10.0[b]	44.0[b]	.23[b]	124.0[c]
1956–1960	16.0[d]	46.0[d]	.35[d]	133.4
1961–1965	21.0[e]	42.0[e]	.50[e]	146.6
Taiwan				
1902–1905	2.0	26.9	.07	43.4
1906–1910	3.6	26.0	.14	44.4
1911–1915	5.8	30.5	.20	55.2
1916–1920	11.2	28.1	.42	61.2
1921–1925	9.8	33.5	.29	68.9
1926–1930	13.1	46.7	.29	95.1
1931–1935	16.3	50.4	.32	105.2
1936–1940	15.9	49.6	.32	105.3
1951–1955	21.0[f]	36.0[f]	.58[f]	94.8[e]
1956–1960	26.3[g]	37.2[g]	.71[g]	104.8
1961–1965	34.0[e]	35.0[e]	.97[e]	130.1[h]
Japan				
1881–1885	1.9	20.4	.09	42.6
1886–1890	3.5	24.8	.14	56.5
1891–1895	4.8	30.7	.20	66.9
1896–1900	7.0	33.0	.21	80.6
1901–1905	7.3	34.3	.21	86.8
1906–1910	9.1	35.0	.26	95.5
1911–1915	13.3	39.6	.34	112.4
1916–1920	19.1	37.4	.51	122.0
1921–1925	22.1	38.5	.57	147.7
1926–1930	30.3	38.5	.79	182.7
1931–1935	41.8	36.0	1.16	218.1
1936–1940	63.8	40.3	1.58	248.8
1951–1955	47.0[b]	32.0[b]	1.47[b]	246.1
1956–1960	66.0[d]	34.0[d]	1.94[d]	347.0
1961–1965	117.0[i]	38.0[i]	3.08[i]	513.3[h]

Sources: For the sources of data and the method used to compute these figures, see my unpublished doctoral dissertation, "A Study of the Changes in the Structure of Manufacturing Industry and in the Trade Pattern of Manufactured Products in Korea, Taiwan and Japan," (Columbia University, 1966), Chapter 3.

[a] South Korea only for the post-World War II period. [b] 1953 figures. [c] Average of 1953–1955. [d] 1958 figures. [e] 1963 figures. [f] 1954 figures. [g] 1957 figures. [h] Average of 1961–1964. [i] 1962 figures.

determine whether any of them has significant peculiarities that can be called exceptions.

Because comparisons among countries are most meaningful when they pertain to similar stages of development, I shall attempt a rough approximation of developmental stages in this section. Since it has been established that economic development is closely correlated with the increasing share of manufacturing industry and with rising per capita income, I shall use the percentage share of manufacturing in total national product and the per capita income levels as indexes of economic development.

Early Phase of Industrialization. Korea was a colony of Japan from 1910 to 1945, and Taiwan was Japan's colony from 1896 to 1945. They seem to have been in an early phase of industrialization before World War II; their manufactured product was less than 10 per cent of GNP, and per capita income was less than $100. In the same sense, Japan seems to have been in an early phase of industrialization before 1910.

Approximate levels and trends in per capita product are shown in Table 1. Because the estimates of per capita income are crude, the simple ratio of net manufactured output to net agricultural output (A/B) is also used as an index of economic development.

The per capita income of Korea increased from about $40 to $90 (at 1951 dollar prices) during 1911–1940, and that of Taiwan from about $45 to $105 during 1902–1940. These figures correspond to those for Japan during 1881–1910, when its per capita income increased from about $40 to $95. In Korea, the ratio of net manufactured output to net agricultural output increased from about .05 to .28 during 1911–1940; in Taiwan, from about .07 to .32 during 1902–1940; and in Japan, from about .09 to .26 during 1881–1910. Comparing these three countries and using both indicators, it seems reasonable to draw a parallel and assert that they were at roughly the same stage of economic development during the respective periods.

During these years, Korea, Taiwan, and Japan achieved remarkable growth in total national output, especially in manufactured output. In Korea, per capita income increased about 2.3 times during the 30-year span 1911–1940; per capita agricultural output, 1.8 times; per capita manufactured output, 11 times; and population by about 50 per cent. The gross value of manufactured product increased by about $850 million, and that of agriculture by almost as much.

In Taiwan, per capita income increased about 2.7 times during the 40-year span 1902–1940; per capita agricultural output, 1.9 times; per capita manufactured output, 8 times; and population by about 80 per cent. The gross value of manufactured output increased by about $300 million, and that of agriculture by about $250 million.

In Japan, per capita income increased about 2.3 times during the 30-year span 1881–1910; per capita agricultural output, 1.8 times; per capita manufactured output, about 5 times; and population by about 30 per cent. The gross value of manufactured output increased by about $1,250 million, and that of agriculture by about $1,150 million.

In all three countries, growth rates of per capita income were higher than 3 per cent per annum. If the data used in this computation are correct, these rates rank among the highest overall rates of growth observed in early stages of economic development. The growth rates might be overstated early in each period because of incomplete census data, but these possible deficiencies in the data do not rule out a comparison of Korea's 1911–1940 period, Taiwan's 1902–1940 period, and Japan's 1881–1910 period for the purpose of analyzing the changing composition of manufactured output and trade.

A Transitional Stage. Converted at the official exchange rate, the per capita income of Korea rose from approximately $113 in 1953 to $158 in 1965, while the per capita income of Taiwan rose from $94 in 1953 to $157 in 1964. These per capita income ranges correspond to the first half of Japan's 1900–1940 period.

There was substantial industrialization in Korea before World War II, but, because of the partition and the heavy damage inflicted by the Korean War, manufacturing comprised only about 8 per cent of South Korea's GNP in 1953. This figure had risen to 18 per cent in 1965. In Taiwan, manufacturing was about 14.3 per cent of GNP in 1953 and had risen to 25.5 per cent by 1964.

During 1900–1940, Japan's per capita income rose from about $90 to $260 (from about $90 to $150 during 1900–1920, and from $150 to $260 during 1920–1940), and the share of manufacturing in GNP expanded from 8 to 32 per cent (from 8 to 16 per cent during 1900–1920, and from 16 to 32 per cent during 1920–1940). Thus, the development of Korea and Taiwan during 1953–1964 seems to correspond to Japan's development from 1900 to 1940; that of Korea to the first half of the Japanese period (1900–1920), and that of Taiwan, which was slightly more advanced, to the middle portion (roughly 1910–1930).

According to Rostow, Japan went through "takeoff" and arrived at "maturity" during 1900–1940. Surely, neither Korea nor Taiwan has arrived at Japan's 1940 stage of development. However, it does not seem absurd to assume that Korea and Taiwan will arrive at maturity within a decade or two, and I shall call the period 1953 to the present a transitional stage for these two countries.

CHANGES IN THE COMPOSITION OF MANUFACTURED OUTPUT AND IMPORTS

The Early Phase. We shall regard—somewhat arbitrarily—1911, 1902, and 1881 as the starting points of industrialization in Korea, Taiwan, and Japan, respectively. These points have some similarities: per capita income was about $40, and per capita manufactured product was about $2. Since then, there has been a marked growth in national income and a relatively rapid growth in manufacturing. In consequence, we may expect similar patterns of development.

This section compares the patterns of change in manufactured output and imports in Korea, Taiwan, and Japan during their early phases of industrialization. It covers roughly the period 1911–1937 for Korea and the period 1902–1936 for Taiwan (when these countries were colonies of Japan), and the period 1881–1910 for Japan.

The Japanese pattern is used as a standard of comparison. This choice is easily justified. Chenery compared Japan's production and imports in 1914 and 1935 with his "typical" patterns of production and imports. He found that Japan's structure was not very dissimilar from that of present-day developing countries at corresponding income levels, and that the deviations of Japanese patterns from "typical" patterns were no greater than those of a country chosen at random. There was only one apparent exception—an abnormally large amount of textile production in Japan due to the large volume of Japanese textile exports.[8]

Table 2 attempts to provide a crude approximation of the demand patterns in Korea, Taiwan, and Japan during this phase. Demand is defined as the sum of domestic production and imports minus exports. Owing to inconsistencies in classification among trade and production data and changes in the method of classifying industrial production, these figures are inaccurate, but will have to do. Examination of the figures in Table 2 reveals greater growth in the demand for machinery

[8] H. B. Chenery, S. Shishido, and T. Watanabe, "The Pattern of Japanese Growth, 1914–1954," *Econometrica*, XXX (January 1962), 98–129.

Table 2

Manufactured Products: the Composition of Demand, Output, and Imports in the Early Phase (per cent of total[a])

	Demand				Output				Imports			
Korea	1911	1920	1930	1935	1911	1920	1930	1937	1911	1920	1930	1935
Machinery	5.9	6.0	6.9	7.4	1.9	1.8	0.9	1.1	8.9	12.0	11.9	14.0
Metals	8.1	5.4	8.0	6.0	3.8	5.2	5.9	4.9	11.2	10.6	12.1	15.4
Building materials	6.5	6.5	5.6	5.5	5.4	6.2	5.9	5.1	7.0	5.8	5.4	6.1
Chemicals	8.0	11.0	13.9	19.7	2.3	7.4	9.6	28.8	12.2	18.1	19.6	20.7
Textiles	34.8	29.2	22.7	19.0	16.7	8.9	13.2	13.2	46.2	36.9	31.5	25.8
Food and kindred	28.5[b]	28.6[b]	34.2	34.4	51.0	36.6	59.2	42.4	9.3	9.8	8.8	5.2
Taiwan	1914	1922	1930	1935	1914	1922	1930	1938	1914	1922	1930	1935
Machinery	2.8	8.6	9.1	9.4	—	2.5	2.3	3.5	4.7	8.1	11.0	11.8
Metals	5.9	7.7	7.4	9.1	1.3	1.5	1.8	5.4	7.7	11.4	9.1	15.9[c]
Building materials	10.4	13.2	13.1	12.1	3.4	5.0	6.4	4.3	12.6	9.1	7.3	10.3
Chemicals	17.3	25.3	23.7	26.6	2.6	7.9	6.7	10.3	29.1	25.3	29.6	30.5
Textiles	13.0	10.3	11.1	11.1	0.4	1.8	1.0	1.6	22.3	14.2	19.1	16.6
Food and kindred	44.1	26.6	27.4	24.1	88.7	75.7	76.4	69.0	18.2	24.6	15.5	15.3
Japan	1881	1891	1901	1911	1881	1891	1901	1911	1881	1891	1901	1911
Machinery	0.5	1.9	4.9	12.5	0.3	0.6	2.0	9.4	2.2	5.7	12.8	17.7
Metals	6.6	1.9	5.7	8.4	6.3	2.0	4.2	5.0	7.8	12.8	17.9	27.9
Building materials	1.7	4.2	3.7	3.8	2.8	5.4	4.5	4.7	0.9	1.1	1.6	1.9
Chemicals	4.7	8.2	9.1	9.8	4.5	6.6	6.8	6.5	8.9	19.0	20.8	26.1
Textiles	25.4	41.5	33.2	35.2	15.8	42.8	42.5	41.4	51.1	35.5	17.2	16.5
Food and kindred	59.4	38.1	37.2	26.0	68.3	37.2	34.0	25.9	15.5	20.5	26.0	6.2

Source: Hong, "A Study of Changes," p. 46.

[a] Demand for each manufactured product as a percentage of total demand for manufactured products, and output (or imports) of each manufactured product as a percentage of total manufactured output (or imports). [b] Figures for the demand for food and kindred products are underestimated because of the exclusion of the rice-cleaning industry before 1924. [c] 1934 figure.

and chemicals relative to the demand for textiles and food products. But it is less easy to identify consistent and uniform changes in the three countries' patterns of demand for each manufactured product. In Taiwan, for example, the demand for textiles was relatively small, and the demand for chemicals and building materials was relatively large. In fact, the demand patterns of Korea and Japan are more similar to each other than to those of Taiwan. Also, there was a relatively small demand for machinery in Japan before 1900.

But there are similarities in the demand patterns, especially between Korea and Japan, and one would therefore expect similar patterns of change in the composition of manufactured output, as well as in manufactured imports. One would forecast a rapid rise in textile production and an increase in the share of other industries during later periods. But, despite similarities in the growth of per capita incomes, demand patterns, and the growth rates of manufactured output, there were substantial dissimilarities in the composition of manufactured output and in manufactured imports.

In Korea, the share of textiles in total manufactured output was less than 17 per cent throughout the early phase of industrialization. In Taiwan, the share never exceeded 2.2 per cent. In Japan, on the other hand, the textile industry expanded from about 15 per cent to more than 40 per cent of total manufactured output during the early phase of industrialization. The import patterns of Korea and Taiwan reflect the slow expansion of the textile industry. In Korea, textiles accounted for about 40 to 50 per cent of total manufactured imports during the first half of the period; their share was reduced to less than 30 per cent thereafter, the result of a relative reduction in domestic demand and a slightly increased production of textiles in the later period. In Taiwan, textile imports fluctuated around 20 per cent of total manufactured imports throughout the period. In Japan, on the other hand, the share of textile imports was reduced from more than 60 per cent to less than 20 per cent during the period. This rapid rate of reduction reflected the sharp rise in domestic textile production. It may, perhaps, be inferred that the textile industries of Korea and Taiwan were victims of the colonial economy, whose textile demand was met by Japanese supply.[9]

[9] Korea and Taiwan were designed to supply primary products to Japan and to be supplied by Japan with industrial products. The trade of Korea and Taiwan depended heavily on Japan: In 1933, Taiwan imported 80 per cent of its total imports from Japan, and 93 per cent of its total exports went to Japan. In the same year, 85 per cent of Korea's total imports were from Japan, and 86 per cent of its total exports went to Japan. See *Foreign Trade of Japan: A Statistical Survey* (Tokyo: Oriental Economist Inc., 1935).

In Korea, the share of the food industry fell from 60 per cent in 1930 to about 40 per cent in 1937. In Japan, it fell from about 60 per cent in 1881 to 40 per cent in 1890, and to less than 30 per cent at the end of the period. Thus, Korea and Japan show similar trends. In Taiwan, however, the share of the food industry was extremely large, about 70 to 80 per cent, until the end of the period. More than half of Taiwan's total manufactured output was from sugar refining, which had been developed vigorously by the Japanese.

Another dissimilarity appears in the chemical industry. In Japan and Taiwan, shares remained stable in the 5 to 10 per cent range; in Korea, the share of chemicals expanded to about 30 per cent. The rapid expansion in Korea seems to have been due to the introduction of improved technology in producing chemical fertilizers and Japanese efforts to make Korea, Japan's main rice supplier, self-sufficient in producing fertilizers.[10]

In Taiwan, the stagnant and insignificant share of chemicals is reflected in high imports. And, even in Korea, where the production of chemical fertilizers grew rapidly after 1930, the share of chemicals in total manufactured imports remained at about 15 to 20 per cent. In Japan, too, the share of chemical imports increased steadily, from about 10 to 30 per cent. These phenomena suggest the difficulty of expanding the chemical industry in the early period of industrialization, despite the relatively high and rapidly increasing demand for fertilizers and other chemicals.

More international similarities are shown by the machinery industry. In the three countries, the share of the machinery industry in total manufactured output remained negligible throughout the period. The share of machinery in imports expanded steadily in all three countries, reaching about 15 per cent of total manufactured imports at the end of the period. Excluding the 1901–1910 period in Japan, when, owing partly to armaments production, the share of the machinery industry was expanding a little, output and import patterns were quite similar in Korea, Taiwan, and Japan. The machinery industry did not develop rapidly, and the domestic demand for machinery was met mostly by imports.

During this early phase, Japanese industrialization was due mainly to rapid import substitution and to large exports of textiles. In Korea and

---

[10] Korean fertilizer production in 1930 was valued at only 2 million yen, less than 10 per cent of total chemicals output. By 1935, fertilizer output had reached 37 million yen, or roughly one-third of total chemicals production. Chosen Government General, *Annual Statistical Report of Chosen Government General* (Chosen Sotokufu Tokei Nenpo).

Taiwan, the textile industry was partly or completely deprived of its role as a leading industry. But, even without its leadership, these two countries managed to achieve a rapid rise in agricultural and industrial production. In Korea, the chemical industry played a significant role at the end of the period, and, in Taiwan, sugar refining was dominant throughout the early phase of industrialization. In brief, it seems that established relationships between growth and structural change are not displayed by colonial economies, which are deprived of independence in tariff, foreign exchange, and development policies.

If the atypical patterns of change shown by Korea and Taiwan could be attributed principally to their colonial status, there would be no apparent reason for these countries to depart from typical patterns after World War II. We have therefore to look at the period after 1953 to compare Korea and Taiwan with Japan in its own transitional stage from 1900 to 1940.

The Transitional Stage. There were roughly similar increases in the share of manufactured output in GNP in Korea, Taiwan, and Japan during the periods covered here: in Korea, from 8 to 18 per cent during 1953–1965; in Taiwan, from 14 to 25 per cent during 1953–1964; and in Japan, from 8 to 16 per cent during the first half of the period, 1900–1920, and from 16 to 32 per cent during the second half, 1920–1940. Underlying these increases in the share of manufactured output, there were similar, substantial changes in the composition of demand and output.

I have conducted a logarithmic regression analysis using per capita demand, value added, and imports of each product group as the dependent variables and per capita income as the independent variable, and have called the resulting coefficients "industrialization" elasticities. (The results for Taiwan are presented in Table 3, as an illustration.) In all cases, the elasticities of demand for machinery, electrical machinery, metal products, nonmetallic mineral products, paper products, and chemicals are greater than for total demand, while the elasticities for textiles and food products are smaller than for total demand. This pattern of changes in the composition of demand accords well with the "typical" pattern derived from the experience of developed countries.

All sectors, except printing, metal products (Korea), and nonmetallic mineral products (Japan during 1920–1940), which had elasticities of demand greater than that for total demand, had elasticities of output

Table 3

Logarithmic Regressions of Demand, Output, and Imports on Income:
Taiwan (1953–1964)

	Demand	Output	Imports
Machinery	2.372[a]	3.701[a]	2.060[a]
Electrical machinery	3.038[a]	4.027[a]	2.456[a]
Transport	2.594[a]	3.630[a]	2.121[a]
Base metals	1.089[a]	1.326[a]	1.680[a]
Metal products	2.179[a]	3.210[a]	0.482
Nonmetallic mineral products	2.039[a]	2.759[a]	−2.189[a]
Wood products	0.687[a]	2.144[a]	−3.768[a]
Paper	1.601[a]	1.788[a]	2.191[a]
Petroleum	1.212[a]	1.350[a]	0.587
Rubber	0.888[a]	1.770[a]	−3.093[a]
Chemicals	1.975[a]	2.286[a]	1.628[a]
Textiles	0.300	1.008[a]	−0.831
Furniture	—	—	3.822[a]
Printing	—	—	0.970
Leather	−0.492	0.839	−3.873[a]
Wearing apparel	—	—	−1.684
Food and kindred	1.037[a]	1.059[a]	0.350
All sectors	1.315[a]	1.643[a]	1.458[a]

Source: Hong, "A Study of Changes," pp. 61, 73.
[a] Statistically significant at the .05 level.

greater than for total output. These results suggest the continuous adjustment of the industrial structure to changing demand patterns.

I have also attempted to measure the effect of import substitution and of the expansion in demand on imports of manufactured products, and to compare the results for each country. Table 4 is constructed according to the method used by Maizels.[11] The change in imports from the base year to the current year can be written as $dM = m_1 S_1 - m_0 S_0$, where m represents the import content of supplies, S. The change can be divided into two elements: $dM = S_1(m_1 - m_0) + m_0(S_1 - S_0)$, where the first term measures gross import substitution, and the second term measures the influence of home demand. The growth of home production does not, on this definition, count as import substituting unless it results in a falling share of imports in home consumption.

Import substitution of such manufactured products as nonmetallic mineral products, petroleum and coal products, rubber products, and textiles and consumer goods was very rapid in all these countries; the

[11] A. Maizels, *Industrial Growth*, pp. 150–51.

import content of total supply, as well as the share of each product in total manufactured imports, declined. There was also significant import substitution in electrical machinery, transport equipment, and paper products. But, because of the great increase in demand, these products were still imported in large quantity, and the direction of change in their share of manufactured imports was not always negative. Despite significant import substitution in metals and chemicals, the expansion in demand usually outweighed import substitution, and the share of these products in total manufactured imports increased. Finally, a rapid increase in demand and a low rate of import substitution caused a steady increase in machinery imports.

On the whole, unlike the early phase of industrialization, the changing patterns of demand and the composition of manufactured output and imports in Korea, Taiwan, and Japan show remarkable similarity in the transitional stage.

Apart from the direction of change, the absolute amounts of production and imports are likely to be affected by the size of a country, its sector-specific natural-resource endowment, and its export opportunities. Thus, despite very similar demand patterns, there are some marked differences in production and import patterns among these countries (see Table 5).

In Korea and Taiwan, the share of the consumer-goods industries declined from about a half to a third of total manufactured output. It declined from a third to a sixth during 1900–1920 in Japan, where, by 1940, its share was only one-tenth of total manufactured output. In Korea and Taiwan, the share of textiles was about a fifth of total manufactured output, and showed some tendency to decline; in Japan, it was nearly 40 per cent until the early 1930s. The Japanese consumer-goods industry had a relatively small share, and the textile industry had an abnormally large share (about twice as large as that indicated by Chenery's typical pattern). It is argued, however, that small-scale production was more important in Japan than is now typical of developing countries, and the small share of consumer products might be the results of underestimating food and kindred products by excluding nonfactory, small-scale food and kindred production. This interpretation is mere conjecture, as reliable data on hand production in Japan or other developing countries are not available.

In Korea, more than a third, and, in Taiwan and Japan, generally more than half of total manufactured imports were metals, machinery,

Table 4

Effects of Import Substitution and of Expansion in Demand on Imports of Manufactured Products: Korea (1955–1964), Taiwan (1953–1963), and Japan (1909–1919, 1919–1929, 1929–1936) (millions of dollars[a])

	Changes in Imports Due to		
	Import Substitution	Expansion in Demand	Total
Machinery			
Korea	+6	+14	+20
Taiwan	−3	+37	+34
Japan I	−48	+72	+24
Japan II	+6	+46	+52
Japan III	−168	+159	−9
Electrical machinery			
Korea	−39	+37	−2
Taiwan	−10	+18	+8
Japan I	−27	+24	−3
Japan II	+4	+6	+10
Japan III	−25	+14	−11
Transport equipment			
Korea	−19	+13	−6
Taiwan	−4	+8	+4
Japan I	−42	+47	+5
Japan II	+17	−2	+15
Japan III	−17	+26	+9
Base metals			
Korea	−9	+23	+14
Taiwan	+3	+14	+17
Japan I	—	—	—
Japan II[b]	−258	+226	−32
Japan III	−277	+349	+72
Metal products			
Korea	+1	+1	+2
Taiwan	−6	+7	+1
Japan III	−43	+28	−15
Nonmetallic mineral products			
Korea	−4	+2	−2
Taiwan	−5	+4	−1
Japan I	−11	+8	−3
Japan II	+4	+3	+7
Japan III	−10	+6	−4
Wood Products			
Korea	0	0	0
Taiwan	0	0	0
Japan I	0	+5	+5
Japan II	+60	+11	+71
Japan III	−44	+22	−22
Paper products			
Korea	−19	+21	+2
Taiwan	0	+3	+3
Japan I	−16	+19	+3
Japan II	−32	+37	+5
Japan III	+37	+24	+61
Petroleum and coal products			
Korea	−42	+40	−2
Taiwan	−3	−3	0

	Import Substitution	Expansion in Demand	Total
Rubber products			
Korea	−2	+2	0
Taiwan	−2	+1	−1
Japan III	−11	+6	−5
Chemicals			
Korea	−45	+76	+31
Taiwan	−12	+32	+10
Japan I[c]	−110	+134	+24
Japan II[c]	+31	+123	+154
Japan III[c]	−130	+331	+201
Textiles			
Korea	−39	+24	−15
Taiwan	−6	+5	−1
Japan I	−207	+175	−32
Japan II	+26	+5	+31
Japan III	−50	+24	−26
Printing and publishing			
Korea	—	—	—
Taiwan	—	—	—
Japan I	0	0	0
Japan II	0	+2	+2
Japan III	−1	+1	0
Furniture and fixtures			
Korea	0	0	0
Leather products			
Korea	0	0	0
Taiwan	−1	0	−1
Japan I	−2	+1	−1
Japan II	+1	+2	+3
Japan III	+1	−2	−1
Wearing apparel			
Korea	−7	+2	−5
Food and kindred products			
Korea	+7	+13	+20
Taiwan	−17	+9	−8
Japan I	−16	+31	+15
Japan II	−50	+49	−1
Japan III	−21	+10	−11
Total manufactured products			
Korea	−149	+207	+58
Taiwan	−38	+118	+80
Japan I	−492	+688	+196
Japan II	−29	+358	+329
Japan III	−467	+708	+241

Source: Hong, "A Study of Changes," pp. 66–71.

[a] Korea at 1960 prices; Taiwan at current dollar prices; Japan at 1951 dollar prices.

[b] Includes metal products.

[c] Includes petroleum and rubber products.

Table 5

The Composition of Demand, Output, and Imports: The Transitional Phase (per cent of total)

Demand

Demand	Korea 1955	Korea 1965	Taiwan 1953	Taiwan 1964	Japan 1920	Japan 1936	Chenery's[c] $113	Chenery's[c] $192
Machinery	9.7	9.8	9.0	14.8	14.7	14.5	4.3	7.2
Metals	3.7	7.6	8.7	9.0	11.5	20.6	8.9	10.6
Building materials	6.2	8.1	6.9	8.6	6.3	4.9	8.7	9.0
Chemicals	17.0	19.6	26.6	29.0	14.4	24.3	11.6	13.4
Textiles	24.0	18.1	24.5	16.8	31.9	22.6	23.5	25.2
Consumer goods	38.0	30.4	30.0[a]	26.4[b]	16.8[a]	12.9[a]	44.9	34.4

Output

Output	Korea 1953	Korea 1965	Taiwan 1953	Taiwan 1965	Japan 1901	Japan 1920	Japan 1936	Japan 1940
Machinery	5.7	8.5	2.1	9.3	2.0	4.9	11.4[d]	23.9
Metals	4.5	7.5	4.4	5.8	4.2	5.7	5.5	19.8
Building materials	7.0	9.1	6.5	13.9	4.5	3.7	6.0	6.4
Chemicals	12.6	16.6	18.5	22.4	6.8	9.1	11.9	20.1
Textiles	23.8	18.9	20.8	17.5	42.5	33.2	41.7	17.0
Consumer goods	44.5	32.6	47.1[a]	32.8[b]	39.4	41.8	16.5[a]	11.7[a]

Imports

Imports	Korea 1955	Korea 1965	Taiwan 1953	Taiwan 1964	Japan 1900	Japan 1920	Japan 1936	Japan 1940
Machinery	26.9	22.8	24.9	36.0	33.2	32.4	15.1	13.0
Metals	3.2	12.6	15.8	18.0	12.1	15.1	39.2	23.0
Building materials	1.9	0.4	1.5	0.5	2.9	3.3	3.8	5.8
Chemicals	40.0	50.3	29.6	33.5	24.0	24.4	23.3	49.7
Textiles	16.2	10.1	11.0	3.5	14.3	10.8	8.2	3.1
Consumer goods	10.3	1.6	12.8	8.4	13.5	14.2	9.6	4.0

Source: Hong, "A Study of Changes," p. 77.   [a] Excluding furniture and wearing apparel.   [b] Excluding furniture.

[c] The percentage shares for Chenery's typical pattern are computed using a per capita income of $113 with a population of 52.6 million, and a per capita income of $192 with a population of 69.2 million. These somewhat arbitrary figures are selected in order to utilize the figures compiled in H. B. Chenery, S. Shishido, and T. Watanabe, "Pattern." The share of each industry is computed on the basis of value added.

and transport equipment. But Japan imported much less machinery and transport equipment and imported more metals than did Korea and Taiwan.

Even with these dissimilarities, however, demand patterns and the composition of manufactured output and imports cannot be said to differ drastically from country to country. Even the high degree of Japanese industrialization at a low per capita income level is not a strange phenomenon. To be sure, it violates many generalizations based on the experience of old advanced countries. However, during the periods for which this comparison was made, the amount of manufactured products increased 1.9 times per decade in Japan, and 2.2 times in Korea (1955–1964) and Taiwan (1953–1963). These rates of increase suggest that the present developing countries, such as Korea and Taiwan, can do better than, or as well as, Japan did during the 1900–1940 period.

INDUSTRIALIZATION AND EXPORTS
OF MANUFACTURED PRODUCTS

Because of the limited prospects for the substantial expansion of traditional exports of primary commodities, it is recognized that the rapid enlargement of exports of manufactures may be of strategic importance for developing countries. During recent years, exports of manufactures from such countries, though still small, have exhibited a substantially higher rate of growth than that recorded by exports of primary commodities. In 1961, manufactured exports totaled about $2.6 billion, compared with $1.8 billion in 1955. This increase reflected an annual growth rate of 6.5 per cent, compared with 2.2 per cent for primary commodities over the same period.[12] Exports of manufactures, however, have been dominated by a few developing countries. In 1961, for example, East Asia alone accounted for almost three-quarters of the manufactured exports from all developing countries. It is the purpose of the rest of this essay to explore, by means of a comparative study of some East Asian countries, some general characteristics of changes in the export pattern of manufactures of developing countries.

Although there was a steady increase in the share of manufactured products in total exports during the course of Japanese industrialization,

[12] United Nations, *Trade and Development: Trade in Manufactures* (New York, 1965), pp. 3–9.

Table 6

Changes in the Share of Manufactured Products in Total Gross National Product and in Total Exports: Korea, Taiwan, Japan, India, and Hong Kong (per cent)

	Japan			Korea		Taiwan		India		Hong Kong
Year	MP[a] GNP	MP[b] EX	Year	MP GNP	MP EX	MP GNP	MP EX	MP GNP	MP EX	DO[c] EX
1868	—	5	1910	—	—	—	7	—	17	—
1870	—	8	1915	—	—	—	14	—	28	—
1875	2.7[d]	7	1920	—	6	—	8	—	34	—
1880	3.0	17	1925	—	4	—	7	—	22	—
1885	4.2	20	1930	—	9	—	7	6.0[e]	23	—
1889	6.7	24	1935	9.6[f]	13	14.8[f]	7	8.0[g]	23	—
1891	6.0	31	1953	8.0	2	14.3	11	11.1[h]	43	23
1892	6.2	31	1954	8.8	3	16.4	21	12.5	38	28
1893	6.8	35	1955	10.2	9	16.8	17	12.3	37	29
1894	5.9	35	1956	11.4	8	17.1	11	11.6	37	24
1895	7.1	36	1957	11.7	14	18.2	15	12.2	43	22
1896	8.0	40	1958	11.9	14	17.5	21	11.3	42	39
1897	7.7	37	1959	12.3	12	18.9	31	11.8	43	63
1898	6.0	44	1960	12.7	15	17.5	40	12.0	46	68
1899	8.4	43	1961	12.4	16	18.0	51	12.7	48	71
1900	8.1	48	1962	13.4	20	18.9	59	13.1	47	72
1910	10.9	50	1963	14.5	45	21.8	46	—	47	73
1920	15.6	68	1964	16.1	51	25.5	45	—	48	77
1930	18.1	59	1965	17.9	60	—	—	—	—	—
1940	31.6	77	1966	—	—	—	—	—	—	—

Sources: Hong, "A Study of Changes," pp. 30–31, 92–95; India, Office of the Superintendent of Government Printing, *Annual Statement of the Sea-borne Trade and Navigation of British India* and *Review of Trade of India;* India, Department of Commercial Intelligence and Statistics, *Accounts Relating to the Sea-borne Trade and Navigation of British India,* and *Monthly Statistics of the Foreign Trade of India;* United Nations, *Yearbook of National Accounts Statistics;* and A. Maizels, *Industrial Growth and World Trade* (London: Cambridge University Press, 1963), pp. 486, 533.

[a] Percentage share of manufactured products in total gross national product.

[b] Percentage share of manufactured products in total exports. (*Note:* In the case of Taiwan, refined sugar is excluded from manufactured products. If refined sugar is included, the figures become 66 per cent for 1910, 62 per cent for 1915, 74 per cent for 1920, 50 per cent for 1925, 66 per cent for 1930, and 50 per cent for 1935.)

[c] Percentage share of products of domestic origin, mostly manufactured products, in Hong Kong's total exports.

[d] 1878 figure.   [e] 1929 figure.

[f] Refer to Tables 1 and 2 as well as to the footnotes to those tables for the sources of data and method used to compute these figures.

[g] 1937 figure.

[h] Figures for India's manufactured products in the United Nations' *Yearbook of National Accounts Statistics* include products of gas, electricity, and construction industries. If we could assume that India and Pakistan have similar industrial structures, the share of manufactured product would be about 70 per cent of those figures. Figures in Table 7 are computed on this tenuous assumption.

exports were mainly raw silk, foodstuffs, and other primary products until 1890. However, the share of manufactured products in total exports started to expand rapidly during 1889–1900, changing from a quarter of total exports in 1889 to a half in 1900 (see Table 6). During the 40-year span 1900–1939, moreover, the share of manufactured products in GNP consistently increased, and their share in total exports also rose. Japan seems to have gone through something like a takeoff stage in exports of manufactures during 1891–1900, and fully escaped from its primary export structure after 1900.

In Korea, too, there had been a slow but steady increase in manufactured exports before World War II. However, Korean exports were dominated by rice and other primary products such as mineral ores. After World War II, there was a steady increase in the share of manufactured products in total exports, yet exports were still dominated by primary products (and total exports were exceedingly low during 1952–1960). Only since 1961 have total exports and the share of manufactures in total exports expanded rapidly. By 1963, the share of manufactured products became nearly half of total Korean exports, and, in 1965, manufactured products accounted for about 60 per cent of total exports. In this sense, Korea seems to have escaped from its primary export structure after 1963, although its per capita manufactured exports are still very small.

Taiwan's exports were composed mainly of sugar and rice during the sixty-year period 1896–1956. The share of manufactured products (excluding sugar) fluctuated around 10 per cent of total exports, and the manufactures involved were mainly food products such as canned pineapple or alcohol (a by-product of sugar refining). Since 1957, however, there has been a rapid development of manufacturing industry, and the share of manufactured products (excluding sugar) in total exports has expanded rapidly—from 15 per cent in 1957 to 40 per cent in 1960 and to 45 per cent in 1964. Since 1960, manufactured products have accounted for about half of Taiwan's total exports.

There was a consistent increase in the share of manufactured products, mainly textiles, in India's total exports before World War II. The share of manufactures in total exports fluctuated around 40 to 50 per cent during 1947–1954. However, there has been a steady and definite expansion in the share of manufactured exports since 1955; that share increased consistently from 37 per cent in 1955 to 48 per cent in 1964. Although the rate of expansion in the share of manufactured products and in India's total exports was not particularly impressive in this period, India seems to have escaped from its primary export structure after the war, as nearly half of its total exports are manufactured products.

Hong Kong ceased to be a mere transit port and became a major exporter of manufactures after 1959, when the share of domestic-origin exports, mainly manufactured goods, was 63 per cent of total exports.

In general, there has been a steady expansion in the share of manufactures in total exports with the increase in the share of manufactures in total GNP (i.e., with the progress of industrialization).

Another notable phenomenon is the rapid change in the export structure during a short period at a certain point of industrialization. For instance, in Japan, the share of manufactures in total exports expanded from 24 to 48 per cent during 1889–1900; in Korea, from 15 to 60 per cent during 1960–1965; in Taiwan, from 15 to 45 per cent during 1957–1964; in India, from 23 to 42 per cent during 1935–1947; and in Hong Kong, from 23 to 77 per cent during 1953–1964. All these structural changes occurred within a decade or so and, more importantly, when the share of manufactured output in GNP was between 6 and 20 per cent and per capita income was about $100.

OTHER FACTORS INFLUENCING THE EXPORT PERFORMANCE OF MANUFACTURED PRODUCTS

Maizel's analysis of manufactured exports suggests that the share of manufactured products in total exports tends to increase as industrialization progresses.[13] In Korea, Taiwan, Japan, India, and Hong Kong, this trend was also easily identified. A significant correlation between the percentage share of manufactured products in a country's total exports and the level of industrialization (measured by the share of manufactured output in GNP) was also identified for the eleven Asian countries listed in Table 7.

In 1963, however, the level of industrialization in Korea, Pakistan, India, Burma, and Thailand was quite similar, but the importance of manufactured exports was very different. Hence, some other factors may influence a country's manufactured exports. Chenery's study of the

[13] A. Maizels, *Industrial Growth*, pp. 60–63.

Table 7

Relationship between the Resource Endowment and the Proportion of Manufactured Products in Total Exports, 1963

Country	Share of Manufactured Products in Total Exports (%)	Share of Manufactured Products in GNP (%)	Population Density per Sq. Km.	Share of Primary Exports in GNP[a] (%)
Hong Kong	94	33[b]	3,481	3.86
Taiwan	74	22	325	5.08
Japan[c]	68	16	170	2.90
India	47	13	151	2.47
Korea	44	15	273	1.73
Philippines	28	19	101	9.06
Pakistan[d]	26	10	104	4.03
Indonesia	19	8	67	10.91
Thailand	7	12	56	14.88
Malaya[d]	7	8	58	31.88
Burma	3	16	35	17.31

Kendall's rank correlation coefficients:
Share of manufactured products in
total exports .53[e] .86[e] .56[e]

Sources: United Nations, *Statistical Yearbook: 1964 Bulletin for Asia and the Far East, Yearbook of International Trade Statistics,* and *Yearbook of National Accounts Statistics.*

[a] Smallest figure was given the highest rank in computing the correlation coefficient.

[b] 1955 figure. Source: E. Szczepanik, *The Economic Growth of Hong Kong* (London: Oxford University Press, 1958), p. 178.

[c] 1920 figures. [d] 1962 figures.

[e] Statistically significant at the .05 level.

effects of resource availability on growth patterns suggests a significant correlation between resource endowments and trade patterns; well-endowed countries tend to export more primary products than resource-poor countries.[14]

Unfortunately, we do not have a satisfactory way to measure natural-resource endowments. One common approach is to classify countries as overpopulated or underpopulated on the crude assumption that an overpopulated country is apt to be poorly endowed with natural resources such as arable land, and one may be able to obtain a rough measure of resource supplies by examining population density. But since there may

[14] H. B. Chenery, "The Effects of Resources on Economic Growth," in Kenneth Berrill (ed.), *Economic Development with Special Reference to East Asia* (London: Macmillan Co. Ltd., 1965), pp. 19–52.

be no close correlation between population density and other natural-resource endowments, such as minerals, another method should be used. To this end, I measure primary exports as a percentage of gross national product (not the percentage share of primary exports in total exports), on the assumption that these exports reflect the exportable natural-resource endowments of the country. In this section, then, I use population density and primary exports divided by GNP as indexes of resource endowments. I study 11 Asian countries in which the share of manufactured output in GNP was more than 8 per cent in 1963, and present a series of rank correlation tests. I seek to determine whether there is any significant correlation between resource endowments and export performance in manufactures.

The results are set out in Table 7. There are significant correlations between population density and primary exports, on the one hand, and the share of manufactures in total exports, on the other. Resource-poor countries (those with high population density and low primary exports) tend to export more manufactured products than resource-rich countries. Thus, it seems that the effects of industrialization on exports of manufactured products depend partly on the natural-resource endowment of a country.

Apart from high population density, there are some peculiarities in the cases of Korea, Taiwan, and Hong Kong which seem also to have influenced their performance in manufactured products. In both Korea and Taiwan, a large proportion of imports has been financed by U.S. aid.

In Taiwan, the increase in imports outstripped the rise in exports until 1961, and the gaps (generally 40–50 per cent of total imports) were financed by U.S. aid. For several years, warnings were repeatedly addressed to Taiwan that U.S. aid would cease in the near future. For this and other reasons, the Taiwan government has vigorously promoted export expansion to achieve a better balance of trade in the absence of U.S. aid. Low-interest loans have been extended to manufacturing export industries, which were encouraged to adopt new methods of production and to expand productive capacity. Market surveys have been conducted by the government; quality control has been applied to several products; industries which export 50 per cent or more of output are exempt from (or entitled to reductions in) business taxes.[15] All

[15] Republic of China, Foreign Exchange and Trade Commission, Executive Yuan, *Foreign Trade Quarterly* (Taipei); and United Nations, *World Economic Survey: 1965* (New York, 1965), p. 114.

these encouragements to export have produced favorable results. The unfavorable trend in the trade balance took a turn for the better in 1962, when the increase of exports surpassed that of imports. In 1963, exports rose 50 per cent while imports went up 3 per cent, and, in the same year, for the first time since 1949, Taiwan's trade balance registered an export surplus (about $20 million). Soon thereafter, it was announced that U.S. aid would be terminated by 1965.

In Korea, the proportion of imports financed by U.S. aid has been even larger. Until 1961, more than 70 per cent of total imports were financed by U.S. aid. Warnings that U.S. aid might cease within a few years have also been addressed to the Korean government since the beginning of the 1960s. To complicate matters, the Korean government initiated an ambitious Five-Year Plan in 1962, which required a large amount of foreign exchange. When the Five-Year Plan encountered difficulty because of a shortage of foreign exchange, the government quickly acknowledged the necessity of a drastic expansion in exports and initiated a vigorous export-promotion policy. Tax incentives and low-interest-rate bank loans were provided to export industries, and an export subsidy system was instituted during the latter half of 1961. In an attempt to encourage exports and restrict imports, the government established an export "link" policy, which seems to have been quite effective. Under this "link" policy, only those who exported more than a certain amount during a given period were authorized to import commodities classified as permission-required items. From an average of about $25 million during 1950–1960, exports increased to $41 million in 1961, to $87 million in 1963, to $119 million in 1964, and to $172 million in 1965. The target for 1966 was $250 million, and the target for 1971, the final year of the Second Five-Year Plan (1967–1971), is $550 million. The government vows that, within ten years from 1966, Korea will be exporting more than $1 billion worth of commodities, mainly manufactured products. It is not certain whether the government's somewhat ambitious goal will be realized, but one thing is clear: The government is expending great efforts to expand exports.

The export-promotion policies of Korea and Taiwan were not limited to manufactured products, but, because of the lack of exportable primary products, the principal beneficiaries of these policies have been the manufacturing export industries, and the policies have resulted in a further rapid increase of manufactured exports.

The situation in Hong Kong is even more peculiar. Its population (nearly 3.5 million in 1965) is crowded into a very small area, about a thousand square kilometers of rocky and mountainous land. Its population was about one-half million until the end of World War II, but doubled in 1946. During 1947–1956, moreover, net immigration was about three-quarters of a million, and, with the natural increase of half a million, the population reached 2.5 million by 1956.[16] Pressed by the need to find employment for its burgeoning population, Hong Kong began to transform its economy from its historic entrepôt base to an industrial network capable of manufacturing a variety of products for export. It has emerged as a major exporter of manufactures.

CHANGES IN THE COMPOSITION OF MANUFACTURED OUTPUT AND OF MANUFACTURED EXPORTS

The purpose of this section is to examine in more detail the relationship between industrialization and changes in the export pattern (i.e., to examine the relationship between changes in the composition of manufactured output and of manufactured exports).

Korea, Taiwan, India, and Hong Kong started only recently to export significant amounts of manufactures. Hence, it is impossible to study the relationship between changes in the composition of manufactured output and of manufactured exports on a long-run, time-series basis. The investigation of this long-run relationship is confined to Japan.

Before 1899, the proportion of machinery output in total Japanese manufactured output was negligible, as reflected in the insignificant share of machinery in total manufactured exports. During 1900–1929, the share of machinery output expanded considerably, but there was no matching increase in exports of machinery and transport equipment. During 1930–1940, however, there was another round of expansion in the share of machinery output, and the share of machinery in manufactured exports also grew rapidly. Since World War II, expansion in the output and export shares has been almost identical.

There was a rapid growth in the share of textile output before 1899, and a rapid rate of expansion in textiles' share of total manufactured exports. In 1899, about half of total manufactured exports were textiles.

[16] Data from E. Szczepanik, *The Economic Growth of Hong Kong* (London: Oxford University Press, 1958), p. 154.

During 1900–1929, the share of textile output fluctuated within 40 to 50 per cent; and its share in exports was near 50 per cent. After 1930, and until the 1960s, textiles' share in manufactured output and manufactured exports declined rapidly and continuously. By 1962, the share in output was about 10 per cent; and the share in exports about 20 per cent.

Only after 1930 did Japan's industrial structure begin to show large changes toward the pattern of the presently developed countries. The share of machinery in manufactured output expanded sharply from one-tenth to about one-quarter; chemicals increased from one-seventh to one-fifth. There was a sharp reduction in the share of textiles and consumer goods. These changes in the industrial structure were reflected in the export pattern: There was a sharp increase in the export shares of machinery, metals, and chemicals, and a sharp fall in the share of textiles.

During the 30-year period 1900–1929, textiles and consumer goods constituted about 60 to 70 per cent of total manufactured exports. In this period, the share of manufactured output in GNP increased from about 8 to 18 per cent and per capita income rose from about $90 to $180. After 1930, the share of textiles and consumer goods declined continuously. During 1930–1964, the share of manufactured output in GNP expanded from about 18 per cent to about 32 per cent, and per capita income increased from about $200 to $600. Japan's movement toward increased exports of machinery and metals began after 1930, following a further increase in output of the machinery and metals industries. This movement has intensified since World War II, especially since 1955, when machinery and metals represented nearly one-third of total Japanese manufactured exports.

The export patterns of Korea, Taiwan, India, and Hong Kong in the 1960s are not very different from those of Japan during 1900–1929. As Table 8 shows, textiles and consumer goods constitute the dominant share of total manufactured exports. One notable difference is that, in Korea and Taiwan, the share of products other than textiles and consumer goods is about 49 to 54 per cent, and these countries are exporting significant amounts of electrical machinery, metal products, and wood products (mainly plywood). The manufactured exports of India (in 1964), like those of Japan (in 1900–1929), are almost exclusively textiles and consumer goods.

If the presently developing countries followed the same pattern as Japan, they would require some three decades from their emergence as

Table 8

Changes in the Composition of Manufactured Output and Exports: Japan, India, Korea, Taiwan, and Hong Kong (per cent of Total)

Japan	Output				Exports			
	1900	1909	1919	1929	1900	1909	1919	1929
Machinery	1.2	5.3	11.4	9.2	0.4	1.3	2.9	3.2
Metals	5.4	2.2	5.4	9.3	14.4	12.3	7.3	3.4
Building materials	4.6	5.6	5.2	5.5	5.3	7.6	6.3	7.4
Chemicals	6.7	10.3	11.9	14.8	11.7	11.7	11.0	8.9
Textiles	44.6	49.7	51.0	40.8	57.7	49.4	55.0	58.3
Consumer goods	35.2	22.8	14.7	19.0	5.4	22.8	14.0	17.7

Japan	1939	1953	1962	1939	1953	1964
Machinery	21.7	15.3	32.0	14.7	17.2	31.1
Metals	21.9	17.7	14.4	8.5	16.9	19.1
Building materials	5.3	7.5	8.0	8.3	6.5	4.5
Chemicals	19.7	17.4	16.2	12.4	6.9	10.0
Textiles	14.0	18.2	8.5	36.4	34.2	16.5
Consumer goods	11.9	21.5	16.6	16.8	10.9	8.9

India	Output			Exports				
	1951	1957	1964	1938	1947	1951	1957	1964
Machinery	4.4	7.9	11.1	—	—	—	0.7	2.0
Metals	12.8	11.1	17.5	6.1	—	0.1	0.7	3.8
Building materials	2.7	3.4	3.9	—	—	—	0.9	0.6
Chemicals	9.4	13.7	17.0	1.0	2.0	1.1	4.9	4.8
Textiles	50.8	45.4	35.7	81.1	90.1	92.1	75.8	70.6
Consumer goods	19.8	18.5	14.8	11.9	7.9	6.7	14.9	15.8

	Taiwan				Korea		Hong Kong	
	Output		Exports		Output	Exports	Exports	
	1959	1965	1959	1965	1965	1965	1959	1964
Machinery	4.1	9.3	1.6	5.2	8.5	3.7	3.5	5.3
Metals	7.2	5.8	11.3	9.0	7.5	17.9	6.4	4.4
Building materials	9.1	13.4	11.8	22.1	9.1	20.4	1.0	0.6
Chemicals	17.8	22.4	18.7	12.1	16.6	2.0	2.4	1.5
Textiles	20.3	17.5	29.4	21.9	18.9	25.6	20.0	16.6
Consumer goods	40.3	32.8	26.8	24.3	32.6	25.7	51.4	48.3

Sources: Hong, "A Study of Changes," pp. 92, 94, 106; and India, Department of Statistics, Cabinet Secretariat, *Monthly Statistics of the Production of Selected Industries of India.*

exporters of manufactures to be transformed from textile and consumer goods exporters into exporters of other manufactures. The short experience of other developing countries prevents a definite conclusion, but the experience of developing countries like Korea, Taiwan, India, and Hong Kong suggests that they may not take so long. Since the emergence of India as an exporter of manufactures, the share of textiles in its manufactured exports has declined steadily, from 92 per cent in 1951 to 76 per cent in 1957 and to 71 per cent in 1964; in Taiwan, it fell from 29 per cent in 1959 to 22 per cent in 1964; and in Hong Kong, it fell from 20 per cent in 1959 to 17 per cent in 1964. In Korea, about half of the total manufactured exports are products other than textiles and consumer goods. The share of consumer goods other than textiles has also been declining slightly in these countries. This more rapid transformation may reflect the problems faced by presently developing countries when exporting textiles and other consumer goods—the severe protective policies imposed by developed countries, ever-increasing competition among developing countries, and the absence of easy colonial markets such as those that were available to Japan before World War II.

ROGER LAWRENCE

Primary Products, Preferences, and Economic Welfare: The EEC and Africa

THE TREATY OF ROME, WHICH ESTABLISHED the European Economic Community, committed six sovereign nations of Western Europe to the ambitious task of merging their national economies into a single integrated economy. The principal means to this end was the creation of a customs union among the six nations. This undertaking and its economic implications have rightly held the center of attention in recent years.

The Treaty of Rome, however, also stipulated that overseas (i.e., non-European) states and territories maintaining special relationships with the six member countries would enter into "association" with the EEC; that is, they would take on some, but not all, of the duties and privileges of members. The association arrangements provided preferential markets for the exports of the Overseas Associated Members (OAM): OAM products were to enter the EEC duty-free, while a common external tariff was to be raised against comparable goods from third countries. Thus, as regards tariff policy, OAM exports were to be treated as if the OAM were full members of the customs union.

If the association of the OAM with the Common Market entailed nothing more than the creation of new tariff preferences for OAM exports, there would be a *prima facie* case for concluding that the OAM have gained by association. A good many of the OAM, however, enjoyed preferential trading arrangements with their own metropolitan countries before the EEC came into being, and the terms of these separate arrangements were usually quite favorable to the overseas areas—particularly in the case of the French associates. In fact, the tariff protection granted overseas exports in the French market was generally greater than that afforded by the EEC. In consequence, the French overseas areas, which constitute the largest group of overseas associates, found themselves exchanging protection behind a high French tariff wall for protection behind a lower EEC common external tariff—in effect, they exchanged a lower degree of preference for a larger preferential market.

The following pages explore the chief determinants of the comparative-static effects of this change. The first section reviews briefly the tariff policies of the metropolitan countries with respect to their overseas territories and the tariff policy of the EEC with respect to its overseas associates. The second section develops a schematic framework that isolates the principal variables determining the direction of the comparative-static welfare changes produced by the switch from metropolitan to EEC preference schemes. The argument in this section, although developed specifically in terms of the EEC and its overseas associates, is quite general. It presents a useful device for analyzing the welfare effects of enlarging a trade-preference area (or a customs union) and shows that the direction of static welfare changes resulting from the enlargement can be ascertained with a minimum of information. The third section examines the actual course of the relevant variables for some important OAM exports.

NATIONAL AND EEC COMMERCIAL POLICIES TOWARD ASSOCIATED AREAS

Of the six EEC members, all but Germany and Luxembourg maintained special relations with overseas areas in the mid-1950s, but the importance of the various members' overseas areas in world trade, and the commercial policies of member countries toward these areas, varied greatly. On the one hand, the exports of Italian Somaliland averaged a mere $8 million per annum in 1955–1956 and consisted primarily of bananas. These exports were highly protected in the Italian market; Italy imposed a 36 per cent tariff on banana imports from other countries, and channeled all imports through a state monopoly whose main purpose was to assure an advantageous outlet for Somaliland's banana crop. On the other hand, the exports of the Belgian Congo and Ruanda-Urundi averaged almost $600 million in 1955–1956. These, however, received very little preference in the Benelux (the main exceptions being bananas and crude vegetable oils), and the greatest part of these same exports, consisting of mineral ores, will not receive tariff preferences from the EEC. Excluding mineral ores in order to obtain a broad group of commodities, mainly agricultural, on which EEC preference will obtain, preference-eligible exports from the Belgian Congo and Ruanda-Urundi averaged about $190 million.

The French overseas areas are by far the most important group of associates in terms of the value of trade subject to preferences before and after the establishment of the EEC. The average annual value of exports from tropical French Africa and Madagascar, other than mineral ores, was about $580 million in 1955–1956, and comprised 75 per cent of all such exports from overseas associated areas. At the same time, French preferences for overseas exports were substantial; in 1957, roughly 55 per cent (by value) of the combined exports of French West Africa and French Equatorial Africa benefited from some tariff protection in the French market. Hence, the effect of the EEC association arrangements on trade in tropical products depends primarily on what happens to the French associates, and the discussion below will be focused almost exclusively on those areas.

Preference for overseas goods in French markets was effected in three main ways: preferential tariff treatment of overseas exports, quantitative controls on imports from third countries, and price-guarantee schemes.[1] Tariff preference for overseas goods was accomplished by admitting those goods to metropolitan France duty-free and by imposing tariffs on comparable goods originating in third countries. The rate of preference

---

[1] For one product, cotton, there were also direct subsidies to producers. At certain times and for certain products, moreover, there was a system of "pairing" (*jumelage*). Under this system, an importer's authorization to import nonoverseas products was made contingent on his agreeing to purchase given amounts of the same goods from overseas producers.

enjoyed by the overseas territories varied from product to product. For some goods, there was no French duty on competing third-country imports, and thus no tariff preference; in other instances, third-country goods bore duties as high as 30 per cent.

The degree of tariff preference that France could grant to overseas products was circumscribed by her adherence to the General Agreement on Tariffs and Trade. Article I of the GATT stipulates that departures from most-favored-nation treatment may be continued among areas that were dependent on a single authority before July 1, 1939. The margin of preference that may be accorded to such areas, however, is limited to that which existed on April 10, 1947.[2]

Lacking complete freedom to grant tariff preferences, France resorted to the other devices mentioned above. These arrangements supplemented tariff preferences or substituted for them. For some products, the government simply set a "guaranteed" price each year that was generally intended to be above the world price. If the French price threatened to fall below this guaranteed price, French importers were required to diminish or eliminate their purchases from third countries.[3] For other products,[4] quantitative restrictions on imports from third countries were established as a matter of principle—that is, regardless of the evolution of prices.

The commercial policy of the EEC with respect to the overseas areas was established by the Treaty of Rome and further elaborated by two implementing conventions, signed in 1957 and 1963. Pursuant to the provisions of the Treaty and conventions, the EEC countries are eliminating their tariffs on imports originating in overseas associates, following schedules established for the EEC transition period. At the same time, they are moving their tariffs on goods from third countries toward the common external tariff (which, it should be recalled, is zero for some products). A select group of OAM exports, however, was accorded immediate duty-free entry into the EEC in mid-1964, and the full common external tariff was applied to imports from third countries, albeit at lower rates than those originally envisaged for these commodities.[5]

---

[2] GATT, *Articles of Agreement*, Article I, paragraphs 2 and 4.

[3] Products subject to these measures included cotton, sisal, gum arabic, palm and copra oil, and coconuts. See F. Bloch-Lainé et al., *La Zone Franc* (Paris: Presses Universitaires de France, 1956), p. 435.

[4] Coffee, tapioca, and bananas. See Bloch-Lainé et al., *La Zone Franc*.

[5] The products in question are pineapples, coconuts, coffee, tea, pepper, cloves, nutmeg and cocoa beans.

Table 1

Total Exports of French West Africa and French Equatorial Africa in 1957; French and EEC Tariffs

Product	Value (millions of CFA francs)	French Tariff[a] (%)	EEC Tariff[a,b] (%)
Unroasted coffee	16,139	20	9.6
Shelled peanuts	14,918	10[c]	—
Cocoa beans	6,579	25[c]	5.4
Cattle	271	—	—
Crude oil	480	—	—
Unprocessed wood	7,064	10[c]	—
Processed wood	1,475	15	10
Cotton	4,398	—	—
Diamonds	424	—	—
Fresh bananas	1,839	20	20
Palm nuts	1,839	10	—
Crude peanut oil	7,315	18	10
Refined peanut oil	1,196	18	15
Oil cake	1,759	10	—
Other	9,479	4.4[d]	2.7[d]
Total	75,175		
Weighted average (all items)		8.1	4.8
Weighted average (preference items)		8.7	5.1

Sources: France, Ministère des Affaires Economiques et Financières, Institut National de la Statistique et des Etudes Economiques, *Bulletin Mensuel de Statistique d'Outre-Mer*; France, Ministère des Finances et des Affaires Economiques, *Tarifs des droits de douane d'importation et d'exportation*; and *Customs Tariff of the European Communities* (London: Her Majesty's Stationery Office, 1962).

[a] Tariffs for aggregated commodity groups should be treated as approximations, because it was not always possible to reconcile trade returns with tariff classifications.

[b] Common external tariff as of 1960, except for coffee and cocoa, for which the recorded tariff rate is the one effective in mid-1964.

[c] Suspended in 1957, valued at zero in computing the average tariffs.

[d] Weighted average. Nonpreference items are included in this category.

For two commodities, further provisions diluted the impact of the tariff changes; tariff quotas were granted to Germany for bananas, and to Italy and the Benelux for coffee, allowing substantial duty-free imports of these commodities from third countries.

The nontariff preferences that France had used are not being continued by the EEC. The most recent Association Convention set forth a time-table for the elimination of French price-support schemes and, as a *quid pro quo*, earmarked $230 million in aid to the overseas associates to finance rationalization and diversification projects, that is, to enlarge profitable production at world prices and, if necessary, to help producers transfer into new lines of production. Although there have been diffi-culties in adhering to the original timetable, the expectation remains that direct price supports will shortly be eliminated.

Under EEC arrangements, then, the full burden of providing privileged status for OAM exports will fall on tariff policy. This tariff policy is summarized in Table 1, which shows the principal export products of former French West Africa and French Equatorial Africa, along with the French and EEC tariffs on these commodities. The table shows clearly that the level of tariff protection afforded by the EEC, as measured simply by the height of the nominal tariff, will be less than that provided by the pre-EEC French preference system. Thus, in associating themselves with the EEC, the French overseas areas surrendered a relatively high degree of preference in the French market for a relatively low degree of preference in the larger EEC market. The next problem is to isolate the variables which determine the impact of this change on the welfare of the overseas associ-ates, of the EEC members, and of excluded exporting countries.

WELFARE CHANGES IN AN ENLARGED
TRADE PREFERENCE AREA

Consider Figure 1, where D_F is France's import demand for the export products of the OAM, where D_F' is French import demand reduced by a specific French tariff (which does not apply to imports from the French OAM), and where D_F^T is French demand reduced by the EEC's common external tariff, which is assumed to be lower than the pre-EEC French tariff (and which, again, does not apply to imports from the OAM). Let D_{CM} be the combined import demand for OAM products of all EEC members, and D_{CM}^T be the combined EEC demand reduced by the common

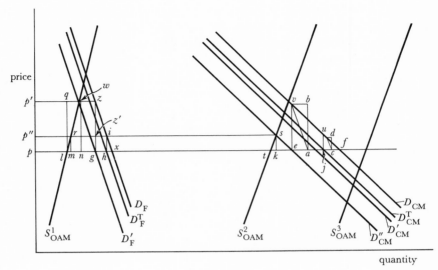

Figure 1

external tariff. D'_{CM} and D''_{CM} are two alternative versions of total EEC demand reduced by pre-EEC national tariffs, depending on whether the national tariffs of the EEC members other than France were less (D'_{CM}) or greater (D''_{CM}) than the common external tariff.[6] In Figure 1, the height of the tariff in non-French EEC members implied by D''_{CM} is given by the distance ab, and the height of the non-French tariff implied by D'_{CM} is given by cd.[7]

[6] As drawn, D'_{CM} lies to the left of D^T_{CM}, reflecting the fact that the French national tariff exceeded the common external tariff by more than the amount by which other members' national tariffs fell short of the CXT. This is not a necessary result, and D'_{CM} could equally well be placed to the right of D^T_{CM}.

[7] These distances are derived geometrically as follows. To "wash out" France's contribution to the position and slope of D''_{CM}, move horizontally to the right from any point on D''_{CM} by a distance equal to the horizontal distance between D_F and D_F' (in Figure 1, from e to a). Join this point to D_{CM} by a line drawn parallel to D_F. The point given by the intersection of this line with D_{CM} will then lie above the price solution from which the operation was begun by the amount of the non-French members' tariff. This result may be checked as follows. In adding the demand schedule of France (with and without tariff) to the combined schedule of the other EEC members (with and without national tariffs) we get:

$$m_{CM} = m_t + m_o$$

where m_{CM} is the horizontal distance between the demand schedule for the Common Market and that schedule reduced by the "aggregate" tariff, and m_t and m_o are the horizontal distances between the French and other members' demand curves, respectively,

Let S_{OAM}^1, S_{OAM}^2, and S_{OAM}^3 be three alternative versions of the export supply schedule of the French OAM. S_{OAM}^1 represents that family of possible OAM supply schedules characterized by the fact that the OAM cannot satisfy completely French demand at prices ruling in the French market. S_{OAM}^2 represents that family of possible OAM supply schedules characterized by the fact that OAM supply exceeds French demand at prices ruling in the French market, but is less than (or equal to) total EEC demand at prices ruling in the Common Market. S_{OAM}^3, in turn, represents a situation in which OAM supply exceeds total EEC demand at prices ruling in the Common Market.

Consider now the effects of enlarging the preference area between France and the OAM to include France's EEC partners.[8] Assume that perfect competition reigns in all markets. Ignore for the moment S_{OAM}^2 and S_{OAM}^3, and suppose that the quantity of OAM exports forthcoming at ruling prices is less than French import demand; that is, that S_{OAM}^1 is the overseas associates' supply schedule.

Before the EEC, the French price is p' and OAM exports, which are directed entirely toward the French market, are equal to pn. The gain to the OAM from the preferential arrangement with France is measured by the area $plwp'$, and France's loss is measured by the rectangle $pnwp'$. The gain to the OAM results from a simple shifting of the terms of trade between the OAM and France on the volume of OAM exports that

---

and these schedules reduced by the appropriate tariffs. Rearranging and expressing the distances in terms of Figure 1, we have (for the case in which D_{CM}'' is the relevant aggregate demand schedule *cum* tariff):

$$(1) \quad af = ef - ea$$

Likewise, designating b as the slope of the relevant demand curve, we may write:

$$b_o = b_{CM} - b_t$$

or, in terms of Figure 1:

$$(2) \quad af/ba = ef/ve - ea/ve$$

where the distance ve equals ba. The height of the non-French members' tariff, however is:

$$t_o = m_o(1/b_o)$$

or, substituting from (1) and (2):

$$(3) \quad t_o = af(ba/af) = ba$$

[8] The discussion below assumes that tariffs are the only form of commercial preference, and that transport costs are zero. It also relies on the familiar notion of Marshallian consumers' and producers' surplus, and makes the usual assumptions associated with those concepts.

would have been forthcoming at world prices (pl), plus an increase in producers' surplus, equal to lwq, on the additional exports elicited by the preferential arrangement. The loss to France results from the shifting of the terms of trade on pl of OAM exports, plus the terms-of-trade loss resulting from shifting ln of import demand from other sources to the OAM.

What are the consequences of enlarging the preference area? Initially, the EEC common external tariff yields a price in the EEC market (including France) of p''. Total exports of the French OAM are reduced from pn to pm, and the quantity of imports demanded by France increases from pg to ph. The French OAM lose: Their gain from EEC preferences is measured by the area $plrp''$, which is smaller than $plwp'$. France, on the other hand, gains: The terms-of-trade burden of providing a preferential market for OAM exports has been reduced from $pnwp'$ to $pmrp''$, and a consumers' surplus gain, equal to ziz', has been obtained on the additional imports. If, in addition, OAM exports continue to be directed entirely toward France, the other EEC members bear none of the cost of providing preferences for OAM exports.

These, then, will be the primary welfare changes resulting from enlargement of the preference area. There will, however, be a secondary set of welfare changes due to the impact of the change in the preference area on the world market price of OAM export commodities.

Consider the effects of the enlargement on over-all demand and supply (not shown in Figure 1). At any given world price, the French OAM now supply fewer exports, and France demands more imports. These changes, taken by themselves, imply a rise in world price. But adjustment of the non-French EEC members' tariffs to the common external tariff will also affect overall demand. If the other EEC members' pre-union tariffs were above the CXT (as shown by D''_{CM} in Figure 1), reduction to the level of the CXT would increase the quantity demanded, reinforcing the effect of the change in the French tariff. If the other members' tariffs were below the CXT (as shown by D'_{CM} in Figure 1), adjustment to the CXT level would tend to offset or reverse the price-raising effect of the change in the French tariff. Likewise, the effect of expanding the trade-preference area on the export supply of the non-French OAM (included, for the first time, in a preferential zone) could offset or reinforce the contraction of the French OAM supply, depending on whether pre-EEC production in non-French OAM areas took place at a price below or above the EEC price implied by the CXT. These other factors, then, make the effect of enlarging the trade-preference area on the world market price considerably less clear. Nonetheless, there is a large variety of circumstances in which the result of the enlargement would be a higher world price. This would tend to limit the French gains and French OAM losses described earlier. More important, if world price rises, exporters excluded from the preferential market actually gain (relative to their pre-EEC position) from enlargement of the preferential area. This is, at first blush, a paradoxical conclusion: The exporting area included in the preference area loses, while the excluded area gains.

All these conclusions, however, depend entirely on the relative sizes of French OAM supply and French demand at ruling prices. Quite different results obtain when we alter the OAM supply schedule. Ignoring now S^1_{OAM} and S^3_{OAM}, suppose that S^2_{OAM} represents the French OAM export supply; that is, assume that at ruling prices OAM export supply exceeds French import demand, but is less than (or equal to) total EEC demand. Under these conditions, the French preference system would not have given rise to an "operative" tariff preference[9] for OAM goods in the French market; OAM exports to France would have taken place at the world price. To see that this must be so, one need only note that, in this case, some OAM export production is of necessity directed toward third markets. Any tendency for the French price of OAM exports to rise above the world price would thus create an incentive for producers shipping to third markets to redirect their output toward France. Such a process would continue until prices in French and third markets were equalized.

The advent of the EEC will change market relationships so as to make tariff preference for OAM exports "operative" for the first time. After formation of the EEC, the French OAM will receive a premium on exports to the EEC, while France and other EEC members must now pay the world price plus the CXT for their imports. (In Figure 1, the OAM gain is given by the area $ptsp''$; France's loss by $pxip''$; and the loss of the other EEC members by $hksi$.) The quantity of OAM exports supplied will increase (from pt to pk in Figure 1), and the quantity of French imports will decrease (from px to ph). These two developments, taken by themselves, will depress the world price of goods exported by the OAM, and inflict losses on third-country exporters. As before, secondary adjustments in the non-French OAM and non-French EEC member

[9] The term "operative preference" describes a situation in which suppliers of goods subject to preference actually receive a higher price because of the preference than they would have received without the preference.

could work to offset this outcome, or even to reverse it.[10] (In addition, the change in world price would alter the magnitude, but not the direction, of the welfare changes spelled out above.) On the whole, however, there is a strong presumption that enlargement of the French OAM preferential market results in gains for the OAM, and in losses for EEC members (including France) and for excluded exporters.

There will be still another outcome if, ignoring for the moment S^1_{OAM} and S^2_{OAM}, we assume that OAM output at relevant prices is greater than total EEC demand, as shown by S^3_{OAM}. Under these circumstances, enlargement of the OAM preferential market is insufficient to render tariff preferences operative: OAM exports will be marketed at world prices before and after the expansion of the preference area. By the same token, excluded exporters will not be damaged by the preference extension, and France and the EEC will not incur welfare changes.

The assumption that all markets are organized under a regime of perfect competition is, of course, unrealistic, and we must now explore the implications of relaxing this assumption to some degree. Suppose, for example, that the marketing of OAM exports was centralized in one organization capable of engaging in price discrimination. This change in assumptions would not alter the analysis just presented if S^1_{OAM} were the relevant supply schedule of OAM exports. But if OAM supply is S^2_{OAM}, important alterations must be made in the argument. Before the existence of the EEC, it would have been possible for the OAM to limit the volume of exports directed toward France. Assuming adequate information concerning the position and shape of the French demand schedule, the OAM would have been able to direct the quantity pg toward France, thereby obtaining the full benefit of French preferences on this quantity of exports. (Any quantity less than pg would also obtain full preference in the French market, but the quantity pg is the largest that the OAM could direct toward France and still obtain the full margin of preference.) In this case, the advent of the EEC would not initiate operative preferences, but would merely modify an operative system and might not increase OAM gains. The OAM gain from its preference in France might be represented by an area as large as $p'zgp$. With EEC preference, the gain to the OAM will be represented by an area such as $p''stp$. One cannot say whether $p''stp$ is greater or smaller than $p'zgp$ without additional

---

[10] If, for example, non-French OAM production took place at prices exceeding world prices by more than the CXT, and national tariffs in the other EEC members were above the CXT.

information about the magnitude of OAM exports, French import demand, the pre-EEC French tariff, and the CXT. It should be noted, however, that, even if the OAM lose from expansion of the preferential area, the excluded exporters are likely to lose, since the enlargement will elicit additional OAM production, implying, *ceteris paribus*, a fall in the world price. The introduction of price discrimination does not alter the conclusions regarding welfare changes for the other EEC members.

Consider now the consequences of expanding the trade-preference area when S^3_{OAM} represents French OAM export supply. Under these circumstances, and assuming, as before, that the centralized exporting organization practices effective price discrimination, the OAM would have realized a net welfare benefit equal to the area $p'zgp$ before enlargement of the preferential area, and, after expansion of the area, will realize a gain equal to $p''ujp$. As before, it is not possible to ascertain whether this change represents a gain or loss without further knowledge of various magnitudes, but note that, in any case, excluded exporters are not likely to be damaged by the enlargement, because production in the OAM will continue to be governed by world prices. Here, moreover, the welfare burden borne by France may increase or decrease (depending on whether $p'zgp$ is less or greater than $p''ihp$), but the other EEC members will suffer losses (equal to $iujh$).

THE EEC AND THE OVERSEAS ASSOCIATES: SOME TENTATIVE FINDINGS

The argument of the preceding section has served to identify the kind of information necessary to make statements about the comparative-static welfare effects of enlarging French preference arrangements to include the entire Common Market. Clearly, the most important consideration is the relation of French OAM export supply, before and after formation of the EEC, to French and total EEC import demand. We must also ask whether or not French OAM producers were successful in exercising price discrimination under the pre-EEC regime. In addition, we must examine the relation of pre-EEC national tariffs to the CXT, and take into account the likely effects of the association arrangements on output in the Belgian OAM.

The relevant information for major OAM export products is given in Table 2. The first column sets forth the relationship between French

Table 2

Factors Determining the Direction of Welfare Changes Resulting from Association: Selected OAM Exports

Product	Market Relationships Prior to EEC[a] (1)	Price Discrimination (2)	CXT (%) (3)	French Tariff Lowered or Raised (4)	All National Tariffs Lowered or Raised (5)	Belgian Preference for Belgian OAM (6)	Likely Direction of Welfare Changes[b] OAM French	OAM Belgian	Excluded Exporters	France	Other EEC Members
Cocoa	2	No	5.4	raised	raised	0	G	G	L	L	L
Bananas	2	Yes	20.0	NC[b]	raised	15%	G	G	L	NC	L[c]
Coffee (Robusta)	3	Yes	9.6	lowered	lowered	0	L	G	G	G	L[d]
Wood	2	No	0	NC	lowered	0	NC	NC	NC	NC	NC
Cotton	1	—	0	NC	lowered	0	L[e]	NC	G[e]	G[e]	NC
Peanut oil	2	Yes	10.0	lowered	NC	5%	L[f]	G	L	G	L
Peanuts	1	—	0	NC	lowered	0	L[e,f]	NC	G[e]	G[e]	NC

[a] Key: 1 = OAM export supply less than French import demand; 2 = OAM export supply greater than French import demand, but less than combined import demand of all EEC countries; 3 = OAM export supply greater than the combined import demand of all EEC countries.

[b] Key: G = gain; L = loss; NC = no change.

[c] Limited by tariff quotas granted to Germany.

[d] Limited by tariff quotas granted to Italy and the Benelux.

[e] Reflects solely the planned termination of French price-support schemes for overseas production, and does not allow for the increased financial aid to the OAM that serves as a *quid pro quo*.

[f] Does not include possible benefits to the OAM arising from the inclusion of edible oils and oilseeds in the EEC's common agricultural policies.

OAM supply and French and EEC demand.[11] Most of the products fall into that class of goods (class 2) for which OAM export supply is greater than French import demand, but less than EEC import demand. This is significant, because it is precisely in this circumstance that enlargement of the preferential area promises gains to the OAM. Column (2) then records the existence or nonexistence of price discrimination on the part of the French OAM. Since direct evidence on price discrimination was lacking, its existence was inferred whenever OAM supply exceeded French demand and French import prices exceeded world prices by as much as (or more than) the French tariff.

Column (3) records the CXT for the seven products, and columns (4) and (5) show whether the French tariff (whose movements are strategic for changes in French OAM welfare) and the combined national tariffs of all EEC countries must be raised or lowered to align them with the CXT. When some national tariffs were above and some below the CXT, a weighted average of the national tariffs was taken (using the volume of imports in 1956–1957 as weights), and the relation of the weighted average to the CXT was used to determine the entry in column (5). Column (6) records the state of pre-EEC preferences for the exports of the Belgian OAM in Belgium. Prior to the EEC, the Belgian OAM enjoyed tariff preferences on two commodities, bananas and peanut oil.

These bits of information can be pieced together to make statements about the direction of comparative-static welfare changes; conclusions regarding those changes are summarized in the remainder of the table.[12]

The results are straightforward for the first commodity, cocoa. French OAM exports exceeded French import demand prior to the EEC, but the total export supply from areas receiving preference was less than total EEC demand. Before the Common Market, moreover, the French tariff on cocoa was suspended, and cocoa produced in the Belgian OAM received no tariff preference in Belgium. Furthermore, the alignment of individual tariffs to the CXT entailed an increase of tariffs in the EEC countries. The shift from national to EEC preferences thus worked to reduce the quantity demanded in the EEC and to elicit additional production in the

[11] Strictly speaking, the relevant comparison after the EEC is between total OAM supply and EEC import demand. But the addition of the non-French OAM does not change the market relationships shown in Table 2.

[12] There is the additional possibility that welfare will be redistributed among the countries making up the groups listed in Table 2. This possibility is not examined in the subsequent analysis.

OAM, generating gains for the French and Belgian OAM and losses for excluded exporters (since additional OAM production and reduced EEC demand tend to reduce the world price for cocoa). All EEC members sustain losses by taking up OAM exports at prices exceeding the world price.

The EEC policy concerning bananas leads to similar welfare changes. In this case, however, the CXT was set at the same level as the pre-EEC French tariff; hence, no welfare changes occur for France. Prior to the EEC, moreover, the French OAM practiced price discrimination and made good the 20 per cent preference on their bananas in the French market. As a result, the gains from enlargement of the preferential area will obtain only on the excess of their production over French demand. Finally, a tariff quota was granted to Germany allowing duty-free imports from excluded exporters. This provision reduces substantially the immediate welfare loss of EEC members other than France.

Robusta varieties of coffee are the only product in Table 2 for which total OAM output exceeds total EEC demand. In accordance with the preceding section, then, we can assert that excluded exporters will not be damaged by expansion of the preferential area, since marginal OAM output will continue to be governed by world prices. In fact, since the level of tariffs on EEC coffee imports will be reduced, the effect on excluded exporters may be favorable. French OAM producers, on the other hand, appear likely to lose: Before the EEC, they exercised price discrimination and obtained a premium over world prices of about 20 per cent (the full amount of France's tariff) on exports shipped to France. Under EEC arrangements, they will obtain at most a 9 per cent premium on the (larger) volume of exports they will be able to ship to the EEC. On a static basis (assuming, that is, that the relevant supply and demand parameters and the world price are the same after as before the EEC), this involves losses for the OAM: a 9 per cent premium on the volume of exports equal to total EEC imports in 1957 is worth less than a 20 per cent premium on the volume of exports equal to France's pre-EEC imports. Belgian OAM exporters, on the other hand, will gain from the EEC arrangements if they are able to practice price discrimination in the marketing of their coffee exports. France gains insofar as the burden of providing a privileged market for OAM exports has been reduced, while other EEC members, who take on this burden for the first time, lose. (This loss is reduced, however, by the tariff quotas granted to Italy and the Benelux permitting substantial tariff-free imports from third countries.)

National and EEC commercial policies toward tropical woods are not such as to generate welfare changes in the passage from national to EEC systems. The tariff policies of France and the EEC also fail to cause welfare changes in the case of cotton. In this case, however, France ran a price-support scheme in favor of the French OAM and this will not continue in the EEC framework. The welfare changes entered in Table 2 for the French OAM, France, and the excluded exporters reflect the dismantling of this scheme and the expectation that its demise will result in reduced French OAM cotton production.[13]

Tariff changes for peanut oil will, other things equal, lead to losses for the French OAM. Before the EEC, the OAM obtained an 18 per cent preference on shipments to France; after the EEC, they will obtain at most a 10 per cent premium on total exports. At constant world prices, however, a 10 per cent premium on a volume of exports equal to total EEC imports in 1957 is worth less than an 18 per cent premium on a volume of exports equal to France's pre-EEC import demand. But increased production nonetheless seems likely to occur in the French and Belgian overseas associates. With pre-EEC exports greater than French import demand, output before the EEC was governed by world prices rather than French prices, whereas output after the EEC will be governed by the preferential price in EEC markets. Prices will rise in the Belgian OAM because the preference on exports will increase from 5 to 10 per cent. In each case, output should rise, and the changes in output should result in gains for the French and Belgian OAM and losses for excluded exporters. France will gain too, by reducing the burden of providing preference for OAM exports, and other EEC members will lose by taking up part of that burden.[14]

Tariff changes for peanuts will not cause welfare changes for the OAM, but the termination of French price supports will penalize the French OAM. Furthermore, the elimination of these schemes should reduce production in the OAM and put some upward pressure on peanut prices; hence, excluded exporters should gain. France will gain by eliminating her price supports for OAM exports, and, since there is no

---

[13] As a *quid pro quo* for eliminating price supports, the OAM are to receive financial aid from the EEC earmarked for "the rationalization and diversification" of production. Since Table 2 attempts to show only changes in welfare arising from trade, no account has been taken of these capital flows.

[14] This statement takes no account of the distribution of costs and benefits resulting from the EEC common agricultural policy for edible oils and oilseeds.

tariff preference in the EEC, there should be no gains or losses for other EEC members.[15]

All in all, the welfare changes listed in Table 2 show no pervasive welfare gain for the French OAM. In fact, gains are indicated for only two commodities, while losses seem likely for four commodities. The magnitude of the gains in the two cases could, of course, outweigh the magnitude of the losses in the other four cases; the procedure adopted here does not allow us to make statements about sizes of welfare changes. It should be noted, however, that two products, coffee and peanuts, made up more than 40 per cent of the combined value of French West Africa's and French Equatorial Africa's exports in 1957, and on both of these products the direction of welfare change is negative.

Likewise, Table 2 does not show pervasive welfare losses for the excluded exporting countries: In three cases, there may actually be welfare gains for these countries. Again, however, little can be said about the magnitudes of the welfare changes. The direction of welfare changes for France is, with one exception, favorable, and the changes for the other EEC members are clearly unfavorable. Hence, the most clear-cut conclusions emerging from this part of the analysis are that the EEC arrangements will result in welfare gains for France, and that these gains will occur at the expense of other EEC members.

The argument summarized in Table 2 can be translated into statements regarding the changes in trade patterns to be expected from the EEC arrangements. Reverting to the argument of the preceding section, gains to the OAM and losses to excluded exporters will be accompanied by a rise in OAM exports and a decrease in excluded countries' exports. This pattern of gains and losses, then, implies an increase in the French OAM's share in world trade. If, however, an increase in the OAM's share of world trade is to be attributed unambiguously to EEC commercial policies, it must be accompanied by a rise in the OAM's share of EEC imports and by an increase in the portion of OAM exports directed toward EEC markets.

Evidence on market shares can thus provide some indication of the relative importance of the comparative-static welfare effects described above. If the static effects of the association arrangements were of prime importance in determining the pattern of trade flows, the evolution of

---

[15] This statement, as well as the attribution of losses to the OAM, takes no account of the cost and benefits of increased financial aid provided to the OAM by EEC members as a *quid pro quo* for the elimination of the price-support scheme.

trade patterns should be roughly as indicated by the argument above. If trade patterns develop differently, one can only conclude that circumstances other than the EEC's association arrangements were of overriding importance.

Table 3 presents data on the relevant trade patterns for the seven commodities examined earlier. In an attempt to detect the effects of association, trade patterns in 1963–1964, the latest two years for which data are available, were compared with trade patterns in 1956–1957, the last two years before the EEC came into being. The period examined is not sufficiently long to capture all the effects of association. For some selected OAM exports, the full margin of preference in EEC markets materialized only in mid-1964 (cocoa and coffee fall in this category), and, for other products, the transitional tariff adjustments were not complete at the end of 1964. In consequence, the short-run effects of association will not be fully reflected in the data. Furthermore, the long-run sensitivity of OAM supply to price changes may be greater than the short-run sensitivity; thus, the full response of OAM producers to tariff preference may not yet be evident. Nonetheless, an examination of the changes in trade patterns that have occurred does allow at least some tentative conclusions regarding the relative importance of the comparative-static effects of association.

The changes in trade patterns shown in Table 3 are not generally consistent with those predicted by the previous argument. For products on which gains were indicated for the OAM, the latter's share in world trade should increase; where losses were indicated, the share should remain unchanged or decline. This pattern actually emerged for only one of the commodities listed in Table 3—cocoa. The share of OAM cocoa in EEC markets also increased, but the portion of OAM cocoa exports directed toward EEC markets fell, suggesting that the larger share of the OAM in world markets was not the result of the EEC tariff preference, but emanated from unrelated factors on the supply side. Thus, for the seven products examined in Table 3, the change in trade patterns does not support the view that the EEC arrangements have been a strong force affecting the welfare of associated and excluded exporting countries.

At the same time, the pattern of imports into EEC member countries is sometimes consistent with the argument that the EEC arrangements result in a shifting of the burden of providing preferential markets from France to her Common Market partners. For cocoa, bananas, and coffee,

Table 3

Changes in Trade Patterns for Selected OAM Exports: 1956–1957 to 1963–1964

Product	Memo Item: Indicated Outcome for French OAM[a]	French OAM Share in World Trade (%)		French OAM Share in EEC Imports (%) 1956-57			French OAM Share in EEC Imports (%) 1963-64			Portion of French OAM Exports Directed toward EEC Markets (%)	
		1956-57	1963-64	Total	France	Other	Total	France	Other	1956-57	1963-64
Cocoa	G	16	20	32	81	20	38	80	28	73	71
Bananas	G	10	9	39	98	2	32	90	5	89	87
Coffee	L	9	10	26	72	1	24	71	4	66	59
Wood	NC	n.a.	n.a.	14	44	9	27	60	19	78	83
Cotton	L	1	2	4	n.a.	n.a.	5	16	1	94	75
Peanut oil	L	35	28	51	94	7	28	96	2	81	20
Peanuts	L	25	26	56	84	4	41	66	2	100	82

Sources: FAO, World Trade Yearbook; Statistical Office of the European Communities, Foreign Trade Statistics: Associated Overseas Areas; OECD, Foreign Trade, Series C and Series IV; France, Institut National de la Statistique et des Etudes Economiques, Bulletin Mensuel de Statistique d'Outre-Mer.

[a] See Table 2.

the share of the OAM in France's market fell somewhat, while the share of the OAM in the markets of other Common Market countries rose.

In setting forth conclusions regarding the OAM and the excluded exporters, it should again be emphasized that data running through 1964 may not show the full impact of association. For some commodities, however, there is additional evidence that the OAM themselves consider their tariff preferences to be relatively unimportant sources of potential gain. Thus, OAM coffee producers belong to the 1962 International Coffee Agreement, and the most important cocoa producers (the Ivory Coast, Cameroon, and Togo) belong to the Cocoa Alliance. In both cases, the future market shares of the members of the agreement will be determined by the workings of the agreement. This presumably means that higher prices for OAM producers resulting from EEC preferences will not be translated into increased total exports by the OAM.[16] The decision of the OAM to join these agreements may well reflect a judgment that joint action to influence world commodity prices is more important to the OAM than a single-minded exploitation of the OAM tariff advantage in EEC markets. Thus, for coffee and cocoa—two important OAM export products—little, if any, distortion in trade patterns seems indicated in the future. For other commodities, the longer-run impact of association seems less clear. For bananas, however, the 20 per cent preference for OAM exports, which has not yet come into full effect, may be capable of inflicting significant losses on excluded exporters.

The apparent insignificance of the association arrangements, as a factor affecting world trade patterns, results, in part, from factors unrelated to the EEC. Two aspects of the EEC's own policies, however, have also contributed to this outcome:

1. When the Second Association Convention was signed in 1963, the common external tariff for a number of important OAM export products was reduced, diminishing preferences for these goods. In fact, the degree of preference provided by the new common external tariff was generally identical with the degree of preference that had emerged at that point from the gradual process of aligning national tariffs to the original CXT. The decision to freeze the degree of preference in non-French markets at the point reached in 1963, together with evidence that the OAM share in total world exports was not increased by this

---

[16] Preferences in the EEC could still result in a redirection of OAM exports from third markets to EEC markets, entailing gains for the OAM. If total OAM exports remain unchanged, however, this would not involve losses for excluded exporters.

preference, may indicate that the EEC sought to regulate preferences in a way that would maintain, but not enhance, the OAM position in export markets.

2. The Second Association Convention substituted capital flows (production and diversification aids) for price-support schemes. This technique has been used to compensate the OAM for the dismantling of France's nontariff preferences that were not to be continued by the EEC.

Taken together, these two moves appear to indicate a desire on the part of the EEC to prevent the association arrangements from increasing distortions in world trade.

CONCLUSION

The examination of market structures and tariff changes has not revealed a clear pattern of gain for the French OAM from the EEC association arrangements. Nor has it revealed systematic losses for excluded countries. So far, even where comparative-static gains for the OAM are indicated, actual trade patterns do not generally reflect these gains. By implication, factors other than EEC tariff preferences have been instrumental in determining producing countries' export performances. On the whole, the most clear-cut welfare change resulting from the EEC association arrangements is that of France, which has reduced significantly the burden of maintaining privileged markets for OAM products. Likewise, the non-French EEC members appear to have sustained some losses by assuming part of the costs of providing preferences for the OAM. Thus, the main effects of the association arrangements may simply be welfare shifts among the EEC members, rather than a redistribution of welfare between associated and excluded exporters.

III

INTERNATIONAL FINANCIAL POLICIES AND THE INTERNATIONAL MONETARY SYSTEM

JOHN PATRICK

The Optimum Policy Mix:
Convergence and Consistency

THIS ESSAY EXTENDS THE MODEL of balance-of-payments adjustment
presented by Robert Mundell in his pioneering article in the IMF
Staff Papers.[1] A presentation of Mundell's original discussion is followed
by the exposition of mathematical techniques that can be applied to it.
I then utilize those techniques to extend Mundell's analysis. I employ a
two-country model which takes explicit account of changes in the outside
world and their effects on the country under consideration. I analyze the
consequence of changes in stocks of capital, rather than flows, responding
to interest-rate differentials; I ask what happens when interest rates move
together rather than independently, and study the problems that arise
when incomes, as well as interest-rate differentials, have an influence on
capital movements. I show that the explicit inclusion of the rest of the
world does not invalidate Mundell's original discussion of the proper

This essay is based on a dissertation in preparation. I thank Professor Robert Mundell
for his observations on my dissertation proposal and on the meaning of his own work
in this area.

[1] R. A. Mundell, "The Appropriate Use of Monetary and Fiscal Policy for Internal
and External Stability," *IMF Staff Papers* IX (March 1962), 70–79.

policy response to internal and external disequilibrium. However, the other complications introduced raise the possibility that Mundell's conclusions are inappropriate. A final section discusses the results of conflicting balance-of-payments targets.

MUNDELL'S ANALYSIS

In his 1962 paper, Mundell demonstrated that the monetary and fiscal authorities of a single country can attain full employment and equilibrium in the balance of payments by the proper assignment of monetary and fiscal-policy instruments to the two policy targets. The argument is shown quite simply in Figure 1. There, the vertical axis measures the

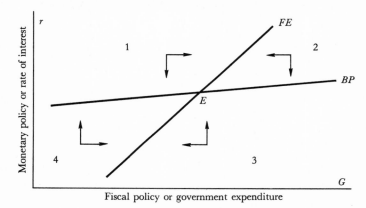

Figure 1

rate of interest, and the horizontal axis represents government expenditure. The *FE* line is the locus of combinations of the rate of interest, r, and government expenditure, G, that produce the full-employment level of income. It has a positive slope since, as government expenditure is increased, the rate of interest must be raised in order to stabilize total employment.[2] All points above *FE* involve unemployment; all points below involve overemployment.

The line *BP* represents combinations of the rate of interest and government expenditure that produce equilibrium in the balance of payments. It also slopes up to the right because an increase in government spending

[2] It is assumed throughout that the monetary authorities offset any monetary effects of changes in government expenditure, so that there is no link between G and r.

increases imports by increasing income and requires an offsetting rise in the interest rate to reduce expenditure and to attract foreign capital. All points above *BP* represent a surplus in the balance of payments; all points below represent a deficit. Overall equilibrium occurs at *E*, where both full employment and external balance are attained.

The slope of *BP* is less than that of *FE* because of the influence of the interest rate on international capital flows, over and above its effect on imports through its effect on expenditure. Without this capital-account effect, the slopes of the two lines would be the same; the trade-off between the two instruments with respect to each policy target would be determined solely by the instruments' effects on expenditure. The addition of interest-sensitive capital flows, however, makes the interest rate a comparatively more powerful influence on the balance of payments and thereby makes *BP* less steep than *FE*.

The direction of policy adjustment to disequilibrium is determined by the assignment of instruments to targets, as indicated by the arrows in Figure 1. The interest rate is assigned to the maintenance of balance-of-payments equilibrium, and government expenditure is assigned to full employment. Thus, whenever there is a balance-of-payments deficit, the interest rate is raised; it is lowered for a surplus. Whenever there is unemployment, government expenditure is increased; it is decreased for overemployment.

This arrangement is stable. If the policy makers find themselves in area 4 of Figure 1, with a deficit and unemployment, they will simultaneously increase expenditure and the rate of interest, moving up and to the right toward *E*. If the direction of change does not exactly head toward *E*, the path of policy adjustment will bump against *FE* or *BP*, but cannot go outside area 4. If the path hits *BP*, the rate of interest will cease to rise, and a continuing increase of *G* will pull the policy combination back into area 4. If the path hits *FE*, *G* will cease to rise while *r* will continue to do so, pulling the path back into area 4. This process will go on until *E* is reached. A similar argument holds for area 2, where there is an external surplus and overemployment. From area 1 (unemployment and surplus) or area 3 (overemployment and deficit), this assignment can pass through *BP* or *FE* and thus overshoot one of the targets. If this happens, however, the system will have moved into one of the two stable areas, 2 or 4.

An analogous argument presented in Figure 2 demonstrates that the opposite assignment of instruments to targets, with interest rates adjusted

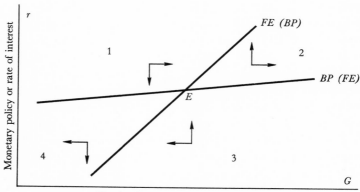

Fiscal policy or government expenditure

Figure 2

according to the state of employment and government expenditure according to the state of the balance of payments, will be unstable. In the critical areas, 2 and 4, the policy path will always be away from equilibrium.

This figure also demonstrates that, if the rate of interest has a stronger effect on employment than on the balance of payments (if *FE* and *BP* are interchanged as indicated in parentheses), the original Mundell prescription of Figure 1 will be unstable. Assigning the rate of interest to external balance and government expenditure to internal balance will cause the policy path to move away from equilibrium in the critical areas, 2 and 4. The principle illustrated here is that, for successful adjustment, one assigns each instrument to the target on which it has the stronger relative effect.[3]

The unique power and appeal of this simple model is that it prescribes a set of policy responses that converge on equilibrium even when the policy makers have limited knowledge of the economic system. They have merely to know the actual and target values of employment and the balance of payments (so that they can decide whether to raise or lower the policy instruments), and the relative slopes of the two lines (so that the proper assignment of instruments to targets can be made). Further knowledge of the parameters of the economic system is not necessary.[4]

[3] R. A. Mundell discusses this guide to "effective market classification" in "The Monetary Dynamics of International Adjustment under Fixed and Flexible Exchange Rates," *Quarterly Journal of Economics*, LXXIV (May 1960), 250.

[4] I am greatly indebted to Professor Mundell for calling my attention to this most important attribute of his model. Of course, he may not precisely agree with my statement on this point.

A MATHEMATICAL MODEL[5]

Two basic requirements must be met for Mundell's model to be stable—for the policy path to converge on E. First, the slope of FE must be steeper than that of BP; second, the instruments must be adjusted in the right direction (represented by the arrows in the diagram).

To derive a mathematical statement of the first stability condition, that FE be steeper than BP, let the level of income (Y) and the balance of payments (B) be linear functions of the policy instruments, the rate of interest (r), and the level of government expenditure (G):

$$Y = c_1 + a_{11}G + a_{12}r \tag{1}$$

$$B = c_2 + a_{21}G + a_{22}r \tag{2}$$

The constant terms represent the effect on Y and B of all other variables in the economy (which other variables are held constant in this analysis). The four coefficients a_{ij} are the partial derivatives of Y and B with respect to the instruments G and r. The coefficients a_{11} and a_{22} are assumed to be positive; an increase in government expenditure increases income, and an increase in the rate of interest improves the balance of payments. On the other hand, a_{12} and a_{21} are assumed to be negative; an increase in the rate of interest lowers income, while an increase in government expenditure worsens the balance of payments.

The slope of FE, dr/dG with Y held constant, is $-a_{11}/a_{12}$ and is positive because a_{11} is positive and a_{12} is negative. The slope of BP, dr/dG with B held constant, is $-a_{21}/a_{22}$ and is also positive since a_{22} is positive and a_{21} is negative. Hence, the first condition for stability, that FE be steeper than BP, is that $-a_{11}/a_{12} > -a_{21}/a_{22}$ or $a_{11}a_{22} - a_{12}a_{21} > 0$. In other words, Mundell's policy prescription is stable if the determinant of the two-equation system is positive.

The second stability condition is that the policy instruments be adjusted in the right direction, given the nature of the economic system. To put this mathematically, let us first specify the assignment of instruments to targets. The directions and amounts in which they are adjusted per unit

[5] This discussion of the mathematics of policy-adjustment mechanisms draws very heavily on three important sources: Richard N. Cooper, "On the Theory of Policy in an Integrated Economy," unpublished manuscripts; Mundell, "Monetary Dynamics," Appendix; Paul A. Samuelson, *Foundations of Economic Analysis* (Atheneum, New York, 1965), pp. 269–74, 380–439.

of time may be specified by making the change in each instrument proportional to the difference between the equilibrium value and actual value of the target variable to which it is assigned:

$$\frac{dG}{dt} = k_1(Y^* - Y) \tag{3}$$

$$\frac{dr}{dt} = k_2(B^* - B) \tag{4}$$

Here, Y^* is the equilibrium level of income, that which produces full employment, and B^* is the equilibrium level of the balance of payments. The k's are constants, relating changes in the instruments to the extent of the disequilibria. The assignment of each instrument is represented by the disequilibrium to which it is linked (G to Y, and r to B); the direction and amount by which it is adjusted per unit of time is represented by the algebraic value of the corresponding k.

Now replace Y and B in equations (3) and (4) with the arguments of equations (1) and (2) to produce two simultaneous differential equations in G, r, and t:

$$\frac{dG}{dt} = k_1Y^* - k_1c_1 - k_1a_{11}G - k_1a_{12}r \tag{5}$$

$$\frac{dr}{dt} = k_2B^* - k_2c_2 - k_2a_{21}G - k_2a_{22}r \tag{6}$$

These equations can be solved for G and r as functions of time, but this need not be done to determine the stability of the adjustment process. For the system to converge on an equilibrium, it is necessary and sufficient that all the coefficients of the following equation be positive:[6]

$$\begin{vmatrix} k_1a_{11} + \lambda & k_1a_{12} \\ k_2a_{21} & k_2a_{22} + \lambda \end{vmatrix} = 0 \tag{7}$$

or:

$$\lambda^2 + (k_1a_{11} + k_2a_{22})\lambda + k_1k_2(a_{11}a_{22} - a_{12}a_{21}) = 0 \tag{7a}$$

This is true because the solutions to equations (5) and (6) are sums of terms of the type $e^{\lambda t}$, and they will not disappear as t increases unless the

[6] Samuelson, *Foundations*, p. 431.

real parts of all roots of λ are negative.[7] These real parts will be negative if, and only if, the coefficients of (7a) are positive.

Now policy makers can easily ensure that $(k_1 a_{11} + k_2 a_{22})$ is positive by choosing the proper signs for k_1 and k_2. Each k should have the same sign as the corresponding coefficient—the coefficient pertaining to the impact of the instrument on the target to which it is assigned (i.e., k_i should have the same sign as a_{ii} so that $k_i a_{ii} > 0$). This is, indeed, the common-sense method of policy adjustment. If a_{11} is positive, as assumed, indicating that an increase in government expenditure will increase income, common sense argues that government expenditure should be raised when income is low, and k_1 should be positive. Similarly, if a_{22} is positive, indicating that an increase in the rate of interest improves the balance of payments, an increase in interest rates is the natural response to an unfavorable balance of payments, and k_2 should be positive. If, instead, we had assigned the rate of interest to the level of income rather than government spending, k_2 would have had to be negative according to our rule; the partial derivative of income with respect to the interest rate is negative, and, to raise income, one has always to *lower* the rate of interest. In terms of Figure 1, the arrows should point toward the targets to which they are assigned, not away from those targets.

Whether $k_1 k_2 (a_{11} a_{22} - a_{12} a_{21})$ in (7a) is positive depends on the signs of the k's and on the sign of the determinant of the partial derivatives relating instruments to targets. If $k_1 k_2$ is positive, the determinant must be positive; if $k_1 k_2$ is negative, the determinant must be negative. In the Mundell model, of course, a_{11} and a_{22} are positive; hence, the assignment rule will make $k_1 k_2$ positive. Therefore $(a_{11} a_{22} - a_{12} a_{21})$, the determinant, must also be positive (i.e., *FE* must be steeper than *BP*).

What would happen if the second term were negative—the case of improper assignment? In the two-target case, interchanging the assignment of targets and instruments would produce a stable system. This can be shown as follows. Reversing the assignment of targets and instruments interchanges arguments in equations (5) and (6), replacing (7) and (7a) with:

$$\begin{vmatrix} k_1 a_{21} + \lambda & k_1 a_{22} \\ k_2 a_{11} & k_2 a_{12} + \lambda \end{vmatrix} = 0 \qquad (8)$$

[7] *Ibid.*, pp. 399–400. Note that I use a "characteristic equation" of the form $|a + \lambda I| = 0$, rather than the traditional $|a - \lambda I| = 0$. Had I chosen to use the traditional form, I would have had to define disequilibrium as $(Y - Y^*)$ or $(B - B^*)$ and to change the sign of k_1 and k_2 in equations (3) and (4). I chose the mathematically unorthodox definitions because they made the economic analysis simpler.

or:

$$\lambda^2 + (k_1 a_{21} + k_2 a_{12})\lambda + k_1 k_2 (a_{12} a_{21} - a_{11} a_{22}) = 0 \qquad (8a)$$

Note, now, that the assignment rule makes k_1 negative, as is a_{21}; government expenditure is assigned to the balance of payments and will be reduced when the balance of payments shows a deficit. Similarly, k_2 has a negative sign, as does a_{12}; the interest rate is assigned to employment policy and will be reduced when there is unemployment. Hence, $k_1 a_{21} + k_2 a_{12}$ in (8a) is positive, as required. Furthermore, $k_1 k_2$ is positive, as before, since both k's are negative. Therefore, $k_1 k_2 (a_{12} a_{21} - a_{11} a_{22})$ must be positive when $k_1 k_2 (a_{11} a_{22} - a_{12} a_{21})$ is negative, and stability is restored by the reassignment of instruments.[8]

It should be noted that we have not had to discuss the size of the k's in order to study stability. The signs alone are important.

In some cases, reassignment will not affect the stability of the system; it will be stable no matter what the assignment. This occurs, for example, if a_{11} and a_{22} have the same signs while a_{12} and a_{21} are of opposite sign. In this case $(a_{11} a_{22} - a_{12} a_{21})$ must be positive, since both pairs of terms are positive. The reassignment of instruments to targets will change the sign of this argument, but now $k_1 k_2$, by which it is multiplied, will also change sign, leaving the sign and absolute value of the whole term unchanged. In diagrammatic terms, this is the case in which one of the loci is positively sloped and the other negatively sloped. Such cases are stable regardless of the assignment of instruments to targets. (The approach to equilibrium may be cyclical, however.)

It would be interesting to know the general conditions on the coefficients a_{ij} of any matrix that will permit an arbitrary assignment of instruments. This knowledge might greatly simplify policy making. In this essay, however, I am concerned primarily with the use of monetary and fiscal policies, where the assignment is important.

Another interesting case is that in which an unstable adjustment mechanism can be made stable without the reassignment of instruments to

---

[8] More generally if a_{11} and a_{22} have the same signs, $k_1 k_2$ will be positive, and the unstable outcome, $a_{11} a_{22} - a_{12} a_{21} < 0$, implies that a_{12} and a_{21} will have the same signs. In consequence, the reassignment of instruments will not change the sign of $k_1 k_2$ and must change the sign of the term which it multiplies in (8a), restoring stability. If, instead, a_{11} and a_{22} have opposite signs, $k_1 k_2$ will be negative, not positive, and $a_{11} a_{22} - a_{12} a_{21} > 0$ would threaten instability, for $k_1 k_2 (a_{11} a_{22} - a_{12} a_{21})$ would then be negative. But, if a_{11} and a_{22} had opposite signs, $a_{11} a_{22} - a_{12} a_{21} > 0$ would mean that a_{12} and a_{21} had opposite signs, so that reassignment would not change the (negative) sign of $k_1 k_2$ and would make for stability.

targets. This can be done by instructing the managers of one instrument to act against common sense in choosing the sign of k. Imagine that $k_1 a_{11}$ and $k_2 a_{22}$ are both positive, but that $k_1 k_2 (a_{11} a_{22} - a_{12} a_{21})$ is negative, making the system unstable. If $k_2 a_{22}$ can be made smaller than $k_1 a_{11}$, the monetary authorities can change the sign of k_2, lowering the interest rate in the face of an external deficit, and still maintain the condition that $k_1 a_{11} + k_2 a_{22}$ be positive. Doing so, they would change the sign of the determinant $k_1 k_2 (a_{11} a_{22} - a_{12} a_{21})$, making it positive and making the system convergent. Reassignment might be a more efficient method of stabilization. But, if political pressures or the ignorance of the fiscal authorities prevented reassignment, an independent monetary authority might be able to impose stability unilaterally by reversing the direction of adjustment.

This line of argument raises an interesting possibility for adjustment in an integrated world economy. One country or a group of countries might be able to impose stability on the international system when other countries refuse to cooperate in an international reassignment of instruments to targets along Mundell's lines. A general discussion of the conditions under which such action would be successful should be attempted.

THREE TARGETS AND THREE INSTRUMENTS

Mundell's model can easily be extended to cover the case of three targets and three instruments. Imagine a system in which a second country, linked to the first through international trade and payments, strives to attain full employment through the use of fiscal policy. Assume that the second country is passive with respect to its balance of payments, allowing the first country to seek its payments target unimpeded. Such an assumption is necessary to produce viable adjustment. In a two-country model, the balance of payments of one country is equal (with opposite sign) to that of the other, provided the same definitions of balance are used in both countries.[9] If both countries attempted to pursue different balance-of-payments targets, a conflict would arise. (The problem of conflicting balance-of-payments targets is discussed in a later section).

[9] See Cooper, "Theory of Policy."

The two-country economy is described by the following linear equations:

$$Y_I = c_1 + a_{11}G_I + a_{12}r_I + a_{13}G_{II} \tag{9}$$

$$B_I = c_2 + a_{21}G_I + a_{22}r_I + a_{23}G_{II} \tag{10}$$

$$Y_{II} = c_3 + a_{31}G_I + a_{32}r_1 + a_{33}G_{II} \tag{11}$$

The subscripts I and II indicate whether the variable is that of the first or the second country.

We can also specify that the fiscal authorities in II will adjust G_{II}, government expenditure in II, to satisfy:

$$\frac{dG_{II}}{dt} = k_3(Y_{II}^* - Y_{II}) \tag{12}$$

Here, k_3 will be positive, as were k_1 and k_2 of equations (3) and (4).

By substituting (9), (10), and (11) into (3), (4), and (12), we obtain a system much like (5) and (6), but with three equations in three unknowns. This new system will converge on equilibrium if all the roots of the following equation have negative real parts:

$$\lambda^3 + (k_1a_{11} + k_2a_{22} + k_3a_{33})\lambda^2$$

$$+ [k_1k_2(a_{11}a_{22} - a_{12}a_{21}) + k_1k_3(a_{11}a_{33} - a_{13}a_{31})$$

$$+ k_2k_3(a_{22}a_{33} - a_{23}a_{32})]\lambda + k_1k_2k_3 \, |a| = 0 \tag{13}$$

Here, $|a|$ is the determinant of partial derivatives of the whole economic system.

Here are the necessary and sufficient conditions for the three roots of (13) to have negative real parts:

(i) $(k_1a_{11} + k_2a_{22} + k_3a_{33}) > 0$

(ii) $k_1k_2k_3 \, |a| > 0$

(iii) $(k_1a_{11} + k_2a_{22} + k_3a_{33})[k_1k_2(a_{11}a_{22} - a_{12}a_{21}) +$

$$k_1k_3(a_{11}a_{33} - a_{13}a_{31}) + k_2k_3(a_{22}a_{33} - a_{23}a_{32})] - k_1k_2k_3 \, |a| > 0$$

Condition (i) is the familiar one: each k should have the same sign as the coefficient linking the instrument and the target to which it is assigned. Condition (ii) states that the determinant of the whole system should have the same sign as the product of all the k's. Given conditions (i) and (ii), part of condition (iii) is that the sum of all "partial stability conditions" must be positive.[10] These partial stability conditions are similar to $k_1 k_2 (a_{11} a_{22} - a_{12} a_{21})$, one of the necessary and sufficient conditions for stability in the two-target Mundell model. It should be noted, however, that $k_1 k_2 (a_{11} a_{22} - a_{12} a_{21}) > 0$, necessary for stability in the two-target case, is not required for the three-target system. Put differently, an improper assignment of instruments would lead to instability in a two-target system, but, in a larger system, certain errors in assignment might not be fatal. It is easily shown, in fact, that the stability conditions of small systems are included in, but are not decisive for, the stability conditions of large systems.[11]

So far, we have been dealing with "continuous adjustment." Our assumptions about the behavior of the policy makers are stated in terms of dx/dt, a continuous rate of change over time. In effect, we have assumed that the fiscal and monetary authorities are willing and able to adjust their policies promptly and steadily in response to disequilibria, and that these disequilibria can be measured at every instant in time.

But monthly estimates of income and the balance of payments are the best that can be made with any degree of accuracy, and, in practice, policy makers probably make significant policy changes on a quarterly basis or less frequently. Certain aspects of monetary policy, open-market operations for example, can be made virtually continuous, but this is not true of fiscal policy, where even annual changes seem difficult. This is unfortunate, since the stability conditions of a discontinuous model, one adjusted monthly or quarterly, are more difficult to fulfill than those of a continuous model.

A discontinuous model may be specified in the following manner.

$$\Delta G_{\mathrm{I}}(t) = k_1 [Y_{\mathrm{I}}{}^* - Y_{\mathrm{I}}(t-1)] \tag{14}$$

$$\Delta r_1(t) = k_2 [B_{\mathrm{I}}{}^* - B_{\mathrm{I}}(t-1)] \tag{15}$$

$$\Delta G_{\mathrm{II}}(t) = k_3 [Y_{\mathrm{II}}^* - Y_{\mathrm{II}}(t-1)] \tag{16}$$

where t refers to the current period and $t-1$ to the previous period. The equations state that the change in each instrument between the

---

[10] I am indebted to Professor Kenen for the useful expression, "partial stability condition."

[11] For an expansion of the equation for the roots of λ in a system of n targets, see Cooper, "Theory of Policy."

preceding and current periods is a fraction of the previous period's disequilibrium in the target to which that instrument is assigned.[12]

Let the values of the k's and the a's be the same for the discontinuous model as for the continuous one. This will allow us to compare the conditions for stability in the two models.

With a two-target model and continuous adjustment, it was necessary and sufficient for stability that the two coefficients of equation (7a) be positive. Call those coefficients b_1 and b_2. Then conditions for stability in a two-target, discontinuous model are three: that $b_2 > 0$, $b_1 - b_2 > 0$, and $4 - 2b_1 + b_2 > 0$.[13]

In the three-target, continuous-adjustment model, stability depended on certain conditions regarding the coefficients of equation (13), namely, conditions (i), (ii), and (iii). If we call these coefficients c_1, c_2, and c_3, conditions (i), (ii), and (iii) state that: $c_1 > 0$, $c_3 > 0$, and $c_1c_2 - c_3 > 0$. We can then write the stability conditions of the three-target, discontinuous-adjustment model as: $c_3 > 0$, $2c_2 - 3c_3 > 0$, $c_1c_2 - (c_2 - c_3)^2 - c_1c_3 - c_3 > 0$, and $8 - 4c_1 + 2c_2 - c_3 > 0$.[14]

The greater complexity of the discontinuous stability conditions derives from the fact that the roots of the critical equation have to be smaller than unity in absolute value, not merely negative as in the continuous model.[15] Hereafter, I should like to discuss the stability of

[12] We would obtain an adjustment model with the same properties by assuming that there is a lag between changes in the instruments and the resulting changes in the targets, rather than a lag in the measurement of disequilibrium or in the reaction to disequilibrium.

[13] The discontinuous analogs of equations (5) and (6) are:

$$\Delta G(t) = k_1 Y^* - k_1 c_1 - k_1 a_{11} G(t-1) - k_1 a_{12} r(t-1)$$

and:

$$\Delta r(t) = k_2 B^* - k_2 c_2 - k_2 a_{21} G(t-1) - k_2 a_{22} r(t-1)$$

These equations can be solved to define the values of the instruments as functions of the number of periods, N, which have elapsed since the initial period. Each instrument at N will be represented by a sum of terms of the type $A\beta^N$, where the values of β are the roots of the following equation:

$$\beta^2 + (k_1 a_{11} + k_2 a_{22} - 2)\beta + k_1 k_2 (a_{11}a_{22} - a_{12}a_{21}) - (k_1 a_{11} + k_2 a_{22}) + 1 = 0$$

Here, $(k_1 a_{11} + k_2 a_{22})$ and $k_1 k_2 (a_{11}a_{22} - a_{12}a_{21})$ are the coefficients of equation (7a) which we call b_1 and b_2. If all roots of this equation are smaller than unity in absolute value, all the terms $A\beta^N$ will approach 0 as N increases, and the instruments of the discontinuous model will approach limiting values, indicating that the system is stable. But, from Samuelson (*Foundations*, p. 436, equations 183), we can establish that the roots of β will be less than unity in absolute value if $b_2 > 0$, $b_1 - b_2 > 0$, and $4 - 2b_1 + b_2 > 0$.

[14] These are derived by extending the analysis in note 14 to a three-target model and by application of equations 190 in Samuelson, *Foundations*, p. 437.

[15] See note 11.

discontinuous as well as continuous models. However, the conditions for stability in discontinuous models are so very complicated (especially in the three-target, three-instrument case) that their evaluation requires more knowledge of the economy than I wish to assume. Fortunately, it is easily proved that the necessary and sufficient conditions for stability in continuous models appear as necessary conditions for stability in two- and three-target discontinuous cases.[16] Hence, by analyzing the stability conditions pertaining to continuous models, I will have established necessary conditions for the stability of discontinuous models. If a continuous model is unstable, the corresponding discontinuous model will, *a fortiori*, be unstable. If the continuous model is stable, the discontinuous model may be stable.

THE TWO-COUNTRY MODEL WITH PASSIVE RESPONSES

It remains for us to put economic content into the coefficients of equations (9), (10), and (11) by building a short-term economic model. Imagine, then, a world of two countries, I and II, whose economies are described by the following sets of equations.

First there are four definitional equations:

$$Y_I = I_I + C_I + G_I + X_I - M_I \tag{17}$$

$$B_I = X_I - M_I + F_I \tag{18}$$

$$Y_{II} = I_{II} + C_{II} + G_{II} + X_{II} - M_{II} \tag{19}$$

$$B_{II} = -\frac{B_I}{R_I} \tag{20}$$

---

[16] The necessary and sufficient conditions for stability in the two-target discontinuous model are $b_2 > 0$, $b_1 - b_2 > 0$, and $4 - 2b_1 + b_2 > 0$. Obviously, these conditions imply that $b_2 > 0$ and $b_1 > 0$, the necessary and sufficient conditions for the continuous model. For the three-target model, discontinuous adjustment is stable if $c_3 > 0$, $2c_2 - 3c_3 > 0$, $c_1c_2 - (c_2 - c_3)^2 - c_1c_3 - c_3 > 0$, and $8 - 4c_1 + 2c_2 - c_3 > 0$. Since $c_3 > 0$, however, the second condition implies that $c_2 > \frac{3}{2}c_3 > 0$. Therefore, from the third condition, we can establish that c_1 must be positive; otherwise we cannot have $c_1(c_2 - c_3) > 0$. If c_1, c_2, and c_3 are positive, the third condition implies that $c_1c_2 - c_3 > 0$. Thus, we have shown that the necessary conditions for stability in a discontinuous model are that $c_1 > 0$, $c_3 > 0$, and $c_1c_2 - c_3 > 0$, which are the necessary and sufficient conditions for stability in the continuous model.

where subscripts I and II indicate to which country the variable refers, I is investment, C is consumption, G is government expenditure, X is exports, M is imports, B is the balance of payments, F_I is the net flow of capital into I, and R_I is the rate of exchange (units of I's currency *per* unit of II's currency). Henceforth, I assume that the exchange rate is fixed, and that the units of currency are defined so that $R = 1$.

Now make the following behavioral assumptions:

$$I = I^0 - ir + zY \tag{21}$$

where I^0 is a constant, $-i$ is the partial derivative of I with respect to the rate of interest, r is the rate of interest (the instrument of monetary policy), z is the proportion of income invested at the margin, which argument is an unsatisfactory attempt to reflect the fact that income has an effect on investment. Next:

$$C = C^0 + c(1 - tx)Y \tag{22}$$

where C^0 is a constant, c is the marginal propensity to consume out of disposable income, and tx is the proportion of income taken by taxes at the margin. Government expenditure, G, is autonomously determined by government decision and is the fiscal-policy instrument. Also:

$$X_I = M_{II} = M_{II}^0 + m_{II}Y_{II} \tag{23}$$

$$X_{II} = M_I = M_I^0 + m_I Y_I \tag{24}$$

where m is the marginal propensity to import. Finally:

$$F_I = F^0 + f(r_I - r_{II}) \tag{25}$$

where F^0 is a constant and f is the partial derivative of net international capital flows into country I with respect to the interest-rate differential between the two countries.

In these behavioral equations, i, z, c, tx, m_I, m_{II}, and f are assumed to be positive. Any negative relationship between the dependent and independent variables of an equation is indicated explicitly by placing a minus sign in front of the coefficient, as in equation (21).

If we substitute equations (21), (22), (23), (24), and (25) into (17),

(18), and (19) and simplify, we will obtain the following equations for income and the balance of payments in the two countries:

$$Y_{\rm I} = Q_1 + \frac{(h_{\rm II} + m_{\rm II})}{D} G_{\rm I} - \frac{i_{\rm I}(h_{\rm II} + m_{\rm II})}{D} r_{\rm I} + \frac{m_{\rm II}}{D} G_{\rm II} - \frac{i_{\rm II}m_{\rm II}}{D} r_{\rm II} \quad (26)$$

$$B_{\rm I} = Q_2 - \frac{m_{\rm I}h_{\rm II}}{D} G_{\rm I} + \frac{(Df + i_{\rm I}m_{\rm I}h_{\rm II})}{D} r_{\rm I} + \frac{m_{\rm II}h_{\rm I}}{D} G_{\rm II}$$

$$- \frac{(Df + i_{\rm II}m_{\rm II}h_{\rm I})}{D} r_{\rm II} \quad (27)$$

$$Y_{\rm II} = Q_3 + \frac{m_{\rm I}}{D} G_{\rm I} - \frac{i_{\rm I}m_{\rm I}}{D} r_{\rm I} + \frac{(h_{\rm I} + m_{\rm I})}{D} G_{\rm II} - \frac{i_{\rm II}(h_{\rm I} + m_{\rm I})}{D} r_{\rm II} \quad (28)$$

$$B_{\rm II} = -B_{\rm I} \quad (29)$$

where Q_1, Q_2, and Q_3 are constants, and $h = 1 - c(1 - tx) - z$. Since $c(1 - tx)$ is the proportion of total income consumed at the margin, and z is the proportion of income invested at the margin (when interest rates are unchanged), h may be viewed as the proportion of an increment in total income that is not spent by the private sector. Assume that h is positive. The determinant, D, is $(h_{\rm I}h_{\rm II} + h_{\rm I}m_{\rm II} + h_{\rm II}m_{\rm I})$, the usual national-income multiplier with foreign repercussions with h replacing s, the marginal propensity to save.

The values of the coefficients a_{ij} in equations (9) through (11) of the preceding section are given by the arguments of (26) through (28). Thus, $a_{\rm II} = (h_{\rm II} + m_{\rm II})/D$, $a_{12} = -i_{\rm I}[(h_{\rm II} + m_{\rm II})/D]$, and so on.

We have already demonstrated that, when k_1 and k_2 are given the same signs as a_{11} and a_{22}, the stability of Mundell's original policy prescription requires that $k_1k_2(a_{11}a_{22} - a_{11}a_{22}) > 0$. If we take these coefficients from equations (26) and (27), *holding government expenditure and the rate of interest constant in country II*, we see that this expression is equal to $k_1k_2f[(h_{\rm II} + m_{\rm II})/D]$. Since all these parameters are positive while k_1 and k_2 are positive, this expression is positive and the Mundell prescription is stable. Note that the response of capital flows to interest-rate differentials is critical here; the Mundell prescription is stable or unstable as f is positive or negative, and, if $f = 0$ (if interest-rate differentials exert no influence on international capital flows), there will, in general, be no equilibrium because the determinant of the partial derivatives will vanish.

If we wish to think in terms of the slopes of FE and BP, the slope of FE will be $1/i_I$ and the slope of BP will be $1/[i_I + (Df/m_I h_I)]$; if, then, $f > 0$, the slope of BP will be less than that of FE; if $f < 0$, the slope of BP will be greater than that of FE, indicating instability; if $f = 0$, the slopes of the two lines will be the same. All this is just as Mundell put it in his 1962 article.

Let us make some modifications in the initial assumptions. What would happen if the location of stocks of capital, rather than flows of capital, were dependent on the interest-rate differential?[17] This would create a problem for balance-of-payments adjustment because the balance of payments is a flow. If an enduring external imbalance must be corrected by inducing an inflow of capital, equilibrium will require a continuing change in the interest-rate differential rather than a fixed interest-rate differential. The changing interest-rate differential would lead to a continuous shifting of stocks (i.e., a continuing flow).

In consequence, no equilibrium level of the instruments would be possible. The rate of interest would have to continue changing in order to maintain external balance. As a result, income would have a tendency to change, and this tendency could be offset only by continuous change in government expenditure. Equilibrium would be achieved by the proper rates of change in the instruments rather than by the proper levels. For a long period, however, a continuously rising or falling interest rate might be intolerable, and some other instrument would have to be found to cope with an enduring disturbance.

Yet the situation is not entirely hopeless. While a good part of the response of capital movements to interest rates may be stock adjustment, some of the response may be flows of new saving, and, if some such flows can be induced by the interest-rate differential, it will be possible to achieve equilibrium at a fixed level of the instruments. In this case, the value of the term critical to stability of the adjustment mechanism is

$$k_1 k_2 [f_1(h_{II} + m_{II})/D(1 + k_2 f_2)],$$

where f_1 is the partial derivative of capital *flows* with respect to the interest-rate differential, and f_2 is the partial derivative of capital-stock

[17] Mundell discusses this problem briefly in "Appropriate Use of Monetary and Fiscal Policy," p. 71, note 2.

transfers with respect to changes in the interest-rate differential.[18] Both f_1 and f_2 are assumed to be positive. The term $[f_1(h_{II} + m_{II})/D(1 + k_2 f_2)]$ is smaller than the corresponding term without stock adjustment, but is still positive, indicating stability for the Mundell assignment.

What happens if interest rates in the two countries are linked? Suppose that an increase of r_I, causing capital to flow in, reduces the supply of capital in II and causes r_{II} to rise. Formally, let:

$$r_{II} = r_{II}^0 + w_{II} r_I \qquad (30)$$

where r_{II}^0 is a constant and w_{II} shows the relationship between changes in r_I and in r_{II}. If we substitute into equations (26) and (27), *ignoring* G_{II}, the equations for the economic system will be:

$$Y_I = Q_1 + \frac{(h_{II} + m_{II})}{D} G_I - \frac{[i_I(h_{II} + m_{II}) + w_{II} i_{II} m_{II}]}{D} r_I \qquad (31)$$

$$Y_{II} = Q_2 - \frac{m_I h_{II}}{D} G_I$$

$$+ \frac{[(1 - w_{II})Df + i_I m_I h_{II} - w_{II} i_{II} m_{II} h_I]}{D} r_I \qquad (32)$$

When $w_{II} = 0$, the system reverts to its original form, and, as w_{II} increases, the negative effect of interest rates on income increases while its positive effect on the balance of payments decreases and may eventually change sign. If this point is reached, we will have a situation in which the diagonal elements of the matrix of coefficients are of opposite sign while the off-diagonal elements have the same sign. In this case, assignment is not a necessary condition for stability, as shown above (p. 270). Either assignment will be stable.

However, it can be shown that, before the effect of r_I on the balance of payments becomes negative, the determinant of partial derivatives will become negative. And as $k_1 k_2$ will be positive until a_{22} becomes negative,

[18] In this case:

$$Y_I = Q_1 + \frac{(h_{II} + m_{II})}{D} G_I - i_I \frac{(h_{II} + m_{II})}{D} r_I$$

$$B_I = Q_2 - \frac{(m_I h_{II})}{D} G_I + \frac{(Df_1 + i_{II} m_{II} h_I)}{D} r_I + f_2 \frac{dr_I}{dt}$$

When substituted into the adjustment equations, $dG_I/dt = k_1(Y_I{}^* - Y_I)$, and $dr_I/dt = k_2(B_I{}^* - B_I)$, these arguments yield the stability condition in the text.

the increase in w_{II} will carry the system into a region of instability.[19] If, then, interest rates are linked, there will be a region of strong linkage in which the Mundell assignment is improper and a reversal of assignment will be needed for stability. This is true because the effect of the interest rates on expenditure in I is augmented when r_{II} moves with r_I, while their effect on the balance of payments will be weakened. Since the effect of fiscal policy remains unchanged, a point will be reached where interest rates have a more powerful influence on income than on the balance of payments, compared to fiscal policy. At this point, the Mundell assignment becomes inappropriate.[20]

In this case, we can no longer say which assignment is appropriate if we know only the signs of the coefficients. It might then be safest to use the Mundell assignment and try to make w_{II} as small as possible. This would require a degree of international cooperation, for the strength of the linkage between interest rates in I and II is affected by monetary policy in II. Stability of the Mundell types will be fostered if the monetary authorities of II try to minimize the links between their own interest rate and that of the country experiencing balance-of-payments difficulty, thus allowing capital to flow freely toward the country in difficulty.

Another complication can arise which may have an important influence on the assignment problem. Incomes may have an effect on international capital flows. Interest rates are an important indicator of the rate of return to investment, but they are not the whole picture by any means. The addition of incomes is an attempt to include the effect of economic activity in the two countries on rates of return. Much of what I shall say on this point was anticipated in an important article by Harry Johnson. His discussion, however, was not framed in terms of a Mundell-type adjustment model.[21]

To take account of income effects, redefine the capital-movements

[19] As $a_{11}a_{22} - a_{12}a_{21} = (1 - w_{II})f(h_{II} + m_{II}) - w_{II}i_{II}m_{II}$, this term will be zero when $f(h_{II} + m_{II}) = w_{II}(h_{II} + m_{II}) + w_{II}i_{II}m_{II}$. Solving for w_{II}, we find the point at which increasing w_{II} will cause the determinant of partial derivatives to become negative. At this point, $w_{II} = [f(h_{II} + m_{II})]/[f(h_{II} + m_{II}) + i_{II}m_{II}]$. By similar analysis, a_{22} will become negative when $w_{II} = (Df + i_{II}m_I h_{II})/(Df + i_{II}m_{II}h_I)$. By inspection, the w_{II} required to turn a_{22} negative is larger than the w_{II} required to turn $a_{11}a_{22} - a_{12}a_{22}$ negative. Therefore, there is a region of instability where $[f(h_{II} + m_{II})]/[f(h_{II} + m_{II}) + i_{II}m_{II}] < w_{II} < (Df + i_{II}m_I h_{II})/(Df + i_{II}m_{II}h_I)$.

[20] Remember, however, that G_{II} is held constant in this analysis; hence, changes in r_{II} affect Y_{II} and, through Y_{II}, affect B_I.

[21] Harry G. Johnson, "Some Aspects of the Theory of Economic Policy in a World of Capital Mobility," *Revista Internazionale di Scienze Economiche e Commerciali* XII (June 1965), 545–59. I am grateful to Richard Ablin for showing me this article and pointing out its importance.

function:

$$F = F^0 + f(r_{\text{I}} - r_{\text{II}}) + f_{\text{I}}(Y_{\text{I}} - Y_{\text{II}}) \tag{33}$$

Here, f_{I} is the partial derivative of capital flows with respect to the difference of income in the two countries. If we substitute this argument into equation (18), along with the other behavioral equations, and then hold the instruments of II constant, we will obtain the following equations for income and the balance of payments of I:

$$Y_{\text{I}} = Q_1 + \frac{(h_{\text{II}} + m_{\text{II}})}{D} G_{\text{I}} - i_{\text{I}} \frac{(h_{\text{II}} + m_{\text{II}})}{D} r_{\text{I}} \tag{34}$$

$$B_{\text{I}} = Q_2 + \left[f_{\text{I}} \frac{(h_{\text{II}} + m_{\text{II}} - m_{\text{I}}) - m_{\text{I}}h_{\text{II}}}{D} \right] G_{\text{I}}$$

$$+ \left[\frac{Df + i_{\text{I}}m_{\text{I}}h_{\text{II}} - i_{\text{I}}f_{\text{I}}(h_{\text{II}} + m_{\text{II}} - m_{\text{I}})}{D} \right] r_{\text{I}} \tag{35}$$

First, consider the term $(k_1 a_{11} + k_2 a_{22})$ which must be positive for stability. With the Mundell assignment (G_{I} to Y_{I} and r_{I} to B_{I}), k_1 will always be positive, as it was before, since $(h_{\text{II}} + m_{\text{II}})$ is positive. However, the sign of k_2 is no longer certain. If $(h_{\text{II}} + m_{\text{II}}) > m_{\text{I}}$ and if f_{I}, the influence of income on capital flows, is large, r_{I} will have a negative, rather than a positive, effect on the balance of payments. The decrease in income caused by raising the interest rate will cause an outflow of capital so strong that it will outweigh the direct inflow of capital caused by raising the interest rate and the reduction in imports due to lowering income. If this is true, a_{22} will be negative and k_2 will be made negative in order to make $(k_1 a_{11} + k_2 a_{22}) > 0$.

The second stability condition will be unchanged by the effect of income on capital movements; it is equal to $k_1 k_2 f [(h_{\text{II}} + m_{\text{II}})/D]$. When, therefore, f_{I} is large and the point is reached at which the sign of k_2 is changed from positive to negative, this second expression will become negative; the system will be unstable. We can conclude that, if the effect of income on capital movements is sufficiently strong to reverse the net effect of interest rates on the balance of payments, the Mundell prescription will be unstable and reassignment will be necessary. Interest rates must then be assigned to full employment, and fiscal policy to external balance.

There is also a region in which the assignment is not important for stability. The partial derivative of B_{I} with respect to G_{I} is:

$$f_{\text{I}}[(h_{\text{II}} + m_{\text{II}} - m_{\text{I}}) - m_{\text{I}}h_{\text{II}}]/D.$$

If $(h_{II} + m_{II}) > m_I$ and if f_I is large, this term will change signs from negative to positive. When, however, this coefficient becomes positive because of a large f_I, the coefficient a_{22}, equal to $f + i_I[m_I h_{II} - f_I(h_{II} + m_{II} - m_I)]/D$ will not yet be negative. In this case, the diagonal elements of the matrix of coefficients will have the same signs, while the off-diagonal elements will have opposite signs; either assignment produces stability.

Now combine the effect of income on the capital account with the interest-rate linkage discussed previously. In this case, the economic system is:

$$Y_I = Q_1 + \frac{(h_{II} + m_{II})}{D} G_I - \frac{[i_I(h_{II} + m_{II}) + w_{II}i_{II}m_{II}]}{D} r_I \quad (36)$$

$$B_I = Q_2 + \frac{[f_1(h_{II} + m_{II} - m_I) - m_I h_{II}]}{D} G_I$$

$$+ \frac{\{(1 - w_{II})Df + i_I[m_I h_{II} - f_I(h_{II} + m_{II} - m_I)]}{D} \frac{+ w_{II}i_{II}[f_I(h_I + m_I - m_{II}) - m_{II}h_I]\}}{} r_I \quad (37)$$

The value of $a_{11}a_{22} - a_{12}a_{21}$ is given by $\{(1 - w_{II})f(h_{II} + m_{II}) + w_{II}i_{II}(f_I - m_{II})\}/D$. This critical term will become negative as w_{II} increases, indicating unstable adjustment if $m_{II} > f_I$ (i.e., if the net effect of decreasing income in II is to worsen the balance of payments. But, if f_I is large enough to make $i_{II}f_I > i_{II}m_{II} + f(h_{II} + m_{II})$, an increase in w_{II} will not cause this term to become negative. Thus, interest-rate linkage may no longer reverse the sign of the determinant if the additional influence of income on capital flows is very strong.[22]

THE TWO-COUNTRY MODEL WITH ACTIVE RESPONSES

Thus far, we have included the second country in a passive way. Its income and interest rate have responded to policy actions taken by the first country; its authorities have taken no initiative to achieve their

[22] The same thing can be said of the coefficient a_{22}. If $h_I + m_I > m_{II}$, and if f_I is very large, an increase in w_{II} will not cause this term to become negative. However, if f_I is large while w_{II} is small to begin with, a_{22} may actually start out negative and become positive as w_{II} increases. Here, the condition for stability becomes rather complicated to analyze.

own targets. This is unrealistic. Economic policy makers abroad will not sit by idly while their targets are disturbed by policy changes in other countries. Imagine, therefore, that the fiscal authorities of the second country act to attain full employment in II while the fiscal and monetary authorities of I strive for full employment and balance of payments in I. Country I is given sole responsibility for the balance of payments in order to avoid conflict.

We might first assume that II starts at a position of full employment, which is disturbed only by policy changes in I and not by any autonomous changes in employment in II itself. In this case, the authorities in II would adjust their fiscal policy to offset the disturbances emanating from I. In effect, we could assume that Y_{II} is constant, and analyze the policy mix in I to see if it is stable.

I shall not analyze this case because it is unrealistic on two grounds. First, it assumes that the fiscal authorities of II have perfect knowledge of the workings of the economic system. Otherwise, they would not be able to offset exactly disturbances emanating from I. In this essay, moreover, I am trying to see just how much knowledge of the system is necessary to achieve stability, and I would defeat my purpose if I assumed that policy makers in II possess full knowledge. Second, in order to offset disturbances exactly, the authorities in II would have to know precisely where the disturbance originated, whether in I or in their own economy. Yet disturbances in the level of employment do not carry labels saying what caused them: shifts in autonomous expenditure in I, shifts in autonomous expenditure in II, or changes in the coefficients.

Therefore, I want to assume that the authorities of II look only at the disturbances in their economy without trying to discover the causes, and adjust to those disturbances in exactly the same way as authorities in I.[23] Thus, the adjustment of G_{II} will be described by the following equation:

$$\frac{dG_{II}}{dt} = k_3(Y_{II}^* - Y_{II}) \tag{38}$$

Here, k_3 gives the relationship between changes in government expenditure and disequilibria in employment in II.

First, assume that there is no interest-rate linkage and no income effect on capital movements. The equations of the economic system will be

---

[23] I do not mean to imply that a knowledge of the causes of disturbances cannot improve the efficiency of policy making. My objection is that such knowledge is difficult to obtain, and I would like to see if successful policy can be made without it.

given by (26), (27), and (28) with interest rates in II held constant. The first stability condition is that $c_1 = (k_1a_{11} + k_2a_{22} + k_3a_{33}) > 0$, and it will hold if each k always has the same sign as the coefficient to which it is assigned. Moreover, since a_{11}, a_{22}, and a_{33} are all positive, all k's will be positive. The second condition is that c_3, the determinant of partial derivatives, be positive. The value of this determinant is $k_1k_2k_3(f/D)$, and it will be positive as long as f, the response of capital flows to the interest-rate differential, is positive. If f is zero, the system will have no solution; if f is negative, the Mundell prescription will be unstable. The third condition for stability, $(c_1c_2 - c_3) > 0$, will also be satisfied when all assumptions underlying (26), (27), and (28) hold.[24]

Therefore, the inclusion of a second country in the Mundell model, in which the authorities try to achieve full employment through the use of fiscal policies, does not make the Mundell assignment unstable. Furthermore, we can prove that reversing the assignment in I will create an unstable policy mix, just as for one country acting alone. Assigning r_I to Y_I and G_I to B_I, the coefficients from which k_1 and k_2 take their signs become $-i_I(h_{II} + m_{II})$ and $-m_Ih_{II}$, respectively. Thus, both k_1 and k_2 will be negative and the product of the k's, $k_1k_2k_3$, will still be positive. In reversing the policy assignment, however, we will have interchanged two rows of the determinant of partial derivatives, changing the sign of that determinant. Therefore, c_3 will now be equal to $-k_1k_2k_3f/D$, indicating an unstable adjustment. Thus, stability with the second country included requires that the Mundell prescription be followed.

We assumed before that r_{II} is held constant or is related to r_I by the constant w_{II}. What will happen if we assume that the authorities of II vary their interest rate independently in order to achieve full employment, rather than using fiscal policy? This is a realistic example because many important countries around the world rely heavily on monetary policy to achieve internal stability.

In this case, the change in interest rates in II will be related to the disequilibrium in employment in the usual way:

$$\frac{dr_{II}}{dt} = k_3(Y_{II}^* - Y_{II}) \tag{39}$$

The economic system will be given by equations (26), (27), and (28) with G_{II} rather than r_{II} held constant. The adjustment coefficients k_1 and k_2

[24] It can be shown that $c_1c_2 - c_3$ equals $\{[k_1(h_{II} + m_{II}) + k_2(Df + i_Im_Ih_{II}) + k_3(h_I + m_I)][k_1k_2f(h_{II} + m_{II}) + k_1k_3 + k_2k_3(f(h_I + m_I) + i_Im_I)]\}/D^2 + \{k_1k_3[k_1(h_{II} + m_{II}) + k_2i_Im_Ih_{II} + k_3(h_I + m_I)]\}/D^2$. This term is positive under our assumptions.

will be positive as before, but k_3 will be negative; in order to increase income in II one must lower interest rates. In consequence, $(k_1a_{11} + k_2a_{22} + k_3a_{33})$ will be positive. In addition, c_3 is equal to $-k_1k_2k_3(f_{II}/D)$ and is positive because k_3 is negative. The condition $c_1c_2 - c_3 > 0$ is also satisfied.[25]

Again, reversing the assignment in I will produce instability. Thus, as long as the Mundell prescription is followed by I, II can use either monetary or fiscal policy, and equilibrium will be attained in both I and II. The adjustment of interest rates in II in response to income changes will have side effects on the balance of payments through both the current and the capital accounts, but it is the interest-rate differential rather than the level of interest rates which determines the capital flows. Hence, country II can choose whatever interest rate it needs for full employment; country I has only to alter its interest rate around r_{II} to create the requisite differential and induce the capital flow needed for external balance. At the same time, by varying G_I, it can reach full employment.

The addition of an interest-rate linkage and an income effect on capital flows greatly complicates the analysis of adjustment when the second country actively seeks full employment. We can prove that a weak interest-rate linkage will not cause the Mundell assignment to be unstable. A stronger linkage, however, introduces the possibility of instability, the conditions depending on the other parameters of the system. A large income effect on capital flows will also produce instability with the Mundell assignment if $(h_{II} + m_{II}) > m_I$. If this occurs, reassignment of r_I to Y_I and of G_I to B_I will restore stability to the adjustment mechanism.

It may be useful to summarize. Using a continuous-adjustment model, we have shown that the assignment of monetary policy to external balance and fiscal policy to internal balance is stable when: policies in I have repercussions on expenditure in II to which II does not react; II simultaneously attempts to achieve full employment by the use of either monetary or fiscal policy. But these conclusions may not hold when there is a linkage of interest rates in I and II or when the effect of incomes on capital movements is large. If there is an interest-rate linkage, the model in which II is passive always has an unstable region, and the model in which II is actively striving for full employment may have an unstable region. If there is a large positive income effect on capital flows,

---

[25] Here, $c_1c_2 - c_3 = [k_1(h_{II} + m_{II}) + k_2(Df + i_{II}m_Ih_{II}) - k_3i_{II}(h_I + m_I)]\{[k_1k_2f(h_{II} + m_{II}) - k_2k_3f(i_{II}(h_I + m_I) + i_Im_I) - k_2k_3i_Ii_{II}m_I] - k_1k_3[k_1(h_{II} + m_{II}) + k_2i_Im_Ih_{II} - k_3i_{II}(h_I + m_I)]\}/D^2$. This expression is positive because k_3 is negative.

the system will become unstable whether II actively seeks full employment or not. When an interest-rate linkage and income effect on capital flows are combined, the results are unclear. The Mundell assignment may be unstable. In every case of instability, however, the reassignment of G_I to the balance of payments and r_I to full employment is sufficient to eliminate instability.

CONFLICTING BALANCE OF
PAYMENTS TARGETS

Finally, suppose that the two countries pursue conflicting balance-of-payments targets. This would happen if both were trying to achieve external surpluses (on the same statistical definition) in order to accumulate reserves.

To analyze this case, assume first that fiscal policy is unchanged in each country and that each country assigns its monetary policy to the balance of payments. Specify the adjustment of interest rates in the usual way:

$$\frac{dr_I}{dt} = k_1(B_I{}^* - B_I) \tag{40}$$

$$\frac{dr_{II}}{dt} = k_2(B_{II}^* - B_{II}) \tag{41}$$

Moreover, with the exchange rate held constant $(R = 1)$, $B_{II} = -B_I$. Substituting into equation (41), we find that:

$$\frac{dr_{II}}{dt} = k_2(B_{II}^* + B_I) \tag{42}$$

Equations (40) and (42) show that no equilibrium is possible with conflicting targets. When $B_I = B_I{}^*$, the monetary authorities in I will cease to adjust r_I. However, this value of B_I will not equal $-B_{II}^*$, and the monetary authorities of II will continue to adjust r_{II}, pulling the balance of payments away from $B_I{}^*$. Similarly, if $B_I = -B^*$, country I would continue to adjust r_I, pulling B_I away from II's target. No equilibrium can exist.

To solve for the path of the balance of payments over time, we use equation (27) with G_I and G_{II} held constant:

$$B_I = Q_2 + \frac{(Df + i_I m_I h_{II})}{D} r_I - \frac{(Df + i_{II} m_{II} h_I)}{D} r_{II} \qquad (43)$$

Differentiating this equation with respect to time and substituting into the resulting equation the time rate of change of the interest rates, given by (40) and (42), we obtain a first-order differential equation for B_I with the following solution:

$$B_I = \frac{[k_1(Df + i_I m_I h_{II})B_I{}^* - k_2(Df + i_{II} m_{II} h_I)B_{II}^*]}{k_1(Df + i_I m_I h_{II}) + k_2(Df + i_{II} m_{II} h_I)} + Ce^{-vt} \qquad (44)$$

Here, C and v are constants that are not expanded because they are not important to what I want to say; the exponential term to which they pertain will decay asymptotically toward zero as time passes, and the balance of payments will approach a definite limit. The value of this limit is an average of the two countries' balance-of-payments targets.

Now substitute this new expression for B_I into equations (40) and (42) and integrate in order to ascertain the time paths of the rates of interest:

$$r_I = Q_I + \frac{k_1 k_2 (Df + i_{II} m_{II} h_I)(B_I{}^* + B_{II}^*)}{k_1(Df + i_I m_I h_{II}) + k_2(Df + i_{II} m_{II} h_I)} t + b_1 e^{-vt} \qquad (45)$$

$$r_{II} = Q_{II} + \frac{k_1 k_2 (Df + i_I m_I h_{II})(B_I{}^* + B_{II}^*)}{k_1(Df + i_I m_I h_{II}) + k_2(Df + i_{II} m_{II} h_I)} t + b_2 e^{-vt} \qquad (46)$$

Again, the exponential terms disappear over time, but the rates of interest are linear functions of time. Thus, both rates of interest will rise or fall indefinitely depending on whether $(B_I{}^* + B_{II}^*)$ is greater or less than zero (i.e., whether, on balance, the two countries desire a surplus or a deficit).

We could extend this analysis to study the simultaneous use of fiscal policy to achieve full employment. The resulting equations would be difficult to solve explicitly, but would show that no equilibrium is possible in this case either. The instruments will be changed indefinitely, and the two countries will be unable to achieve either their balance-of-payments targets or their employment targets.

This discussion underscores a basic proposition. The *sine qua non* of successful adjustment in an integrated world economy is an agreement on consistent balance-of-payments targets. Without such an agreement, both external and internal goals will be frustrated.

Such an agreement could be obtained in a number of ways. Explicit targets which sum to zero could be assigned to all countries; surplus countries could agree not to pursue explicit balance-of-payments policies, thereby allowing the deficit countries to approach zero balance unhindered; or countries with large reserves could agree not to eliminate deficits until their reserves reached a more moderate level. But it may be discovered that all countries would like to run surpluses. In this case, new reserves must be created if their goals are to be fulfilled.

CONSTANTINE MICHALOPOULOS

Imports, Foreign Exchange, and Economic Development: The Greek Experience

A FOREIGN-EXCHANGE SHORTAGE CAN BECOME the effective barrier to a country's economic development by denying the country access to imported commodities essential for its economic growth. This proposition, which development planners have stressed for years, has recently been demonstrated in theoretical studies by Chenery, McKinnon, and others.[1] These studies, involving construction of highly formal models, have nevertheless neglected to examine in detail the conditions that must be fulfilled for foreign exchange to become the effective constraint on growth.

[1] H. B. Chenery and M. Bruno, "Development Alternatives in an Open Economy: The Case of Israel," *Economic Journal*, LXXIII (March 1962), 79–103; H. B. Chenery and A. M. Strout, "Foreign Assistance and Economic Development," *American Economic Review*, LVI (September 1966), 679–733; I. Adelman and H. B. Chenery, "Foreign Aid and Economic Development: The Case of Greece," *Review of Economics and Statistics*, XLVIII (February 1966), 1–19; R. I. McKinnon, "Foreign Exchange Constraints in Economic Development and Efficient Aid Allocation," *Economic Journal*, LXXIV (June 1964), 388–409.

The first objective of this essay is to examine these conditions, their theoretical implications, and their empirical justification. The second objective is to investigate the main constraints inhibiting the economic development of Greece since World War II. The investigation will utilize a version of the simple constraints model constructed by McKinnon, and will concentrate on Greek growth during the period 1952–1962.

Though some aspects of Greek development are not typical of most other developing countries, it is hoped that this application of the model will enhance understanding of the operative constraints in other countries. In addition, the case of Greece has itself generated international interest in recent years. Chenery, for instance, has more than once commented on the Greek experience in his studies of growth constraints,[2] and Greece also provides the example of a recipient of U.S. economic aid that has made major strides in development, permitting a drastic reduction in aid.

IMPORTS AS A CONSTRAINT ON GROWTH

Let us first examine the growth of an underdeveloped, nontrading economy. In this context, economic development involves increases in productive capacity that come about from investment in physical plant and equipment, or from improvements in technology, in the skills of the labor force, and in the organization of production. The rate of increase in productive capacity will depend on: (a) the quantity of capital goods that can be produced with given domestic resources—dependent in turn on the willingness of the population to abstain from current consumption and generate savings; and (b) the ability of the educational system (defined in a broad sense) to improve the technical and managerial skills of the population—dependent in turn on the willingness of the country to forgo the use of some of its resources for current consumption. Within this framework, then, the rate of savings is likely to operate as the effective constraint on the country's growth.

Next, let us turn to an underdeveloped economy that engages in international trade, and assume that such an economy suffers from a comparative disadvantage in the production of most capital and intermediate products, while enjoying an advantage in the production of

---

[2] His study with Adelman covers some of the same ground explored in this essay, but our findings differ in significant respects.

primary commodities and simply processed consumer goods. The operational significance of this assumption is that there is little substitutability between domestically produced and imported capital goods. A developing economy will be able to produce efficiently some capital goods (e.g., building materials), but, in most lines of production, attempts to manufacture capital goods will merely lead to steeply rising costs.

Empirically, this assumption may be justified by examining the trade patterns of most developing countries. It can be demonstrated without much difficulty that capital-goods imports form a large portion of those countries' import bills, and that developing countries' exports consist to a large extent of primary commodities and simply processed goods.[3] Comparative advantage in capital goods requires a highly skilled labor force, efficient entrepreneurs, and large-scale production. None of these requirements is likely to be met in a developing economy.[4]

Under these circumstances, international trade has an important role to play in the process of development: By engaging in international trade, an underdeveloped country can lift the ceiling on its growth rate; domestic production of capital goods, skills, and technology can be supplemented by imports of such goods, skills, and technology, increasing the real value of domestic savings. In other words, the feasible rate of growth for a country engaged in international trade may be higher than the growth rate the country could achieve under autarky. Trade provides a means of exchanging goods with a small growth potential—such as consumer and primary commodities—for capital goods, thereby accelerating the development that can be extracted from a given amount of domestic savings.[5]

Given this beneficial impact of trade, what constraints operate on the growth rate of a trading country? Let us retain our assumption about comparative advantages and also suppose that unlimited possibilities are open to the country for the export of consumer goods and primary commodities. This assumption can be formalized in either of two ways: It may be taken to imply that the price elasticities of demand and supply

[3] Alfred Maizels, *Industrial Growth and World Trade* (Cambridge: Cambridge University Press, 1963), p. 174.

[4] See A. O. Hirschman, *The Strategy of Economic Development* (New Haven: Yale University Press, 1958), pp. 18–19, 25–26; H. B. Chenery, "Patterns of Industrial Growth," *American Economic Review*, L (September 1960), 643.

[5] J. Hicks, "National Economic Development in the International Setting," *Essays in World Economics* (Oxford: Clarendon Press, 1959), p. 182. Goods with a small growth potential are those that do not add to a country's productive capacity.

for the country's exports are infinite, so that the amount of consumer and primary commodities exports can be expanded at will—thus leading to unlimited increases in foreign-exchange receipts. Alternatively, it may be taken to imply that the foreign demand for the country's exports is expanding at a pace rapid enough to absorb all the consumer goods the country is able to export (i.e., that the demand and supply curves for exports are shifting to the right so that, irrespective of the relevant price elasticities, foreign-exchange receipts are increasing).

If these conditions are met, and the price elasticity of supply of the country's imports is infinite, domestic goods can be transformed into imported capital goods at constant terms of trade, and the inability of the underdeveloped country to produce some capital goods efficiently need not affect adversely the growth potential of a given amount of savings. The rate of output growth will not be influenced by the composition of domestic output, but will be determined solely by the rate of savings the economy is able to generate, just as in the closed economy.

Suppose, also, that some capital goods necessary for investment cannot be produced domestically at all. This supposition implies that the available technology utilizes certain inputs in fixed proportions (i.e., that the elasticity of substitution between some subset of inputs is zero and that some of these inputs must be imported because their domestic costs of production are infinite). Suppose, in addition, that only one type of technology is in fact available in each sector of the economy—that domestic and imported inputs must be used in certain fixed proportions— and that the structure of domestic demand is fixed so that no change in input requirements may occur because of changes in the pattern of consumption.

Retaining the assumption of unlimited export possibilities, let us examine in detail the constraints operating on a country's growth rate. This may be done by the use of a simple Harrod-Domar model.

From the fixed-proportions assumption above, it follows that productive capacity (P) in a given economy will depend on the use of a minimum of domestically produced inputs (aK_d) combined in fixed proportions with imported inputs (bK_m). Hence:

$$P = \min (aK_d, bK_m), \quad \text{where } a > 0, b > 0 \tag{1}$$

An increase of one unit in total capacity requires additional units of each of the inputs. Put formally, each additional unit of productive capacity requires a permanent increase in the stock of capital goods equivalent to

$1/a + 1/b$ units of domestic output.[6] Furthermore, the number of units of domestic output available to increase capacity depends on the propensity to save. Assume that there is a maximum average propensity to save in the economy equal to a fraction of domestic income (Y):

$$\max S = sY \tag{2}$$

and that income equals productive capacity:[7]

$$Y = P \tag{3}$$

At any given time, investment equals domestic savings (assuming there are no net capital transfers from abroad):

$$I = S \tag{4}$$

Thus, the change in productive capacity over time will be given by:

$$\frac{dP}{dt} = \frac{1}{1/a + 1/b} \cdot I = \frac{1}{1/a + 1/b} \cdot sY \tag{5}$$

Finally, noting that the expression $1/(1/a + 1/b)$ is the output/capital ratio, which we shall denote by r, we may write:

$$\frac{dP}{dt} \cdot \frac{1}{P} = rs \tag{6}$$

The maximum rate of growth that the economy can attain will be determined by rs.[8] If, in turn, the output/capital ratio is assumed to be technologically determined or, at any rate, not variable in the relevant time interval, the maximum rate of growth that can be achieved will be determined by the maximum rate of savings, s, the economy is able to generate.

It has thus been demonstrated that, if unlimited possibilities for export expansion exist, the savings rate will be the effective constraint on output growth, even under the limiting assumptions of a fixed technology, fixed production coefficients, and no substitution of factors through changes in the composition of consumption.

Suppose, next, that the assumption of unlimited export possibilities is dropped and the opposite extreme assumption is adopted—that the short-term possibility of expanding exports is zero, so that there is a

[6] The use of the Harrod-Domar model requires the statement of all parameters and variables in constant prices (i.e., it implies constant terms of trade).

[7] That is, there are no unemployed factors.

[8] More precisely: $dP/dt = rsY$ and, if $Y_t = Y_0 e^{rst}$, then $P_t = P_0 e^{rst}$ and the growth of capacity over time is equal to rs.

maximum of foreign exchange that can be obtained in the short run. There are several possible reasons why additional exports may not be possible without a sharp deterioration in the terms of trade. The supply elasticity of exportables may be very low, or additional exports of old or new commodities may not be possible because additional exports require a degree of internal resource mobility that is lacking.

If the other assumptions made earlier are retained, and the technologically determined capital-goods requirement exceeds the fixed amount of foreign exchange provided by domestic exports, the maximum growth rate of the economy will be limited by the amount of capital-goods imports that can be purchased with available foreign exchange.[9]

A simple formal model leading to this conclusion has been elaborated by McKinnon.[10] In order to maintain the output growth at the rate rs, a certain level of investment in imported capital goods (I_m) will be necessary during each time period. If export possibilities are unlimited, the portion of domestic output exported in each time period (xP) can always be made to exceed these import requirements (provided savings suffice to attain the growth rate rs). If, however, the supply of foreign exchange is fixed in the short run, I_m may exceed xP. In this case, the assumption of complementarity between domestic and imported inputs leads to the conclusion that the amount of investment undertaken and the growth rate depend on the imports of capital goods that can be secured with available exports. Thus, an import constraint will exist.

The precise condition that must be satisfied if a country's growth is to be subject to an import constraint is, following McKinnon:

$$bx < rs \qquad (7)$$

where b is, as before, the reciprocal of the domestic output equivalent of capital-goods imports necessary to change productive capacity by one unit, x is the portion of total output exported, and r and s are, as formerly, the output/capital ratio and average savings rate.[11] Of course, the foreign-exchange supply may be fixed in the short run, but $bx > rs$. In this case, the savings rate would again be the effective constraint.

So far, it has been assumed that all export receipts may be utilized to

---

[9] This is the conclusion also reached by Chenery, McKinnon, and others; see note 1. See also S. Linder, "Economic Development: The Role of Trade" (unpublished paper; New York: Columbia University, 1963).

[10] R. I. McKinnon, "Foreign Exchange Constraints."

[11] *Ibid.*, p. 391. Here is the reasoning which leads to this conclusion. As: $I_m = P/b = rsP_0e^{rst}/b = rsP/b$, a fixed foreign-exchange supply, and $I_m > xP$ means that $bx < rs$.

import capital goods. Put differently, it has been assumed that the possibilities of import substitution in products other than capital goods are infinite, so that the upper limit to imports of capital goods is given by the foreign exchange received from the sale of all exports. Yet it may not be possible to utilize all foreign-exchange earnings for the importation of capital goods; some foreign exchange may be needed to import inter-mediate goods that the country cannot produce domestically. More simply, assume that import substitution cannot be carried into a certain portion of total imports—that some imported inputs, other than capital goods, are necessary for domestic production.

This proposition implies that the production function of a developing country has the following form, instead of the one given in (1):

$$P = (aKd, bK_m, nM), \quad \text{where } a > 0, b > 0, \text{ and } n > 1 \qquad (8)$$

This condition asserts that each additional unit of capacity requires a permanent increase in the stock of capital goods, equal to $1/a$ and $1/b$ units of domestic output, plus a current flow of imported intermediate goods equal to $1/n$ units of domestic output. If this is the case, the effective constraint from the export side will be bf, not bx, where $f = x - 1/n$ and $bf < bx$. If $bf < rs$, foreign-exchange earnings are the effective constraint on a country's output growth; if $bf > rs$, savings are the effective con-straint. If $bf = rs$, any additional capital goods that can be imported through capital transfers (F) have a beneficial impact on growth in that they represent additions to both available domestic savings and the capacity to import capital goods.

If imports are the effective constraint on output growth, the maximum rate of growth possible without foreign transfers will be bf; if savings are the effective constraint, rs will be the maximum rate of growth. Foreign transfers increase the rate of growth possible in each case. Thus, the maximum rate of growth with foreign transfers will be $b(f + F^*)$ or $r(s + F^*)$, where F^* is the ratio of foreign transfers to gross domestic product.

It must be noted that $bf < rs$ need not imply that $b(f + F^*) < r(s + F^*)$, because b must always be larger than r except in the limiting case where all capital goods are imported. Hence, the country's maximum rate of growth after transfers will be determined by $b(f + F^*)$ when $b(f + F^*) < r(s + F^*)$ rather than when $bf < rs$; similarly for $r(s + F^*)$.

To summarize briefly, the foregoing analysis has shown that, under the assumptions of fixed production coefficients, a fixed supply of foreign exchange inadequate to meet the technologically given requirements for capital-goods imports will subject the growth of the economy to a constraint arising from the structure of its foreign trade. Let us call this the import constraint.

CONSTRAINTS ON GREEK GROWTH—A PRELIMINARY VIEW

Greek economic development since World War II can be divided into two distinct periods—the first from 1945 to 1952; the second from 1952 to the present. Before 1952, chaotic conditions due to the communist insurrection and war destruction prevailed in the Greek economy. Thus, in the period 1945–1952, the political situation, which did not allow postwar reconstruction to proceed smoothly, can probably be considered the effective constraint on Greek growth.[12] After 1952, however, the Greek economy generated an impressive growth of output within a framework of relative price stability. Between 1952 and 1962, the period on which this study is focused, Gross Domestic Product at constant prices grew at an annual rate of 5.7 per cent; manufacturing production increased at an annual rate of 7.6 per cent; and agricultural output grew at 4.4 per cent.[13]

What were the effective constraints on Greek economic growth during this period? Two such possible constraints have been identified by the model developed earlier: imports and savings. Before proceeding to apply the constraints model, it is appropriate to pause and ask another question: It is likely that constraints other than those identified in the model limited Greek economic growth?

Two possible alternative constraints will be considered briefly: labor supply and entrepreneurial skills. As Chenery has shown, the growth rate of labor supply, in conjunction with the annual growth in labor productivity, can set an upper limit to output growth.[14] Similarly, the lack

[12] For a discussion of conditions in Greece before 1953, the best English reference is E. A. Eliades, "Stabilization of the Greek Economy and the 1953 Devaluation of the Drachma," *IMF Staff Papers*, IV (September 1954), 22–72; see also X. Zolotas, *Monetary Equilibrium and Economic Development* (Princeton: Princeton University Press, 1965), pp. 25–45.

[13] The Greek source for all production, income, and investment figures cited in this study is: Greece, Ministry of Coordination, *National Accounts of Greece*, No. 9 (1948–1959) and No. 12 (1958–1962).

[14] H. B. Chenery and M. Bruno, "Development Alternatives."

of an entrepreneurial class or organizational skills has often been considered a prime factor inhibiting economic growth in less-developed countries.[15]

There is strong evidence that neither constraint was operative in the Greek case. First, during the decade 1952–1962, substantial unemployment existed in both Greek agriculture and industry, while labor productivity grew at the rapid annual rate of 5.1 per cent.[16] Furthermore, throughout the period considered there was large-scale emigration of Greek labor. Between 1955 and 1964, emigration from Greece to Australia, the United States, and Western Europe averaged about 54,000 per annum, out of a total population of about 8.5 million. Emigration on such a scale would hardly have taken place (or would have been allowed to take place) had the growth in labor supply been the effective constraint on output growth.

Second, it can be safely asserted that Greece is amply endowed with entrepreneurial talent. Indeed, Greek entrepreneurial talent overflows the Greek borders and has spread to many other countries, developed and underdeveloped. One might argue that, as in other underdeveloped countries, Greek organizational skills are attracted to activities such as trade and services that allow quick returns on invested capital, and that they show a distinct aversion for investment in manufacturing. This, however, is more a problem of allocation than an outright shortage of necessary talent.

EXAMINING THE CONDITIONS

For imports to have been the effective constraint on Greek output growth, certain strict conditions must be fulfilled. Briefly, these conditions are:

1. A single technology must exist for the production of a given output mix, implying that the elasticity of substitution between inputs is zero. If alternative technologies of equal efficiency exist, one of them utilizing no imported capital goods or other imported inputs, a developing economy

[15] A. O. Hirschman, *The Strategy of Economic Development.*

[16] A. Papandreou, *A Strategy for Greek Economic Development* (Athens: Contos Press, 1962), p. 24; A. Pepelasis and P. A. Yotopoulos, *Labor Surplus in Greek Agriculture* (Athens: Contos Press, 1962), pp. 44–45. However, the authors fear that, if present trends persist, seasonal agricultural labor shortages may occur in the future.

need never be subject to an import constraint; it can substitute domestic inputs for the imported ones it cannot procure from abroad.[17]

2. The structure of domestic demand must be fixed. If it is not, substitution in consumption might furnish an output mix utilizing infinitely small amounts of imported capital goods.[18]

3. The supply of foreign exchange must be fixed in the short run. If it is not, the f parameter in the constraint formula could become infinitely large, making it impossible for a country's growth to be arrested because of a lack of imported inputs.

The conditions having been postulated in an absolute, extreme way, it is imperative to note that an import constraint may arise even if these conditions are not strictly satisfied. An import constraint may arise if the relevant elasticities have values that are low, though not equal to zero. If, for example, the elasticity of substitution between inputs is low, a country cannot freely substitute domestic for imported inputs and, at some point, attempts at further import substitution will run into rapidly rising costs. This, again, implies that, because of foreign-exchange limitations, the country is not attaining the maximum rate of growth permitted by its available savings.

Similarly, to say that the growth of foreign exchange receipts is not zero need not mean that it is large, and an import constraint may exist even if the country can increase its foreign receipts in the short run, provided its input-import requirements are quite high. It would therefore suffice for this analysis to evince an empirical presumption that the relevant elasticities are low and that it is impossible to use alternative technologies with much lower import requirements.

There is considerable empirical evidence indicating that these conditions are satisfied in less-developed countries in general and in Greece in particular.

1. With respect to the uniformity of production techniques, the results of investigations by Chenery, Bhatt, and others show substantial similarity in production coefficients for the same economic activities in different countries.[19] The industrial technology employed by less-developed

[17] Naturally, if many equally efficient technologies exist, but each requires similar capital-goods imports, the condition will also be satisfied.

[18] The b parameter in the constraint formula would approach infinity.

[19] H. B. Chenery and T. Watanabe, "International Production Structures," *Econometrica*, XXVI (October 1958), 500–501; R. Bhatt, "Capital Intensity in Industries," Oxford University Institute of Statistics, *Bulletin*, XVIII (May 1956), 180–81. See also C. Michalopoulos, "Interindustry Relations, External Economies, and Regional

countries tends to be imported from the industrially advanced economies and to use factors in proportions suitable to factor availability in the latter. This tendency often calls for the employment of large quantities of capital and skill-intensive methods of production.

Available evidence also suggests a complementarity between domestic and imported capital goods; import-substitution possibilities in the capital-goods sector are limited and costly. For example, statistical studies show that less-developed economies tend to import a large share of their total capital goods and that import substitution in the capital-goods sector has been negligible.[20]

In the case of Greece, there is evidence that, though the production techniques usually employed are somewhat antiquated, additions to productive capacity undertaken during the period considered employed modern techniques borrowed from abroad.[21] Furthermore, investment in Greece between 1952 and 1962 was heavily dependent on imports of capital goods. The share of imported capital goods in domestic capital formation was constant and large, amounting to about 23 per cent of gross annual investment.[22] Despite increases in the domestic production of capital goods, there was negative import substitution in the capital-goods sector. The share of imported capital goods in the total supply of capital goods increased in the period.[23] These findings, taken in conjunction with price trends favorable to import substitution in capital goods,[24] strongly suggest that, in Greece, the low observed substitution between domestic and imported inputs is a result of a low elasticity of substitution between inputs.

2. Little can be said with certainty about the substitutability between domestic and imported inputs through changes in the composition of consumption. Substitution in consumption varies directly with the range

---

Economic Development" (paper to be presented at the United Nations Inter-regional Seminar on Industrial Location and Regional Development, Minsk, August 1968), for an extension of the Chenery and Watanabe findings.

[20] Maizels, *Industrial Growth*, pp. 267, 277. See also G. E. Eleish, "The Input-Output Model in a Developing Economy: Egypt," in T. Barna (ed.), *Structural Interdependence and Economic Development* (New York: St Martin's Press, 1962), pp. 213–16.

[21] G. Coutsoumaris, *The Morphology of Greek Industry* (Athens: Center of Economic Research, 1963), pp. 308–309.

[22] C. Michalopoulos, "Trade and Development in Light of the Greek Experience" (unpublished doctoral dissertation; Columbia University, 1966), p. 80 and Table IV-6.

[23] *Ibid.*, pp. 85–88.

[24] *Ibid.*, p. 89.

of commodities that make up domestic demand, and with factor mobility.[25] The former is a function of per capita income and market size. In less-developed economies, and in Greece in particular, per capita income is low, market size is limited, and factor mobility is small. There is, then, a presumption that input substitution through changes in the output mix is quite narrowly limited.

3. Naturally, the range of products over which inputs can be substituted increases a great deal with the introduction of international trade. A country can expand the production and export of commodities which are heavy users of domestic inputs and can thereby purchase the capital goods it needs for domestic-capital formation. The assumptions previously made, that the supply of foreign exchange is fixed and that there are limitations to import substitution, are thus the corollaries to a more general assumption that the overall output mix cannot be changed at will.

A limitation on foreign-exchange earnings can be attributed to several additional constraints: The world demand for a country's exports may be sluggish because the income elasticity of demand is low; the price elasticity of demand for its exports may be low; or the elasticity of supply of its exportables may be low.

There is considerable controversy over the price and income elasticities of demand for developing economies' exports and their impact on these countries' foreign-exchange receipts. At this point, it is sufficient to cite evidence that the income elasticity of demand for a great many commodities exported by developing countries is, in fact, quite low; this fact accounts for the relatively sluggish export growth in some of those countries.[26] The industrial countries' import restrictions on goods

[25] R. Bharadwaj, "On Factor Substitution and Full Employment," *Indian Economic Journal*, XI (October–December 1965), 200–201; V. Lutz, *Italy: A Study in Economic Development* (New York: Oxford University Press, 1962), pp. 15–16.

[26] Some selected references: R. Nurkse, *Patterns of Trade and Development* (Oxford: Blackwell, 1961); United Nations ECLA, *The Economic Development of Latin America and Its Principal Problems* (New York: United Nations, 1950); C. P. Kindleberger, *The Terms of Trade: A European Case Study* (Cambridge, Mass.: The Technology Press, 1956); T. Morgan, "Trends in the Terms of Trade and Their Repercussions on Primary Producers," in R. Harrod and D. Hague (ed.), *International Trade Theory in a Developing World* (New York: St. Martin's Press, 1963), pp. 52–95. On the income elasticities of less developed countries' exports, see T. Schultz, *Economic Organization of Agriculture* (New York: McGraw-Hill Book Co., 1957), pp. 44–81; L. M. Goreny, "Agricultural Commodities Projections for 1970," *FAO Commodity Review*, 1962 Special Supplement (Rome: 1962); H. Neisser and F. Modigliani, *National Incomes and International Trade* (Urbana: University of Illinois Press, 1953); Maizels, *Industrial Growth*, p. 47.

exported by less-developed economies,[27] the difficulties of breaking into new markets, particularly for industrial exports,[28] and supply deficiencies[29] have also tended to limit the foreign-exchange earnings of less-developed economies.

Furthermore, since most of the developing countries' exports are primary commodities, there is a presumption that price elasticities of demand are low, though this need not mean that the price elasticity of demand facing an individual country is equally low. In Greece, for example, there is some evidence that the price elasticity of demand for exports is low, but this finding is offset by the considerable substitutability between Greece's main export staple, tobacco, and Turkish tobacco.[30]

In addition, Greek merchandise exports (except tobacco) and service exports, which account for a large share of total foreign-exchange receipts, have an income-elastic demand. In consequence, there has been a considerable increase in Greek foreign-exchanges earnings in the decade examined.[31] Indeed, the main obstacles to a further rise in Greece's foreign-exchange earnings appear to stem from the supply side. Deficiencies in the supply of traditional exportables, as well as an apparent inability to generate new exportable commodities, have inhibited the growth of foreign-exchange earnings from the sale of merchandise exports.[32]

On balance, Greek foreign-exchange availabilities cannot be regarded as fixed. The crucial question, however, is somewhat different: Assuming that increases in foreign-exchange receipts were possible, would they have sufficed to cover the growing need for imports of capital and intermediate goods, thereby enabling Greece to avoid an import constraint? This question will occupy a central position in the remainder of this study.

[27] J. H. Richter, "Reflections on a Policy for Agricultural Trade," and G. Blau, "Commodity Export Earnings and Economic Growth," in *New Directions for World Trade* (London: Oxford University Press, 1964), pp. 52, 176–78.

[28] C. Miles, "The Market for Manufactures of Underdeveloped Countries," in *New Directions in World Trade*, pp. 116–22.

[29] A. K. Cairncross, *Factors in Economic Development* (New York: Praeger, 1962), p. 208.

[30] C. Michalopoulos, "Trade and Development," pp. 94–98. See also, A. Gerakis and H. Ward, "Economic Stabilization and Progress in Greece," *IMF Staff Papers*, XI (March 1964), 133.

[31] C. Michalopoulos, "Trade and Development," pp. 94–98.

[32] *Ibid.*, pp. 99–102; see also X. Zolotas, *Monetary Equilibrium*, p. 138.

THE IMPORT AND SAVINGS
CONSTRAINTS IN GREECE

The investigation of constraints operating on Greek growth during 1952–1962 involves estimation of the parameters entering the constraints model developed earlier. Specifically, estimates must be made of f, foreign-exchange availability; b, the import component of domestic investment; r, the output/capital ratio; and s, the savings rate.

Conceptually, the identification of the last three parameters offered no difficulties: r was defined as the incremental output/capital ratio for Greece between 1952 and 1962; s, as the average savings rate out of gross domestic product for the same period. To estimate b, it was assumed that the actual imports of capital goods reflected the need for imported capital goods by the Greek economy. This assumption implied, in effect, that these imports could not have been produced domestically within reasonable cost limits. The assumption does not appear too drastic in view of the evidence already offered on substitution between inputs in the Greek economy.

Foreign-exchange availability, f, presented conceptual and practical problems, because availability is a vague term lending itself to many interpretations. The formal definition of foreign-exchange availability adopted for this study includes foreign-exchange receipts from exports, services, and emigrants' remittances. Foreign transfers, both governmental and private, have been excluded for a number of reasons. First, foreign official transfers can be considered as accommodating finance and, as such, it would be inappropriate to include them in the identification of growth constraints. For example, a government facing the prospect of an import constraint on output growth in the near future might seek foreign aid to break through the bottleneck. Success in procuring foreign assistance might disguise the actual *ex ante* constraint operative on growth.[33]

Second, foreign-exchange availability implies that there is reasonable certainty that the foreign-exchange receipts will be forthcoming. The notion of "reasonable certainty" is admittedly quite subjective. Some uncertainty attaches to foreign-exchange receipts from any source. It can be argued, however, that foreign aid involves more uncertainty

---

[33] Recall that $bf < rs$ does not imply that $b(f + F^*) < r(s + F^*)$; see p. 295.

than most other sources of foreign exchange. The very fact that that aid is allocated annually by a foreign legislature, over which the recipient has no control, makes for a great deal of uncertainty concerning the level of aid forthcoming. In the case of Greece in the decade 1952–1962, U.S. aid and loans fluctuated so widely (the average year-to-year change was 36 per cent) that Greece could hardly count on constant or rising levels of aid with any "reasonable" certainty.[34]

For similar reasons, capital inflow from private sources has been excluded from the formal definition of availability. A considerable part of the private capital coming into Greece consisted of funds owned by Greek citizens residing in foreign countries and repatriated as a result of unsettled conditions abroad, as in Egypt and the Congo. The level of the annual inflow of private capital fluctuated erratically. Foreign-exchange availability is thus defined as foreign exchange earned through the use of domestic resources.

In consequence, one has to ask a double question: What would have been the effective constraint on Greek growth and the corresponding growth rate if Greece had been left to its own devices, and was the growth rate raised by the net inflow of foreign private and governmental capital? The analysis to follow, however, will not be restricted by the formal definition of exchange availability given above. Instead, a critical value of foreign exchange "needed" will be calculated, and alternative combinations of foreign-exchange sources will be compared with this need, in order to assess the importance of different sources of foreign exchange in eliminating bottle-necks to Greek economic expansion.

All concepts of foreign-exchange availability relate to the availability of foreign exchange for importing capital goods. The amount of foreign exchange devoted to the purchase of nonsubstitutable imports necessary for current domestic production (M_n) must therefore be deducted from each total availability estimate.[35] The total of invisible receipts used in defining exchange availability is net of invisible payments. (This procedure was adopted because invisible payments can be considered totally nonsubstitutable and are the bare minimum compatible with the service needs of the country. All foreign-exchange outlays for travel, foreign services, and capital outflow are strictly regulated through licensing by the Bank of Greece.)

[34] C. Michalopoulos, "Trade and Development," p. 130.
[35] This is the M_n term which must be deducted from x to arrive at f in the constraint formula. For values and methods of estimation of M_n, see Table 2.

Table 1

Parameter Values

	1952–1954	1955–1958	1959–1962	1952–1962
Output/capital ratio (r)†	.435	.321	.280	.343
Savings rate (s)‡	.109	.160	.192	.163
Import component of investment (I_m)§	.236	.230	.228	.230
$r/I_m = (b)$ ‖	1.84	1.40	1.22	1.49

Sources: For investment, output, and savings, Greece, Ministry of Coordination, *National Accounts of Greece*, No. 9 and No. 12; for imports, Greece, National Statistical Service, *Statistical Yearbook of Greece*, 1954–1962.

† r is an incremental measure, relating gross annual investment to the increase in gross annual output one year later; it is averaged for each period.

‡ s is total domestic savings divided by gross domestic product (GDP) for each period.

§ I_m is capital-goods imports (SITC category 7 except 737.01 and ships) divided by gross fixed capital formation.

‖ McKinnon ["Foreign Exchange Constraints in Economic Development and Efficient Aid Allocation," *Economic Journal*, LXXIV (June 1964), pp. 388–409], suggests that an estimate of b, the domestic output equivalent of imports required for a unit change in productive capacity, can be given by r/I_m. For some methodological problems, see C. Michalopoulos, "Trade and Development in Light of the Greek Experience" (unpublished doctoral dissertation, Columbia University, 1966), Appendix B.

The calculation of the parameters in the constraints formula has been approached in two ways. Estimates of the constraint are given for the period as a whole, but three subperiods have also been identified: 1952–1954, 1955–1958, and 1959–1962.

The method of analysis used in describing the possible constraints is the following: Estimates were made of the output/capital ratio, the capital-goods imports component of capital formation, and the savings rate, for each of the three subperiods and for the period as a whole. These are given in Table 1. Then the constraint formula was solved for f, giving a critical level of foreign exchange expressed as a percentage of gross domestic product, the critical level being the one at which the import and savings constraints would be equally effective. This figure was then converted into drachmas, using the appropriate value of gross domestic product. If the foreign exchange actually available for importing capital goods fell short of this amount, an import constraint was operative. If available foreign exchange exceeded this amount, savings were the effective constraint on Greek growth.

The result of these computations are shown in Table 2. In the formal sense (exchange availability = exports + invisibles), the Greek economy was subject to an import constraint for the period 1952–1962 taken as a whole. Greek output growth was also limited by imports in two of the three subperiods. In the early part of the decade, 1952–1954, available foreign exchange almost sufficed to furnish required capital imports. In the second subperiod, the import constraint strengthened, partly as a result of rising import prices. However, in the last subperiod, 1959–1962, large increases in foreign-exchange receipts from services and remittances enlarged foreign-exchange availability, and the import constraint gave way to a savings constraint on Greek output growth.

These results partially contradict the findings of Adelman and Chenery regarding the nature of the constraints operative on Greek growth during a period (1951–1961) similar to the one examined here. One conclusion of that study is that the savings constraint was limiting in the years up to

Table 2

Import and Savings Constraints in the Greek Economy (million drachmas at 1954 prices)

	1952–1954 Average	1955–1958 Average	1959–1962 Average	1952–1962 Average
1. Critical value of exchange needed $[(r \cdot s/b) \cdot V]$†	1,247	2,231	3,295	2,343
2. Exports (X)	5,241	6,446	7,125	6,364
3. Invisibles (D)	1,499	3,209	7,330	4,241
4. Nonsubstitutable current imports (M_n)‡	5,695	8,280	11,062	8,587
5. Foreign-exchange availability (f): $f \cdot V = X + D - M_n$	1,045	1,375	3,393	2,018

Sources: For product, Greece, Ministry of Coordination, *National Accounts*; for imports, Greece, National Statistical Service, *Statistical Yearbook of Greece*, No. 9 and No. 12; for exports, invisibles, and all other foreign-exchange receipts and transfers, Bank of Greece, *Monthly Statistical Bulletin*.

† V = Gross Domestic Product at constant prices. For estimates of r, s, and b, see Table 1.

‡ M_n = raw materials, intermediate goods, and agricultural consumer goods, imports of which accounted for over 20 per cent of domestic supplies in 1961. For details, see C. Michalopoulos, "Trade and Development in Light of the Greek Experience" (unpublished doctoral dissertation, Columbia University, 1966), Appendix B.

1957 and that the import constraint was effective in the period 1957–1961.[36]

There are two conceptual differences between the constraint model used in this study and the one used by Adelman and Chenery. First, in this model, an attempt has been made to account for possibilities of import substitution in areas other than capital goods and intermediate inputs. In the Chenery study, actual imports in all categories were employed to define foreign-exchange requirements.[37] The latter definition of foreign-exchange requirements makes the implicit assumption that the elasticity of substitution between all domestic and imported inputs is zero in production and consumption alike, an assumption that seems rather drastic and not really necessary for the existence of an import constraint.

Second, the concept of foreign-exchange availability employed by Chenery and Adelman included receipts from government aid and private-capital inflows. This concept differs from the one used here, for reasons outlined earlier, and probably accounts for most of the difference in the findings. Foreign transfers accounted for a large part of total foreign-exchange receipts in the early part of the period considered, but diminished steadily thereafter.[38] Their exclusion from foreign-exchange availability would tend to make an import constraint much more effective in the early part of the period than later on.[39]

These conceptual differences notwithstanding, there is considerable indirect evidence supporting the hypothesis that a foreign-exchange shortage was more effective in the earlier part of the period than in later years.

An excess of supply of savings over the demand for investable funds

[36] I. Adelman and H. B. Chenery, "Foreign Aid," pp. 8–9. It is interesting to note that Chenery's recent findings partly contradict his earlier conclusion that the balance of payments provided the limit to Greek growth in the period up to 1953. See H. B. Chenery, "The Application of Investment Criteria," *Quarterly Journal of Economics*, LXVII (February 1953). In another study, Chenery implied that, for the period 1950–1961 as a whole, the savings rate was not the effective constraint on Greek growth, a finding consistent with ours. See AID, Program Coordination Staff, "Investment, Savings and Flow of External Resources, Selected Underdeveloped Countries" (paper presented by H. B. Chenery, Columbia University, December 1963).

[37] I. Adelman and H. B. Chenery, "Foreign Aid," p. 8.

[38] C. Michalopoulos, "Trade and Development," p. 93, Table IV-8.

[39] An additional difficulty with the Adelman and Chenery model results from their computation of capital-goods requirements. These are partly based on a somewhat arbitrary estimate of the existing capital stock as three times domestic output. See Adelman and Chenery, "Foreign Aid," p. 19.

can be taken to indicate the absence of a savings constraint. Adelman and Chenery suggest that this was the case in Greece after 1957.[40] However, it appears that an excess of savings prevailed in earlier years as well.[41]

Another characteristic of an economy subject to an import constraint is a low level of capacity utilization in industry and in other sectors. Capacity utilization is limited if plants are unable to operate fully for lack of nonsubstitutable imported inputs.[42] However, in Greece, capacity utilization rose over the decade examined.[43]

An increase in import restrictions or a decrease in exchange reserves can also be taken as indirect indications of an effective import constraint. In Greece, import restrictions—though still important—were relaxed during the period examined, while foreign-exchange reserves increased, pointing in both instances to a relaxation of the import constraint.

Finally, if an import constraint became effective after 1957, the share of import-intensive investment activities should have declined. Though there is little detailed information about the import component of Greek investment, there are indications that the reverse occurred: Investment in the relatively low-import-intensity construction sector declined, while it rose in the more import-intensive sectors of transportation and communication.[44]

There is little doubt that, during the period examined, the Greek rate of savings increased rapidly. But so did capital requirements, as seen from the growth in the capital/output ratio from 2.6 in 1952–1954 to 3.6 in 1959–1962 (Table 1). At the same time, capital-goods import requirements formed a constant and large share of rising domestic capital formation. Thus, the available evidence indicates that, until late in the decade, low levels of foreign-exchange availability posed the effective limit on output growth. In the last subperiod, the growth of foreign-exchange receipts reduced the importance of the import constraint.

---

[40] *Ibid.*, p. 9. The evidence cited is from H. S. Ellis et al., *Industrial Capital in Greek Development* (Athens: Contos Press, 1964).

[41] X. Zolotas, *Monetary Equilibrium*, p. 54.

[42] H. B. Chenery and A. M. Strout, *Foreign Assistance and Economic Development*, AID Discussion Paper No. 7 (Washington, D.C.: 1965), pp. ii–8.

[43] C. Michalopoulos, "Trade and Development," pp. 144, 173–76, 179. Capacity utilization correlates well with imports of raw materials and intermediates and with foreign-exchange availability.

[44] Greece, Ministry of Coordination, *National Accounts*.

THE ROLE OF INVISIBLES AND CAPITAL TRANSFERS

The model employed here is a useful tool with which to analyze the importance of changes in foreign-exchange availabilities, foreign transfers, and their components on Greek economic growth. Table 3 provides a basis for comparing the critical value of foreign exchange needed to avoid an import constraint (row 1) and different hypotheses about foreign-exchange developments (rows 4–11).

Row 4 shows that exports alone, though they grew at the quite respectable rate of 6.6 per cent per annum, could not fill the need for capital-goods imports (implied by s, r, and b); they hardly sufficed to provide the flow of imports needed for current production.

Row 5 gives the figures for foreign-exchange availability as formally defined earlier (see pp. 302–303 and Table 2), including receipts from

Table 3

Greek Foreign Exchange Sources and Needs: 1952–1962
(million drachmas at constant 1954 prices)

	1952–1954 Average	1955–1958 Average	1959–1962 Average	1952–1962 Average
1. Critical value of foreign exchange needed $[(r \cdot s/b) \cdot V]$	1,247	2,231	3,295	2,343
2. Aid, reparations and loans (F_a)	3,173	1,264	2,243	2,141
3. Private-capital inflow (net) (F_c)	945	1,553	1,899	1,513
4. $X - M_n$†	−454	−1,834	−3,937	−2,223
5. $X + D - M_n$‡	1,045	1,375	3,393	2,018
6. $X + D + F_c - M_n$	1,990	2,928	5,292	3,531
7. $X + D + F_c + F_a - M_n$	5,163	4,192	7,535	5,672
8. $X + F_c + F_a - M_n$	3,664	983	205	1,431
9. $X + D^* - M_n$§	1,045	10	−1,899	−404
10. $X + D^* + F_c - M_n$	1,990	1,563	0	1,109
11. $X + D^* + F_c + F_a - M_n$	5,103	3,827	2,243	3,250

Sources: See Table 2.

† X = Exports, M_n = nonsubstitutable imports (other than capital-goods inputs).

‡ D = invisibles.

§ D^* = invisibles, had they grown at the same rate as exports between 1952–1954 and 1959–1962.

services. According to this definition, an import constraint existed through two of the subperiods and for the period as a whole.

Row 8 shows that, if foreign transfers from all sources are added to exports but invisibles are not, total available foreign exchange falls short of the critical capital-goods import level, except in the first subperiod.

Rows 9–11 include calculations of foreign-exchange availability, had invisibles grown no faster than exports (6.6 per cent per annum) between 1952–1954 and 1959–1962. An import constraint would have been effective for the period as a whole and for most of the subperiods, even when the concept of availability is broadened to take in private-capital flows (row 10). These calculations underscore the importance of the very rapid growth of net receipts from service transactions, especially shipping and tourism (compare row 10 with row 6).

Despite the existence of an import constraint, Greece was able to achieve a substantial rate of economic growth, partly as a result of large private and governmental transfers. Row 7 shows that Greece received foreign transfers sufficiently large to break through the import-imposed barrier on its growth. When foreign governmental and private transfers are added to exports and invisibles, the sum total of foreign exchange received was more than adequate to cover the capital-goods import needs of Greece throughout the period. There is little doubt that, in the absence of foreign transfers, the growth rate of Greek output after World War II would have been much slower.

The contribution of foreign transfers to Greek growth can be estimated using the following relationships: Maximum Greek growth after transfers would have been $b(f + F^*)$ if $b(f + F^*) < r(s + F^*)$, or $r(s + F^*)$ if $b(f + F^*) > r(s + F^*)$, where $F^* = (F_a + F_c)/V$. The contribution of foreign transfers to Greek growth would then have been $b(F^*)$ or $r(F^*)$ depending on whether $b(f + F^*)$ is smaller or larger than $r(s + F^*)$.

Since changes in the level of external reserves have the same impact on growth as a foreign transfer, the concept of foreign transfers employed must be adjusted for changes in reserve levels. For simplicity, it is assumed that, at the end of each subperiod (3–4 years), reserves were at an optimum level, and that any changes from one period to another reflected changes necessary to reach that optimum level. Accordingly, foreign transfers were adjusted for net reserve changes for each subperiod.

Table 4 attempts to estimate the maximum feasible growth in Greek output in the period 1952–1962 and to gauge the contribution of foreign-capital transfers to such growth. Row 1 shows the growth rate that would

Table 4

Greek Growth Rates, Estimated and Actual in 1952–1962
(per cent per annum)

	1952–1954	1955–1958	1959–1962
	$b(f+F^*)>r(s+F^*)$	$b(f+F^*)>r(s+F^*)$	$b(f+F^*)>r(s+F^*)$
1. Growth possible without foreign transfers	$rs = 4.7$	$rs = 5.1$	$rs = 5.4$
2. Contribution of adjusted foreign transfers to Greek growth (F^*)†	$rF^* = 2.9$	$rF^* = 1.5$	$rF^* = 1.2$
3. Estimated feasible growth $[(1) + (2)]$	7.6	6.6	6.6
4. Actual growth	5.4	6.2	5.0

Sources: See Table 1 for values of b, r, and s, and Table 3 for values of f, F_a, and F_e.
  † F^* was calculated by subtracting from $F_a + F_e$ the net change in gold and foreign-exchange reserves for each subperiod. This net change in reserves has been calculated from the annual balance of payments statements of the Bank of Greece, as shown in its *Monthly Statistical Bulletin.*

have been possible without foreign transfers. Row 2 shows the contribution of foreign transfers to Greek growth after adjustment for changes in reserves. Finally, rows 3 and 4 compare the estimated limits to Greek growth calculated through the constraint model to actual Greek growth during each of the three subperiods.

The feasible rates of growth estimated from this model are close to the actual rates shown in row 4. In all three subperiods, however, the estimated rates exceed the actual rates by a small margin. This slight over-estimation does not imply that a third constraint (other than savings or imports) was effective on Greek growth during the period discussed. The calculation of the parameters of the model leading to the estimate of maximum feasible growth rates entailed a large number of assumptions all along the way, and some error is inevitable. It is, in fact, reassuring for the validity of the assumptions employed that the error was so small.

Table 4 also illustrates vividly the importance of foreign transfers in Greek economic growth. The contribution of foreign transfers to Greek growth is especially large in the first subperiod, 1952–1955, where these transfers account for about one-third of the feasible rate of output growth of the Greek economy. In subsequent periods, the role of foreign transfers shrank, relative to the role played by domestic resources. However, even in the last subperiod, almost one-quarter of Greek output growth could be attributed to foreign transfers.

It is instructive to note that the role of foreign transfers in growth shrank as the import constraint was relaxed. Just as there is an unmistakable trend in the relaxation of the import constraint, there is a definite decline in the role played by foreign transfers. This finding is consistent with the hypothesis put forth by Chenery and McKinnon that the contribution of foreign transfers to the growth of domestic output is larger when the import constraint is dominant than when the domestic savings rate sets a ceiling on a country's output growth.

CONCLUDING REMARKS

The main hypothesis examined in this study was that an inadequacy of capital-goods imports can set the effective barrier to a country's growth. It was argued that trade in general, and imported capital goods in particular, are so important to the growth of an underdeveloped country that the country's ability to import necessary goods—rather than the savings it can generate—limits the maximum growth it can achieve.

It has been demonstrated that in one developing country, Greece, imports rather than savings constituted the main constraint on growth through most of the period 1952–1962. The import constraint was more stifling in the early part of the period, and was relaxed toward the end.

Despite the existence of the import constraint over the period as a whole, Greece was able to generate a rapid rate of growth, primarily because it was fortunate enough to obtain large foreign-capital transfers in the form of U.S. aid and private foreign capital. These transfers enabled Greece to achieve increases in its output far greater than would have been possible had domestic resources alone been used.

During the early 1950s, when the contribution of the foreign transfers to Greek economic growth was most crucial, these transfers consisted largely of U.S. aid, and took the form of grants. The analysis thus brings out the contribution of U.S. aid, a contribution that was large not only in the immediate postwar years, but well into the 1950s.

The analysis, indeed, provides an excellent demonstration of the importance of timely economic assistance and, more generally, foreign transfers to any developing country. Over the decade considered, Greek output grew at a pace only slightly higher than the 5 per cent per annum rate which the United Nations has recommended as a target rate for developing countries. And, though Greece expanded its foreign-exchange receipts quite rapidly, its rate of output growth led to increases in capital-goods imports so huge that the need for foreign transfers persisted. The need for foreign transfers would be even larger in developing countries less able to expand their foreign-exchange receipts.

JOHN R. KARLIK

The Costs and Benefits of Being

a Reserve-Currency Country:

A Theoretical Approach Applied

to the United States

DISCUSSIONS OF INTERNATIONAL MONETARY REFORM and of U.S. balance-of-payments difficulties have repeatedly asked whether use of the dollar as a reserve asset is advantageous to the United States.[1] The following analysis

The doctoral dissertation summarized in this essay was written with the financial assistance of the Federal Reserve Bank of New York. Professors Donald Keesing and Benjamin J. Cohen offered valuable criticism, suggestions, and encouragement. Of course, I assume sole responsibility for the analysis and conclusions, which do not necessarily represent the views of either my advisers or the Federal Reserve.

[1] See, for example, Commission on Money and Credit, *Money and Credit* (Englewood Cliffs: Prentice-Hall, Inc., 1961), p. 233; the testimony of Robert V. Roosa before the U.S. Congress, Joint Economic Committee, Subcommittee on International Exchange and Payments, *Hearings, Outlook for the United States Balance of Payments*, 87th Congress, 2nd Session, 1963, p. 119; the testimony of Alan R. Holmes before the U.S. Congress, Joint Economic Committee, Subcommittee on International Exchange and Payments, *Hearings, Outlook for the United States Balance of Payments*, 87th Congress, 2nd Session, 1963, p. 154; the testimony of C. Douglas Dillon before the U.S. Congress, Joint Economic Committee, *Hearings, the United States Balance of Payments, Part 1: Current Problems and Policies*, 88th Congress, 1st Session, 1963, p. 28; and Henry G. Aubrey, *The Dollar in World Affairs* (New York: Harper & Row, 1964), pp. 127, 234, 237.

offers a limited and heavily qualified answer to this question. The answer is limited in that costs and benefits are viewed historically and evaluated solely in terms of real national income. Thus, other factors, such as the political prestige gained from reserve-currency status and the constraints that this responsibility may place on our foreign military activities or programs for economic development, are excluded from consideration. Furthermore, this analysis is not concerned with the future; instead, it seeks to determine whether *to date* the United States has gained or lost from reserve-currency status. The conclusion is qualified because it is derived from an appraisal of what would have happened if the international monetary system had developed along very different lines. Any such estimate rests largely on the opinions of the analyst. Some readers will disagree, perhaps fundamentally, with my suggestions as to the way the international monetary system would have evolved without the dollar as a reserve asset.

ALTERNATIVE GROWTH PATHS

In any attempt to evaluate the advantages and disadvantages of being a reserve-currency (center) country, the alternative option of retaining non-reserve-currency (peripheral) status must be viewed in its entirety. As the following discussion demonstrates, the gains and losses from reserve-currency status are not independent of one another; on the contrary, the magnitudes of various costs and benefits are interrelated. Thus, costs and benefits cannot be estimated individually (as if they were independent) and totaled. Instead, starting with the date when the nation in question became a reserve-currency country, one must construct a hypothetical non-reserve-currency growth path. This alternative path must be traced using an assumed set of plausible, consistent policies that do not involve reserve-currency status. The sign of the compounded difference between the actual and hypothetical real national income streams can then be used to determine whether reserve-currency status has resulted in a net gain or loss.[2,3]

[2] For a discussion of the interest rate to be used for compounding, see John R. Karlik, "The Costs and Benefits of Being a Reserve-Currency Country: A Theoretical Analysis Applied to the United States" (unpublished doctoral dissertation, Columbia University, 1966), pp. 97–100.

[3] Three articles have been published which attempt to compare the costs and benefits of being a reserve-currency country: William A. Salant, "The Reserve-Currency Role

In addition to the errors that will almost certainly result if costs and benefits are estimated independently, another analytic pitfall should be mentioned. It is incorrect to select major decisions or events occurring at intermediate points in a nation's career as a center country and then ask what the nation would have done if it had been a non-reserve-currency country. This procedure is faulty because the choice or problem selected might never have arisen if the nation had been a peripheral country. Furthermore, even if a particular option did arise independently of reserve-asset status (i.e., would have arisen whether or not the nation's money was used internationally as a reserve asset), earlier events might already have produced a gap between the reserve-currency and non-reserve-currency income growth paths. Thus, the study of policy choices arising at intermediate points ignores any previous divergence between reserve-currency and peripheral growth paths.

THE RESERVE-CURRENCY ACTIVITIES OF A CENTER COUNTRY

The possible reserve-currency activities of a center country are acquiring gold, supplying reserves, furnishing financial and commercial services to foreigners, and coping with constraints on economic policy arising from reserve-currency responsibilities. Any reserve-currency income effect can be attributed to one or a combination of these four activities. The fact that a nation is a reserve-currency country need not imply that it engages in each of these activities during its career. On the other hand, it may pursue two or more of them simultaneously. The test for distinguishing reserve-currency income effects is to ask the following question:

---

of the Dollar: Blessing or Burden to the United States ?," *Review of Economics and Statistics*, XLVI (May 1964), 165–72; Herbert G. Grubel, "The Benefits and Costs of Being the World Banker," *National Banking Review*, II (December 1964), 189–212; Robert Z. Aliber, "The Costs and Benefits of the U.S. Role as a Reserve Currency Country," *Quarterly Journal of Economics*, LXXVIII (August 1964), 422–56. Aliber's article appeared in revised and condensed form as Chapter III in his recent book, *The Future of the Dollar as an International Currency* (New York: Praeger, 1966). Of these three discussions, Salant's is the least comprehensive; he does not even present a complete list of the costs and benefits of being a center country. The other two each attempt to measure costs and benefits as if they were independent; thus, these two discussions add up mutually inconsistent estimates of individual costs and benefits. For a more extensive criticism of these studies, see Karlik, "Costs and Benefits," pp. 102–108.

Would income have been altered if a center country had consistently avoided reserve-currency status? In the subsequent analysis, this test is applied first to individual activities, in each case ignoring the income effects of other reserve-currency activities. Interrelationships between these activities are then briefly outlined. This manner of exposition should not be taken to imply that the income effects of distinct activities can be separated when constructing a hypothetical non-reserve-currency growth path for an actual center country.

THE COST OF ACQUIRING GOLD

A nation cannot become a reserve-currency country if: (1) its currency is not widely accepted as an international medium of exchange and traded actively in foreign-exchange markets; (2) the country does not have a large, diversified domestic financial market, and (3) if it is not a net international creditor. These requirements reflect structural characteristics of its national economy that determine its fundamental capability to be a reserve-currency country. In addition to satisfying these requirements, however, the nation must also have a sufficient stock of reserves, typically in the form of gold, to make its national currency acceptable as a reserve asset. If its gold stock is not adequate for this purpose and its authorities desire to make the national currency a reserve currency, policies fostering gold acquisition must be implemented.

Any peripheral country must suffer some reduction in real national income, relative to its maximum zero-balance level of income,[4] when running payments surpluses to acquire reserves. A nation's economic authorities can employ a variety of policies to achieve a balance-of-payments surplus and a gold inflow, including devaluation, deflation induced through fiscal measures, increases in domestic interest rates, and trade or exchange restrictions. All of these involve reductions in income. The cost of acquiring gold for reserve-currency purposes is the loss of income (both current and discounted future income) caused by the least-cost combination of policies required to produce the desired gold influx.

[4] This level is achieved through the optimum combination of exchange rates, monetary and fiscal policies, and trade and exchange restrictions. If a nation is willing to run balance-of-payments deficits, deviations from this optimum zero-external-balance combination can always produce some increase in real national income. Deviations that lead to payments surpluses always entail some decline in real national income.

If the gold which subsequently makes a currency acceptable or more desirable as a reserve asset was originally obtained for some other purpose, there is no reserve-currency gold-acquisition cost. But continuing to hold that gold for reserve-currency purposes entails a cost. For example, suppose that the economic authorities of a nation desire to reduce unemployment but cannot reduce interest rates or follow expansionary fiscal policies. They may resort to devaluation, consequently inducing a gold influx.[5] The gold acquired as a side effect of internal employment policies may make the national currency highly desirable as a reserve asset. If so, and if employment once again attains a satisfactory level without the stimulus of an undervalued exchange rate, the nation's authorities face the choice between exchanging gold for goods, services, or assets and holding gold for reserve-currency purposes. The cost of accumulating it must be attributed to peripheral considerations, but, if the authorities decide to hold the gold, nothing else can be obtained in its place.[6] Hence, there is an opportunity cost of holding gold for reserve-currency purposes. This cost is the increase in income that would be associated with the use of the gold to acquire goods, services, or assets.

THE INCOME EFFECTS OF
SUPPLYING RESERVES

Use of a currency as a reserve asset is reflected initially in the gain from supplying reserves. To the extent that a reserve-currency country attempting to maximize national economic welfare has larger balance-of-payments deficits than it would have as a peripheral nation, it enjoys an immediate (or direct) benefit from supplying reserves. Whether these additional deficits are financed through gold losses or the accumulation of liabilities to official foreigners is immaterial; the benefit arises from the fact that deficits are indeed larger. The amount by which deficits are larger than they would have been if a peripheral growth path had been followed does not necessarily equal the portion of actual deficits financed

[5] Assuming that foreign retaliation does not wipe out the exchange-rate change desired by the potential center country.

[6] Of course, goods, services, or assets may subsequently be obtained in exchange for liabilities to official foreigners. The accumulation of such liabilities constitutes the immediate benefit from supplying reserves (discussed in the next section) and is the direct offset to the cost of acquiring or holding gold.

through reserve creation. Foreign official reserve-asset preferences determine the distribution of a center country's deficit financing between gold losses and the accumulation of liabilities to foreign official institutions. Consequently, the increase in a nation's total deficit resulting from reserve-currency status may either exceed or fall short of the quantity of currency reserves actually supplied.

When a positive demand for reserves, or any other factor, causes foreign countries to run balance-of-payments surpluses with a welfare-maximizing reserve-currency country, the latter can reduce or eliminate its corresponding deficits only by incurring some income loss. A reserve-currency country is not different from a peripheral one in this regard; policies to limit deficits reduce its real national income. However, because of its special position, a center country may not have to limit its net external expenditures; it may be able to finance the deficit by supplying gold or currency reserves. The immediate (or direct) benefit from supplying reserves is the gain in income, relative to the maximum zero-balance level, that results from deficits permitted by a nation's reserve-currency role. This gain is the counterpart of income foregone by foreigners seeking to acquire reserves.

An increase in foreign reserves also has a subsequent (or indirect) impact on the income of the country supplying reserves; this impact may produce either a gain or a loss. Apart from acquisition costs, an increase in reserves enables foreign nations to attain higher levels of real national income and capital formation by permitting them to finance subsequent balance-of-payments deficits that would otherwise force income losses on them. At worst, an expansion of foreign reserves can prove to be superfluous and lead to no subsequent increase in foreign income, capital formation, or economic growth.

Yet the more rapid expansion of foreign incomes permitted by additions to foreign reserves (still excluding the cost to foreigners of acquiring these reserves) may or may not redound to the advantage of the reserve-currency country. Faster economic growth abroad may enhance or worsen the terms of trade of the center country, depending on the production and expenditure biases associated with increments in foreign income. The net effect of these biases cannot be presumed to favor trade expansion or the terms of trade of the center country.[7] Hence, the subsequent income effect of supplying reserves may constitute either a gain or a loss.

[7] See Harry G. Johnson, "Economic Expansion and International Trade," *Manchester School*, XXIII (May 1955), 95–112. For an alternative view, see Henry G. Aubrey, *The Dollar*, p. 128.

THE IMPACT OF INCREASED DEMAND FOR FINANCIAL AND COMMERCIAL SERVICES

Reserve-currency status is likely to increase foreigners' demand for financial and commercial services available in a center country.[8] Foreign central banks will make use of its foreign-exchange and domestic financial markets. Foreign individuals and corporations may be induced by the reserve status of the currency to purchase assets denominated in it as a hedge against economic instability elsewhere. Such purchases would most likely be executed through banks or brokers in the center country. These additional dealings, in turn, could make foreigners more familiar with other available services, inducing them to seek short- and medium-term financing in the reserve-currency country and to use commodity exchanges and factoring and insurance companies there.

If a nation so desires, it can prevent the use of its currency as a reserve asset without impairing the usefulness of its money as a private international trading medium. A variety of measures can be employed to discourage official foreigners from holding assets denominated in its currency. An informal expression of governmental displeasure might suffice, and, if persuasion were ineffective, a tax on interest payments to official foreigners or a threat to freeze reserve assets valued in its currency would undoubtedly suffice. None of these measures would interfere with the ability of commercial banks and security dealers, domestic and foreign, to satisfy the needs of private international commerce and investment.[9] Such measures, however, might well reduce the private foreign

[8] A. C. L. Day, *The Future of Sterling* (Oxford: The Clarendon Press, 1954), Chapter 10; Robert V. Roosa, *Monetary Reform and the World Economy* (New York: Harper & Row, 1965), pp. 23–24; Grubel, "Benefits and Costs," pp. 191–96; Aliber, "Costs and Benefits," pp. 446–47.

[9] For a similar argument, see James Tobin, "The Future of the Dollar as International Money," in U.S. Congress, Joint Economic Committee, Subcommittee on International Exchange and Payments, *Hearings, Guidelines for International Monetary Reform, Part 2: Supplement*, 89th Congress, 1st Session, 1965, p. 229; Grubel, "Benefits and Costs," p. 207; testimony by Lester V. Chandler before the U.S. Congress, Joint Economic Committee, Subcommittee on International Exchange and Payments, *Hearings, Guidelines for International Monetary Reform, Part 1*, 89th Congress, 1st Session, 1965, p. 15; testimony by Warren L. Smith before the U.S. Congress, Joint Economic Committee, Subcommittee on International Exchange and Payments, *Hearings, Guidelines for International Monetary Reform, Part 1*, 89th Congress, 1st Session, 1965, p. 64; Robert Triffin, "Guidelines for International Monetary Reform," in U.S. Congress, Joint Economic Committee, Subcommittee on International Exchange and Payments, *Hearings, Guidelines for International Monetary Reform, Part 1*, 89th Congress, 1st Session, 1965, pp. 171–72.

demand for financial and commercial services offered in the potential center country.

The impact of a reserve-currency role, therefore, arises from the additional foreign private and official demand for financial and commercial services which would be lost if a center country's money were merely an international trading currency. The initial income effect of increased foreign demand for these services is surely positive, since the terms under which private banks and brokers furnish their services normally ensure profits. But the interest payments to foreigners on investments induced by reserve-currency status constitute an offset to this initial gain, and it is conceivable, though unlikely, that the net income effect of additional foreign demand for services might be negative.

RESERVE-CURRENCY CONSTRAINTS ON INCOME

Reserve-currency status leads to income losses if being a center country creates additional payments imbalances which are costly to overcome, or raises the real cost of eliminating those disequilibria that would occur even if the nation were a peripheral country. Whether or not reserve-currency status induces additional costly disequilibria can be determined only by comparing, according to the particulars of each individual case, the actual course of events with a plausible hypothetical non-reserve-currency growth path. Although special factors are important in any such comparison, some generally applicable remarks can be made concerning the impact of reserve-currency status on the use of adjustment mechanisms and, consequently, on the costs of adjustment.

An excessive balance-of-payments deficit can be reduced or eliminated by deflation, domestic interest-rate increases, trade restrictions, capital-export controls, or devaluation. The efficacy of deflation, interest-rate increases, capital-export limitations, or trade restrictions is not greatly influenced by the international status of a nation's currency. Virtually nothing about reserve-currency status affects either the mechanisms by which higher interest rates and direct controls reduce capital outflows or the means by which deflation, tariffs, and quotas curtail imports. The international bargaining power a nation acquires as a center country may, however, supplement the effectiveness of these adjustment methods by discouraging foreign retaliation.

Of all possible adjustment mechanisms, the efficacy of devaluation is most likely to be altered by reserve-currency status. This change in the impact of devaluation occurs because any reduction in the gold price of a reserve currency becomes a major factor influencing its subsequent desirability as a reserve asset.

When any nation devalues, some others are likely to devalue also in order to avoid payments deficits. Given the size of an initial devaluation, in terms of gold, the number of other currencies devalued tends to increase with the number of countries substantially affected (i.e., with the share in world trade of the nation first altering its exchange rates). As the group of devaluing countries expands, the proportion of global trade affected by exchange-rate adjustments also grows, and imposes pressure to devalue on nations that have not done so. Thus, an important (possibly the most important) factor determining the number of subsequent devaluations is the structure and value—relative to all international transactions—of the international trade and capital flows of the country initiating the process, rather than the international status of its currency.

But the international status of the initiator's currency may also have a significant influence on the extent of subsequent devaluations. A reduction in the gold value of a reserve currency changes the size of a peripheral nation's reserve stock, if that stock includes assets denominated in the devalued currency, relative to the same nation's net external receipts. If devaluation of a reserve currency reduces the size of a peripheral nation's reserves relative to either its expected payments deficits or anticipated fluctuations in its net external receipts, some further incentive to devalue arises, since that nation's demand for reserves is likely to expand.

The tendency of devaluations to spread is a powerful deterrent to an increase in the gold price of any country's currency, because ensuing devaluations vitiate attempted exchange-rate changes and the benefits of such changes. Reserve-currency status is an additional constraint to the extent that subsequent devaluations tend to be more widespread or larger if the currency first devalued is used as an international reserve asset, not merely as a private trading medium. Nor is the greater number of subsequent devaluations the only deterrent. Devaluation of a reserve currency can shift foreign official asset preferences away from the devalued currency, toward gold or other reserve currencies. This shift may be so substantial as to terminate the currency's reserve-asset role or to drain the issuing country of most of its gold and exchange reserves. The former eventuality would preclude any future benefit from center status; the latter would leave the nation in a greatly weakened position as either a reserve-currency or a peripheral country.

The risk of losing reserve-currency status, gold, or both may prevent a reserve-currency country from resorting to devaluation when confronted with disequilibria which, if the nation were a peripheral country, would demand an exchange-rate change as the optimal adjustment. It must then employ more costly adjustment mechanisms. The resulting loss of income due to reserve-currency status is equivalent to the difference between the cost of adjusting as a center country and the cost of devaluing as a peripheral nation.[10]

Both the direct benefit from supplying reserves and the cost of income constraints depend, in part, on the quantity of gold a nation acquires (or holds) for reserve-currency purposes, and, hence, on the amount of income sacrificed in order to acquire (hold) gold. When a center country can finance payments deficits by accumulating liabilities to official foreigners, it avoids income constraints arising from the need to reduce deficits. But, if it cannot finance deficits in this manner, its choice of policies to reduce or eliminate deficits may be limited by outstanding liabilities to official foreigners. Thus, *ceteris paribus*, the more gold a country acquires (holds) for reserve-currency purposes, the greater is the amount of currency reserves it can supply to foreign authorities without encountering constraints on real national income. Similarly, if a center country supplies a given quantity of currency reserves, constraints limiting its income are likely to be less stringent, and thus less costly, the greater the size of its reserve-currency gold acquisitions.

RESERVE-CURRENCY INCOME EFFECTS
THROUGH 1949

The income effects of U.S. reserve-currency activities through 1949 can be described briefly. Although this account merely presents, without substantiation, the more important steps in the argument, it provides the background necessary for analysis of the 1950s and 1960s.[11]

[10] However, these costs are comparable only if the disequilibrium necessitating an adjustment would have been the same regardless of whether or not the nation in question was a reserve-currency country. Few actual cases are likely to meet this requirement.

[11] For a detailed consideration of U.S. reserve-currency activities from the early 1920s through 1949, see Karlik, "Costs and Benefits," Chapter III, pp. 134–79.

The United States was a reserve-currency country from at least the early 1920s, but for two reasons it is expedient to assume that through 1933 there was no appreciable net reserve-currency income effect. First, data for U.S. liabilities to official foreigners are not available for years before 1934; thus, one can only guess the size and nature of this country's reserve-currency activities in earlier years. Second, those indicators that are available suggest that, after having reached a total of about $1 billion in 1927, U.S. liabilities to official foreigners declined to practically nothing by the end of 1933.

From the beginning of 1934 through 1949, the United States acquired $18.5 billion of gold, $2.7 billion of which came from the reserves of other nations rather than from production or private dishoarding. In the same period, dollar liabilities to official foreigners grew about $3.4 billion. Thus, gold acquisitions from official foreigners may be viewed *ex post* as the consequence of switching from gold to dollars.[12]

Three factors acting in succession caused most of this huge gold influx: first, dollar devaluation in 1933–1934; second, threats of another major war induced fears that mounted steadily through the late 1930s; and third, large postwar U.S. payments surpluses resulting from wartime devastation. (The only period from 1934 through 1949 when the United States did not have external surpluses was 1942–1945.) Since none of these factors reflected a desire on the part of American officials to strengthen or expand the reserve-currency role of the dollar, this country paid no reserve-currency gold-acquisition cost from 1934 through 1949. The dollar was devalued in an attempt to raise domestic prices, particularly agricultural prices. Later in the 1930s, nothing could be done to ease the well-founded fears of impending war. An upward revaluation of the dollar not only would have failed to stem the gold influx; it would also have had adverse effects on domestic employment. Similarly, in the early postwar years the IMF urged that exchange-rate adjustments be delayed, since premature adjustments would probably have increased inflationary pressures abroad without appreciably reducing payments imbalances.

If the dollar had not been a reserve currency, the United States could have easily financed its wartime (1942–1945) payments deficits from its gold reserves; there would have been no need to curtail these net external payments.[13] Thus, U.S. deficits during this period were no larger than

[12] *Ibid.*, pp. 147–49.
[13] *Ibid.*, pp. 163–76 and especially pp. 172–76.

they would have been if this country had been a peripheral nation, and no additional reserves were supplied to foreigners. From 1934 through 1949, therefore, this country enjoyed no benefit from supplying reserves, and the size of foreign reserves was unaffected by the reserve-currency role of the dollar. Similarly, at no time from 1934 through 1949 were dollar liabilities to official foreigners large enough to impose constraints on American economic policy or to create disequilibria that were costly to overcome.

Only one reserve-currency income effect is evident: the probable gain from having satisfied the increase in foreign demand for financial and commercial services that was induced by reserve-currency status. Since this gain represented the difference between a variety of service charges and interest payments to official foreigners,[14] it was probably small. Thus, through 1949 the income effects from reserve-currency activities were hardly significant. If the dollar had not been a reserve currency and if all settlements with official foreigners had been made in gold, U.S. reserves at the end of 1949 would merely have been smaller by the amount of outstanding dollar liabilities to official foreigners. This country's reserves would have totaled approximately $21.2 billion rather than $24.6 billion.

THE WILLINGNESS OF THE UNITED STATES TO SUPPLY RESERVES IN THE EARLY 1950s

In 1950, the United States expanded its role in the development of the postwar gold-exchange standard. At that time, this country began to contribute more actively to the reestablishment of convertibility, both through a donation of capital assets to the EPU and through policies which encouraged foreign nations to accumulate gold and dollar reserves. With the exception of 1952 and 1957, 1950 marked the beginning of a long series of annual balance-of-payments deficits.

The objectives of U.S. postwar international economic policy were the reconstruction of foreign productive capability, the reestablishment of interconvertibility between national currencies, and the reduction of trade barriers. A reconstitution of foreign reserves was essential for achieving the last two of these objectives—objectives that the United States

[14] See the discussion on pp. 319–320.

would have pursued even if it had been a peripheral nation. Thus, it is reasonable to presume that the policies adopted would have been substantially the same as those actually followed until gold losses forced the elimination of balance-of-payments deficits. A review of the U.S. balance of payments during the 1950s shows that no action to limit deficits would have been likely before the beginning of 1956.

Under peripheral status, the U.S. gold stock at the beginning of 1950 would certainly have been excessively large. With merchandise imports of $6,879 million during that year, the ratio of reserves (calculated at $21,205 million, in accordance with the argument of the preceding section) to imports would have been 308 per cent. This ratio is two to six times the ratios of reserves to imports typically maintained by peripheral nations. Robert Triffin has observed that "the overall record of the eight postwar years [1950–1957] strongly suggests that most of the major countries would aim at maintaining a reserve level of not less than 40 per cent" of merchandise imports.[15] The IMF study of reserves and liquidity noted that, with the exception of the Scandinavian countries, Portugal, and Switzerland, industrial nations "in general appear to have tried to achieve ratios of between 30 and 50 per cent, or perhaps 40 or 50 per cent, in the sense that if reserves were below these levels they tried to increase reserves, and if reserves rose beyond some such level, they saw fit to adopt a more expansionist policy."[16]

As another comparison: Twelve industrial nations' maximum year-end ratios of reserves to merchandise imports for 1960 through 1965 are presented in Table 1.[17] In order to produce the greatest possible ratios, these countries' reserve positions in the IMF were added to their gold and exchange reserves. In no case do the ratios approach 300 per cent.

Table 2 presents the actual U.S. balance of payments measured by official settlements for the period from 1950 through 1960. On the basis of these actual settlements, Table 3 lists several statistics which are helpful in judging when, under peripheral status, gold losses might have prompted American authorities to curtail payments deficits. For example, the second column of Table 3 shows how the size of the U.S. gold stock would have declined if gold reserves had totaled $21 billion at the end of 1949 and if American officials had adopted policies identical with those

[15] Robert Triffin, *Gold and the Dollar Crisis* (New Haven: Yale University Press, 1960), p. 45.

[16] International Monetary Fund, *International Reserves and Liquidity* (Washington, D.C. 1958), p. 48.

[17] These are the same twelve industrial nations mentioned in the IMF study.

Table 1

Maximum Year-End Ratios of Reserves[a] to Imports (c.i.f.), 1960–1965

Country	Year of Maximum	Reserves as Percentage of Merchandise Imports
Norway	1965	22
Denmark	1964	25
Sweden	1962	25
Belgium	1961	40
Japan	1960	44
Netherlands	1961	45
Germany	1960	59
France	1965	61
Italy	1961	70
Austria	1963	72
Switzerland	1962	95
Portugal	1960	146

Source: *International Financial Statistics* (September 1966).
[a] Gold and exchange reserves plus reserve position in the IMF.

that were actually implemented. Such policies presumably would have led to deficits and surpluses equivalent to those which actually occurred. The size of the resultant hypothetical gold stock can be compared, year by year, with the growing 25 per cent gold reserve requirement on Federal Reserve note and deposit liabilities. Table 3 also gives the size of the hypothetical gold stock as a percentage of actual annual merchandise imports and as a percentage of actual liquid liabilities to private foreigners.

By the end of 1955, the U.S. gold stock would have declined to within $1.3 billion of the 25 per cent minimum required level. Shrinkage of the "free" gold stock (gold in excess of required reserves) from $2.2 billion at the beginning of the same year might have provoked official concern about the size of American deficits. On the other hand, at the end of 1955 the gold stock would have exceeded the level of annual imports by a modest amount; hence, the ratio of reserves to imports would have been well above that maintained by most other peripheral nations. Moreover, gold reserves would have been substantially more than double outstanding liquid liabilities to private foreigners (if these had grown as they actually did); this country could have used about $6.5 billion of additional gold

Table 2

U.S. Balance of Payments: 1950–1960 (millions of dollars)

Year	1950	1951	1952	1953	1954	1955	1956	1957	1958	1959	1960
Increase (+) in U.S. reserves: gold and convertible currencies	−1,743	53	379	−1,161	−249	−41	306	798	−2,275	−1,075	−1,702
Increase (−) in IMF dollar holdings	−15	−20	36	−95	−182	−141	363	367	−17	−260	−741
Increase (−) in official dollar holdings of foreign countries	−1,554	505	−1,237	−848	−1,043	−559	−930	−20	−735	−948	−1,149
Special transactions: nonscheduled repayments (−) of government loans	—	—	—	—	—	—	—	—	—	−435	−53
Balance of payments financed by official transactions (surplus +)	−3,312	538	−822	−2,104	−1,474	−741	−261	1,145	−3,027	−2,718	−3,645

Sources: 1950–1959: Walter S. Salant et al., *The United States Balance of Payments in 1968* (Washington, D.C.: The Brookings Institution, 1963), p. 10. Nonscheduled repayments of government loans in 1959: *Survey of Current Business* (June, 1961). 1960: *Survey of Current Business* (June 1964).

Note: Changes in the U.S. gold stock include IMF purchases of dollar securities with gold amounting to $200 million in 1956 and $300 million in 1960. The 1959 figure reflects a net gold payment to the IMF of $44 million, the difference between the $344 million U.S. gold subscription and IMF gold sales in exchange for dollar assets totaling $300 million. Changes in IMF holdings equal variations in the U.S. gold tranche position plus these purchases of dollar assets in 1956, 1959, and 1960; they do not include the 1959 dollar subscription.

Table 3
U.S. Gold Reserves (millions of dollars)

End of Year	Actual Gold Stock	Hypothetical Gold Stock as a Non-reserve-Currency Country	Gold Stock Necessary to Satisfy 25% Reserve Requirement	Hypothetical Reserves as a Percentage of Annual Merchandise Imports	Hypothetical Reserves as a Percentage of Liquid Liabilities to Private Foreigners
1949	24,563	21,205	10,753	308	544
1950	22,820	17,893	11,005	196	430
1951	22,873	18,431	11,720	164	368
1952	23,252	17,609	12,054	163	336
1953	22,091	15,505	12,151	141	293
1954	21,793	14,031	11,812	135	264
1955	21,753	13,290	11,975	116	233
1956	22,058	13,029	12,087	102	203
1957	22,857	14,174	12,069	107	203
1958	20,582	11,147	12,006	89	148
1959	19,507	8,429	12,150	55	94
1960	17,804	4,800	11,852	33	52

Sources: Federal Reserve Bulletin; Supplement to Monetary and Banking Statistics, Section 14; Survey of Current Business, 1963 Balance-of-Payments Supplement, and June 1964; and Walter S. Salant et al., The United States Balance of Payments in 1968, p. 10.

for financing payments deficits and still have retained enough gold to match existing liquid liabilities to private foreigners. Thus, although action might have been taken during 1956 to curtail payments deficits, any move in that direction before the beginning of 1956 would have been most unlikely.

But, under peripheral status, the adoption of policies to end (rather than reduce) deficits could hardly have been delayed past the end of 1959 and probably would have been undertaken at an earlier date. To defer the complete elimination of chronic deficits for so long, even if net payments to foreigners had previously been curtailed, would have necessitated reduction of the gold-reserve requirement. Moreover, by the end of 1959, the ratio of reserves to annual imports would have declined until it fell within the range apparently desired by other industrialized peripheral nations—nations whose currencies were not so widely used in international trade. In addition, gold reserves might not have been adequate to cover liquid liabilities to private foreigners, and surely would have been inadequate if measures restricting deficits had not been adopted before 1959. Finally, the sheer size of U.S. gold losses, which could have approached $12.8 billion by 1959 and reduced the stock from a year-end maximum of $21.2 billion to only $8.4 billion, would probably have raised demands for an end to deficits. Even small continued deficits into the 1960s would most likely have forced U.S. reserves well below the desired minimum level. Therefore, a move to eliminate chronic deficits, not merely to reduce them, and achieve a mean zero balance of payments would have been a virtual certainty by the close of 1959.

Given the pattern of actual deficits and surpluses, 1958 would probably have been the first year when concern about the diminishing size of the U.S. gold stock might have caused the adoption of policies to end, rather than merely reduce, chronic deficits. Fears that gold reserves might become inadequate might have spread in 1955 or 1956, but several factors would have tended to ease such apprehensions. Official settlements in favor of foreigners declined rapidly and steadily from 1953, when the deficit totaled $2,104 million, through 1956, when the deficit amounted to only $261 million. As the result of the Suez crisis, moreover, this country enjoyed a substantial surplus in 1957. Without any move to curtail deficits (i.e., with no departure from policies actually adopted), "free" gold reserves would have risen to $2.1 billion by the end of 1957. Furthermore, many respected analysts of the U.S. balance of payments believed that the dollar shortage would remain an international monetary problem for years to come and that chronic surpluses might be difficult to avoid in the future.[18] Thus, although some action to limit deficits might have been initiated in 1956 if the United States had been a peripheral nation, measures intended to end deficits probably would have been deferred until 1958 or 1959.

MEASURES TO END DEFICITS

Some measures that might have been taken to terminate U.S. payments deficits could have forced real national income well below the growth path actually attained under reserve-currency status. Perhaps the most severe of all possible remedies would have consisted of tight monetary policy in combination with government budget surpluses. This choice of policies might have been based on the hypothesis that U.S. payments deficits were the consequence of domestic inflation. Inflation did occur until 1958, and was the source of considerable official concern, particularly when prices continued to rise during the downward phase of the 1957–1958 recession.[19] Clearly, the United States *could* have fared much worse as a peripheral nation than it did as a center country. The more difficult and more relevant question, however, is whether the United States *would* have enjoyed as high or higher levels of real national income as a peripheral nation than it actually did as a reserve-currency country.

Either of two methods could have been employed to eliminate deficits without curtailing U.S. real national income. First, dollar devaluation, if successful, could have ended deficits without impairing employment and, indeed, might have stimulated domestic economic activity sufficiently to overcome the adverse income effects of the required deterioration in terms of trade.[20] Second, high interest rates in combination with large

[18] For factors which could have caused reemergence of chronic U.S. balance-of-payments surpluses, see D. C. A. MacDougall's *The World Dollar Problem* (London: Macmillan and Co., Ltd., 1957). William M. Scammell, writing in 1956, argued that the dollar shortage was not a problem of postwar adjustment but a structural phenomenon likely to persist. See his *International Monetary Policy* (London: Macmillan and Co., Ltd., 1957), pp. 333–34.

[19] See, for example, *The Annual Report of the Council of Economic Advisers*, Transmitted to the Congress January 1959 (Washington, D.C.: U.S. Government Printing Office, 1959), pp. 17–20, 32, 48, 52–53; 1960, p. 51.

[20] Since the U.S. economy was operating at a suboptimal level, devaluation might have permitted the elimination of deficits without a decline in income. But, if the economy had initially been fully employed, as was assumed in the foregoing theoretical analysis, any method of eliminating deficits would necessarily have entailed some reduction in real national income.

government budget deficits and, perhaps, fiscal incentives to encourage domestic investment could have produced the same outcome.

Even if the United States had been a peripheral country, American and foreign monetary authorities would have resisted dollar devaluation in 1958 or 1959. The factors listed above which would have tended to ease fears about the continuation of U.S. deficits (the rapid decline in deficits from 1953 through 1956, the surplus in 1957, and predictions by academicians of an extended dollar shortage) would have made devaluation seem an extreme solution for a problem that might soon vanish.[21] Furthermore, American authorities would probably have feared a postponement of foreign-currency convertibility if the dollar had been devalued during 1958, or the possible reintroduction of exchange controls abroad if devaluation had come the following year.

The other way in which the United States might have ended deficits in the late 1950s consists of a substantial increase in interest rates accompanied by large government budget deficits and, possibly, special fiscal measures to offset the depressing effect of high interest rates on domestic investment.[22] But, in the unlikely event that this solution had been proposed by the Republican Administration in power, it is virtually certain that Congress could not then have been persuaded to accept budget deficits. Considering the three-year lag in enacting the 1964 tax reduction, and given the fears about a resurgence of domestic inflation that were prevalent during the late 1950s among both Congressmen and the Administration's economic policy makers, there is little reason to believe that high interest rates and large government deficits could have been adopted then as a means of terminating deficits with no loss of income.

Initial steps to curtail U.S. deficits probably would have relied on a variety of partial measures, rather than on a fundamental adjustment technique. These measures, perhaps similar to those actually employed

[21] Robert E. Aliber has also argued ("Costs and Benefits," pp. 450–52) that dollar devaluation relative to other currencies would not have been possible because other countries would not have allowed the consequent deterioration in their trade balances and international competitive positions with respect to a nation as large as the United States.

[22] Higher interest rates tend to shift domestic demand toward consumption at the expense of investment. See Paul A. Samuelson, "Fiscal and Financial Policies for Growth," in American Bankers Association, *A Symposium on Economic Growth* (February 25 1963), pp. 96–100; and James Tobin, "Economic Progress and the International Monetary System," *Domestic and International Financial Policies of the United States*, Proceedings of the Academy of Political Science (May 1963), p. 85.

since 1959, might well have included the reduction of foreign aid and military expenditures, an effort to raise the proportion of economic and military assistance outlays spent in the United States, the removal of incentives to travel abroad, an export promotion scheme with liberalized export financing, and tax revision to deter American investment abroad or to promote foreign investment in this country.[23] Remaining net deficits might have been eliminated by a combination of tighter monetary policies and direct restrictions on capital outflows. The deflationary impact of higher interest rates, if counteracted at all, probably would not have been fully offset through expansionary fiscal policies. Especially after the 1957–1958 recession, a government budget surplus—as additional insurance against inflation and excessive domestic liquidity—was more likely than a deficit.[24]

The termination of U.S. deficits in the late 1950s would probably have entailed some loss of income. If fiscal policy had been more or less the same as it actually was, and if only a small part of the burden had been placed on monetary policy (with most of the burden placed on partial remedies and capital-export limitations), the amount by which real national income would have deviated from actual income might have been quite small. By contrast, if monetary policy had been used vigorously to curtail capital outflows, and if fears of continued inflation had also led to government budget surpluses, the loss of income could have been quite large. Domestic unemployment could have been much larger than it was, and the 1957–1958 recession could have become a near depression. Although the most likely outcome would necessarily have fallen somewhere between these extremes, an income loss could have been expected. Given the predispositions of the Republican Administration, initial measures to eliminate deficits would probably have relied more heavily on restrictive monetary and fiscal policies than on capital export controls.

---

[23] For a description of the growth of concern about U.S. deficits that in fact did occur in 1958 and 1959, and for an outline of measures first adopted—as well as others only considered—to curtail net payments to foreigners, see Henry C. Wallich, "Government Action" in *The Dollar in Crisis*, Seymour E. Harris (ed.) (New York: Harcourt, Brace and World, Inc., 1961), pp. 97–113.

[24] Wallich suggests that balance-of-payments considerations, which were much less critical than they would have been if the United States had been a non-reserve-currency country, had some impact on the actual decision at the end of 1958 to propose a balanced budget for the 1960 fiscal year. A cash surplus of $800 million actually occurred in that year. See "Government Action," pp. 99–100.

ZERO-BALANCE INCOME DURING THE
1960s

Assuming that U.S. deficits would have been terminated during 1958 or 1959, the impact on domestic and foreign incomes of the methods used to do so would have had an important influence on the selection of policies to prevent the resumption of gold losses in subsequent years. The size and persistence of deficits that have actually occurred since 1959 indicate that continuing action would have been necessary to prevent the recurrence of deficits. If policies initially used to achieve zero balance had produced highly undesirable domestic side effects, American officials presumably would have used alternative methods for avoiding new deficits—methods that would not have entailed the same consequences. Similarly, if the policies first adopted had injured other countries, foreign authorities would surely have urged the use of an alternative. If, instead, the termination of U.S. deficits had caused little hardship here and abroad, the policies initially adopted would probably have been continued.

The elimination of U.S. payments deficits could have produced large subsequent foreign income losses in two ways: first, if a substantial deflation had occurred here, it would undoubtedly have spread to other nations; second, a severe shortage of reserves could have halted the growth of international trade and capital flows and could conceivably have produced a downturn in the volume of these international transactions. It is impossible to calculate the probability that the methods used to terminate deficits in 1958–1959 would have induced a serious domestic recession. But it is clear that, with no expansion in the supply of reserves from other sources, a severe liquidity shortage would have developed after this country stopped supplying gold.

The total actual increase in foreign countries' gold and exchange reserves from the end of 1959 through 1965 amounted to the equivalent of $15.2 billions. But gold production and Soviet sales accounted for only $3.2 billion of this gain in reserve assets.[25] Furthermore, the total reported liabilities of France to Franc Area monetary authorities and of the United Kingdom to Sterling Area monetary authorities declined in this period, and net drawings by foreign countries from the IMF increased by only $2.1 billion.[26] Hence, the remaining $9.9 billion addition to

[25] *International Financial Statistics* (September 1966), pp. 16–17.   [26] *Ibid.*, p. 5.

foreign countries' reserves (or nearly two-thirds of the total expansion in foreign reserves) consisted of U.S. gold losses and additions to official dollar stocks. In the absence of large-scale creation of reserve assets, a global shortage of reserves would almost certainly have developed after the elimination of U.S. deficits.

Foreign countries could have adopted either of two approaches to avoid serious injury resulting from deflation in the U.S. and global reserve inadequacy. These two approaches may be characterized respectively as autarchic and cooperative. The autarchic approach would have entailed the retention or erection of barriers to international trade and capital flows. In this manner, each individual nation would have attempted to limit its own need for reserves and to insulate its domestic economy from the impact of deflation in other nations, including the United States. The cooperative approach would have embodied a joint effort by most noncommunist nations to effect a planned increase in the global stock of reserve assets, either through a uniform general increase in the price of gold or through a reform of the international monetary system. A full cooperative approach would have also entailed an attempt to eliminate international economic disequilibria, including exchange-rate disequilibria, that prevented countries from utilizing productive resources fully and efficiently. While the cooperative solution could have produced long-run benefits for both this country and the rest of the world, weighed against these gains would have been the losses—including tentative moves toward the autarchic approach—necessary to stimulate action and to hasten agreement.

The actual outcome might have been some combination of these two extreme solutions. Short of monetary reform or worldwide devaluation, IMF quotas might have been enlarged by greater amounts than they actually were. At the same time, trade and exchange restrictions might not have been relaxed, and new restrictions might have been imposed to a limited degree. But, from this country's viewpoint, the more important question is whether the United States would have been able to switch to a nondeflationary method for preventing the reemergence of payments deficits.

The two nondeflationary methods for eliminating payments deficits are (1) devaluation relative to other currencies and (2) high interest rates (possibly supplemented by capital-movement restrictions) offset domestically by government budget deficits.

It is doubtful that the dollar could have been devalued in the midst of a global liquidity shortage. Since U.S. payments deficits would already have been eliminated, foreign officials could easily have interpreted any move to devalue the dollar as an attempt to export unemployment at a time when many other nations were also trying to counter deflationary forces. If, on the other hand, a worldwide increase in the price of gold had occurred, deflationary tendencies and the shortage of reserves inducing them might have been avoided. But, as in the 1930s, the round of devaluations would not have ended until it was clear that the United States had gained no trading advantage over foreign countries through a devaluation of the dollar relative to other currencies. Exchange-rate adjustments would probably have continued until the same basic structure of exchange rates had been reestablished. Thus, devaluation of the dollar relative to other currencies would have been unlikely.

If dollar exchange rates could not be altered, an appropriate combination of fiscal and monetary policies would have embodied the remaining nondeflationary possibility for preventing the reappearance of U.S. payments deficits. It is definitely possible, and perhaps even likely, that fiscal policy in the 1960s would have been sufficiently expansionary to keep unemployment rates from rising above the fairly high levels that actually existed.[27] If the methods initially employed to terminate gold losses had induced an especially severe recession in 1958–1959, expansionary fiscal techniques might well have been used earlier and more vigorously than they actually were. But a fall in unemployment rates to levels substantially below the actual rates would have been unlikely. And, if unemployment rates as a peripheral nation had not declined below actual rates, the probable losses from initially eliminating deficits would not have been offset by subsequent gains.

Subsequent gains, if any, can hardly be estimated, but, given the strong congressional bias against governmental activities which tend to be inflationary, there is little reason to believe that gains in the 1960s would have been large enough to offset any substantial amount of earlier losses. Of course, the earlier losses might have been moderate or even small, but then the incentive to use expansionary fiscal policies during the 1960s would also have been reduced. Although the distribution of all possible

[27] Unemployment rates during the 1960s are as follows: 1960, 5.6 per cent; 1961, 6.7 per cent; 1962, 5.6 per cent; 1963, 5.7 per cent; 1964, 5.2 per cent; 1965, 4.6 per cent. Source: *Economic Report of the President*, Transmitted to Congress January 1966 (Washington: U.S. Government Printing Office, 1966), p. 235.

net outcomes for the period from 1958 through 1966 is dispersed over a broad range, it appears that this distribution has a negative mean. An alternative way of stating the same conclusion is to say that, as a non-reserve-currency country, the United States would have had few opportunities to enjoy higher levels of real national income than it actually did, and that risks of declines in income below historical levels would have been numerous. Consequently, the United States has probably produced a greater income stream as a center country than it would have produced as a non-reserve-currency country.

RECAPITULATION

Having reached this point, the reader may be puzzled by the lack of any explicit reference to the list of reserve-currency costs and benefits presented above. He may wonder if some cost or benefit mentioned there has not been overlooked.

The possible costs and benefits of being a reserve-currency country are the following: the cost of acquiring or holding more gold than the center country would have if it had been a peripheral nation; the expansionary income effect of being able to run greater balance-of-payments deficits than the country otherwise could have; the cost or benefit, through changes in foreign incomes, of expanding the global supply of reserves; the benefit from increased foreign demand for financial and commercial services available in a center country; and the cost of reserve-currency constraints on income.

If the United States had been a peripheral country in the 1950s, it would not have needed a gold stock as large as its gold reserves would have been. Thus, some gain would have been realized from reducing excess gold reserves. The cost to a reserve-currency country of holding excess gold reserves is the income forgone through failure to run the enlarged payments deficits that would cause excess gold holdings to be eliminated. However, if a center country is able to finance equivalent deficits through the accumulation of liabilities to foreign authorities, no net change in income occurs. Since the United States, as a center country, ran deficits at least as large as those it would have had as a peripheral nation, no net cost resulted from holding excess gold reserves. Conversely, because the United States, if it had been a peripheral nation, would presumably have had total deficits during the 1950s equivalent to excess gold reserves at the end of 1949, this country could actually derive no net benefit from balance-of-payments deficits until such time as its excess gold holdings had been eliminated.

When, however, the actual increase in outstanding U.S. liabilities to official foreigners during the 1950s outstripped the decline in gold reserves which would have occurred during the same period had this country been a peripheral nation, benefits from enlarged deficits began to accumulate. If the United States had been a peripheral nation, excess gold reserves would have been run off completely by at least 1958 or 1959, when aggregate gold losses would have totaled $8 to $12 billion. Thus, after 1958–1959, when chronic payments deficits and gold losses would have ended, the ability of the United States to incur further deficits led to some benefit.

The fact that the United States supplied more reserve assets to foreign nations than it would have done as a non-reserve-currency country also had an impact on U.S. real national income. Expanding the global supply of reserve assets may have either a positive or a negative impact on the income of a center country. But failure of the United States to supply additional reserves would almost certainly have led to a global scarcity of reserves. Thus, the supply of reserves from the United States after 1958 or 1959 most likely had a net expansionary impact on foreign incomes. Although the impact on U.S. income of providing foreign authorities with gold and dollar reserves and of expanding foreign incomes could conceivably have been negative, this effect was probably positive.

A reserve-currency income constraint is any factor that creates additional disequilibria which are costly to overcome, or that raises the cost of disequilibria a center country would face regardless of the reserve-asset status of its currency. For the reasons given above, devaluation of the dollar relative to other currencies probably would not have been possible even if the dollar had not been a reserve currency.

Since the use of monetary policy and capital-export controls has not been appreciably hampered by reserve-currency status, there is little reason to presume that these adjustment mechanisms would have been used much more effectively if the United States had been a peripheral country. In fact, a global shortage of reserves could have expanded potential U.S. deficits and induced the use of tighter monetary policies than were actually employed. Consequently, when compared with actual requirements, fiscal policy might have been called on to bear an even greater burden in preventing domestic deflation, and unemployment might have been higher than it actually was in the early 1960s. Although clearly not impossible, it seems unlikely that, if the United States had been a peripheral country, unemployment would have been reduced below historical rates. It is even less likely that this reduction in the number of idle workers would have been large enough to offset the probable costs of initially eliminating payments deficits in 1958–1959.

Finally, no attempt has been made to estimate the probable benefit to the United States from satisfying the increase in foreign demand for financial and commercial services induced by reserve-currency status. But this additional gain, which was not included in the foregoing considerations, tends to reinforce the conclusion that the United States probably enjoyed higher levels of real national income as a reserve-currency country than it would have enjoyed as a peripheral nation.

PETER B. KENEN and ELINOR B. YUDIN

The Demand for International

Reserves

IF ECONOMISTS COULD MEASURE THE NEED for reserves, they might be able
to agree on the right way to reform the international monetary system.
Most of the economists who propose drastic reform do so because they
anticipate a shortage of reserves; some even believe that the shortage is
upon us. Those who advocate more gradual change believe that reserves
are adequate now and for the next several years; some even believe that
reserves are excessive.

Unfortunately, there is no way to measure the adequacy of reserves—
not even to make historical comparisons. Scitovsky's comments illustrate

Reprinted, by permission of Harvard University, from *The Review of Economics and
Statistics*, XLVII (August 1965), 242–50. We are indebted to fellow members of the
International Economics Workshop, Columbia University, and to the Seminar in
International Economics, Harvard University, for criticism and suggestions. Professor
Jon Cunnyngham provided valuable guidance in the design of computations. Research
on the project was financed by a Ford Foundation grant to the International Economics
Workshop, Columbia University.

several of the problems involved in appraising the global stock of reserves:

If the world supply of reserves were adequate, the drawing down of some countries' reserves to unduly low levels would be matched by some other countries' excessive accumulation of reserves, and the desire to eliminate balance-of-payments deficits in the former would be matched by the desire to eliminate the surpluses in the latter.[1]

On this definition, global reserves would not be adequate unless countries behaved symmetrically toward surpluses and deficits. By implication, Scitovsky's criterion assumes that every government or central bank has a precise demand for reserves; if it acts to restrict aggregate expenditure when its reserves fall below a certain level, it will also act to stimulate expenditure when reserves exceed that same level. Behavior, however, may not be this simple. A government willing to tolerate losses of reserves without taking restrictive action may still prefer to accumulate more reserves than to expand demand and court inflation. Even if each country had a unique demand for reserves, moreover, a fixed global total of reserves could be more or less "adequate" depending on its distribution. Finally, Scitovsky's criterion, like most others, involves important normative judgments, implicitly endorsing global price stability as a policy objective and assuming that a symmetrical response to deficits and surpluses will accomplish payments adjustments with appropriate speed.[2]

It is even difficult to measure the stock of reserves, as the several reserve assets and reserve credits now in use are not perfect substitutes for one another; equal amounts of gold, currency, and credit may make unequal contributions to a nation's external liquidity. Liquidity is a state of mind. Most of the economists concerned with these problems take account of central-bank gold and foreign currency, IMF gold tranches, and automatic drawing rights under bilateral credit arrangements. Others count all assets susceptible of mobilization at moments of crisis—all IMF drawing rights, the long-term foreign assets of official institutions, and

---

[1] Tibor Scitovsky, in U.S. Congress, Subcommittee on International Exchange and Payments of the Joint Economic Committee, *Hearings: International Payments Imbalances and Need for Strengthening International Financial Arrangements* (Washington, D.C., 1961), p. 208.

[2] Several recent studies stress these important normative issues—the links between the question of adequacy and the problem of adjustment. See R. E. Caves, "International Liquidity: Toward a Home Repair Manual," *Review of Economics and Statistics*, XLVI (May 1964); F. Machlup et al., *International Monetary Arrangements: The Problem of Choice* (Princeton: Princeton University Press, 1964), pp. 53–54; and *Ministerial Statement of the Group of Ten and Annex Prepared by Deputies* (August 1964), pp. 4–5.

"potential" bilateral credits. Some prefer to deal with gross assets and gross drawing rights, others make allowance for "liquid" liabilities.

Yet quantitative methods may still answer important factual questions about liquidity. We may ask, for example, if national holdings of reserves, defined consistently if not perfectly, exhibit any marked regularity or rational pattern. If they do, we may be able to describe the national demand for reserves of a "typical" country, then to appraise the distribution of global reserves.

THE MEASUREMENT OF PAYMENTS
DISTURBANCES

Measurement always requires a yardstick. A dollar total of reserves, gross or net, is meaningless. But the yardstick generally used to measure liquidity—the ratio of reserves to imports—does not tell us very much. This familiar ratio merely shows how long a country could finance its imports if it were suddenly deprived of all its foreign-exchange earnings. A better yardstick would direct our attention to the more likely contingency. It would compare the level of reserves to the variations in payments and receipts that countries actually expect to experience.

Governments have many reasons for holding reserve assets, including the requirements of domestic monetary legislation or long-standing custom. But the paramount reason for holding reserves is the commitment to maintain stable exchange rates in the face of payments disturbances. Trade and private service flows, government transactions, and capital movements are subject to several disturbances—secular, cyclical, seasonal, and random. Under a system of flexible exchange rates, the net current impact of all these disturbances would be manifest as changes in the exchange rates. If exchange rates were perfectly rigid, by contrast, the net current impact of these disturbances would be manifest as changes in official reserves and official liabilities—the counterparts of central-bank intervention supporting the exchange rates. Under the arrangements that actually prevail, small changes in exchange rates occur automatically, absorbing some disturbances.[3] Changes in policy, moreover, especially in

---

[3] In one important case studied here (Canada), the exchange rate was allowed to fluctuate extensively. More important, the rate was deliberately altered. In two other cases (Germany and the Netherlands), there were smaller but significant changes in exchange rates, interrupting the continuity of the data.

exchange controls, have suppressed or offset significant disturbances. However, most of the countries surveyed in this study have been compelled to intervene in the foreign-exchange market, and the larger disturbances afflicting payments and receipts are usually reflected in their reserves.

The adequacy of official reserves and credit facilities must be appraised in relation to expected future disturbances, not in relation to those of the past. But the size and duration of future disturbances may perhaps be gauged by examining past disturbances, manifest as changes in official reserves. In Triffin's words:

The order of magnitude of deficits calling for reserve financing might first be gauged quantitatively on the basis of past experience. This first approximation should then be revised, upward or downward, in the light of other pertinent evidence about the probable course of external and internal developments.[4]

Admittedly, changes in reserves do not measure past disturbances with any great accuracy—even with respect to countries that have abjured exchange control and have not altered their exchange rates. Changes in domestic policy, especially in monetary policy, can offset substantial disturbances, and the endogenous responses of the private sector have also been important in many instances. Finally, reserves may sometimes change autonomously, as central banks may intervene in the foreign-exchange market when there has been no apparent disturbance, selling gold and foreign currency when the exchange rate is above its "lower support point," and buying when the rate is below its "upper support point." They also engage in forward foreign-exchange operations and intergovernmental credit transactions that distort statistics on reserves and thereby distort any measure of disturbances derived from those statistics. Yet changes in reserves remain the best available measure of disturbances. In their very nature, moreover, they are certain to reflect the disturbances sufficient in size or duration to compel official intervention—disturbances requiring the use or acquisition of official reserves.

Inspection of the major countries' published reserve statistics suggested that the monthly changes in each nation's reserves can be described stochastically—that the changes may even be normally distributed.[5] If

---

[4] Robert Triffin, *Gold and the Dollar Crisis* (New Haven: Yale University Press, 1961), p. 35.

[5] The reserve statistics used in this study span the five-year period 1958–1962. They include official holdings of gold and convertible foreign exchange, the net IMF position (whether positive or negative), and, prior to 1959, the net EPU position of member countries. All data were drawn from *International Financial Statistics*. It might have been better to include credits available through EPU, rather than credits drawn or granted,

this were so, a country's balance of payments could be described as a simple random walk. But the monthly changes in reserves also displayed a significant serial correlation; successive observations were not independent. If, then, a country's balance of payments is to be described stochastically, one must use a Markov process rather than a random walk. We consequently sought to describe each country's balance of payments by a simple autoregressive scheme:

$$\Delta R_t = \rho \Delta R_{t-1} + \epsilon_t, \quad 0 < \rho < 1 \tag{1}$$

where ϵ_t has $N(\bar{\epsilon}, \sigma_\epsilon^2)$. In other words, the monthly "surplus" or "deficit" in the balance of payments, as measured by the change in gross reserves, ΔR_t, was treated as reflecting a current disturbance, ϵ_t, drawn from a normal population with mean $\bar{\epsilon}$ and variance σ_ϵ^2, and the "carry-forward" of all past disturbances embodied in $\rho \Delta R_{t-1}$. The past disturbances will be subject to cumulative decay when $0 < \rho < 1$.[6] This compound hypothesis, if valid, would be quite convenient, allowing the complete description of a country's payments experience in terms of three parameters: $\bar{\epsilon}$, the mean of the net disturbance; σ_ϵ^2, its variance; and ρ,

---

and to have included the IMF gold tranche which cannot turn negative, rather than the net IMF position which does turn negative when countries draw on their credit tranches. But these substitutions would not have altered many of the month-to-month changes. The monthly changes in reserves were computed directly from the gross reserve figures, but adjusted to exclude the discontinuities introduced by the termination of EPU (January 1959). One might also have adjusted the published statistics for drawings on bilateral credit facilities, for the creation of and drawings on IMF "standby" credits, for changes in "liquid" liabilities, or for "special" intergovernment capital transactions such as debt prepayments. These adjustments would have had significant effects on the British statistics and, at the end of the period under study, on the statistics of several continental European countries.

[6] The supposition that ϵ_t is normally distributed obtains support from theory, not just casual observation. If the balance of payments can be viewed as a sum of separate transactions, each of them subject to a stochastic disturbance, the change in reserves will itself display a disturbance equal to the sum of the component disturbances. Although the components of the sum may not be normally distributed, the Central Limit Theorem suggests that the sum will have a normal distribution. The supposition that $0 < \rho < 1$ also obtains support from theory. Some of the constituent disturbances are likely to vanish soon after they appear. Others are likely to endure for several months or years unless they are offset by endogenous responses or by public policy. These offsets, however, will only take hold with the passage of time, eroding the disturbance gradually. A disturbance ϵ_0, therefore, may be deemed to have a net effect $\rho^k \epsilon_0$, k months later. These points are discussed at much greater length in a paper by the junior author, Elinor B. Yudin, *The Demand for Reserves* (International Economics Workshop, Columbia University, 1964 mimeo.). That paper also contains a detailed description of the computations presented below.

its carry-forward or duration.[7] To test this hypothesis, we have computed simple least-squares estimates of:

$$\Delta R_t = \bar{e} + p\Delta R_{t-1} + u_t \tag{1a}$$

where $\bar{e}$ approximates $\bar{\epsilon}$, p is an estimate of ρ, and σ_u (the standard error of estimate) is an estimate of σ_ϵ.[8] We then ran separate statistical tests on the several parts of our composite hypothesis—that $0 < \rho < 1$, that u_t is normally distributed, and that a simple Markov scheme suffices to describe the monthly balance of payments.

Estimates of $\bar{e}$, p, and σ_u for 14 countries are arrayed in Table 1.[9] Eight countries' data displayed significant positive values for p; one more series (Germany) displayed a positive value just short of statistical significance.[10] Five other national series gave negative values for p, but only one of these (Finland) was significantly different from zero. In the majority of cases, then, our results were consistent with the supposition that $0 < \rho < 1$. An even larger majority of countries conformed to the next supposition; ten sets of residuals u_t satisfied a χ^2 test for normal fit at the .05 level of significance.

---

[7] The values of the parameters, $\bar{\epsilon}$, $\sigma_\epsilon{}^2$, and ρ, obtained below, will, of course, reflect the choice of time interval (the use of monthly data). But the relative national values of each parameter should not be much affected by this arbitrary choice. Although quarterly estimates of the three parameters would probably differ from the monthly estimates studied here, they are apt to differ in similar degrees from one country to the next. It is the relationship among national values, moreover, that matters for the cross-sectional analysis in the next section.

[8] If the residuals u_t are normally distributed, implying that the ϵ_t are normally distributed, a simple least-squares estimate of $\bar{e}$ and p will approach the desirable large-sample properties of asymptotic consistency and efficiency.

[9] Additional estimates were made for the changes in reserves reported by 13 other countries (Brazil, Chile, Colombia, El Salvador, Greece, India, Iran, Iraq, Lebanon, Mexico, Pakistan, Peru, and the Philippines) usually classified as "less-developed" countries. Nine of these countries' reserves gave values for p that were not significantly different from zero; two (Greece and Pakistan) gave significant positive values, two more (Iran and Iraq) gave significant negative values. The latter pair also showed significant (negative) second-order autocorrelation. Four countries' residuals (Brazil, El Salvador, Iraq, and Lebanon) failed the χ^2 test for normality at the .05 level, but only one (Lebanon) failed the Bartlett test for homoscedasticity. One would expect—and one finds—that the changes in reserves for these countries are more nearly random than those for the countries in Table 1. Most of the underdeveloped countries still use strict exchange controls and have small reserves. Any enduring payments disturbance is usually met by changes in direct controls, so that the monthly changes in reserves should be regarded as the consequence of imperfect synchronization in exchange control, rather than the measure of the payments disturbances.

[10] When the most recent past *quarterly* change in reserves was substituted for ΔR_{t-1}, the German data gave a significant positive p.

Table 1

Autoregressive Equations: Monthly Changes in Reserves, 1958–1962

Country	Parameters (and Standard Errors)		Standard Error of Estimate	
	$\bar{e}$ (millions of dollars)	p	(σ_u) (millions of dollars)	u_t Normally Distributed[b]
Austria	5.40 (2.66)[a]	0.4664 (0.1198)[a]	18.9958	yes
Belgium	7.65 (4.47)	0.4216 (0.1165)[a]	32.4678	yes
Canada	2.99 (8.64)	0.4914 (0.1149)[a]	66.3340	no
Denmark	2.70 (2.14)	−0.2176 (0.1306)	16.4670	yes
Finland	1.32 (1.12)	−0.3785 (0.1280)[a]	8.3367	yes
Germany	10.12 (33.14)	0.2022 (0.1284)	256.4864	no
Italy	22.32 (9.05)	0.4661 (0.1139)[a]	61.5243	yes
Japan	9.16 (5.02)	0.6457 (0.1001)[a]	33.2173	yes
Netherlands	20.17 (6.87)[a]	−0.0853 (0.1294)	49.3806	no
New Zealand	0.22 (1.97)	0.4331 (0.1177)[a]	15.2923	yes
Norway	1.91 (1.34)	−0.1796 (0.1303)	10.2767	yes
Sweden	3.36 (2.21)	0.3307 (0.1237)[a]	16.4466	yes
Switzerland	17.08 (8.78)	−0.0631 (0.1494)	66.6481	yes
United Kingdom	14.69 (16.77)	0.3302 (0.1244)[a]	127.4753	no[c]

[a] Significantly different from zero at the .05 level.

[b] Distributions listed as "yes" are those that satisfied the χ^2 test for normality at the .05 level of significance.

[c] Would satisfy the χ^2 test for normality at the .01 level of significance.

There is no satisfactory test for the sufficiency of the simple Markov scheme, but two imperfect tests give consistent results. The first test was performed by inserting an additional term into equation (1a):

$$\Delta R_t = \bar{e} + p_1 \Delta R_{t-1} + p_2 \Delta R_{t-2} + u_t' \tag{1b}$$

Not one computed p_2 was significantly different from zero, suggesting that the simple scheme set forth by equation (1) provides a sufficient stochastic description of the payments disturbances.[11] The second test applied the Durbin-Watson ratio to the residuals, u_t, generated from equation (1a). There was no evidence of autocorrelation, positive or negative.[12]

Our hypothesis, however, involves one additional supposition—that σ_ϵ^2 is constant through time. To test this assumption of homoscedasticity, we split each country's residuals, u_t, into two equal groups at the mid-point of the monthly series (June 1960), made separate estimates of σ_u^2 for the two subperiods, and applied the Bartlett test. Our results, arrayed in Table 2, were less satisfactory than expected. Six of the 14 sets of residuals showed a change in variance during the five-year period 1958–1962.

Viewed from a different standpoint, however, these same results inspire more pleasure than chagrin, supporting the contention that reserves must grow through time. The Brookings group endorses this important hypothesis:

While the range of potential swings in the balance of payments will probably continue to be a moderate percentage of the total volume of international transactions, these swings have widened greatly in recent years, and the trend of recent developments suggests that they are likely to widen further in the future.[13]

We have obtained additional support for the Brookings view by running a set of simple trend estimates, displayed in Table 2. Treating every u_t^2 as a point-estimate of σ_u^2, we have made regression estimates of linear trend:

$$u_t^2 = u_0^2 + \lambda T \qquad (2)$$

Four of the λ's were statistically significant, and nine of the 14 λ's were positive, suggesting gradual growth in the amplitude of payments disturbances.

Our composite hypothesis ($0 < \rho < 1$, ϵ_t normal, and σ_ϵ^2 constant) is rarely satisfied by any one country's data. Belgium and New Zealand are the only ones whose data pass all tests at the .05 level of significance. (The Italian, Japanese, Swedish, and British statistics could do so too,

---

[11] This test is imperfect because ΔR_{t-1} and ΔR_{t-2} will be intercorrelated when $p_1 > 0$.

[12] This test is also imperfect, as the Durbin-Watson test should not be applied to data generated from an autoregressive transform. See J. Durbin and G. S. Watson, "Testing for Serial Correlation in Least Squares Regression. I," *Biometrica* (1950), 410.

[13] See W. Salant et al., *The United States Balance of Payments in 1968* (Washington, D.C.: The Brookings Institution, 1963), p. 136; also the *Report of the Group of Ten*, p. 8. Triffin (*Gold*, Chapter 3) made the same point much earlier, but did not explicitly relate his argument for growth in reserves to the evolution of payments disturbances.

Table 2

Tests for Stability of the Standard Errors (σ_e)

Country	Bartlett Test (χ^2)	Linear Trend Coefficients and Standard Errors	
		λ	σ_λ
Austria	7.908[b]	14.3987[a]	4.4660
Belgium	0.017	1.5601	13.0310
Canada	30.603[b]	305.0469[a]	86.5924
Denmark	0.290	1.9199	3.0062
Finland	2.228	−0.9648	0.7330
Germany	0.835	−370.1011	1141.2093
Italy	4.275[a]	87.3123	53.7158
Japan	6.231[a]	27.6118[a]	13.1164
Netherlands	1.405	−82.6399	58.6199
New Zealand	0.008	−1.1795	1.9708
Norway	2.116	1.4701	1.1071
Sweden	5.070[a]	−2.2450	4.7838
Switzerland	5.544[a]	172.4060[a]	69.6477
United Kingdom	0.971	161.9592	186.5336

[a] Significantly different from zero at the .05 and .01 levels.
[b] Significantly different from zero at the .05 level, but not at the .01 level.

but only if the tests for normality and homoscedasticity were substantially relaxed by accepting the hypotheses of normality and homoscedasticity unless they are contradicted at the .01 level of significance rather than the .05 level.) A majority of national estimates, however, passed each of our tests taken one at a time—even the test for homoscedasticity. Hence, we were content to use our computed parameters, $\bar{e}$, p, and σ_u^2, as yardsticks with which to appraise the need for reserves—as the input to a series of cross-sectional relationships seeking to measure the demand for reserves.

THE DEMAND FOR RESERVES

If countries hold reserves to cope with disturbances—to maintain stable exchange rates—the demand for reserves should depend on expectations as to the size and duration of those disturbances. Each country's demand for reserves should therefore depend on the central bank's expectations concerning the anticipated mean disturbance, $\bar{\epsilon}$, the variance of disturbances, σ_ϵ^2, and the "carry-forward," ρ.[14] Yet any attempt to measure the "typical" demand for reserves by a cross-sectional analysis of information on national reserves and payments disturbances must make two heroic assumptions:

First, we are obliged to assume that each central bank or government holds the reserves it desires. This assumption can never be fulfilled with precision, if only because the stock of reserves circulates continuously.[15] Nor can it be fulfilled for all countries together unless the total of reserves is sufficiently large.[16]

Second, we are obliged to assume that the distribution of future disturbances, as forecast by the central banks, resembles the distribution of past disturbances. The values of $\bar{e}$, p, and σ_u must be regarded as satisfactory proxies for $\bar{\epsilon}$, ρ, and σ_ϵ, and these, in turn, must be thought to resemble the parameters that the authorities contemplate when they appraise the sufficiency of their reserves. This assumption cannot be exactly fulfilled because recorded changes in reserves will always reflect the influence of policies initiated to control the nation's balance of payments and regulate its stock of reserves. A country that deems itself short of reserves may act directly to reduce payments disturbances—or will willingly accommodate a "structural" surplus—thereby compressing σ_u, reducing p, and enlarging $\bar{e}$. We shall assume that the values of σ_u and p shown in Table 1 are not materially affected by national policies— that they are satisfactory proxies for σ_ϵ and ρ, the "true" parameters. We shall also assume that these "true" parameters do not greatly differ from those that central banks project for the future. But we do not have similar

[14] Alternatively, the demand for reserves might be deemed to depend on the distribution of a single number, jointly generated by these three parameters—on the distribution of anticipated *cumulative* surpluses and deficits. One could derive such a distribution from the three parameters studied in the text, but this would be extremely laborious and should not be necessary. The three parameters, $\bar{\epsilon}$, σ_ϵ^2 and ρ, specify that distribution completely and sufficiently. One might also try to link the level of reserves to the *total* variance, rather than the variance around $\bar{\epsilon}$. This procedure would avoid the necessity for separate consideration of $\bar{\epsilon}$ and ρ in the equations that follow. But it would also misrepresent the stochastic character of the balance of payments adduced in the previous section.

[15] One might, perhaps, surmount this first objection by seeking to explain *average* national reserves over a period of years. But experiments along these lines gave similar results to those reported in the text (the experiments on single-year reserves).

[16] This second *caveat* does not much impair the validity of our approach because we do not study all the major countries simultaneously. We have deliberately excluded the United States—the main supplier of reserves over the past few years. We have also excluded France because its reserve data were not sufficiently continuous.

confidence in our estimates of $\bar{\epsilon}$, as any deliberate attempt to adjust reserve holdings is certain to affect the mean monthly change and, therefore, our values for $\bar{\epsilon}$. A country that anticipates a "structural" deficit ($\bar{\epsilon} < 0$) and lacks sufficient reserves to finance such a deficit is obliged to defend its position. In consequence, its observed $\bar{\epsilon}$ may differ substantially from its anticipated mean disturbances, $\bar{\epsilon}$.[17]

We now suppose that the demand for reserves depends on $\bar{\epsilon}$, σ_ϵ, and ρ. As a linear approximation:

$$R_{it} = \beta_0 - \beta_1 \bar{\epsilon}_i + \beta_2 \rho_i + \beta_3 \sigma_{\epsilon i} \tag{3}$$

where R_{it} measures the ith country's gross reserves at the start of the tth month. To compute a cross-sectional least-squares estimate of this relationship, we employed the parameters arrayed in Table 1, but made systematic adjustments in those statistics. When p was not significant (or significant but negative), it was arbitrarily fixed at zero. The corresponding estimate of $\bar{\epsilon}$ was replaced by the mean change in reserves, and the corresponding estimate of σ_u was replaced by the simple standard deviation of the monthly change in reserves.[18] Our first least-squares estimates sought to "explain" the distribution of gross reserves at December 31, 1957 ("initial" reserves). Out second estimate sought to "explain" gross reserves at December 31, 1962 ("terminal" reserves):[19]

$$R_{57} = 68.11 + 5.77\bar{e} + 77.17p + 19.34\sigma_u, \quad \bar{R}^2 = .95 \tag{3a}$$
$$\quad (177.81) \quad (15.96) \quad (378.12) \quad (2.16)*$$

$$R_{62} = -159.80 + 95.89\bar{e} + 1136.62p + 16.69\sigma_u, \quad \bar{R}^2 = .96 \tag{3b}$$
$$\quad (206.91) \quad (18.57)* \quad (440.00)* \quad (2.51)*$$

[17] In the period under study, of course, the several national values of $\bar{\epsilon}$ jointly reflected the massive United States deficits of 1958–1962. These deficits may be viewed as "structural" disturbances afflicting other countries—as an overwhelming increase in the "supply" of reserves, posing an intractable identification problem. We think it equally correct, however, to view them as reflecting European policies deliberately designed to acquire reserves, and, therefore, overlaying or distorting the "true" $\bar{\epsilon}$. One can hardly accuse the European countries of excessive zeal in accomplishing a restoration of payments equilibrium. On the contrary, the major European countries were quite content to acquire reserves by way of the United States deficit.

[18] Computations using the "unadjusted" values of $\bar{\epsilon}$, p, and σ_u suggested that this adjustment did not have much effect on our final results. As expected, it did increase the standard error of β_2 (pertaining to ρ), but not by enough to alter our conclusions. Estimates were also made using σ_u^2, "adjusted" and "unadjusted," and the results of these computations were slightly different from those described below. In general, the coefficient of multiple correlation ($\bar{R}^2$) was lower, and the influence of ρ was sometimes less pronounced.

[19] The standard errors of the regression coefficients appear in parentheses beneath the coefficients. Asterisks denote statistical significance at the .05 level.

These equations offer strong support for our hypothesis that the demand for reserves depends on the size and duration of disturbances. They attribute great explanatory power to σ_ϵ (represented by the "adjusted" values of σ_u). They also apply the anticipated sign to β_2, the coefficient attached to ρ, and β_2 is significant with respect to "terminal" reserves. In both equations, however, β_1 takes the "wrong" (positive) sign, and the influence of $\bar{e}$ attains striking significance in the second equation. These results support our *caveat* concerning the computed mean of the disturbances, $\bar{e}$. The $\bar{e}$ may reflect intended reserve accumulation, not the projected mean disturbance determining demand. We therefore delete this variable from subsequent equations.[20]

When $\bar{e}$ is deleted from our first two equations, we obtain these results:

$$R_{57} = 89.80 + 70.23p + 19.95\sigma_u, \quad \bar{R}^2 = .95 \qquad (3a')$$
$$(160.61) \ (362.40) \qquad (1.26)*$$

$$R_{62} = 200.96 + 1021.19p + 26.98\sigma_u, \quad \bar{R}^2 = .88 \qquad (3b')$$
$$(355.51) \quad (802.14) \qquad (2.78)*$$

The equations still "explain" the distribution of reserves quite well, but β_2 (pertaining to ρ) is no longer significant in the "terminal" equation. Furthermore, the coefficient of multiple correlation, $\bar{R}^2$, declines abruptly with respect to "terminal" reserves, falling below the $\bar{R}^2$ for "initial" reserves. As the "terminal" $\bar{R}^2$ was consistently lower than the "initial" $\bar{R}^2$ in other experiments, we may perhaps infer that the very large increase in reserves generated by the United States payments deficit was not well distributed among other countries.

One would expect the demand for reserves to reflect additional circumstances and considerations, not just expectations concerning disturbances. We have sought to take account of two such considerations—the opportunity cost of holding reserves and the level of "liquid" liabilities that governments regard as claims on their reserves—but have not been successful.

We did not try to devise a direct measure of opportunity cost. Instead, we supposed that reserve accumulation is usually accomplished at the expense of capital formation—public or private, domestic or foreign—and that the "social marginal product" of capital varies inversely with per capita income. On this supposition, per capita income should correlate

---

[20] Note, in passing, that $\bar{e}$ and σ_u are highly intercorrelated.

directly with total reserves. A country with a high per capita income should hold more reserves than a country with a low per capita income.[21]

We had equal difficulty measuring "liquid" liabilities, as the published figures are notoriously poor. There are no statistics for Switzerland, a major banking center, and the British data are organized quite differently from other countries' figures. In the end, we added the gross liabilities of central banks and governments to the net liabilities of "deposit money banks," both as reported in *International Financial Statistics*.[22] Once again, we employed a linear approximation:

$$R_{it} = \beta_0 + \beta_2 \rho_i + \beta_3 \sigma_{\epsilon i} + \beta_4 y_i + \beta_5 L_{it} \tag{4}$$

where y_i represents per capita income in the ith country and L_{it} represents that country's liabilities. The addition of per capita income and of liabilities did not much improve the overall fit:

$$R_{57} = -371.78 + 305.95\rho + 20.63\sigma_u + 0.39y_i - 0.02L_{57}$$
$$(275.32) \quad (336.44) \quad (1.19)* \quad (0.21) \quad (0.01)$$

$$\bar{R} = .96 \quad (4a)$$

$$R_{62} = 715.40 + 977.98\rho + 28.06\sigma_u - 0.51y_i - 0.03L_{62}, \quad \bar{R}^2 = .88$$
$$(681.78) \quad (836.39) \quad (2.96)* \quad (0.52) \quad (0.02)$$

$$(4b)$$

Indeed, liabilities took on the "wrong" (negative) sign in both equations, while per capita income took on the "wrong" (negative) sign in the 1962 equation.

In a final experiment, we replaced liabilities with the domestic money supply, M_{it}, to allow for the impact of domestic monetary legislation on the demand for reserves and for the contention that "excessive" domestic liquidity represents a potential claim on reserves.[23] This permutation was

[21] The statistics for per capita income were obtained from income data in *International Financial Statistics*. They pertain to 1960.

[22] For the United Kingdom, we used the "old" series on sterling balances, excluding British indebtedness to the IMF. For the Canadian banks, we used foreign-currency deposits *less* banks' claims on their foreign branches. When "explaining" initial reserves, we used liabilities at December 31, 1957; when "explaining" terminal reserves, we used liabilities at December 31, 1962. We ran several computations using other constructs (central bank liabilities taken alone, then official and bank liabilities without allowance for bank assets), but we did not find significant departures from the pattern described in the text.

[23] See M. W. Holtrop, "Method of Monetary Analysis Used by De Nederlandsche Bank," *IMF Staff Papers* (February 1957). We did not employ liabilities and the money stock in the same equation as they are closely correlated.

Table 3

Excess (+) and Shortfall (−) of Gross Reserves Computed from "Best" Equations

(millions of dollars)

Country	1957			1962			$\bar{e}$
	Actual Reserves	Computed Reserves	Excess (+) or Shortfall (−)	Actual Reserves	Computed Reserves	Excess (+) or Shortfall (−)	
Austria	523.00	491.33	31.67	1,081.00	1,041.72	39.28	5.3991
Belgium	1,148.00	770.89	377.11	1,753.00	1,406.53	346.47	7.8446
Canada	1,926.00	1,432.61	493.39	2,547.00	2,270.03	276.97	2.9886
Denmark	172.00	445.99	−273.99	261.00	982.56	−721.56	1.4833
Finland	180.00	279.37	−99.37	317.00	765.13	−448.13	1.3186
Germany	5,197.00	5,277.10	−80.10	6,964.00	7,286.80	−322.80	29.4500
Italy	1,354.00	1,336.97	17.03	3,644.00	2,145.22	1,498.78	22.3195
Japan	524.00	774.07	−250.07	2,022.00	1,410.68	611.32	9.1578
Netherlands	1,009.00	1,090.82	−81.82	1,946.00	1,824.01	121.99	15.6167
New Zealand	152.00	417.76	−265.76	171.00	945.71	−774.71	.2228
Norway	197.00	319.53	−122.53	304.00	817.54	−513.54	1.7833
Sweden	501.00	440.62	60.38	801.00	975.55	−174.55	3.3577
Switzerland	1,898.00	1,429.63	468.37	2,872.00	2,266.14	605.86	16.2333
United Kingdom	2,374.00	2,648.29	−274.29	3,311.00	3,856.40	−545.40	14.6865

not informative. Our results were much as with liabilities:

$$R_{57} = -320.31 + 351.11p + 20.92\sigma_u + 0.35y_i - 0.02M_{57}, \quad \bar{R}^2 = .96$$
$$(290.16) \quad (383.28) \quad (1.55)* \quad (0.22) \quad (0.02)$$

$$(4c)$$

$$R_{62} = 757.13 + 576.12p + 25.44\sigma_u + 0.47y_i + 0.02M_{62}, \quad \bar{R}^2 = .87$$
$$(720.22) \quad (980.99) \quad (4.25)* \quad (0.57) \quad (0.04)$$

$$(4d)$$

Although central banks insist that "liquid" liabilities and the domestic money supply are relevant to any appraisal of their reserves, we could not establish any connection between either item and actual reserves. The prospective volatility of the balance of payments, measured by σ_u, accounted for the bulk of the total variation in the several central banks' holdings of reserves.

The strong partial correlation between R_{it} and σ_u, however, could conceivably reflect the influence of country size. Large countries, one might argue, hold large reserves and likewise experience large disturbances, as measured by the changes in their reserves. To exclude this possibility, we recomputed each of our cross-sectional equations with the addition of national income as a proxy for size. As national income had no explanatory power and did not alter our other results, we doubt that those results are spurious or accidental.

THE DISTRIBUTION OF RESERVES

Our cross-sectional equations cannot be used to detect an absolute "excess" or "deficiency" of gross reserves. But they can be used cautiously to appraise the distribution of reserves—to estimate the gross reserves each nation would hold if it conformed to "average" behavior, and the relative "excess" or "shortfall" in national holdings compared to "average" behavior. Table 3 presents two sets of calculations based on the "best" regression equations we were able to develop. The first three columns of that table list actual and computed reserves for 1957, along with the relative "excess" (+) or "shortfall" (−), the discrepancy between computed and actual holdings. The next three columns list the corresponding figures for 1962, and the final column lists the computed mean disturbance ($\bar{e}$ adjusted for nil or negative p). Computed reserves are derived from the simple regression relationship between R_{it} and σ_u

(the only consistently significant relationship we have identified):

$$R_{57} = 113.74 + 19.88\sigma_u, \quad \bar{R}^2 = .96 \qquad (5a)$$
$$(98.47) \quad (1.15)*$$

$$R_{62} = 548.99 + 25.95\sigma_u, \quad \bar{R}^2 = .87 \qquad (5b)$$
$$(233.07) \quad (2.73)*$$

We do not attach great significance to these computations, but have been impressed by certain regularities:

First, we detect a considerable change in the distribution of reserves between 1957 and 1962. The correlation between the successive relative national positions (between columns 3 and 6 of Table 3) is a mere .49.

Second, we find support for our contention that "new" reserves were not well distributed over this period. Countries displaying large relative deficiencies in 1957 should, perhaps, have made the largest gains in reserves by 1962. In this case, their data would have displayed the largest mean changes, i.e., the largest values for $\bar{e}$. Had this been so, in turn, there should have been a negative correlation between the third and seventh columns of Table 3. In actual fact, there was no such correlation.[24]

Finally, our computations conform to *a priori* expectations in several strategic respects: They reveal a persistent and substantial relative deficiency in British reserves, sharp gains across the period in the relative positions of Japan and Italy, a deterioration in the relative position of Canada resulting from its payments crisis in 1962, and, surprisingly, a very slight relative deficiency for Germany.[25]

---

[24] As one would expect, the sixth and seventh columns of Table 3 were positively correlated, but not very strongly.

[25] It should be noted in this connection that the level and variation in German reserves caused that country to appear as the extreme observation in the cross-sectional analysis, but that the exclusion of Germany from the entire analysis did not change the pattern or significance of our overall findings. Furthermore, alternative estimates of relative "excesses" and "shortfalls" based on equations including per capita income, liabilities, and p (similar to equations 4a and 4b in the text) did not give very different results in respect of distribution. The relative "excess" of Canadian reserves increased on this computation, while the position and pattern of change for several small countries especially Austria, Belgium, and Sweden, was rather different.

MARGARET L. GREENE

Reserve-Asset Preferences Revisited

As DEBATE ON THE INTERNATIONAL monetary system intensifies, it has become appropriate to reexamine official reserve-asset[1] preferences. I do not intend to appraise the present monetary system or to add yet another plan to the already long list of proposed reforms. I do hope, however, to isolate some of the factors influencing the composition of a country's reserve holdings, and to discover whether a consistent pattern of reserve composition emerges for each country studied. Should such a pattern appear, I shall try to uncover the effect, if any, of increased international monetary cooperation and of measures to restrict the U.S. gold outflow on the composition of reserve holdings. This investigation is clearly relevant to discussions of the future of the international monetary system, since an understanding of the way the current system has functioned is prerequisite to meaningful and viable reform.

By the end of the 1950s, the long-run dilemma of the present gold-exchange system had emerged clearly: If the monetary system is to generate sufficient liquidity, the United States must run a balance-of-payments deficit and allow its reserve position to deteriorate. If, on the other hand, the United States protects its reserve position in order to maintain confidence in the dollar, there will be a shortage of reserve assets. As this dilemma was recognized, cooperation among countries at

---

[1] Throughout this essay, "reserve assets" or "reserves" means gold and foreign-exchange holdings of a country's monetary authorities.

the center of the system became increasingly evident. The participating countries have apparently gradually accepted the notion of collective responsibility for maintaining the viability of the existing payments system.

The bilateral agreements made with the United Kingdom at Basle, in March 1961, were among the first bits of evidence suggesting that central banks feel a responsibility to protect major countries suffering from speculative movements of funds. In the same year, a group of central banks organized the London Gold Pool, a cooperative undertaking designed to share the costs and benefits of intervention in the London gold market to stabilize the price of gold. In 1962, central banks initiated the first "swap" arrangements (mutual credit facilities designed to meet specific short-term needs), and the United States began issuing the so-called "Roosa bonds" (U.S. Treasury nonmarketable obligations of more than one year's maturity denominated in either dollars or foreign currencies) in an attempt to reduce conversion of foreign official dollar holdings into gold. Have these developments been paralleled by a reduction in the official demand for gold?

As a preliminary estimate of reserve-asset preferences before 1960, I shall use the results of Peter B. Kenen's study in which he attempts to measure the official demand for gold as a reserve asset.[2] To obtain a standard basis for subsequent comparisons, I shall recalculate Kenen's regression results using revised data and a slightly different period, I, 1957–III, 1960 (designated period I). Then I shall bring the analysis forward into period II (IV, 1960–II, 1964) to test the stability of these relationships in the 1960s and to look for the effects of international monetary cooperation on central-bank gold transactions.

In order to conduct this analysis, I shall make three provisional assumptions, some of them subject to subsequent test: First, each central bank is assumed to act in a perfectly competitive market for gold and reserve-currency assets; or, more simply, the supply of these assets is assumed to be infinitely elastic to the individual central bank. Second, each central bank is assumed to act without taking into consideration the effects of its action on the functioning of the payments system. And third, the level of reserves is assumed to be given at any point in time by the past and present evolution of the country's balance of payments, so that the expression:

$$\text{Reserves} = \text{gold} + \text{foreign exchange}$$

[2] Peter B. Kenen, *Reserve-Asset Preferences of Central Banks and Stability of the Gold Exchange Standard*, Princeton Studies in International Finance, No. 10 (Princeton, New Jersey: Princeton University, 1963).

may be considered a budget constraint, and not merely an identity. Consequently, for any given level of reserves, an increase in gold holdings may occur only at the expense of foreign-exchange holdings.[3,4]

In fact, countries may no longer act independently in a completely competitive market. Furthermore, the closer cooperation among central banks may have given them direct, though limited, control over the level of their own gross reserves and over the composition of other countries' reserves. By initiating a swap arrangement, for example, any central bank may increase its gross reserves. To this extent, the level of reserves may not constitute an exogenous constraint.[5] Furthermore, the proceeds of drawings, designed to meet specific short-term needs, are held exclusively in foreign exchange. Consequently, any central bank participating in a swap may end up holding a larger proportion of its reserves in foreign exchange than it would otherwise.[6] Decisions concerning the level of reserves may still be regarded as logically anterior to decisions concerning the composition of reserves, but the latter may reflect to some extent central-bank cooperation. Put differently, it may be difficult to obtain reliable estimates of desired reserve composition from data on actual reserve composition.

In the second and third sections of this essay, a two-part estimation procedure is used to test certain of these assumptions—to determine whether, in fact, cooperation has resulted in a composition of reserve assets different from that found for the pre-cooperation period. The recalculation of Kenen's equations will yield estimates of reserve-asset preferences before the era of cooperation. If, in fact, central-bank cooperation has not altered observable preferences, the equations explaining gold holdings or gold purchases in period I should be similar to those pertaining to period II (and to the two periods combined). If, instead, the equations for period II differ from those for period I, the assumption

[3] For further discussion of this point see *Ibid.*, p. 35.

[4] At a later point in the study, an additional assumption will be invoked, namely, that all central banks are assumed to be utility maximizers.

[5] However, the magnitude of drawings under swap arrangements is not particularly large in the period under study and, as they were often initiated by the United States, which is excluded from this study, they were nearly exogenous from the standpoint of the countries examined here. Consequently, resort to this assumption is not likely to distort the results. See "International Gold and Dollar Flows," *Federal Reserve Bulletin*, (March 1962); during this period, only two of the countries studied—the United Kingdom and Canada—initiated swap arrangements.

[6] The "additional" foreign exchange held, however, would be fully hedged—as a result of the swap operation—against exchange-rate changes.

Table 1

Reserves, Gold, and Foreign-Exchange Holdings: All
Countries, June 1964 (millions of U.S. dollars)

Country	Reserves	Gold	Foreign Exchange
Belgium	1,789	1,392	397
Canada	2,418	931	1,487
France	4,737	3,451	1,286
Germany	6,681	4,081	2,600
Italy	2,861	2,148	713
Japan	1,757	289	1,468
Netherlands	1,786	1,601	185
Sweden	720	182	539
Switzerland	2,955	2,599	356
United Kingdom	2,605	2,439	266
Total	28,309	19,113	9,247
World exclusive of U.S.	47,054	24,902	22,153

that decisions regarding the composition of reserve assets are taken without regard for their effect on the functioning of the payments system will no longer be valid, and I will infer that cooperation has changed reserve-asset preferences. In particular, I will look for a reduction in the demand for gold during period II.

The final section will reexamine the method of analysis used in measuring reserve-asset preference. First, I will expand the preliminary estimates by introducing interest earnings on foreign-exchange assets and working-balance requirements into the basic equations. In addition, I will present alternative measurements of the official demand for gold. The first of these will use a stock-adjustment hypothesis intended to measure the rate at which governments attain their desired gold holdings. Next, I will try to adopt a hypothesis often employed to describe the composition of investment portfolios: this approach will seek to take account of expected return and risk as determinants of reserve-asset decisions.

I will limit my discussion to the countries comprising the Group of Ten, minus the United States, plus Switzerland.[7] These countries stand at the center of the international monetary system and account for

[7] The countries studied here are Belgium, Canada, France, Germany, Italy, Japan, the Netherlands, Sweden, Switzerland, and the United Kingdom. Of this group, eight countries were in Kenen's group of "continuous" gold changes; Sweden was in Group IV, "frequent changes"; and Japan was in Group III, "infrequent changes." Of the remaining fifty-seven countries which Kenen studied, only seventeen gave him significant regression results.

more than 77 per cent of the world's monetary gold holdings (see Table 1).[8] I will follow Kenen's convention of country-by-country analysis, as national reserve-asset preferences may differ. The period under consideration spans the seven and one-half years, January 1957 through June 1964, thereby eliminating the effects of the unusually large French gold purchases in early 1965 and the U.K. balance-of-payments crisis in the second half of 1964, which could distort the analysis.

The reserve data used throughout this study include official monetary holdings of gold and convertible currencies as recorded in *International Financial Statistics*.[9] Except where otherwise noted, they exclude the IMF gold-tranche position and, before 1959, the EPU position of the European countries. In general, the U.S. dollar is the dominant reserve currency, but other currencies, including sterling, may be included in particular countries' holdings.[10]

This description of the reserve data becomes less reliable after 1960, as it is sometimes difficult to determine how the assets arising from new cooperative credit arrangements are classified. Some countries treat them as reserve assets; others classify them as "other assets" held by the central bank, and some do not explain their practices. It is consequently impossible to obtain truly comparable data for all countries. By and large, however, net claims arising from London Gold Pool operations, forward foreign-exchange market transactions, and bilateral and multi-lateral credit arrangements are apparently excluded from national reserve assets, save for outright holdings of foreign exchange such as those obtained by drawings on the IMF or by activating a swap agreement. On the other hand, U.S. Treasury certificates of indebtedness maturing in less than one year and Roosa bonds payable in U.S. dollars are apparently included in national reserve data.[11]

---

[8] Furthermore, as most of these countries display continuous gold-stock changes, they are likely to yield the most significant statistical results.

[9] International Monetary Fund, Washington: various issues 1957–1964.

[10] Convertible currency holdings usually exclude securities with maturities exceeding twelve months, even though these longer-term holdings may be considered as substitutes for shorter-term securities when making portfolio decisions between gold and foreign exchange. In some instances, gold or foreign-exchange holdings may be underestimated; for example, the Italian and German central banks ran off currency holdings in 1959 and in later years by arranging forward contracts with their domestic commercial banks.

[11] The Roosa bonds payable in foreign currencies were generally classified as "other assets" except by Germany; these issues have therefore been deducted from the published German data to make the German series more consistent with those of other countries.

Proxies for risk have been developed for the last section of this study, using the official-settlements definition of the U.S. deficit,[12] the quarterly U.S. gold loss,[13] and the ratio of total "liquid" dollar liabilities to the U.S. gold stock.[14] The U.S. treasury bill rate[15] has been used as a proxy for interest earnings on foreign-exchange assets.

The notation used herein is as follows:

G = central-bank holdings of gold, end of current quarter, in millions of U.S. dollars

F = central-bank holdings of convertible currencies, end of current quarter, in millions of U.S. dollars

R = central-bank reserves, end of current quarter, in millions of U.S. dollars $(G + F)$

$\bar{F}$ = mean of central-bank holdings of convertible currencies over the whole period

F_{t-1} = central-bank holdings of convertible currencies, end of previous quarter

I_{US} = U.S. treasury bill rate on three-month issues

Z = proxy for risk

Quarterly changes in G and R are denoted by ΔG and ΔR, respectively.

RESERVE-ASSET PREFERENCES
IN 1957–1960

My estimates of the official demand for gold are based on the work of Peter B. Kenen.[16] His basic hypothesis postulates a functional relationship between the demand for gold and the level or change in total reserves.

[12] Report of the Review Commttee for Balance of Payments Statistics, *The Balance of Payments Statistics of the United States* (Washington, D.C.: Government Printing Office, 1965), Table 9.7, p. 121.

[13] U.S., Department of Commerce, *Survey of Current Business* (Washington, D.C.: June 1960 and June 1965).

[14] Board of Governors of the Federal Reserve System, *Federal Reserve Bulletin; Supplement to Banking and Monetary Statistics: Gold;* and *Supplement* to *Banking and Monetary Statistics: International Finance.* (Washington, D.C.: various issues 1957–1964).

[15] *Ibid.*

[16] Kenen analyzed the demand for gold for sixty-one countries from II 1950 through III 1960. The period studied for each country, of course, depended on the availability of data; for some countries, Kenen used a period similar to my period I. See Appendix Table A.

He obtains evidence of a drift toward gold throughout the period he examines (1950–1960), and also obtains regression estimates of the "marginal propensity to hold gold" and of the "marginal propensity to buy (sell) gold out of the current increase (decrease) in total reserves." Whereas these marginal propensities may differ among countries, for individual countries, he felt, they were sufficiently stable throughout the 1950s to furnish reliable estimates.[17] Finally, Kenen analyzed the speculative fourth quarter of 1960 to find evidence of central-bank participation in the "gold rush." He detected a marked shift toward gold among countries at the periphery of the international monetary system, but the major central banks showed considerable restraint in their gold purchases at that critical time.

In my recalculation of Kenen's equations, minor differences appear. I have used the last fifteen quarters of his original period, (I 1957 through III 1960) and have fewer observations for most countries. In addition, the data for several countries have undergone considerable revision.[18] I shall therefore use my calculations, rather than Kenen's, as the standard for comparison of reserve-asset preferences before and after 1960.

In actual fact, my recalculation of Kenen's equations for period I yielded results very similar to his. To compare these two sets of equations, I looked for similar values of the "marginal propensities," of the significant positive trend terms that he discovered and identified as evidence of a drift toward gold,[19] and of the behavior patterns during the speculative period.

The "marginal propensities" derived from my equations were much the

[17] To obtain estimates of the "marginal propensities," Kenen tried several linear regression equations: a gold-stock equation, relating gold holdings to total reserves; a simple gold-transaction equation, relating net gold purchases (sales) to net increases (decreases) in total reserves; a multiple gold-transaction equation, which introduces an adjustment for "excess" foreign-exchange holdings; and a lagged foreign-exchange equation which relates gold transactions solely to foreign-exchange holdings at the start of the quarter. For a fuller discussion of the hypotheses underlying these equations see Kenen, *Reserve-Asset Preferences* (Princeton), pp. 34–56. For a discussion of the statistical properties of these estimates, see M. L. Greene, "Reserve-Asset Preferences of Foreign Central Banks" (New York: Columbia University, International Economics Workshop, 1966), Chapter II.

[18] See Appendix Table A for a comparison of the mean values of gold and total reserves in the two samples. Notice, in this connection, that changes in the definitions of reserve assets have changed the data considerably in Kenen's and my experiments. Compare, for example, the paired mean values for Italian and Japanese gold and reserves.

[19] For discussion of the trend term in these equations see Kenen, *Reserve-Asset Preferences*, (Princeton), p. 59.

Table 2
Best Equations: Period I

Country	Original Equation		Recomputed Equation		Equation	$\bar{R}^2$
	R^2	d	R^2	d		
Belgium	.787	2.26	.8834	2.44	$\Delta G = -2.91 + .8749\Delta R$†,‡	.8744
Canada	.267	1.07	n.s.	n.s.	n.s.	n.s.
France	.446	1.90	.4458	2.18	$\Delta G = 52.35 + .3628(F_{t-1} - \bar{F})$†	.4031
Germany	.129	.76	n.s.	n.s.	n.s.	n.s.
Italy	.744	1.93	.5031	1.15	$\Delta G = 85.66 + .3049\Delta R$† $+ .2865(F_{t-1} - \bar{F})$†	.4203
Japan	n.s.	n.s.	n.s.	n.s.	n.s.	n.s.
Netherlands	.639	1.52	.8399	1.82	$\Delta G = 12.93 + .5730\Delta R$† $+ .4062(F_{t-1} - \bar{F})$†	.8132
Sweden	.212	1.65	.3964	2.75	$\Delta G = -5.21 + .1720\Delta R$† $+ .1769(F_{t-1} - \bar{F})$	.2958
Switzerland	.888	2.37	.9403	2.19	$\Delta G = 2.30 + .8995\Delta R$†,‡ $+ .5572(F_{t-1} - \bar{F})$†	.9304
United Kingdom	.932	1.34	.8852	1.47	$\Delta G = 25.58 + .5361\Delta R$† $+ 1.0119(F_{t-1} - \bar{F})$†,‡	.8660

Note: $\bar{R}^2$ designates the coefficient of determination, adjusted for degrees of freedom; d designates the Durbin-Watson coefficient.
† Statistically significant from zero at the .05 level of significance.
‡ Not statistically significant from unity at the .05 level of significance.

same as those found by Kenen.[20] In addition, the behavior pattern displayed by each country was unchanged. Whenever significant results were obtainable for a country, the equations which best "explained" reserve-asset preferences were the same in both computations[21] (see Table 2). The single most prevalent reserve-asset pattern is described by the multiple gold-transaction equation. This outcome suggests that gold purchases are explained by increases in total reserves or by "excess" holdings of foreign exchange (reflecting previous increases in reserves not converted into gold).

The drift toward gold, however, did not appear in any of the recalculations.[22] This outcome is not necessarily inconsistent with Kenen's results: any drift to gold which Kenen detected may have pertained to observations prior to 1957 and would not be revealed in the recalculation. In addition, the trend term may not attain significance in the recalculation since there are fewer observations in the sample. However, Kenen may be wrong in claiming that there was a drift toward gold. Only two of the ten countries (Germany and Italy) had significant positive trend terms in his own equations; all other trend terms, though positive, were nonsignificant.[23]

An analysis of the speculative quarters again yielded results similar to Kenen's. Using the recalculated equations in Table 2, I extrapolated for two quarters in order to obtain predicted gold purchases (or sales) for those quarters. The actual gold change was never significantly greater than the prediction, and, in two instances, it was significantly smaller than the prediction (see Appendix Table B).

The countries at the center of the monetary system seem to have restrained their gold purchases during the speculative period, thereby relieving some of the pressure on the reserve currencies. Was this restraint temporary—to be compensated for after the speculative period by an increase of gold purchases? Or was the fourth quarter of 1960 the

[20] Kenen, however, obtained significant equations for Canada and Germany, whereas I could not.

[21] The only exception is Sweden, for which the multiple gold-transaction equation is used even though the coefficient for the foreign-exchange adjustment is not significant. Kenen's best equation for Sweden excluded the last argument. See Greene, "Reserve-Asset Preferences" (Columbia), pp. 18–23 *passim* for further discussion of this point.

[22] It should be noted that none of the constant terms in the "best" equations of Table 2 is significant.

[23] Kenen, *Reserve-Asset Preferences* (Princeton), p. 59. In the recalculated equations, three of these trends turned negative. For further discussion of this point, see Greene, "Reserve-Asset Preferences" (Columbia), Chapter II.

beginning of a longer period of restraint, reflecting the monetary authorities' recognition of their joint responsibility for protecting the reserve
curriencies? To answer these questions, it is necessary to extend the
analysis into the 1960s, when new institutional devices for international
monetary cooperation came into being.

RESERVE-ASSET PREFERENCES
IN 1960–1964

The "best" equations discussed in the preceding section reflect reserve-
asset preferences in the late 1950s. If these behavior patterns were maintained in the 1960s, they should reappear in regression results for period II
(or for the two periods combined). Any major change in the "best"
equations, by contrast, would suggest a change in reserve-asset preferences. In particular, if restraint in gold purchases continued after the
first quarter of 1961, these equations should display a decline in either the
time trend or the "marginal propensity" to acquire gold.

When the same "best" equations were estimated for the period IV 1960
to II 1964, the "marginal propensities" were reduced, and the regression
equations were far inferior to those in period I.[24,25] The noticeable
reduction in the values of the "marginal propensities" suggests that the
demand for gold associated with any given rise in reserves was considerably lower in period II than in period I. To measure more precisely the
change in the demand for gold, I used a standardized value for the
change in each country's reserves (the mean of ΔR across periods I and II
together) to obtain a standardized value for each country's gold purchase
$(+)$ or sale $(-)$ in each period. In effect, I assumed that the change of
reserves was equal in both periods,[26] thereby attributing any change in the

[24] All the equations used for period I were also attempted for period II. See Greene,
"Reserve-Asset Preferences" (Columbia), Appendix B, for all equations for each country.

[25] In only one instance was any equation superior to the corresponding equation for
period I, the lagged foreign-exchange equation for Germany:

$$_{\text{II}}\Delta G = 62.23 + 0.2081(F_{t-1} - \bar{F})\dagger, \quad \bar{R}^2 = .8620, \quad d = 1.68$$

Previously, the only significant result for Germany was the gold-stock equation, which
had yielded a very poor fit.

[26] This test also assumes that the standardized value of $(F_{t-1} - \bar{F})$ is zero. If this
assumption does not hold, error may appear and the test may be distorted when applied
to the multiple gold-transaction equations.

Table 3

Comparison of Results Using the Best Estimating Equation: Period I–Period II (millions of U.S. dollars)

Country	$_I \Delta G$	$_{II} \Delta G$	Period with the Larger Gold Increase	Chow Test F Ratio
Belgium	20.80	16.06	I	5.46†
Canada	n.s.	n.s.	n.s.	n.s.
France	162.26	116.52	I	4.03†
Germany	177.05	−33.62	I	7.02†
Italy	102.18	5.20	I	7.93†
Netherlands	29.37	15.30	I	1.82
Sweden	−3.95	.85	II	5.07†
Switzerland	36.75	37.43	II	8.58†
United Kingdom	31.46	−35.79	I	19.24†
Total	555.92	121.95	I	

Note: In this table and all following tables, Japan has been deleted, as no significant results were obtained.

† Significantly greater than unity at the .05 level of significance.

demand for gold to a change in the "marginal propensity to buy gold" or in the trend term. This test showed that the demand for gold was distinctly lower in the second period (see Table 3).[27] Indeed, in only two of eight cases did the "best" equation imply a larger demand for gold in period II. Furthermore, the eight-country total of quarterly gold purchases based on the standardized ΔR was greater for period I than for period II.

These results suggest that there was a reduction in the demand for gold and, by implication, that the equations for the two periods differ systematically. The Chow test for equality of β coefficients confirms this supposition.[28] Of the eight "best" equations, seven displayed highly significant F ratios (see Table 3).

[27] The equations used in this table are the "best" equations for period I; only in the case of Germany was the "best" equation for period II used.

[28] This procedure postulates and tests the null hypothesis that the regression equation for the full period (I 1957–II 1964) estimates the "true" relationship. The F ratio is used to estimate the reduction in the sum of squared residuals resulting from the use of two separate equations and will not be significant if the two equations do not differ from the full-period equation. Gregory C. Chow, "Tests of Equality between Sets of Coefficients in Two Linear Regressions," *Econometrica*, XXVIII (July, 1960), pp. 591–605; and John Johnston, *Econometric Methods* (New York: McGraw-Hill Book Co., 1963), pp. 136–8.

Table 4

Comparison of Full-Period Results: Simple Gold-Transaction Equation

| | Period I | | Periods I and II | | | | | | | | | |
| | | | Without Dummy | | With Additive Dummy | | | | With Multiplicative Dummy | | | |
Country	$\bar{R}_1^2$	d_1	$\bar{R}^2$	d	$\bar{R}^2$	d	Sign of D'	Sig.	$\bar{R}^2$	d	Sign of $b_{\Delta R_A} - b_{\Delta R_B}$	Sig.
Belgium	.8744	2.44	.5696	1.36	.5559	1.37	−		.6748	1.68	+	†
Canada	n.s.	‡	n.s.	‡	n.s.	‡	++		n.s.	‡	++	
France	n.s.	‡	.1047	2.00	n.s.	‡	++		n.s.	‡	++	
Germany	n.s.	‡	n.s.	‡	n.s.	‡	++		n.s.	‡	++	
Italy	n.s.	‡	.2666	1.56	.4708	1.78	−	†	.3285	1.66	+	
Netherlands	.6207	1.48	.4807	1.68	.4622	1.66	−		.5293	1.60	+	
Sweden	n.s.	‡	n.s.	‡	.2245	2.37	+	†	n.s.	‡	++	
Switzerland	.9055	3.02	.7773	2.21	.7699	2.22	−		.7771	2.29	+	
United Kingdom	.4379	2.29	n.s.	‡	n.s.	++			.3069	2.12	+	†

Notes: Number of significant additive dummy variables: 2. Number of significant differences between multiplicative dummy coefficients: 2.
† Denotes a significant additive dummy or a significant difference between multiplicative dummy coefficients.
‡ Denotes a statistic pertaining to a nonsignificant equation.

Since only four countries yielded significant gold-transaction equations, no attempt was made to choose "best" equations for period II. Instead, all the gold transaction equations were reestimated for the full period, I 1957 to II 1964.[29] One would expect the full-period equations to be less successful than those for period I, and, indeed, these equations explained less of the variation in gold purchases (as measured by $\bar{R}^2$; see Table 4).

In order to impound the difference between periods and thereby improve the full-period equations, two dummy devices were used in subsequent computations. An additive dummy variable, D', was introduced, with $D' = 0$ for I 1957–III 1960, and $D' = 1$ for IV 1960–II 1964. Then, a multiplicative dummy was introduced in lieu of D':

$$\Delta G = b_t + b_{\Delta R_A}(\Delta R_A) + b_{\Delta R_B}(\Delta R_B), \qquad \Delta R_A = \Delta R \text{ for I 1957–III 1960 and zero thereafter,}$$

$$\Delta R_B = 0 \text{ for I 1957–III 1960 and } \Delta R \text{ thereafter}$$

The results obtained using the multiplicative dummy were always consistent with those obtained using the additive dummy. Whenever D' was positive, $b_{\Delta R_A} < b_{\Delta R_B}$; whenever D' was negative, $b_{\Delta R_A} > b_{\Delta R_B}$. In cases where the Chow test had been significant, moreover, this technique improved the full-period equations.

The results of all full-period gold-transaction equations are summarized in Tables 4 to 6.

The full-period simple gold-transaction equations were as good as, or better than, the equations obtained for period II alone; but in only two cases were they superior to the equations for period I alone. Autocorrelation was slightly reduced in the full-period equations; however, the regression coefficients were noticeably smaller than those obtained for period I.[30] The additive dummy was usually negative, reflecting a decline in gold purchases throughout period II. But the introduction of D' into this equation did not usually improve the fit (except in those cases, mentioned above, where the Chow test was significant). The use of the multiplicative dummy gave values of $b_{\Delta R_A}$ similar to those of the marginal propensities to buy gold in the period I equations, and $b\Delta_{R_A}$ always exceeded $b_{\Delta R_B}$. However, only two countries displayed a significant difference between the two marginal propensities.

[29] For all gold-stock and gold-transaction equations, see Greene, "Reserve-Asset Preferences" (Columbia), Appendix B.

[30] For Italy, however, $b_{\Delta R}$ increased.

Table 5

Comparison of Full-Period Results: Multiple Gold-Transaction Equation

Country	Period I		Periods I and II										
			Without Dummy		With Additive Dummy				With Multiplicative Dummy			
	$\bar{R}_I^2$	d_I	$\bar{R}^2$	d	$\bar{R}^2$	d	Sign of D'	Sig.	$\bar{R}^2$	d	Sign of $_m{}^b\Delta R_A - {}_m{}^b\Delta R_B$	Sig.
Belgium	.8734	2.19	.5608	1.33	.6584	1.42	−		.6923	1.79	+	†
Canada	n.s.	‡	n.s.	‡	n.s.	‡	‡	†	n.s.	‡	‡	
France	.4116	2.48	.3109	2.17	.3206	2.19	−		.3044	2.29	+	
Germany	n.s.	‡	n.s.	‡	.3100	.97	−	†	n.s.	‡	‡	
Italy	.4203	1.15	.4995	1.35	.6592	1.74	−		.5423	1.51	+	
Netherlands	.8132	1.82	.6893	1.74	.6871	1.72	−	†	.6957	1.70	+	
Sweden	.2958	2.75	n.s.	‡	.2488	2.42	+		.2973	2.45	+	
Switzerland	.9304	2.19	.8109	1.86	.8496	1.90	−	†	.8136	2.00	+	
United Kingdom	.8660	1.47	.3147	1.44	.3332	1.48	−		.4928	1.84	+	†

Notes: Number of significant additive dummy variables: 4. Number of significant differences between multiplicative dummy coefficients: 2.
† Denotes a significant additive dummy or a significant difference between multiplicative dummy coefficients.
‡ Denotes a statistic pertaining to a nonsignificant equation.

Table 6

Comparison of Full-Period Results: Lagged Foreign-Exchange Equation

| | Period I | | Periods I and II | | | | | |
| | | | Without Dummy | | With Additive Dummy | | | |
Country	$\bar{R}_I^2$	d_I	$\bar{R}^2$	d	$\bar{R}^2$	d	Sign of D'	Sig.
Belgium	n.s.	‡	n.s.	‡	n.s.	‡	‡	
Canada	n.s.	‡	.1620	2.04	.1820	2.06	—	
France	.4031	2.18	.2764	1.94	.2635	1.91	—	
Germany	n.s.	‡	n.s.	‡	.3243	1.08	—	†
Italy	n.s.	‡	.1665	.90	.5308	1.46	—	†
Netherlands	.4619	1.66	.2120	1.51	.2394	1.64	—	
Sweden	n.s.	‡	.1935	2.13	.1833	2.24	+	
Switzerland	n.s.	‡	n.s.	‡	n.s.	‡	‡	
United Kingdom	.4733	2.25	.1968	1.39	.2330	1.49	—	

Note: Number of significant dummy variables: 2.

† Denotes a significant dummy.

‡ Denotes a statistic pertaining to a nonsignificant equation.

In general, the full-period multiple gold-transaction equation was also inferior to that obtained for period I alone, and autocorrelation apparently increased in the full-period equations. Again, the values of $_mb_{\Delta R}$ were lower than in period I. The additive dummy was significantly negative in four cases and brought the estimates of $b_{\Delta R}$ closer to those obtained for period I alone. The multiplicative dummy was also applied, and again $b_{\Delta R_A} > b_{\Delta R_B}$; as before, however, the difference was significant for only two countries.

The full-period lagged foreign-exchange equations were not only inferior to the equations in period I, but also to the significant equations in period II. The German example is most striking; while giving highly significant results for period II alone, this equation was not significant for the full period. The additive dummy was significant in only two cases (and negative in both).

A full-period "best" equation was chosen for each country and compared with the equation for period I to see if a change in reserve-asset composition could be detected.[31] These equations are arrayed in Table 7.

[31] In choosing the "best" equation here and hereafter, I have used a criterion slightly different from Kenen's. He excluded any equation that contained a nonsignificant variable. But in a multiple regression equation, multicollinearity may reduce the significance of a coefficient, even though the inclusion of the corresponding variable helps to explain the variation in the dependent variable. Consequently, I will choose as a "best" equation an equation which includes a nonsignificant variable if the inclusion of that variable increases the coefficient of determination, adjusted for degrees of freedom.

Table 7

Full Period: Best Equations without Dummy Variables

Country	Equation	$\bar{R}^2$	d
Belgium	$\Delta G = -1.45 + .6280\Delta R\dagger$	.5696	1.36
Canada	$\Delta G = -4.12 + .0726(F_{t-1} - \bar{F})\dagger$	.1620	2.04
France	$\Delta G = 68.30\dagger + .1712\Delta R + .1280(F_{t-1} - \bar{F})\dagger$	.3109	2.17
Germany	no significant equation		
Italy	$\Delta G = 40.29 + .3358\Delta R\dagger + .3073(F_{t-1} - \bar{F})\dagger$	.4995	1.34
Japan	no significant equation		
Netherlands	$\Delta G = 11.45 + .5259\Delta R\dagger + .3802(F_{t-1} - \bar{F})\dagger$	.6893	1.74
Sweden	$\Delta G = -3.11 + .0781\Delta R + .0269(F_{t-1} - \bar{F})\dagger$	.2759	2.42
Switzerland	$\Delta G = 4.12 + .7764\Delta R\dagger + .3762(F_{t-1} - \bar{F})\dagger$	.8109	1.86
United Kingdom	$\Delta G = 16.07 + .2817\Delta R\dagger + .3785(F_{t-1} - \bar{F})\dagger$	.3147	1.44

Note: None of the coefficients was statistically equal to unity at the .05 level of significance.

† Statistically different from zero at the .05 level of significance.

Whereas the "best" full-period equations were usually inferior to those for period I, the basic preference pattern displayed by each country was largely unchanged. The full-period equations (without dummies) were similar in form to those of period I, though $\bar{R}^2$ and the Durbin-Watson statistic was slightly inferior in most cases. It was still impossible to obtain significant results for Japan and Germany. The simple gold-transaction equation continued to give best results for Belgium; the multiple gold-transaction equation gave best results for six other countries.

In some cases, however, the "best" full-period equation was of different form. For the first time, Canada yielded significant results (a lagged foreign exchange equation); and, for France, the best equation was the multiple gold-transaction equation, rather than the lagged foreign-exchange equation.

For six of the ten countries, one or another dummy device sufficiently improved the regression results to provide the "best" equation for the full period (see Table 8).[32] Whenever a dummy was used, moreover, it implied a considerable decline in official gold purchases. The additive

[32] A dummy variable which excludes rather than includes the speculative quarters improved the results for France and the United Kingdom. In these equations:

$$D'' = 1 \text{ for II } 1961\text{--II } 1964, \quad \text{zero elsewhere}$$
$$\Delta R_B' = \Delta R \text{ for II } 1961\text{--II } 1964, \quad \text{zero elsewhere}$$
$$\Delta R_A' = \Delta R \text{ for I } 1957\text{--I } 1961, \quad \text{zero elsewhere}$$

These results suggest that the reduction in gold purchases did not take place until after the speculative period.

dummy, D' (or D'' for France), was always negative, and served to offset the time trend when it reappeared for the first period. The multiplicative dummy gave $b_{\Delta R_B} < b_{\Delta R_A}$, a decline in the "marginal propensity to buy gold."

Although the devices provided new equations, the underlying preference patterns remained the same. In most cases, the inclusion of the dummy variables merely improved the "best" equation in Table 7; it did not suggest an alternative form. Two countries showed changes in their preference patterns; but neither involved a radical departure from previous results. For Belgium, the foreign-exchange argument $(F_{t-1} - \bar{F})$ and, for Germany, the lagged foreign-exchange equation became significant. The single most prevalent reserve-asset pattern in the final full-period equations is again described by the multiple gold-transaction equation. In the final full-period equations (shown in Tables 7 and 8),

Table 8

Full Period: Best Estimating Equations with Significant Dummy Arguments

Country	Equation	$\bar{R}^2$	d
Belgium	$\Delta G = 3.15 + .8945\Delta R_A$†·‡ $+ .3118\Delta R_B$† $+ .0661(F_{t-1} - \bar{F})$	.6923	1.79
Canada	(See Table 7)		
France	$\Delta G = 124.84$† $+ .2290\Delta R$† $+ .2512(F_{t-1} - \bar{F})$† $- 136.5227D''$†	.4151	2.30
Germany	$\Delta G = 196.27$† $+ .1724(F_{t-1} - \bar{F})$† $- 212.2422D'$†	.3243	1.08
Italy	$\Delta G = 89.42 + .2299\Delta R$† $+ .2727(F_{t-1} - \bar{F})$† $- 86.4412D'$†	.6592	1.74
Japan	no significant equation		
Netherlands	(See Table 7)		
Sweden	$\Delta G = -2.82 + .1473\Delta R_A$† $+ .0408\Delta R_B + .0274(F_{t-1} - \bar{F})$†	.2973	2.45
Switzerland	$\Delta G = 38.38 + .8169\Delta R$† $+ .7046(F_{t-1} - \bar{F})$† $- 67.3580D'$†	.8496	1.90
United Kingdom	$\Delta G = -2.76 + .6212\Delta R_A'$† $- .1092\Delta R_B' + .3079(F_{t-1} - \bar{F})$†	.5372	1.91

Note: A dummy variable which excludes rather than includes the speculative quarters improved the results for France and the United Kingdom. In these equations:

$$D'' = 1 \text{ for II } 1961\text{–II } 1964, \text{ and zero elsewhere}$$
$$\Delta R_B' = \Delta R \text{ for II } 1961\text{–II } 1964, \text{ zero elsewhere}$$
$$\Delta R_A' = \Delta R \text{ for I } 1957\text{–I } 1961, \text{ zero elsewhere}$$

It suggests that the reduction in gold purchases did not take place until after the speculative period.

† Statistically different from zero at the .05 level of significance.

‡ Not statistically different from unity at the .05 level of significance.

Table 9
Full Period: Residual Analysis

Country	Best Estimating Equations without Dummy Variables					Best Estimating Equations with Dummy Variables				
	Variance of Residuals			Coefficient of Determination†		Variance of Residuals			Coefficient of Determination†	
	$\sigma^2_{u_I}$	$\sigma^2_{u_{II}}$	$F = \sigma^2_{u_I}/\sigma^2_{u_{II}}$	$\bar{R}^2_I$	$\bar{R}^2_{II}$	$\sigma^2_{u_I}$	$\sigma^2_{u_{II}}$	$F = \sigma^2_{u_I}/\sigma^2_{u_{II}}$	$\bar{R}^2_I$	$\bar{R}^2_{II}$
Belgium	1,001.69	1,780.37	1.78	.7216	.2405	595.28	1,242.31	2.09	.8008	.3809
Canada	727.34	5,194.86	7.14‡	nil	.2210					
France	13,826.90	4,166.49	.30‡	nil	.1802	10,994.82	3,671.71	.33‡	.0398	.2148
Germany		no significant equation				13,312.87	2,942.33	.22‡	.0994	.5716
Italy	4,690.49	4,835.63	1.03	.5254	.0373	3,814.00	2,532.07	.66	.5749	.4521
Japan		no significant equation								
Netherlands	552.05	1,027.08	1.86	.7757	.4098					
Sweden	70.91	11.90	.17‡	.1062	.2969	67.97	9.66	.14‡	.2224	.3799
Switzerland	761.45	4,889.27	6.42‡	.7441	.7415	426.72	3,878.16	9.09‡	.8420	.7771
United Kingdom	28,299.68	34,208.38	1.21	.4688	nil	22,798.96	18,433.42	.81	.5720	.2806

† $\bar{R}^2_I$ and R^2_{II} do not refer to the separate subperiod equations, but denote coefficients of determination computed from the residuals of the full-period equations, for period I and period II separately.
‡ Statistically significant at the .05 level of significance.

the use of dummy arguments restored the marginal propensities, $b_{\Delta R}$ and $b_{\Delta R_A}$, to the values obtained for period I. Furthermore, positive and significant time trends reappeared for two countries, giving results more similar to Kenen's than I had previously obtained.[33] However, there is still little evidence of a drift toward gold: in both cases in which the trend reappeared, it is confined to period I (being offset in period II by the coefficient of D'). In the remaining seven equations, four trend terms were positive and three were negative.

These final, full-period results did not completely account for differences between the two periods. A breakdown of the residual variance indicates heteroscedasticity in half the equations (see Table 9). Also, in every case (except Italy) where there was a significant equation for period I, $\bar{R}^2$ was greater in period I than in the full period. Notice, however, that more of the Durbin-Watson statistics were acceptable in the full period than in period I alone, and that significant relationships were finally obtained for Germany and Canada.

For almost every country, certain reserve-asset preference patterns seem to dominate, regardless of period. Perhaps this finding is spurious; perhaps the full-period equations merely reflect the reserve-asset patterns prevailing in period I. There is some slight evidence that this is, in fact, the case. When significant equations were obtained for period I, the percentage of first-period variation explained by the best full-period equation was ordinarily greater than the percentage of second-period variation explained. When the dummy devices were introduced, the results were improved for period II, but were never as good as for period I (see Table 9). For four countries, however, the best full-period equation explained more of period II gold purchases than of period I gold purchases.[34] And, for all of the final full-period equations shown in Table 8, the adjusted coefficients of determination (shown in Table 9) computed separately for period II were always significant. These results suggest that the reserve-asset patterns prevailing in period I were carried over, albeit weakly, into period II.

The fact that one form of the gold-transaction equation tends to explain each country's reserve-asset preferences throughout the period suggests a fair degree of stability in those preference patterns. The

[33] However, Kenen obtained positive significant trend terms for Germany and Italy, whereas I obtained them for Germany and France.

[34] This result was expected for Canada and Germany, as significant results were not obtained for period I.

deterioration in goodness of fit in the second period may, however, indicate that certain of the assumptions underlying the analysis are less appropriate to the second period than to the first. Indeed, the assumption that central banks act without taking into account the effects of their policies on the payments system appears particularly suspect. In almost every case, the regression results suggest a noticeable reduction in the demand for gold after III 1960, manifest as a linear shift in the regression equation or a reduction in the marginal propensity.[35]

This outcome, in effect, suggests that the fourth quarter of 1960 was the beginning of a sustained period of restraint in gold purchases, reflecting the monetary authorities' recognition of their joint responsibility for maintaining the viability of the international monetary system.

RESERVE-ASSET PREFERENCES: ALTERNATIVE APPROACHES

The final full-period results indicate that this kind of regression analysis—particularly the multiple gold-transaction equation—is a useful device for describing reserve-asset composition. The relationships suggested a fair degree of stability in reserve-asset composition over time, and served to measure the effect of U.S. efforts to reduce foreign official gold purchases. However, the formulation is mechanistic, not economic. In Kenen's original study and in its reexamination here, any change in reserve-asset preferences appeared as a change in the marginal propensity to buy gold or in the time trend. Furthermore, the device used to explain adjustments for "excess" foreign exchange was somewhat simplistic. In brief, no attempt was made to explain central-bank reserve-asset preference in terms of economic arguments such as the costs and risks of holding a particular kind of reserve asset.

In this section I will summarize other experiments performed to obtain a more adequate explanation of reserve-asset preferences. These experiments are exploratory, and are intended to show where further research and refinement would most profitably begin.

I will start by expanding the "best" equations obtained in the preceding

[35] It is probable, moreover, that this reduction of demand has been underestimated. To the extent that the Roosa bonds are considered reserve assets by the central banks holding them, gold acquisitions in period II were even smaller, relative to total reserve acquisitions, than shown by the equations.

sections to include variables representing working-balance requirements and the expected return on foreign-exchange assets. It is, of course, impossible to obtain actual data corresponding to these variables; we must be content with proxies. But these proxies should take on the expected sign and improve the quality of the equations. Finally, I will use the proxies in a more sophisticated analysis of reserve-asset preferences. These refined hypotheses, like those used above, seek to explain gold purchases, and must be appraised from this standpoint.

Since total reserves include both working balances of foreign exchange and portfolio assets, any analysis of reserve-asset preferences should use these variables as arguments explaining reserve-asset choices. Kenen tried to introduce a working-balance term into his multiple gold-transaction equation. He assumed that desired working balances equaled the mean value of foreign-exchange holdings, $\bar{F}$. By introducing the term $(F_{t-1} - \bar{F})$, he hoped to measure the rate at which central banks converted to gold previous increases in reserves held as foreign exchange. His procedure assumes that working-balance requirements are constant throughout the period and equal to the mean of *all* foreign-exchange holdings. These assumptions seem somewhat implausible.

It seems more reasonable to assume that these requirements are directly related to the variability in a country's reserve position.[36] Therefore, as a first approximation, I developed an estimate of working balances using a two-year (twenty-four-month) moving standard deviation of the monthly change in reserves.[37] This estimate is designated $K\hat{S}$, where $\hat{S}$ represents the standard deviation of the change in reserves, and K, the lower-tail normal deviate corresponding to a chosen probability of depleting a given working balance.[38]

When the term $(F_{t-1} - K\hat{S})$ was substituted for $(F_{t-1} - \bar{F})$ to represent the discrepancy between actual foreign-exchange holdings and desired working balances, the quality of the "best" equations changed little

[36] Recorded changes in reserves, however, are not an accurate estimate of past disturbances. Changes in domestic policy may offset such disturbances, or central banks may have operated in the exchange market when there was no apparent disturbance. Yet, reserve changes are the best estimator available, and would probably reflect any disturbance requiring official intervention. Since these data can only show net changes in each month, much of the relevant variation may be concealed and working-balance needs may be understated.

[37] See Greene, "Reserve-Asset Preferences" (Columbia), pp. 54–56, for a fuller discussion of these points.

[38] For example, if the central bank wants no more than one chance in twenty of depleting the working balance, $K = 1.645$, and the working balance would be $1.645\hat{S}$.

Table 10

Full Period: Best Estimating Equations with Working-Balance Estimates

Country	Equation with $\bar{F}$		Equation with Working-Balance Estimate			
	$\bar{R}^2$	d	Equation	Value of K	$\bar{R}^2$	d
Belgium	.6923	1.79	$\Delta G = -6.46 + .8913\Delta R_A + .3173\Delta R_B + .0596(F_{t-1} - K\hat{S}_t)$ (8.71) (.1134)† (.1244)† (.0409)	1.645	.6878	1.78
Canada	.1620	2.04	$\Delta G = -105.08 + .1027(F_{t-1} - K\hat{S}_t)$ (34.93)† (.0346)†	2.33	.2118	2.09
France	.4151	2.03	$\Delta G = 10.63 + .2773\Delta R + .2857(F_{t-1} - K\hat{S}_t) - 188.5064D''$ (24.3848) (.1082)† (.0774)† (71.2601)†	1.645	.3890	2.14
Germany	.3243	1.08	$\Delta G = -182.41 + .2124(F_{t-1} - K\hat{S}_t) - 257.5521D'$ (55.4005)† (.0398)† (53.9838)†	2.33	.4799	1.45
Italy	.6592	1.74	$\Delta G = -146.48 + .2263\Delta R + .2760(F_{t-1} - K\hat{S}_t) - 86.8832D'$ (64.6553)† (.0690)† (.0699)† (23.4834)†	1.645	.6564	1.71
Netherlands	.6893	1.74	$\Delta G = -32.52 + .5362\Delta R + .3349(F_{t-1} - K\hat{S}_t)$ (12.3341)† (.0832)† (.0852)†	1.645	.6574	1.68
Sweden	.2973	2.45	$\Delta G = -12.94 + .1501\Delta R_A + .0464\Delta R_B + .0275(F_{t-1} - K\hat{S}_t)$ (3.4806)† (.0639)† (.0468) (.0092)†	1.645	.2913	2.44
Switzerland	.8496	1.90	$\Delta G = -49.71 + .8169\Delta R + .6962(F_{t-1} - K\hat{S}_t) - 10.8001D'$ (17.4038)† (.0605)† (.1568)† (17.3335)	1.645	.8641	1.87
United Kingdom	.5372	1.91	$\Delta G = -58.32 + .6035\Delta R_A' - .0818\Delta R_B' + .3650(F_{t-1} - K\hat{S}_t)$ (32.5786) (.1371)† (.1450) (.1037)†	2.33	.5267	1.82

† Statistically different from zero at the .05 level of significance.

(see Table 10).[39] But, in cases where the "best" equation suggested that the demand for foreign exchange was solely for working-balance purposes (Canada and Germany), $\bar{R}^2$ increased considerably. These results suggest that $K\hat{S}$ was at least as good as (and perhaps better than) F as an approximation to working balances. If this conclusion is valid, however, previous conclusions regarding the trend terms have to be reconsidered. When $K\hat{S}$ is introduced in lieu of F, most of the trend terms turn negative and significant, rather than positive or nonsignificant as before. This may mean that central-bank cooperation did not reverse a trend toward gold, but merely exaggerated a movement away from gold that had already begun in the 1950s.

This first amendment does not involve any basic change in the analysis. A fall in the demand for gold must still appear as a decline in the marginal propensity to buy gold or in the time trend. Yet any such decline may simply reflect an increase in the cost of holding gold relative to foreign exchange, rather than a change in the underlying reserve-asset preferences. If, for instance, interest earnings on convertible-currency assets were to increase, the opportunity cost of holding gold would rise and central-bank gold purchases might be expected to decline.

To see if reserve-asset choices are sensitive to interest rates, I entered the U.S. treasury bill rate (a proxy for interest earnings on dollar balances) into the "best" equation for each country.[40] Interest sensitivity would imply a negative weight for I_{US} in those equations. In fact, I_{US} showed a negative (although not significant) weight for eight of the nine countries (see Table 11). The chances of this happening if I_{US} has no weight are small (the observed result would occur only 18 times in 1,000). Hence, these results provide evidence of interest sensitivity.[41]

[39] To make the regression estimate, I had to assign arbitrary values to K, using three familiar normal variates: 1.645, corresponding to 95 per cent; 1.96, corresponding to 97.5 per cent; and 2.33, corresponding to 99 per cent.

[40] The three-month bill rate has certain deficiencies as a proxy, since it does not take account of changes in the tax treatment of interest earned by foreign central banks or changes in Regulation Q governing time-deposit rates. Such changes, designed to encourage central banks to hold more dollars, occurred in period II. In 1961 income from U.S. government securities held by foreign central banks was exempt from Federal income tax so as to make the tax treatment of government securities similar to that of bank deposits and bank acceptances. On October 15, 1962, the Federal Reserve Act and the Federal Deposit Insurance Act were amended to exempt deposits of foreign central banks from the regulated rates of interest paid on time deposits.

[41] If gold purchases themselves appear sensitive to changes in the interest rate, the choice among foreign-exchange assets would probably show an even greater responsiveness to interest differentials.

Table 11

Full Period: Best Estimating Equations with Interest Rate

Country	Equation without I_{US}		Equation	Equation with I_{US}	
	$\bar{R}^2$	d		$\bar{R}^2$	d
Belgium	.6923	1.79	$\Delta G = 56.0285 + .7725\Delta R_A + .2834\Delta R_B - 18.1483(I_{US})$ (29.0462) (.1181)† (.1238) (9.5586)	.7034	1.67
Canada	.1620	2.04	$\Delta G = 25.24 + .0773(F_{t-1} - \bar{F}) - 10.2259(I_{US})$ (50.2178) (.0295)† (16.1115)	.1437	2.06
France	.4151	2.30	$\Delta G = 266.91 + .1877\Delta R + .3163(F_{t-1} - \bar{F}) - 41.2626(I_{US}) - 174.3949D''_{ps}$ (79.9164)† (.1077) (.0799)† (31.1052) (67.7103)†	.4317	2.38
Germany	.3243	1.08	$\Delta G = 128.50 + .1826(F_{t-1} - \bar{F}) + 25.4568(I_{US}) - 222.5701D^1$ (123.2673) (.0446)† (25.4403) (60.7377)†	.3243	1.13
Italy	.6592	1.74	$\Delta G = 140.62 + .2113\Delta R + .2954(F_{t-1} - \bar{F}) - 17.0287(I_{US}) - 89.3612D'$ (77.9148) (.0716)† (.0725)† (17.8097) (23.6382)†	.6580	1.74
Netherlands	.6893	1.74	$\Delta G = 51.30 + .4763\Delta R + .3552(F_{t-1} - \bar{F}) + .0285(F_{t-1} - \bar{F}) - 13.4120(I_{US})$ (33.8904) (.0835)† (.0848)† (8.5812)	.7050	1.86
Sweden	.2973	2.45	$\Delta G = 2.65 + .1197\Delta R_A + .0294\Delta R_B + .0285(F_{t-1} - \bar{F}) - 1.8684(I_{US})$ (6.4471) (.0701) (.0483) (.0091) (1.9791)	.2944	2.52
Switzerland	.8496	1.90	$\Delta G = 62.22 + .8052\Delta R + .6726(F_{t-1} - \bar{F}) - 8.6031(I_{US}) - 64.7807D'$ (58.6259) (.0677)† (.1907)† (14.8971) (24.5880)†	.8457	1.94
United Kingdom	.5372	1.91	$\Delta G = 163.49 + .5466\Delta R_A' - .1420\Delta R_B' + .2573(F_{t-1} - \bar{F}) - 55.3564(I_{US})$ (176.12) (.1483)† (.1446) (.1033)† (50.6706)	.5406	1.86

† Statistically different from zero at the .05 level of significance.

These experiments suggest that $K\hat{S}$ and I_{US} are adequate proxies for foreign-exchange working balances and for the opportunity cost of holding gold. Therefore, they are used in subsequent experiments designed to explain reserve-asset composition.

In all the previous experiments it has been assumed that any desired adjustment in reserve composition could be completely accomplished within the quarter. This assumption is probably unjustified, and is even less valid for the 1960s than for the earlier period. Although our experiments indicate that reserve-asset preferences have not changed over time, the deterioration of the goodness of fit in period II suggests that central banks did not substitute gold for foreign exchanges as readily in period II as in period I. One possible explanation of this phenomenon is that central banks did not promptly attain their desired positions in period II. A "stock-adjustment model" that deals explicitly with disequilibrium positions might therefore be more appropriate than the simple models used thus far. With this approach, gold purchases during the quarter are treated as an incomplete adjustment to the desired levels. In other words:

$$\Delta G_t = G_t - G_{t-1} = \gamma(\hat{G}_t - G_{t-1})$$

where γ signifies the rate of adjustment, $\hat{G}_t$, the desired level of gold holdings, and $0 < (1 - \gamma) < 1$. To apply this approach, $\hat{G}_t$ will be treated as a linear function of reserves, the interest rate, a time trend, dummy arguments, and working-balance requirements:

$$\hat{G}_t = \alpha_0 + \alpha_1 R + \alpha_2 T + \alpha_3 I_{\mathrm{US}} + \alpha_4 D + \alpha_5 (F_{t-1} - K\hat{S})$$

Therefore:

$$G_t = \gamma\alpha_0 + \gamma\alpha_1 R + \gamma\alpha_2 T + \gamma\alpha_3 I_{\mathrm{US}} + \gamma\alpha_4 D \\ + \gamma\alpha_5 (F_{t-1} - K\hat{S}) + (1 - \gamma)G_{t-1}$$

The best stock-adjustment equations for each country are shown in Table 12, with summary statistics pertaining to the final full-period equations of the previous section.[42] Satisfactory results were obtained for every country except Canada and Japan. The outcome of the stock-adjustment analysis confirms some of the previous conclusions of this paper. The demand for gold is related to the level or change in total

[42] But pairwise comparisons of these statistics may not be meaningful. Since a first-order autoregressive term appears in the stock-adjustment equation, $\bar{R}^2$ and the Durbin-Watson statistic should be higher in those equations. Furthermore, the autoregressive argument so much dominates the results that a high $\bar{R}^2$ may no longer be evidence of a "good" equation.

Table 12

Full Period: Best Estimating Stock-Adjustment Equations

Country	Final Full-Period Equation		Stock-Adjustment Equation		
	$\bar{R}^2$	d	Equation	$\bar{R}^2$	d
Belgium	.6923	1.79	$G = 101.4025 + .5207R - 28.9990I_{US} - 131.0948D + .4299G_{t-1}$ $\quad (56.8926) \quad (.1005)\dagger \quad (10.7503)\dagger \quad (32.9918)\dagger \quad (.1101)\dagger$	.9532	1.78
Canada	.1620	2.04	no satisfactory equation		
France	.4151	2.30	$G = 37.9137 + .2585R - 7.7578I_{US} + .6624G_{t-1}$ $\quad (76.2270) \quad (.0686)\dagger \quad (25.7509) \quad (.1039)\dagger$	.9905	2.12
Germany	.3243	1.08	$G = 502.9065 + 7.8787T + .0234R + .1096(F_{t-1} - K\hat{S})\ddagger + .7325G_{t-1}$ $\quad (144.3724)\dagger \quad (5.4538) \quad (.0426) \quad (.0441)\dagger \quad (.0596)\dagger$	.9910	1.98
Italy	.6592	1.74	$G = -188.0353 - 1.2018T + .2968R - 2.0913I_{US} + .6813G_{t-1}$ $\quad (84.2786)\dagger \quad (3.9575) \quad (.0607)\dagger \quad (19.0866) \quad (.0837)\dagger$	.9915	1.49
Netherlands	.6893	1.74	$G = -10.3547 + .4183R - 13.3185I_{US} + .5629G_{t-1}$ $\quad (37.2856) \quad (.0603)\dagger \quad (8.5485) \quad (.0629)\dagger$	.9919	1.79
Sweden	.2973	2.45	$G = 33.8416 - .6180T + .0518R - .6060I_{US} - 3.1946D + .7259G_{t-1}$ $\quad (16.1485) \quad (.4985) \quad (.0274) \quad (2.1572) \quad (5.3759) \quad (.0986)\dagger$	.9248	2.55
Switzerland	.8496	1.90	$G = 20.9880 + 3.5505T + .7696R - 12.1964I_{US} - 83.6062D + .1647G_{t-1}$ $\quad (193.7221) \quad (3.6955) \quad (.0909)\dagger \quad (16.1881) \quad (54.6043) \quad (.0857)\dagger$	.9804	1.87
United Kingdom	.5372	1.91	$G = 729.1924 + 20.6818T + .1687R + 159.3327I_{US} - 363.7724 + .6279G_{t-1}$ $\quad (358.3778) \quad (8.2445)\dagger \quad (.1083) \quad (58.8522)\dagger \quad (132.6830)\dagger \quad (.1075)\dagger$	.7828	2.11

Note: The coefficients in this table are those which appeared in the actual regression equations. Therefore $\gamma = 1 - b_{G_{t-1}}$ and $\alpha_i = b_i/\gamma$. For example, the Belgium equation suggests that:

$$G_t = .5701[197.5565 + .9117R - 50.7774I_{US} - 229.5479D] + .4299G_{t-1}$$

The dummy variable used in these equations is D, which measures a shift in gold holdings, and differs from D', which measures a shift in gold purchases. Whereas a negative coefficient for D' represents a reduction in gold purchases throughout the relevant period, a negative coefficient for D represents a decrease of the whole gold stock, which may be caused by a small gold purchase in only one quarter.

reserves, but has fallen off since 1960. Foreign-exchange holdings for working-balance requirements may be an important factor determining reserve-asset composition, particularly for Germany. There is no clear-cut evidence of a "drift toward gold" before 1960, and the demand for gold falls as interest rates rise.

In all the experiments using I_{US}, interest sensitivity appeared. It seems clear, however, that central banks do not merely try to maximize the expected value of their portfolio, as they would then invest all their reserves (in excess of working balances) in the single reserve asset having the highest expected value rather than in several assets. To account for the fact that central banks hold more than one asset, it seems proper to assume that they choose between alternative portfolios by trading expected value against risk.

To analyze reserve-asset composition along these lines I shall start with a special, two-security version of the portfolio model developed by Harry Markowitz.[43] Such an analysis requires an additional assumption: that central banks are risk-averting utility maximizers.

The central bank is assumed to carry out its reserve-asset investment policy subject to a budget constraint. That constraint represents its subjective judgements concerning the anticipated outcomes of various investment decisions as embodied in the expectation (E) and variance (V) of the returns of each portfolio. The central bank's utility is assumed to vary directly with the expected return and inversely with its variance for the entire portfolio.

The empirical counterpart of this analysis is elusive. In order to estimate the slope of the budget constraint (the E/V frontier), one would have to know the equilibrium marginal rate of substitution or frequency distribution for each security, and these are unobtainable. Moreover, as the probabilities of exchange devaluations are purely subjective, changes in the E/V frontier may not be independent of changes in the central bank's indifference map. A risk averter may attach high probabilities to undesired events, thereby affecting his expectations as well as the shape of his indifference map.

[43] Harry Markowitz, "Portfolio Selection," *Journal of Finance*, VII (March 1952), 77–91; *Portfolio Selection*, Cowles Foundation Monograph 16 (New York: John Wiley & Sons, 1959); J. R. Hicks, "Liquidity," *Economic Journal*, LXXII (December 1962), 799–802. This procedure was suggested by John Karlik, "The Costs and Benefits of Being a Reserve-Currency Country" (unpublished doctoral dissertation, Columbia University, New York, 1966), Chapter 1. For fuller discussion of the model, see Greene, "Reserve-Asset Preferences" (Columbia), Chapter IV.

In order to approximate the Markowitz analysis, I will continue to use I_{US} as a proxy for expected return on foreign exchange. But proxies for the expected devaluation of the dollar are more difficult to devise. I have tried four alternatives—the U.S. deficit, the U.S. gold loss, the ratio of foreign-owned liquid dollar claims to the U.S. gold stock, and the change in that ratio. In fact, these proxies for income and risk are not independent of each other: an increase in the U.S. interest rate, for example, may come about because of a U.S. gold loss, a larger U.S. deficit, or an increased expectation of devaluation of the dollar relative to gold.[44]

Using these proxies for income and risk, I sought to explain the proportion of foreign exchange to total reserves. This experiment should yield an estimate of desired foreign exchange as a function of expected return and risk on the portfolio. I then hoped to take account of lags in portfolio adjustment by developing a gold transaction equation to measure the rate at which governments attain their desired gold holdings (where these holdings are implied by the demand-for-foreign-exchange equations). Using the previous notation and denoting the appropriate risk proxy by Z, the basic equation is given as follows:

$$\frac{F - \hat{S}}{R - \hat{S}} = a_0 + a_1 I_{US} + a_2 Z, \quad \text{where } a_1 > 0,\ a_2 < 0$$

Assuming that the correlations between $\hat{S}$, on the one hand, and I_{US} and Z, on the other, are negligible, this equation can be reduced to:

$$\frac{F}{R} = a_0 + a_1 I_{US} + a_2 Z + a_3 \frac{\hat{S}}{R}, \quad \text{where } a_3 = 1 - a_0$$

This final equation was used in the regression analysis.

Unfortunately, the regression equations are unsatisfactory (see Table 13, where the change in the ratio of foreign-owned dollar liabilities to the U.S. gold stock was used as the risk proxy).[45] The income and risk proxies were not well-behaved, the interest-rate coefficients are negative more often than positive, and the risk proxies are seldom significant. The

[44] This joint determination of the risk and income proxies may help to explain why, in the regression results presented below, the proxies seem to take on the same signs.

[45] The high $\bar{R}^2$ obtained in some of the equations may merely reflect a spurious correlation between F/R and $\hat{S}/R$, influenced primarily by changes in R. In almost every attempt to estimate this equation, $\hat{S}/R$ appears highly significant.

Table 13

Estimates of F/R

Country	Equation	$\bar{R}^2$	d
Belgium	$F/R = .3656 - .0143I_{\text{US}} - .1197Z - 6.7929(\hat{S}/R)$ $(.0849)\dagger\ (.0189)\qquad (.5671)\qquad (1.6010)\dagger$	.3545	.27
Canada	$F/R = .3267 + .0119I_{\text{US}} + .7584Z + 6.1302(\hat{S}/R)$ $(.0508)\dagger\ (.0158)\qquad (.4682)\qquad (.7148)\dagger$	.7362	1.17
France	$F/R = .0640 + .0524I_{\text{US}} + 2.4566Z - .2218(\hat{S}/R)$ $(.0688)\ (.0203)\dagger\qquad (.6079)\dagger\ (.2753)$	.3643	1.42
Germany	no significant equation	n.s.	
Italy	$F/R = -.0278 - .0097I_{\text{US}} + 1.1853Z + 13.6344(\hat{S}/R)$ $(.0861)\ (.0187)\qquad (.6632)\qquad (1.2811)\dagger$	.8274	1.20
Japan	$F/R = .9343 - .0263I_{\text{US}} - .8307Z + .2708(\hat{S}/R)$ $(.0246)\dagger\ (.0066)\dagger\qquad (.2039)\dagger\ (.1359)$	.5629	1.15
Netherlands	$F/R = .1488 - .0166I_{\text{US}} + .1025Z + 1.1206(\hat{S}/R)$ $(.0492)\dagger\ (.0122)\qquad (.3965)\qquad (.5756)$	.1130	.67
Sweden	$F/R = .5568 + .0136I_{\text{US}} + 1.4830Z + .7219(\hat{S}/R)$ $(.0984)\ (.0260)\qquad (.7728)\qquad (1.6503)$	.0356	.19
Switzerland	$F/R = .0893 - .0108I_{\text{US}} - .3489Z + 1.1955(\hat{S}/R)$ $(.0214)\ (.0061)\qquad (.1798)\qquad (.5101)$	.1889	1.89
United Kingdom	$F/R = .1332 - .0320I_{\text{US}} + .6117Z + 2.1943(\hat{S}/R)$ $(.1146)\ (.0251)\qquad (.7579)\qquad (1.7042)$	.0471	1.20

† Significantly different from zero at the .05 level of significance.

several risk proxies responded in a similar manner, but the ratio of foreign-owned dollar liabilities to the U.S. gold stock deviated from the general pattern, being significantly positive. Rather than measuring the risk of holding foreign exchange, this variable may be providing an estimate of the available supply of foreign exchange. As my efforts were so unsuccessful, the corresponding gold-transaction equations, designed to measure the rate at which governments attained their desired reserve-asset portfolios, were not computed.

Certainly some, if not all, of these alternative hypotheses offer further explanations of reserve-asset preferences. To recapitulate, a working-balance estimate reflecting recent variations in reserves probably came closer to the true working-balance requirement than $\bar{F}$, which necessarily includes desired foreign-currency investments. Indeed, the success of this estimate, especially in equations where the lagged foreign-exchange argument was the only dependent variable, commends a further attempt to refine this kind of estimate.

By introducing the U.S. treasury bill rate into the "best" equations, I tried to detect elements of rationality in decision-making processes—elements neglected by Kenen's more mechanistic analysis. It is of great interest to observe the clear (although weak) evidence of interest-rate sensitivity in reserve-asset composition. If, in addition, gold purchases themselves appear sensitive to interest rates, the choice among foreign-exchange assets would probably show an even greater responsiveness to interest differentials.

My attempts to explain reserve-asset preferences in terms of cost and risk were not successful. Perhaps the proxies for risk were inadequate. Perhaps the Markowitz model, as I adapted it, is not an adequate basis for empirical work on reserve-asset preferences. By contrast, the regression analysis presented earlier in the study—particularly the multiple gold-transaction equation—appears to be quite useful in describing reserve-asset composition. These relationships, though mechanistic, suggest a fair degree of stability in reserve-asset preferences over time.

APPENDIX

Appendix Table A

	Original Equations (Kenen)			Recomputed Equations (Greene)		
Country	Number of Observa-tions†	Mean of Gold Holdings‡	Mean of Total Reserves‡	Number of Observa-tions	Mean of Gold Holdings	Mean of Total Reserves
Belgium	43	870	959	15	1,099.27	1,179.73
Canada	43	952	1,821	15	1,041.67	1,893.33
France	16	936	1,277	15	936.87	1,283.33
Germany	32	1,538	3,093	15	2,531.13	4,439.80
Italy	16	1,147	1,949	15	1,094.73	2,095.93
Japan	16	110	951	15	162.27	1,118.60
Netherlands	36	822	992	15	1,012.67	1,216.73
Sweden	36	219	387	15	203.73	476.80
Switzerland	43	1,567	1,681	15	1,819.87	1,956.80
United Kingdom	43	2,310	2,627	15	2,399.07	2,818.00

Note: All equations terminate at September 30, 1960. Differences in the number of quarters consequently denote differences in the starting date.

† Kenen, *Reserve-Asset Preferences* (Princeton), Appendix B, Table G, p. 82.

‡ Kenen, *ibid.*, Appendix B, Table A, p. 76.

Appendix Table B

Country	IV 1960			I 1961		
	Actual ΔG	Predicted ΔG	t	Actual ΔG	Predicted ΔG	t
Belgium	76.00	174.69	−3.95†	−38.00	14.59	−1.79
Canada‡						
France	14.00	101.89	.82	242.00	82.30	1.49
Germany‡						
Italy	17.00	54.53	.54	−75.00	6.14	−1.00
Japan‡						
Netherlands	105.00	123.09	−.58	0.00	5.84	−.18
Sweden	−1.00	2.99	−.44	0.00	13.95	−1.35
Switzerland	205.00	189.60	.61	−20.00	195.99	−9.56†
United Kingdom	164.00	144.20	.22	−178.00	−75.81	−1.10

Note: None of the actual variants was significantly greater than the predicted at the .05 level of significance.

† Actual significantly different than the predicted at the .05 level of significance. A dagger next to a negative entry denotes an actual gold purchase smaller than prediction.

‡ No significant equation.

INDEX OF AUTHORS